The Evangelical
# Moment

# The Evangelical
# Moment

## The Promise
## of an American Religion

## Kenneth J. Collins

**Baker Academic**

Grand Rapids, Michigan

Published by Baker Academic
a division of Baker Publishing Group
P.O. Box 6287, Grand Rapids, MI 49516-6287
www.bakeracademic.com

Printed in the United States of America

Library of Congress Cataloging-in-Publication Data
Kenneth J. Collins
    The evangelical moment : the promise of an American religion / Kenneth J. Collins.
        p.    cm.
    Includes bibliographical references and index.
    ISBN 0-8010-2744-6 (pbk.)
    1. Evangelicalism—United States. I. Title.
BR1642.U5C63  2005
277.3′083—dc22                                                        2004018672

To the memory of
Mimi, Richy, and Ann—
like flowers in season,
gone so quickly
but not forgotten

# Contents

# Introduction

# The Many Dialogue Partners of American Evangelicalism

George W. Bush, Jimmy Carter, as well as the current attorney general, the speaker of the House, and the House majority leader all have one thing in common—and it is obviously not that they are Republicans. Rather, they are all born-again American evangelicals. Alan Wolfe, a Boston College sociologist, has maintained that many elements of the "evangelical style" ("its strongly personalist and therapeutic tendencies, its market-savvy approaches")[1] have permeated other faiths, even Roman Catholicism and Judaism, such that "we are all evangelicals now."[2]

While we may not all be evangelicals, the influence of this movement on both the American church and the nation is significant and is likely to continue in the days ahead. According to one estimate, "Every five years since 1965 evangelicals have grown 8 percent, while mainline Protestants have lost 5 percent."[3] And recent Gallup polls paint a similar picture: "Nearly 40% of the American population is born again."[4] Colleen Carroll, a noted Roman Catholic author, has pointed out that the evangelical churches studied by Faith Communities Today showed that "evangelicals founded 58 percent of all new church congregations between 1990 and 2000."[5] And while some cultural

11

observers thought that the rampant pluralistic environment of America would weaken the movement, it has actually done quite the reverse. Sociologists such as Christian Smith, from the University of North Carolina, now maintain that American evangelicalism thrives in a pluralistic, even oppositional, environment.[6] The contrast evidently only increases the popularity, attractiveness, and numbers of evangelicalism.

As popular as this American religion is, it nevertheless has its cultural critics who continually keep the movement out of focus, blurring it with the well-worn stereotypes of an earlier age, of ranting populist preachers and a courthouse in Dayton, Tennessee. Current realities, however, suggest a far different picture. In fact, according to some of the most careful research today, "self-identified evangelicals are among the best-educated Americans and have enjoyed the greatest intergenerational educational mobility among all major American religious traditions."[7] But the myths do die hard, especially in the media and in halls of the academy. Indeed, precisely where there should be an abundance of openness and fair-minded critical thinking, that is, among academics, the stereotypes are puffed again and again, despite significant evidence to the contrary. According to one survey, "nearly one out of three academics said that Evangelicals are a 'threat to democracy.'"[8] Given this environment, with the prospects of tenure and social pressure lurking in the background, who among the educated will speak up for evangelicals? "It's like standing up for the Crusades," Smith observes. "American evangelicals remain one of the last social groups in the United States that people can speak disparagingly about in public and get away with it."[9]

However, according to Mark Noll, a leading historian, evangelicalism (despite the glib definitions offered in the culture) is actually an "extraordinarily complex phenomenon."[10] The movement has always been *"diverse, flexible, adaptable* and *multiform."*[11] And if you ask evangelicals who are actively engaged in the political process today (which is their right, as with any other American), they will reveal not that they have a desire to undermine democracy but that they are interested in "religious freedom and the right of persons to express their religious beliefs free from discrimination."[12] Like any other group, they want liberty to thrive on American soil, they want to be heard, and perhaps most important of all, they want to be understood.

In light of these concerns, this book is principally about understanding American evangelicalism and exploring the promise that it holds for twenty-first-century American religion. It calls, therefore, for an examination of evangelicalism not simply as an isolated entity, one defined apart *by itself* in terms of any number of attributes or traits. Though this popular approach is both helpful and necessary, this book will not leave the matter there. Instead, it will also view the movement as a historical phenomenon that has had not only a number of distinct social locations but also a number of "dialogue partners" across the generations. In other words, American evangelicalism, if it is ever to break through the myths and stereotypes, must be considered not in a static way, simply in terms of self-identified attributes or traits, but in a dynamic and *relational* way, as a movement engaged in various conversations, some of them quite heated, all of which are for the sake of reform. Simply put, given the mission of evangelicalism, which is intimately tied to its identity, the movement must always reckon with "the other," whether it be Roman Catholicism or theological liberalism, whose contrast in turn helps to illuminate, at least in part, the major features of this American religion.

To explore the relational nature of evangelicalism, this book employs the elements of story as identity-making characteristics. That is, American evangelicals often situate themselves in a distinct narrative that gives meaning and purpose to their ongoing efforts. Preeminent in these accounts, of course, is the gospel story itself, whose genius is reflected in various evangelical settings in which the struggles, even defeats, of the movement have become very much a part of the ongoing narrative. Indeed, it is the orality of the movement (a very Protestant trait) that must first of all be grasped and given its proper place if evangelicalism is ever to be properly understood. From the slapdash preaching of a Billy Sunday, to the gentle voice of a mother as she sings a gospel hymn to her baby, to recounting the "heydays" when victories were won or when defeats were acknowledged, evangelicals are simply infatuated with stories. Accordingly, it is the word, not the image or the icon, that is the key to identity here. Put another way, it is not vision or the Greek word *theoreo,* the view of a spectator, that is paramount to evangelical identity. Rather, it is that other Greek word *kaleo,* "to call" or "to call forth," that suggests something of the participatory, relational context as well as the other directedness of much of American evangelicalism.

Given this understanding, the chapters that follow will offer several "conversations," representing different contexts and dialogue partners, the hearing of which should provide clues to the elusive phenomenon that is American evangelicalism. In chapter 1, for example, we will listen to a number of conversations in which evangelical identity emerges, with all of its reforming impulses. Given such diversity, it is no doubt tempting for some to focus on a particular historic expression of evangelicalism, such as Puritan and pietistic evangelicalism or fundamentalist/neoevangelicalism, and then to make it the be-all and end-all for a *contemporary* American movement. We will avoid this tendency and suggest, on the other hand, that a host of narratives actually arise in the evangelical community, the hearing of which invites the listener to a wealth of identities and purposes. Simply put, there are many ways of being an evangelical in America today, and evangelicals delight in that diversity and celebrate such richness.

Whether in terms of individuals or groups, times arise when self-reflection is necessary precisely to go forward and to meet the challenges of the day. Accordingly, chapter 2 considers the dialogue that emerges among evangelicals as they talk among themselves, that is, as they become their own dialogue partners, so to speak, in order to engage in self-correction and thereby become more effective witnesses of the gospel to a hurting world. As I have painstakingly chronicled the literature of the past generation (reading and building databases of books and articles) and have traveled around the country listening, in a more informal way, to expressions of evangelical concern, I have noticed a number of distinct themes that repeatedly emerge in these conversations and that no doubt inform evangelical identity. It is these few though important themes that invariably find their way into so many evangelical conversations. Therefore, it is not simply a matter of diversity among evangelicals, for there are, after all, some common elements that make up much of the substance of evangelical identity. Simply put, American evangelicalism is a movement that embraces distinctiveness and difference and yet has an overarching unity that is displayed in the common bonds of witness, fellowship, and purpose.

Recognizing both the common themes as well as the diversity of American evangelicalism also entails a serious consideration of what both Wesleyan and Reformed voices have contributed to the larger story. Chapter 3, therefore, reconsiders the historic Dayton/Marsden debate and offers fresh insights, new ways of grappling with old problems, that may result in openness, future conversations, and in the end greater mutual understanding and respect. Among other things, Wesleyan evangelicals will be invited to consider other equally valid ways of interpreting their own tradition, some of which clearly overlap with the concerns of contemporary neoevangelicals. Reformed evangelicals, on the other hand, will be invited to grasp in a serious way that Wesleyanism is not a species of liberal "Arminian" accommodations to human effort or initiative but is informed by the theological genius of both John Wesley and Thomas Cranmer. Wesleyanism, therefore, in a way similar to the Reformed tradition, cherishes many of the central insights that arose from the Reformation, insights that make up much of the substance of Protestant witness today. Indeed, the best and most articulate exponent in eighteenth-century England that sinners are saved by faith alone (*sola fide*) and that salvation is a sheer, utter gift from the Most High was none other than John Wesley. In fact, the father of Methodism quipped at one point, "I think on Justification just as I have done any time these seven-and-twenty years, and just as Mr. Calvin does. In this respect, I do not differ from him a hair's breadth."[13]

In a real sense, theology, whether Reformed or Wesleyan, is a careful articulation of the story of the church, the nature of its present liberty, as well as the vitality of its hope for those both within and beyond the community of faith. Again, though theology is undertaken on behalf of the church, to bring clarity and understanding in terms of its own witness, it is also done, in an incarnational sort of way, for the sake of the other. In other words, the church, precisely to be the church, does not simply talk to itself, engaging in uninterrupted monologues, but ever considers the "other," those for whom Christ died but who have not yet found an abundance of grace upon grace. This aspect of the task of theology, then, gives it a public voice, and evangelical theologians as a consequence are currently dialoging and grappling with various intellectual currents, not all of which are open to the prospects of faith. In light of these developments, chapter 4 explores both the challenges as well as the prospects of evangelical theology in light of the cultural and intellectual movements of postliberalism and postmodernism. The good news is that evangelicals are now sitting at the table; the bad news is that they are offered only a diminished, relativistic voice, just one among so many others. But does such a context, despite its apparent openness and inclusiveness, permit the gospel to be heard for what it actually is? Many evangelicals are now wondering.

Beyond this, the public face of American evangelicalism is developed in chapter 5, but this time not so much in terms of intellectual currents as in politics. Here evangelicalism enters the marketplace, where a cacophony of voices can be heard in the competing claims, sometimes strident, for the limited goods of society. Contrary to some popular public perceptions, not all evangelicals are eager to engage in politics or to have their will become the law of the nation, simply because they fear that such involvement will invariably corrupt "the faith once delivered to the saints." Cal Thomas and Ed Dobson have cautioned the evangelical community precisely along these lines. Nevertheless, other evangelicals have become increasingly concerned in the face of secularizing, "politically correct" trends with respect to ethics, education, and public policy—trends that seek to exclude evangelical voices from being heard as a matter of principle or, failing in that, to label such voices so negatively at the outset that few will actually listen. Chapter 5 will push through such rhetoric and maintain that American evangelicals, as with other theists, are not second-class citizens but are both socially relevant and engaged. In fact, evangelical groups are currently involved in some of the most generous and effective programs that are actually making a difference in the lives of the poor.

Though some evangelicals (who haven't quite shaken off their fundamentalist heritage) appeal to the language of a "cultural war" to instill much-needed concern, they often end up fostering monological, and at times simplistic, thinking when issues pertaining to the nature and roles of women are discussed. Consequently, chapter 6 will introduce the voices of some critical evangelicals, from both the Reformed and the Wesleyan tradition, who will maintain that the very genius of the Christian faith transcends the kind of tribalism that emerges in giving "maleness" an ultimacy that it simply cannot bear. To be sure, part of the good news of the gospel, about which contemporary evangelicals are excited, is not only that all people are created in God's image but also that the Christian faith is truly a universal one that transcends the provincialisms of ethnicity, economic status, and gender. As the apostle Paul himself maintained, "There is neither Jew nor Greek, there is neither slave nor free man, there is neither male nor female; for you are all one in Christ Jesus" (Gal. 3:28). Chapter 6, then, explores different hermeneutics, various ways of interpreting Scripture, and suggests which approaches, methodologically speaking, allow the fullness of the gospel to shine through for *all* of God's children. Indeed, in recognizing the biblical equality of men and women—though not without opposition from within the movement itself—contemporary evangelicalism is becoming the more generous and inclusive means of grace that it was always meant to be.

From the beginning of the twentieth century until now, American evangelicalism has undoubtedly had a number of significant dialogue partners, theological liberalism and, more recently, Roman Catholicism among them. Though some of the most prominent identity-defining debates took place among theological liberals, fundamentalists, and evangelicals early on, the American cultural context has shifted to such an extent, especially in terms of religion and ethics, that liberalism is now no longer the dialogue partner that it once was. Instead, Roman Catholicism has reemerged from earlier debates, going back to the sixteenth century, and has found common cause with those Protestants, those "separated brethren," who identify themselves as contemporary evangelicals. Indeed, Roman Catholics and evangelicals today often find themselves on the same side of the debates that take place in broader American culture. From standing up for the dignity of all human life to maintaining the sanctity of marriage, from opposing the hedonistic, even vulgar, substance of much of American entertainment to championing the rights of Christians to be heard in the public square, these two communions of faith have enough in common that they should have been talking long ago. In light of this, chapter 7 explores the ecumenical promise of evangelicalism in terms of the documents "Evangelicals and Catholics Together" and "The Gift of Salvation." Beyond these informal instruments, the official agreement between the Roman Catholic Church and the Lutheran World Federation, that is, *The Joint Declaration on the Doctrine of Justification,* promulgated in 1999, is explored in considerable detail. What promise or challenges does such a historic agreement hold for evangelicals who have placed a premium on both doctrinal orthodoxy and holiness of heart and life and who have been sustained in so many ways by the theological reforms called for by the Reformers of the sixteenth century?

Finally, chapter 8 builds on the insights of the late Heiko Oberman, great Reformation scholar, and underscores the importance of tradition, in conjunction with the primacy of Scripture, in keeping the integrity (both doctrinal and spiritual) of American evangelicalism intact as it meets the challenges of a twenty-first-century world. Moreover, it makes the case that the history of the early church "belongs" as much to evangelical Protestants as it does to Russian Orthodox or Roman Catholics. Indeed, to be stripped of the history of the church, to proceed in a largely ahistorical way (an approach that is championed even by some evangelicals themselves), is to lose important aspects of the larger story—and in the end to suffer the forfeiture of far too much identity. In a way similar to Robert Webber, therefore, this chapter calls for an ancient-future faith, one that opens up American evangelicalism not only to all the conversations in which it has a stake but also to the ones through which it can be nurtured and ultimately thrive. And though some like to gather up these concerns in the language of "evangelical catholicism," I much prefer the terminology of "catholic evangelicalism," for the substance is the evangel, the gospel story of Jesus Christ. The attribute, the description, on the other hand, is that it is a universal story—good news for *all.*

# Who Are the American Evangelicals?

F rom the arrival of the pilgrims in Massachusetts aboard the *Mayflower* in 1620 to the seasoned preaching of Jonathan Edwards in the Connecticut valley during the 1730s; from the "jump and stir" of the camp meeting revival in Logan County, Kentucky, in 1800 to the pointed preaching of the lawyer turned preacher Charles Finney during the 1820s and 1830s; and from the pulpit antics of Billy Sunday, former baseball player and slapdash preacher, well into the twentieth century to the statesmanlike, ever popular preaching of Billy Graham today, American evangelicals have been diverse, vigorous, and earnest. Indeed, while liberal churches currently languish for want of a message that can truly set the captives free, evangelical churches thrive. According to James Davidson Hunter, since 1965, liberal denominations have declined at an average five-year rate of 4.6 percent, while evangelical denominations, on the other hand, have increased at an average five-year rate of 8 percent.[1] And George Marsden, the dean of American evangelical historians, reveals that roughly fifty million Americans now fit the definition of evangelical.[2] Something is clearly going on here.

## Definitions

But just who are the American evangelicals, and how might they best be defined? Here there is much less agreement. Both William Abraham and Robert

19

Johnston maintain that the term *evangelicalism* is a contested one.[3] In other words, there is no consensus among cultural observers as to what constitutes the defining characteristics of American evangelicalism. In the past, faced with this difficulty, scholars such as Timothy Smith employed the terms *mosaic* and *kaleidoscope*,[4] while others such as Jon Stone appealed to the notion of a "coalition," "a dynamic alignment of individuals or groups with common interests or goals."[5] Still others, no doubt influenced by the writings of Wittgenstein, have utilized the language of "family resemblance"[6] to bring some sense of unity.

Despite these important and helpful attempts, many other scholars remain unconvinced. Thus, for example, Martin Wellings, in thinking about the problem of definition from his own British context, observes, "No body or institution within the Protestant world has the power to make such a definition: there is no Protestant equivalent to the Roman Catholic magisterium."[7] Faced with this ongoing perplexity, which constitutes one of the greatest problems in American historiography today, Donald Dayton contends that the term *evangelical* has lost "whatever usefulness it once might have had,"[8] and he, therefore, goes so far as to call for "a moratorium on the use of the term."[9] Despite Dayton's criticism, the terminology of "American evangelicalism" remains valuable in light of its continued use and descriptive power, for it portrays a dimension of Christianity in America that not only warrants serious theological and cultural analysis but also holds much promise for the days ahead.

Given this predicament of naming and identity—Reformed and Wesleyan evangelicals at times even vie with one another for a definition of American evangelicalism that best suits their own interests and agendas[10]—it is perhaps best to use broad and generous definitions that are inclusive rather than exclusive and that accurately reflect the pluralism of American evangelicalism. To accomplish this, we will employ the paradigm of story as a useful device to gather up both the similarities and the differences among American evangelicals. Remarkably, when evangelicals talk about their identity, they often chronicle an account; that is, they detail a "family history" in which key people, places, and events have all played an important role. These stories include not only prominent theological themes, such as the importance of Scripture or the necessity of conversion, but also distinct social locations, both past and present, whether it be Luther's "Here I stand" speech at the Diet of Worms or the fundamentalist-modernist controversy of the early twentieth century.

Therefore, each evangelical story, when compared with others, is marked by both similarity and difference. Wesleyan evangelicals, for instance, will highlight the cruciality of New Testament Christianity as well as the importance of the ante-Nicene fathers. Then in a typically Protestant way, they will perhaps wax eloquently on the genius of the English Reformation as expressed in the work of Cranmer, Edward VI, and the Elizabethan Settlement of 1559 before they go on to explore the energy and creativity of the eighteenth-century Wesleyan revival and its subsequent transformation, at least in some sense, by both American revivalism and the Holiness movement. A Presbyterian evangelical narrative will, of course, be somewhat different. Like its Methodist cousin, however, it too will likely begin with the *evangel* of the first-century church, appreciate the value of Augustine, and then quickly proceed to the Reformation, but this time Calvin, Zwingli, or Beza, not Cranmer, will receive the lion's share of attention. The narrative will then continue with details about the Puritans, in both England and America; it will explore the gracious preaching of Jonathan Edwards during the First Great Awakening; and it will, of course, consider the theology of the great Princeton theologians, Charles Hodge and B. B. Warfield among them, before it reckons with the rise of fundamentalism and the neoevangelicalism that emerged in its wake.

There are, of course, many other American evangelical stories (Anabaptist, Lutheran, Pentecostal, etc.) to be told that will naturally employ different people, places, and events. Accordingly, the following sections of this chapter lift up those elements that form the substance of the accounts that repeatedly emerge in both the literature of American evangelicalism and the oral descriptions of evangelical identity. The bricks and mortar of these historical movements, so to speak, can be used to build remarkably different structures of evangelicalism, but they are yet united in evidencing some common themes. Put another way, these structures are all similar, despite their different social locations and family histories, in paying attention to four enduring emphases: (1) the normative value of Scripture in the Christian life, (2) the necessity of conversion (whether or not dramatic or even remembered), (3) the cruciality of the atoning work of Christ as the sole mediator between God and humanity, and (4) the imperative of evangelism, of proclaiming the glad tidings of salvation to a lost and hurting world. Indeed, each of these four themes has repeatedly emerged in the literature, with more or less emphasis, as evangelicals have grappled with their own identity.[11] They are, therefore, integral to any assessment of the evangelical ethos. They are broad enough to account for evangelical pluralism and yet particular enough to define evangelical self-understanding. They are, therefore, explored in greater detail in the following chapter.

Though common themes do indeed emerge in the midst of diverse stories and historical materials, this by no means suggests that there is a single overarching evangelical narrative. There is not one story to be told but a wealth of stories, no one of which (with the exception, of course, of New Testament

Christianity) that should become the basic paradigm by which all others are measured. Simply put, there is no evangelical metanarrative. There are simply many narratives that in their own distinct way, and out of their own social and theological history, appeal to different historical materials as they evidence some unifying and identity-making themes.

## Movements Integral to Evangelical Identity

### *Historical Evangelicalism*

The story of American evangelicalism begins, in a real sense, with the historical events of first-century Israel and their subsequent interpretation in the Gospels and the letters of Paul. The *euangelion* or good news of the gospel—from which the word *evangelicalism* is derived—concerns the life (incarnation), death, and resurrection of Jesus Christ. In a similar fashion, the verbal form *euangelizomai* is found in Matthew, although it is most often employed in Luke-Acts and in the letters of Paul, where it depicts the proclamation of the good news that *is* Jesus Christ. On this first level, then, in this broad and basic sense, all Christians, as they announce the glad tidings of salvation in words and actions, are evangelicals whether they be Protestant, Roman Catholic, or Eastern Orthodox. Not only, for example, does Donald Bloesch maintain that an "evangelical thrust has not been entirely lacking in the Catholic and Orthodox churches,"[12] but George Gallup, interestingly enough, reveals that 13 percent of American Catholics identify themselves as "born-again Christians."[13] Therefore, the exclusive use of the term *evangelical* by some American Protestants, as if only they were focused on the *evangel,* can appear presumptuous if not arrogant to Christians from other traditions who maintain that they, too, are rooted in the good news of New Testament Christianity. On this basic level, then, this term should unite Christians rather than divide them.

Evangelicalism, whether expressed in terms of the first century or subsequent ones, through the writings of the ante-Nicene fathers or those of Augustine, is ever a *reforming* movement that is in dialogue, and at times in tension, with an earlier tradition. And while New Testament Christianity does indeed issue in a new covenant, that covenant is not utterly discontinuous with the old, as both Calvin and Wesley clearly affirmed. So understood, the good news of the gospel, the *euangelion,* not only is the fulfillment of the words of the prophets but also represents the fruit of Israel, the perfection of God's revelatory acts to this people. The gospel, then, invites both Pharisee and Sadducee to the glory that is Christ, a glory that cannot be grasped, however, apart from the discontinuity of *metanoia* and renewal. On this most basic level, then, the first dialogue partners of evangelicals are neither liberals nor Roman Catholics but Jews.

## *Reformational Evangelicalism*

Though all Christians in telling their story invariably make the connection to the first-century church, American evangelicals are distinct in how they view subsequent history. Unlike Roman Catholics and the Eastern Orthodox, they tend to bypass the Middle Ages and pick up the narrative in the sixteenth century, the time of the Reformation. And though a good case perhaps could be made that Augustine, Bernard of Clairvaux, and John Wycliffe were in some sense evangelicals, such names rarely emerge in the oral histories heard throughout the years, nor do they often appear in the self-reflective literature of American evangelicalism. This particular way of reading the history of the church, what scholars call "historiography," marks much of American evangelicalism as decidedly Protestant. In this setting, the chief dialogue partner to which calls of reform are directed is not Jerusalem, or even Constantinople, for that matter, but Rome.

Moreover, this manner of viewing history makes it difficult for contemporary American evangelicals to maintain that their particular expression of the faith flows through the centuries and therefore can be traced all the way back to the New Testament church.[14] And yet the discontinuity of much of American evangelical historiography, the relative neglect of the Nicene and post-Nicene fathers, for example, actually underscores the reforming impulse of evangelicalism and suggests that it cannot be understood apart from the particular exigencies of the theological and social location to which it was originally addressed. Since the impulse for reform was so greatly evident in the sixteenth century, not during the dark or Middle Ages, this identity-defining period is virtually included in all accounts.

In the first century, the *euangelion* distinguished Christians from those Jews and Gentiles who did not believe in Jesus Christ. In the sixteenth century, however, the German word *evangelisch,* from which the modern term *evangelical* is derived, distinguished the (German) Protestant Reformers and those who followed in their wake from their Roman Catholic counterparts. This polemical use of the term indicates that the dialogue that ever informs the reforming flavor of evangelicalism was now an in-house one. That is,

Christians during the sixteenth century were calling not unbelievers but other Christians to renewal. In fact, Reformers such as Luther, Calvin, and Cranmer believed that an overwrought tradition that had amassed considerably during the Middle Ages was now rendering the gospel virtually opaque.

Luther most likely came to his basic evangelical insight (that sinners are justified in God's sight not by works or by a docile obedience to the magisterium but by grace through faith alone) sometime during 1514–15, that is, well before he reputedly nailed his Ninety-five Theses to the Wittenberg church door on October 31, 1517. Having caused a considerable stir among the people, the German Reformer was summoned by the authorities in 1518 to appear before Cardinal Cajetan at Augsburg. The following year Luther debated Eck at the Leipzig Disputation, where he had the effrontery, in the eyes of many Roman Catholics, to deny the primacy of the papacy as well as the infallibility of General Councils. Luther clarified his views even further in 1520 with the publication of three pivotal treatises: (1) *Address to the German Nobility*, in which he challenged the pope on the interpretation of Scripture; (2) *The Babylonian Captivity of the Church*, in which he criticized not only the subjection of the laity to the hierarchy but also the doctrine of transubstantiation and the notion of the Mass as a sacrifice; and (3) *The Freedom of a Christian*, in which he articulated the gracious liberty of a Christian free from a bondage of works through justifying grace. But it was perhaps Luther's appearance at the Diet of Worms before the emperor Charles V in May 1521 that epitomized his evangelical concerns in the most dramatic way. On that momentous occasion Luther uttered the following words, which have become the evangelical clarion call for reform:

> Since then your serene majesty and your lordships seek a simple answer, I will give it in this manner, neither horned nor toothed: Unless I am convinced by the testimony of the Scriptures or by clear reason (for I do not trust either in the pope or in councils alone, since it is well known that they have often erred and contradicted themselves), I am bound by the Scriptures I have quoted and my conscience is captive to the Word of God. I cannot and I will not retract anything, since it is neither sale nor right to go against conscience. I cannot do otherwise, here I stand, may God help me, Amen.[15]

Observe in these historic words Luther's appeal to Scripture as the final authority of faith and practice. Observe also the weight that this German Reformer gives to the *individual* conscience and reason bound by the Word of God such that the authority of both pope and council can be set aside when they are in error. That is, in tying the normative value of Scripture to reason and the individual conscience, at least in some sense, Luther prepared the way not only for the much-needed criticism of Roman Catholic doctrine but also for the incredible pluralism and separatism that have subsequently come to plague the Protestant *churches*.

Around the world today and especially in Europe, many Lutherans are willing to identify themselves as part of the evangelical movement as understood in this second sense, in which evangelicalism is *principally* informed by a sixteenth-century context. This picture, however, changes considerably if we move to a North American setting. As Mark Ellingsen has so ably pointed out in his own work, the number of Lutherans in North America who identify with the evangelical family is remarkably small.[16] Such a lack of identification is likely because many Lutherans astutely realize that the reigning paradigm of evangelicalism in North America today is not chiefly oriented to the second sense detailed above in which the theological context is sixteenth-century Europe and the chief dialogue partner is Catholicism. Instead, its social location is actually the heady days of the twentieth century with its great and at times acrimonious debates, and its main dialogue partner is theological liberalism.

In terms of the Reformed tradition, and in some contrast to Lutheranism, the earliest phase of the Swiss Reformation arose in Zurich under the steady leadership of Ulrich Zwingli. The influence of this city waned, however, after its defeat at the hands of the Catholic cantons, who were opposed to the reform, and with the death of Zwingli on the battlefield in 1531. After this, the leadership of this wing of the Reformation fell to Geneva, farther west. With the intention of simply passing through this Swiss city in July 1536, John Calvin was nevertheless persuaded by Guillaume Farel to remain there and to assist in the work of renewal. Drawing on all his arts and powers, Farel had actually threatened Calvin and uttered the imprecation that God would curse his retirement and studies if he "should withdraw and refuse to help, when the necessity was so urgent."[17]

Theologically talented in many ways, Calvin had already published his *Institutes of the Christian Religion* in Basel during March of the same year. Drawing on his many rhetorical gifts, no doubt acquired from his study of Christian humanists, Calvin brought forth an enlarged edition of his Latin *Institutes* in 1539, but this Christian classic did not appear in French until 1541. The clarity of the theological themes developed in the *Institutes* (particular election and union with Christ) as well as the beauty and cadence of the French in later editions helped to establish Calvin as a principal leader of Reformed Christians, and his influence naturally spread beyond Geneva to Germany, France, the Netherlands, and even England and Scotland.

There were differences, to be sure, between the German and the Swiss reformations, especially in terms of church discipline, the sacrament of the Lord's Supper, and what theologians deemed "adiaphora," that is, matters of indifference with respect to church customs and practice (are vestments allowed, for example). Nevertheless, both movements were united in calling for the reform of the church, not simply in the area of morals, as Roman Catholics and even Erasmus had preferred to view it, but also in the area of *doctrine*. Thus, for Wittenberg, Zurich, and Geneva, the main dialogue partner was indeed Rome, and the salient issue was restoring the integrity of the gospel, especially in terms of the forensic theme of justification by faith.

When American evangelicals tell their theological story even today, some accounts, however, hardly mention the names of Luther, Zwingli, or Calvin. Such omissions remind us that the multifarious reforms of the sixteenth century may not be best expressed by the simple term *Reformation,* in which one or two scripts hold sway, but by the plural language of "Reformations," in which important differences can be discerned within a larger historical reality. Again, in terms of the family histories of American evangelicals, it is perhaps best to speak not of one or two but of four Reformations: the German and the Swiss, to be sure, but also the Radical (Anabaptist) and the English. These last two Reformations complicate matters somewhat because they did not face simply Rome, as it were, but also Wittenberg and Geneva, thereby at times calling for a "reform of the reform." More to the point, it is precisely the blending of both similarity and difference that marks the Radical and English reformations when they are compared to the German and Swiss movements.

In terms of the Radical Reformation, the Anabaptist reforms found in such diverse communities as the Swiss Brethren, the South German Anabaptists under the leadership of Pilgram Marpeck, the Melchiorites in Germany and the Netherlands, as well as the Mennonites under the careful guidance of Menno Simons called into question the kind of church and state accommodation that had hailed from the time of Constantine and Theodosius the Great (and was assumed both by Luther in his *Address to the German Nobility* and by Calvin in the work of the Consistory in Geneva). The Anabaptist reforms also challenged the theological propriety of infant baptism in a way that the magisterial Reformation did not.[18] In this setting, then, not only Rome was called into account but Wittenberg and Geneva as well. It is this dual directedness of the Radical Reformation that is often expressed even today in Mennonite critiques of American evangelicals who continue to look to the magisterial Reformation for both guidance and illumination. To illustrate, C. Norman Kraus, who has served as the book review editor of the *Mennonite Quarterly Review,* cautions his evangelical cousins, among other things, in terms of their views on church and state, in particular their "accommodation to nationalistic American culture and its tacit espousal of nationalism and capitalism as Christian values."[19] Similar critiques, arising out of a concern for genuine Christian faith and the cruciality of conversion, are directed toward the Protestant practice of infant baptism.

In a similar way, the English Reformation was an enormously complex movement filled with theological subtleties and, at times, political intrigue. However, the reform of the English church had already begun well before Henry VIII squabbled with Clement VII. In the fourteenth century, for example, Parliament had passed the Acts of Praemunire, which were intended to protect the rights and privileges of the Crown from a power-grasping papacy. A statute in 1353, for instance, made it illegal to remove cases from the king's courts to Rome. In the sixteenth century, Henry VIII completed this largely political reform by severing relations with Rome, declaring himself the head of the English church, and confiscating the property of the monasteries.[20]

Theological reform in England began in a real sense during the reign of Edward VI, who, unlike his father, was decidedly Protestant in orientation.[21] Thomas Cranmer, the archbishop of Canterbury at the time, served the boy king and the English church well by crafting the Book of Common Prayer in 1549 (a revised edition appeared in 1552), by composing suitable homilies to be read from English pulpits that articulated the reform in a practical way, and by drawing up the Forty-two Articles of 1553, which were later edited and reduced to the historic Thirty-nine. After the reign of Catholic Mary, who burned Cranmer, Latimer, and Ridley at the stake as heretics, Elizabeth I, the daughter of Anne Boleyn, proceeded to renew the English church in what has come to be known as the Elizabethan Settlement. Among other things, the Prayer Book of 1552 was restored and revised in a 1559 edition, and the Act of Uniformity was passed to bring order to a potentially difficult situation.

Despite the criticism from John Knox, Queen Elizabeth was a remarkable leader, adept at politics and capable of balancing a number of diverse elements. On the one hand, this monarch distinguished the church in her lands from that of Rome. On the other hand, she was reluctant to follow the full course prescribed by the Puritan party, which wanted to transform the English church, with its remaining "rags of popery," along the lines suggested by Geneva. Indeed, the careful balance of the Elizabethan Settlement, in which some continuity with the Middle Ages was indeed affirmed, has been expressed as a *via media* that criticized both Rome and Geneva. Indeed, under Elizabeth's reign, Richard Hooker impugned many of the Puritan arguments in his *Laws of Ecclesiastical*

*Polity,* in which the appeal to natural law was deftly employed, while John Jewel, bishop of Salisbury, undermined much of the criticism from Rome. This means, then, that some contemporary American evangelicals, as found in the Episcopal Church or the United Methodist Church, for example, trace their story through the English Reformation and, therefore, at times agree with Rome *against* Geneva. More important, perhaps, they are no less evangelical for doing so.

## Puritan and Pietistic Evangelicalism

The preceding description of those historical movements that factor into American evangelical accounts of their own identity already reveals a diversity and an inclusiveness that are not always reflected in contemporary assessments. Mark Noll, for instance, makes the claim that "as modern evangelicals, we are spiritual descendents of the Puritans,"[22] and Robert Johnston, for his part, contends that "the American evangelical heritage includes three periods: puritan Evangelicalism, pietistic Evangelicalism and fundamentalist Evangelicalism."[23] However, the American evangelical story cannot begin where Johnston sees it without eliminating important scripts and dialogue partners along the way. Neither can it devolve upon the Puritans as Noll has it for the reasons already indicated. This is not to detract from the considerable value of Puritan spirituality both within the Reformed tradition and beyond but only to suggest that American evangelicals of other traditions will at times take exception to the nature and form of Puritan spirituality, especially, for example, in the areas of worship and liturgy. In a way similar to sixteenth- and seventeenth-century Anglicans, they reject Puritan liturgical iconoclasm, along with its bare church walls, in favor of an aesthetical theology of worship, whereby divine grace and beauty are recognized through the *media* of words, of course, but also through music, colors, forms, processions, and ritual.

Like the Puritans Cartwright, Barrow, and Browne, many of the Pietists of the seventeenth century, such as Philip Jacob Spener and August Francke, not only championed the value of convertive piety but also saw their major task as one of reform. Influenced by the work of Johann Arndt, especially his *Wahres Christentum* (*True Christianity*), Spener labored for renewal in heart and life within the church. His *Pia Desideria* (*Pious Desires*), for example, first published in 1675, called for confession and repentance with respect to those very churches that were the heirs of the Protestant Reformation. With German Pietism, then, we encounter once again the *self-critical* movement of a "reform of the reform," one that was in sharp contrast to the stale Protestantism that, in its fixation on doctrine and orthodoxy, had become "scholastic." To this larger end of correcting conditions in the church, the *Pia Desideria* enunciated six carefully conceived proposals: (1) develop a more extensive use of Scripture, (2) exercise a spiritual priesthood through which laity would become more active, (3) underscore the importance of practical Christian knowledge, (4) avoid needless religious controversy, (5) reform both the lower schools and the universities to inculcate the practical goals of the Christian life, and (6) preach for the purpose not of a display of arcane or irrelevant learning but for the edification of the church.[24]

In a similar fashion, August Francke helped to initiate a revival of pious, godly desires among the students in Leipzig through his *Collegia Philobiblica*. These communions, which displayed the social and corporate dimensions of the faith, underscored the value of both fellowship as well as accountability in the Christian life. Similar patterns of corporate renewal, a genuine *ecclesiola in ecclesia*, were also developed by the Moravians under Count Von Zinzendorf, Spener's godson, and by the Anglicans through the labors of Anthony Horneck, an immigrant Lutheran minister who arrived in London in 1678 and helped to foster the religious societies movement, a movement that, interestingly enough, influenced both Samuel and John Wesley.

If Spener had launched the Pietist movement, Francke saw to its institutionalization. Accordingly, while at Halle, the Lubeck native gave the movement the "prestige associated with academic theologians,"[25] and like Wesley, who followed him, Francke had an outstanding gift for organization, as revealed in the numerous institutions he established, many of which were connected with Halle. They included "an orphanage, . . . a home for widows, a farm, a book store, a hospital, a bakery, a brewery, a library, and an art museum."[26] For the early Pietists, then, personal renewal was ever matched with social reform, especially with the task of ameliorating the plight of the poor.

## *Awakening Evangelicalism*

To explore in an accurate way the ethos and substance of the Great Awakenings that flowered on both British and American soil in the eighteenth century, it is best, perhaps, to make a distinction between an awakening and the revivals that often accompanied them.[27] Thus, the great evangelical awakening in Britain during the eighteenth century, influenced to a certain extent by Moravian Pietism, arose in the midst of the faithful preaching of George Whitefield, Howell Harris, and John and Charles Wesley. Ever attentive to the *means of grace* in the larger life of the church, these godly evangelists patiently waited for renewal, often in the face of harsh and bitter opposition. Moreover, the considerable response to their labors by the common people was not viewed as either a human artifice or a construction but as the gracious gift of the Most High, whose quickening Spirit was the leader and orchestrator of all.

Creative and unconventional in many respects, George Whitefield had already undertaken the practice of field preaching in Bristol during March 1739. At first, John Wesley was horrified at such a practice—with its grass, mud, and rain—and noted that he "could scarce reconcile [himself] at first to this strange way of preaching."[28] "I should have thought the saving of souls *almost a sin*," the Methodist leader added, "if it had not been done *in a church*."[29] Whitefield, however, was persuasive as usual. Though we don't know the substance of all that he said on this topic, Whitefield probably convinced Wesley that he could save more souls outside a church than within it. At any rate, whatever Whitefield said, it worked, for at four in the afternoon on April 2, 1739, Wesley, to use his own words, "submitted to 'be more vile' and proclaimed in the highways the glad tidings of salvation speaking from a little eminence in a ground adjoining to the city, to about three thousand people."[30] Just a few days earlier, Wesley had written to John Clayton and had proclaimed that all the world was his parish. "I judge it meet, right, and my bounden duty to declare unto all that are willing to hear the glad tidings of salvation."[31] Now with the beginning of field preaching, it truly was.

In a similar fashion in the American colonies, it was the faithful preaching of Jonathan Edwards in the Connecticut valley, of William and Gilbert Tennent in New Jersey, and of Theodore Frelinghuysen in New Brunswick that became the means of the Spirit's renewing agency. Remarkably, John Wesley had read Edwards's *Faithful Narrative of the Surprising Work of God* as he walked from London to Oxford in October 1738, but it was actually George Whitefield, fellow member of the Oxford "Holy Club," who tied the awakenings together by his gifted preaching on both sides of the Atlantic. The "Grand Itinerant" preached his way through the American colonies, uniting the labors of others as the churches pulsated with newly found life. This was a word spoken in due season, and the grace of God quickened the hearts of many.

## Revivalistic Evangelicalism

Though the evangelistic efforts of nineteenth-century America evidenced a "convertive piety," as its eighteenth-century forerunners in both Britain and America had done, many in the church began to discern considerable differences and diverse, even disparate, trends. With a population moving westward to exploit the opportunities of the frontier, with new territories to be developed and settled, America experienced a heady freedom in the midst of rapid social and demographic change. The old forms and habits of whatever social order had developed were now in flux, and many of the churches began to rethink just what it meant to be a Christian in America.[32]

Though the Congregational churches of New England were speckled with colorful revivals, and though the "burned over" district in Upstate New York throbbed with enthusiasm, the Presbyterians, Baptists, and Methodists were determined to follow the westward advance of the nation. However, because of their distinct polities and evangelistic techniques, it was really only the last two denominations that thrived on the American frontier. For one thing, the Presbyterians, with their high educational standards for the ministry, were not able to keep pace with the Baptists, who readily formed congregations wherever they went, or with the Methodists, who employed lay preachers to reap the growing harvest.

But all was not well. Those ministers who employed revivals and camp meetings to reach an itinerant population began to receive criticism from friend and foe alike that the revival was rapidly becoming a "technique," an instrument of human, not divine, power. To illustrate, Charles Finney, though remarkably successful in the pulpit, suffered repeated censure for his newfangled methods, which included among other things protracted nightly meetings; the "anxious bench," a prominent spot where those "under conviction" were placed; exhortations by women; and extensive advertisement for his meetings.[33] And to complicate matters even further, thereby giving his critics all the ammunition they needed, Finney himself remarked on one occasion, "A revival is not a miracle or dependent on a miracle in any sense. . . . It is a purely philosophic result of the right use of the constituted means."[34]

Still others thought that Finney had degraded, even cheapened, the gospel by suggesting that redemption, after all was said and done, was largely a human prerogative: "Anyone who was willing to repent could obtain assurance of salvation immediately."[35] Such trends were resented by the Calvinists at the time and were linked to the "liberal" influence of Arminianism and the Methodists.[36] However, upon a closer and more careful examination, a distinction must be made between historic Methodism and the "Arminian" trends of nineteenth-century American religion. Indeed, British Methodism, theologically sophisticated in many respects, especially in the area of soteriology, is best understood not as a species of Calvinism gone wrong, where the Synod of Dort and the ongoing problems of the Continental Reformation become the main interpretive script. Instead, the "Arminianism" of historic Methodism is of the English sort and is best explored in terms of the Caroline divines of the seventeenth century, Jeremy Taylor and Lancelot Andrews among them.[37]

With such distinctions in place, interpreters of American religion, both past and present, would be theologically equipped to realize that when Finney exclaimed that anyone who was willing to repent could obtain assurance immediately, John Wesley would have been his greatest critic. Though the English evangelical would, no doubt, have agreed with Finney that the offer of salvation is genuinely made to all, and therefore preaching should be broad and inclusive, he would have nevertheless rejected any notion that redemption, or the assurance that accompanies it, is within human power or follows *immediately* upon repentance. Thus, in his *Earnest Appeal to Men of Reason and Religion,* Wesley addressed the salient issue as to why all do not have saving faith in the following way:

> We answer, (on the Scripture hypothesis,) "It is the gift of God." No man is able to work it in himself. It is a work of *omnipotence.* It requires no less power thus to quicken a dead soul, than to raise a body that lies in the grave. It is a new creation; and none can create a soul anew, but He who at first created the heavens and the earth.[38]

For Wesley, then, persons can be redeemed if they will ("Ask, and it will be given to you; seek, and you will find; knock, and it will be opened to you" [Matt. 7:7]), always of course as a result of divine efficacious grace, but not *when* they will. In a letter drafted in November 1777, he elaborated:

> To say every man can believe to justification or sanctification *when* he will is contrary to plain matter of fact. . . . That every man may believe if he will I earnestly maintain, and yet that he can believe when he will I totally deny. But there will be always something in the matter which we cannot well comprehend or explain.[39]

In other words, the timetable is never in the hands of sinners, nor are they in control. For Wesley and other English Arminians, salvation is and remains a gift of God, and such truths underscore the sheer gratuity of both divine favor and empowerment. Finney's theology and practice, then, is best understood not in terms of eighteenth-century Wesleyan Arminianism but in terms of its own specific social location in the form of nineteenth-century revivalistic and democratic America.[40]

## Charismatic Evangelicalism

Part of the good news of the gospel for all Christians, of whatever religious tradition, entails not only the person and ministry of Christ but also the reception of the Holy Spirit, who brings numerous gifts and graces to the believing heart. Charismatic evangelicalism, which highlights these truths, is composed of two key groups: Pentecostals, on the one hand, and charismatics, on the other, who both underscore the *charisms* or gifts of the Spirit in the practical Christian life. And though many historians treat this first group largely as a twentieth-century phenomenon, precursors of the movement can actually be found in nineteenth-century American revivalism in general and in the ministries of Charles Finney and Asa Mahan in particular, ministries that proclaimed, among other things, not only the beauty of holiness but also the wonders of "baptism in the Holy Spirit."[41]

Around the turn of the century at a small Bible college near Topeka, Kansas, Charles Fox Parham began to teach that in the book of Acts all instances of baptism in the Holy Spirit were accompanied by the gift of speaking in tongues. Beyond this, he affirmed that this pattern was normative for all Christians. William J. Seymour, a black hotel waiter, soon took up the Pentecostal message and carried it to Los Angeles, where a revival broke out at Azusa Street in 1906. Shortly thereafter, many Wesleyan fellowships were drawn into Pentecostalism through the labors of those who had participated in the Azusa Street mission.[42]

Beyond the theme of baptism in the Holy Spirit, many Pentecostal groups emphasized the reality of healing in Christ, the expectation of the second coming of the Lord, as well as the cruciality of redemption in a way that demonstrated key evangelical themes. Unfortunately, however, a schism occurred in the movement in 1916 over the nature of the Trinity, resulting in the formation of "oneness" or "unitarian" Pentecostals. The larger Pentecostal Fellowship of North America, however, remained orthodox, and its 1948 "Statement of Truth" was taken "verbatim from the 'Statement of Faith' promulgated five years earlier by the National Association of Evangelicals," with but one exception.[43] Today, Pentecostalism ever calls the broader church to reform, especially those congregations that are marked by the *form* of religion yet lack its *power*, that are by and large soteriologically pessimistic and rigid, and that, therefore, live far below the graces and gifts of the Spirit for which Christ died.

Charismatic evangelicalism, the second key group, began in North America in 1960 within several Protestant churches as a loosely structured lay movement that advocated spiritual renewal. As with Pentecostalism, the charismatic movement was characterized by the importance of group worship, the exercise of spiritual gifts that included glossolalia, and the promise of healing. Unlike Pentecostalism, however, charismatics were not willing to draw a tight correlation between speaking in tongues and baptism in the Holy Spirit. By 1967, in the midst of much national turmoil, the joy and serenity of the charismatic movement eventually found its way into Roman Catholic circles, and it was enthusiastically embraced by some faculty members at Duquesne University. Later that year, close to a hundred Catholic charismatics held their first conference at Notre Dame. This renewal movement was finally given a seal of approval by the Vatican when it received representation at the Synod of Bishops held in Rome in 1987. Today, Catholic charismatics number in the millions.[44]

Encompassing Protestants, Roman Catholics, and even some Eastern Orthodox, the North American charismatic movement, as a species of evangelicalism, holds great ecumenical promise for the future, not only in terms of its denominational breadth but also in its appeal to a diversity of social classes.

## *Fundamentalist/Neoevangelicalism*

Though American Protestantism, as other forms of religion, had been legally separated from the state by the Constitution, it had set up a de facto establishment by the time of the Civil War. Thus, the evangelicals of the period, who held together both the importance of personal religion as well as the necessity of social reform, created a "benevolent empire," not only to win the nation for Christ but also to enhance their own social and cultural power. The national organizations that made up this empire, reflecting the goodwill and optimism of the period, operated on an interdenominational basis and included the following: the American Bible Society (1816), the American Colonization Society (1817), the American Sunday School Union (1824), the American Tract Society (1825), the American Temperance Society (1826), the American Peace Society (1828), the American Seamen's Friend Society (1828), and the American Antislavery Society (1833).[45] So equipped, revivalists as well as the more settled parish ministers were remarkably optimistic about the prospects for reform and for ushering in nothing less than the kingdom of God in America.

After the war, however, the worst in America's history, the mood was far less sanguine. The cultural pessimism of dispensationalist premillennialism, an import from Britain, where it was championed by John Nelson Darby, began to take root in the churches. Prophecy conferences soon proclaimed the new perspective and taught, as a part of their broader evangelistic appeal, that American culture would simply deteriorate until the second coming of Christ. This shift from the optimism of postmillennialism, which helped to unify the broad evangelical coalition of the antebellum period and galvanize it for social reform, to the pessimism of premillennialism was even evident in the comments of Dwight Moody, the gifted evangelist, as he reflected on his own call and mission: "I look upon this world as a wrecked vessel. God has given me a lifeboat and said to me, 'Moody, save all you can.'"[46]

Beyond this, the American Protestant empire, composed largely of evangelicals, was challenged intellectually by both Darwinism and German higher criticism, and its cultural predominance was now threatened by waves of immigration that brought increasing numbers of Catholics and Jews to American shores during the latter part of the nineteenth century. The intellectual challenge was particularly acute, and it led to the breakup of a once unified coalition by the time of the establishment of the Federal Council of Churches in 1908.[47] Indeed, many modernists in the church were all too willing to accommodate Christianity to the spirit of the age, to transform the historic truths of the faith in the name of "relevance," and thereby attempt to hold on to their cultural power and influence. As George Marsden points out, "Between 1878 and 1906 almost every major Protestant denomination experienced at least one heresy trial, usually of a seminary professor."[48] Moreover, during the twenty-year period from 1910 to 1930, the architectonic realignment of American Protestantism known as the "Great Reversal" took place. That is, liberal evangelicals, who remained a part of the progressive movement, focused almost exclusively on social reform; fundamentalist evangelicals, on the other hand, who would brook no compromise of the faith, ministered by and large to the soul.[49]

In the swelter of this cultural and theological change, the Presbyterian General Assembly took a stand in 1910 and articulated five fundamentals of the faith that were deemed nonnegotiable: the miracles of Christ, the virgin birth, the satisfaction view of the atonement, verbal inspiration, and the bodily resurrection of Jesus. Over the course of the next five years, in order to strengthen the orthodoxy of the churches, two wealthy California businessmen, Milton and Lyman Stewart, sponsored the publication of *The Fundamentals,* a series of twelve volumes that was produced by leading conservatives including James Orr, Arno C. Gaebelein, Robert E. Speer, B. B. Warfield, R. A. Torrey, C. I. Scofield, H. C. G. Moule, Charles Trumbull, and G. Campbell Morgan.[50] In 1919, conservatives formed the World's Christian Fundamentals Association, though the specific term *fundamentalism* was not applied to those who were "contending for the faith" until the following year, when it was coined by Curtis Lee Laws in the Baptist paper the *Watchman-Examiner.*[51]

J. Gresham Machen, New Testament professor at Princeton Seminary, challenged the modernists in 1923 with the publication of *Christianity and*

*Liberalism* and offered an apologetic for the movement that has never been successfully refuted. Going to the heart of the matter, Machen argued that theological liberalism (as with ancient Christian Gnosticism) employed all the language of historic Christianity but then invested those words with remarkably different meanings. In the end, what emerged was not the apostolic faith but a much different *religion*.[52] The theologically naive at the time, however, failed to notice this subtle change, perhaps because they continued to hear the vocabulary of historic Christianity in the pulpit, to which they had grown accustomed, and now being tied to the leading issues of the day. They simply could not fathom to what extent "the script" had actually changed.

Through the work of Machen, B. B. Warfield, and Charles Hodge of Princeton Seminary,[53] the fundamentalist movement played out principally in those churches that were tied to the Reformed tradition, such as the Northern Baptist Convention and the Presbyterian Church in the U.S.A.[54] And although Holiness groups, such as the Nazarenes and the Wesleyan Methodists, "found their distinctive emphases being reshaped by the fundamentalist-led movement,"[55] their Wesleyan tradition, rooted as it was in Anglicanism and soteriological concerns, prevented them from becoming active participants in the movement itself. Moreover, the Holiness communions, ever aiming at the inculcation of holy love in the hearts of believers, could only look askance at the aggressiveness of many fundamentalist leaders regardless of the issues at stake.

By the time of the Scopes trial in 1925, when William Jennings Bryan, populist leader and champion of fundamentalism, was made to appear foolish through the wily arguments of Clarence Darrow, the cultural leaders of the nation, as well as many average Americans, could only reject this movement as antiquated, rigid, and anti-intellectual. The fundamentalists, in turn, retreated into their churches and Bible institutes. The sectarian spirit loomed so large within the movement that fundamentalists separated themselves not only from the "modernists" but also from those Bible-believing Christians who dared to retain ties with theological liberals. This doctrine of "double separation" became a badge of faithfulness and honor, though it necessarily limited the ongoing influence of fundamentalism both within the church and within the nation.

A complex movement in many respects, American fundamentalism can perhaps best be described in terms of four major characteristics or traits: (1) militancy, that is, aggressive opposition to liberal theology; (2) social ambivalence, in terms of rejecting the social gospel but at the same time wanting greater social power and influence in order to reform the nation; (3) sectarianism, in other words, separating from both the doctrinally heterodox as well as those who associate with them; and (4) the doctrine of verbal inerrancy as a bulwark against the acids of modernity.

Over the course of the twentieth century, key leaders within the movement threw off the label "fundamentalist" and opted for the more irenic title of "new evangelical" or "neoevangelical." In time, however, these *reformers* were simply known as evangelicals, in distinction to liberals such as Harry Emerson Fosdick and fundamentalists such as Carl McIntire, founder of the American Council of Christian Churches. This was a move of considerable and lasting consequence, for a coalition *within* fundamentalism and informed largely by the Reformed tradition had appropriated a name that not only was already in use by a diversity of communions (German Protestants, for example) but also had a long and rich history. Not surprisingly, such a move has added fuel to the fires of the "contested" nature of American evangelicalism.

At any rate, at the organizing conference of the National Association of Evangelicals held at the LaSalle Hotel in Chicago in May 1943, Harold Ockenga delivered the presidential address and thereby laid the groundwork by which the first three emphases of fundamentalism, noted above, would be basically repudiated. To illustrate, both J. Elwin Wright, who had been instrumental in founding the NAE at a conference in St. Louis the year before,[56] and Ockenga himself rejected the militancy of the fundamentalists.[57] Moreover, demonstrating a much more cooperative and less separatist spirit than the fundamentalists, Wright and Ockenga welcomed Pentecostals and Holiness folk into the new coalition.[58] Billy Graham, whose evangelistic career was to take off in 1949 when William Randolph Hearst told his reporters to "puff Graham," was equally eager to be rid of the bellicose and exclusive nature of the "fighting fundamentalists." In fact, during his crusade in New York in 1956, Graham welcomed the support of nonfundamentalists,[59] a gesture that came with a price exacted by his conservative critics. Yet Graham remained undeterred, for the key theme of the new movement was "cooperation without compromise."[60]

In a similar fashion, the neoevangelicals took issue with the social irrelevance of much of fundamentalism, that is, its failure to address the more corporate dimensions of the gospel. Carl F. H. Henry, for example, one of the early neoevangelical leaders, issued a stinging rebuke to fundamentalists in 1947 in his *Uneasy Conscience of Modern Fundamentalism*.[61] In breaking out of some of the polemics and polarities that had marked the earlier fundamentalist and liberal divide, Henry, as with other evangelicals, wanted to unite personal depth with social breadth, the importance of conversion with the necessity of social reform, as earlier nineteenth-century evangelicals such as Theodore Weld, Orange Scott, and Luther Lee had done so well.[62]

By the time of the founding of *Christianity Today* in 1956, a magazine that was distinct from both the fundamentalist *Sword of the Lord* and the liberal *Christian Century,* the rejection of the fundamentalist movement was all but complete. Today the National Association of Evangelicals is a burgeoning voluntary association of individuals, denominations, churches, schools, and organizations and is comprised of over forty thousand congregations from approximately fifty member denominations. One area, however, where the neoevangelicals continued to agree with the fundamentalists was in terms of the doctrine of the divine inspiration of the Bible in general and the teaching of verbal inerrancy in particular. This commitment, Abraham notes, not only made it difficult for the neoevangelicals to be welcomed into the world of scholarship but also demonstrated that "the basic thrust of the fundamentalist tradition was not changed at all."[63] This issue, in one form or another, repeatedly surfaced during the second half of the twentieth century as neoevangelicals continued to grapple with their own identity in terms of their two chief dialogue partners: fundamentalism and liberalism.

Though the NAE was relatively broad and inclusive at its founding and remains so, not one of the predominantly black denominations, such as the African Methodist Episcopal Church or the African Methodist Episcopal Zion Church, became members. The reasons for this are complex. For one thing, because of the racial segregation that isolated them from their white counterparts, blacks "seldom used the term 'evangelical' and their experience is usually regarded as a distinct type in itself."[64] Moreover, since they were never really caught up in the fundamentalist controversy and the neoevangelicalism that emerged from it, the specific term *evangelical* actually has little meaning for many African Americans. To be sure, they much prefer the term "Bible-believing" to "evangelical,"[65] and yet there are black self-identified evangelicals. They can be found in black mainline denominations, within white churches, in Holiness and Pentecostal churches, and as independents. Summarizing this phenomenon, William Bentley states, "With the possible exception of black Pentecostals, black evangelicalism is distinctly a middle-class religious phenomenon and has much more in common with its white counterpart than with the black."[66]

## Some Observations

The preceding stories, though by no means exhaustive, are at least sufficient to demonstrate that there are many ways of being an evangelical in

America. The different historical materials employed in contemporary narratives eventuate in any number of "genealogical" structures. Moreover, as cultural observers pay increasing attention to evangelicals as they chronicle their histories, they will invariably discover three key things: First, there is a feeling of excitement and optimism about what lies ahead for this movement. Indeed, many now believe that American evangelicalism, tempered by both its strengths and weaknesses, will come of age in the twenty-first century and will assume a greater leadership role in American religion. The data from the pollsters appear to support this.[67]

Second, there is an unmistakable sense of pride among evangelicals that has emerged out of the discipline, pain, and fortitude of having remained faithful to Jesus Christ in a shifting American culture, especially when it has not always been popular to do so. From the hodgepodge of historical fact and fiction of Jerome Lawrence and Robert E. Lee's *Inherit the Wind,* a play that reimagined the story of the Scopes trial in a very loose and exaggerated way,[68] to the criticism of Gary Bauer, a contemporary evangelical activist who was recently described at a conference call at the CBS News bureau in Washington as "the little nut from the Christian group,"[69] evangelicals have on occasion been derided and even mocked by the American public media. The truly sad part about this last instance of blatant prejudice, besides the obvious insult, is that not one of the CBS producers at this meeting uttered even a syllable of objection. In fact, according to Public Agenda, a research group, more than two-thirds of American evangelicals believe there is a good deal of prejudice against them. Yet American evangelicals remain firm in their commitments, satisfied with their identity, and open to dialogue with all who will listen. In short, evangelicals know that they are the heirs of a rich legacy, that they are a people with deep and abiding roots.

Third, evangelicalism cannot simply be described in reference to itself as a distinct and separate movement. Indeed, precisely because its identity is ever caught up in mission and reform, evangelicalism will always have a "dialogue partner," whether it be Jews in the first century, Roman Catholics in the sixteenth, Anglicans in the eighteenth, or theological liberals in the twentieth. Given this salient trait, evangelicalism is best defined not in a static way, such as entailed in the characteristics identified in set theory, but in a dynamic one that emphasizes the importance of key *relations* and thereby takes "the other" into account. Put another way, to be an evangelical in America today is not simply a way of being a Christian; it is also a way of *relating to* other Christians and to those beyond the walls of the church.

Though so far we have highlighted some of the different ways of being an evangelical, there are nevertheless a number of elements, both theological and social, that form a common bond among these faithful believers wherever they gather. Transcending the barriers of denominations and other structures, these deeply committed Christians enjoy a fellowship that is almost immediate and a larger lasting purpose that marks them as a distinct people.

# The Evangelical Distinctives

The preceding chapter demonstrated the breadth and diversity of American evangelicalism as it chronicled several narratives that constitute the different ways of being evangelical in America. Though these stories are marked by what is distinctive for each respective tradition, embedded in the accounts are also common themes, that is, a complex of similar practices, theological judgments, and concerns that unite the various traditions. More to the point, the similarities expressed among American evangelicals, the common elements that foster a spirit of community that transcends denominational affiliation, geography, and even at times theological tradition, can best be explored in terms of four major concerns: (1) the normative value of Scripture, (2) the significance of the atoning work of Christ, (3) the necessity of conversion, and (4) the imperative of evangelism.

## Scripture

It would be a Herculean task to examine every American evangelical tradition with respect to its view of the inspiration and authority of Scripture, along with all the appropriate theological nuances. Accordingly, this chapter considers only the view of Scripture that predominated among American evangelicals in the twentieth century and then suggests some reasons for that predominance. The following chapter details alternative assessments of Scripture found in the evangelical community, principally among Wesleyans and Pentecostals, and reveals that though these accounts differ in some important respects from the reigning paradigm or story, they nevertheless are equally serious in their valuation of Scripture and in their affirmation of its normative character.

The reigning view of Scripture found among many contemporary evangelicals, especially from the Reformed tradition, is expressed in the doctrinal basis of the Evangelical Theological Society: "The Bible alone, and the Bible in its entirety, is the Word of God written and is therefore inerrant in the autographs."[1] Though many evangelicals would like to claim that this expression of the authority of Scripture can be found throughout the entire history of the church (and was even the view of Jesus), this expression is best understood in terms of its own historical, social, and theological location.[2] Put another way, this theological judgment has a history, a context out of which it arose, and that context is not early Christianity or even the Reformation period but nineteenth- and twentieth-century America.

Remarkably enough, in the middle of the nineteenth century, the cultural power of American evangelicalism was approaching its height. Not only did the ongoing revivals and camp meetings lead to a nation with a Christian ethos that was far more than a veneer slapped over a secular state, but many of the cultural elites of the period were also drawn from Protestant, evangelical sources. Prior to the publication of Darwin's *Origin of Species* and the introduction of German higher criticism, university and seminary professors found American culture, by and large, congenial to their ongoing theological concerns. Indeed, the science of the period had not yet challenged basic theological truths in a systemic way, and many theologians, Charles Hodge among them, believed that Scottish common sense realism, a philosophy espoused by Thomas Reid and others, paved the way for an acceptable cultural alliance between faith and human wisdom. Moreover, in its critique of the Lockean notion that ideas "represent" reality, Scottish common sense realism held that the truths of common sense are self-evident, discerned through the senses, and in this way it hoped to avoid the skepticism of Hume and other radical empiricists. With such a philosophical orientation in place, many church leaders of the period deemed objective science to be "the best friend of the faith."[3]

Though the church's embrace of common sense realism afforded it greater cultural power, this philosophy, in its empiricist orientation, affected theological method. Charles Hodge, for example, professor at Princeton Theological Seminary, thought of theology as a science: "The Bible is to the theologian what nature is to the man of science. It is a store-house of facts."[4] Hodge was joined in his methodological commitments, which underscored the objective, cognitive nature of the Bible, by fellow Princeton professor B. B. Warfield, who articulated a doctrine of inerrancy that claimed that Scripture was without error (whether it be physical, historical, psychological, or philosophical) when the *ipsissima verba* of the original autographs were considered.[5] A historical resource that helped to sustain the type of arguments that both Hodge and Warfield sought to make in their particular American setting was Francis Turretin's three-volume *Institutes of Elenctic Theology,* a work that, not surprisingly, became a basic text at Princeton for much of the nineteenth century.[6]

For somewhat different reasons, the millenarian movement, during the nineteenth century, focused on the factual, objective nature of the Bible in its emphasis on prophecy in general and on the imminent second coming of Christ in particular. Indeed, Ernest Sandeen is well known for having championed the thesis that the formation of the Princeton theology of Hodge and Warfield, seen in conjunction with the growth of the millenarian movement, especially in its literalistic tendencies, actually helped to determine the character of American fundamentalism.[7] Therefore, when the Presbyterian General Council, which was influenced to some extent by these precursory movements, issued its five fundamentals in 1910, for which it would earnestly contend against the inroads of modernism, biblical inerrancy was one of them. As Stanley Grenz points out, "From then on, adherence to this doctrine became a central feature of the entire fundamentalist coalition."[8]

Though a well-articulated doctrine of biblical inerrancy already existed in the works of Princeton theologians prior to the rise of fundamentalism, the context of this latter movement provides the most significant clues to the ongoing postulation of this doctrine in the current *evangelical* community. In other words, the doctrine of biblical inerrancy, found among American evangelicals, has to be considered *principally* not in terms of seventeenth-century Protestant scholastic forebearers, or of the writings of Turretin for that matter, but in terms of the historical, social, and theological context of "the great struggle" of the American fundamentalists as they took on the theological liberals of the early twentieth century and remained faithful to the truth of the gospel. In this setting, contentious and polarized as it was, inerrancy and the larger theological presuppositions that supported it formed much of the apologetics of not only the classic work *The Fundamentals,* published by Milton and Lyman Stewart from 1909 to 1912,[9] but also the larger movement itself. Moreover, inerrancy, along with its associated views of the authority and inspiration of the Bible, soon became the chief way of distinguishing the heterodox from the orthodox. But could the authority of the Bible have been supported in some other way, a way that would not have been overly tied to the empiricist notions of realism that had filtered into fundamentalist understandings from Princeton sources?

At any rate, the fact that inerrancy was a "theological marker" for many evangelicals, an emblem of the heydays of the movement, became evident during the 1940s when neoevangelicalism distinguished itself, in some important respects, from fundamentalism. Indeed, though Ockenga, Graham, and Henry all wanted to separate themselves from fundamentalists by renouncing a bellicose posture, repudiating a sectarian spirit, and being more socially active, they nevertheless basically continued to uphold a fundamentalist reading of Scripture. This doctrine was simply too ensconced in the identity of fundamentalists, some of whom now called themselves neoevangelicals, to be quietly laid aside.

In 1958, J. I. Packer, a British evangelical, published his *Fundamentalism and the Word of God,* which was warmly received by much of the American evangelical community. In this work, Packer not only argued for a doctrine of inerrancy as the best way to affirm the authority of Scripture, a commonplace by now, but also contended that fundamentalism is "just a twentieth-century name for historic evangelicalism."[10] Beyond this, Harold Lindsell, former editor of *Christianity Today,* published a book in 1976 whose title (*The Battle for the Bible*) suggested that the bellicose nature of evangelicalism had not actually disappeared, as was so often claimed by neoevangelicals, but had now devolved upon the issue of inerrancy, which quickly became a litmus test for Lindsell and others in assessing evangelical identity. In this work, Lindsell stated:

> It is the thesis of this book that biblical inerrancy is a theological watershed. Down the road, whether it takes five or fifty years, any institution that departs from belief in an inerrant Scripture will likewise depart from other fundamentals of the faith and at last cease to be evangelical in the historical meaning of that term.[11]

To the chagrin of not a few American evangelicals, especially from the Wesleyan and Pentecostal communities, Lindsell went on to claim, "I do not for one moment concede, however, that in a technical sense anyone can claim the evangelical badge once he has abandoned inerrancy."[12]

Francis Schaeffer entered the fray during the 1980s with the publication of two key books: *A Christian Manifesto* and *The Great Evangelical Disaster.* In the latter work, Schaeffer not only rejected the use of higher critical methods to study Scripture,[13] which contemporary evangelicals now embrace, albeit with some reservations, but also drew a proverbial line in the sand between evangelicals, a very separatist and fundamentalist thing to do. "Evangelicalism is not consistently evangelical," Schaeffer charged, "unless there is a line drawn between those who take a full view of Scripture and those who do not."[14] And in case the reader missed his point, Schaeffer concluded, "The real chasm is between those who have bowed to the living God and thus also to the verbal, propositional communication of God's inerrant Word, the Scriptures, and those who have not."[15]

More recent works in this genre include *The Coming Evangelical Crisis,* edited by John Armstrong, and *Here We Stand: A Call from Confessing Evangelicals,* edited by James Montgomery Boice and Benjamin Sasse, both published in 1996. Each of these works argues for a doctrine of inerrancy in the form of objective, propositional revelation. In the former, Michael Horton criticizes Bernard Ramm, who called for a broader, more inclusive understanding of the truth of Scripture and who, therefore, impugned biblical inerrancy as the best expression of the authority of Scripture.[16] In the latter work, R. Albert Mohler Jr. bewails the revisioning of evangelical theology undertaken by Stanley Grenz that casts doubt on the suitability of propositional revelation, in a larger doctrine of inerrancy, in order to communicate the full range of the truth of Scripture.[17]

Though the authority of the Bible was expressed by means of a doctrine of biblical inerrancy for most of the twentieth century, principally by those evangelicals whose stories lie in historic fundamentalism, it is unlikely that the majority of twenty-first-century evangelicals will continue in this vein. Such a prediction, no doubt, comes as something of a surprise to those evangelicals who have made inerrancy a litmus test or who have appealed to fear in various forms or to the specious reasoning of slippery slope arguments if such a course is ever contemplated. However, paralleling in some sense the dynamics of the structure of scientific revolutions as detailed by Thomas Kuhn, evangelical thinking about the authority of Scripture in general and inerrancy in particular is already undergoing significant and most likely lasting change. To illustrate, according to Douglas Jacobsen, a "growing number of evangelicals have rejected the traditional inerrantist position."[18] And James Davison Hunter, ever careful in his scholarship, cites the hard data that substantiates all such assertions: "Nearly 40 percent of all evangelical theologians have abandoned the belief in the inerrancy of Scripture."[19]

These modulations in the evangelical community are not all recent, but they are becoming increasingly stronger. Indeed, though he was much criticized at the time, Bernard Ramm warned early on that "the fundamentalist-modernist controversy that was at the eye of the storm . . . warped evangelical theology."[20] And Howard Marshall, noted New Testament scholar, specifically rejected inerrancy "without losing the confidence of the evangelical community."[21] Moreover, as early as 1972, Fuller Theological Seminary discerned good reasons for dropping the language of inerrancy altogether in its statement of faith, a statement that yet amply affirms not only the full authority of Scripture but also its unsurpassed normative value. The current statement reads as follows:

> Scripture is an essential part and trustworthy record of this divine self-disclosure. All the books of the Old and New Testaments, given by divine inspiration, are the written word of God, the only infallible rule of faith and practice. They are to be interpreted according to their context and purpose and in reverent obedience to the Lord, who speaks through them in living power.[22]

Beyond this, Alister McGrath, noted British evangelical, cautioned both the British and the American evangelical communities in his observation that "any view of revelation which regards God's self-disclosure as the mere transmission of facts concerning God is seriously deficient."[23] And Stanley Grenz, for his part, arguing for a more thorough and theologically sophisticated understanding of the truth of the Bible, rightly contended that evangelical theology's acceptance of the fundamentals "oriented it to questions of propositional truth, in contrast to the interest in a person's relationship with God."[24] In a way that illuminates the transforming power of the Bible, Grenz observed, "The Scriptures provide the categories by which we can understand ourselves and organize our narratives."[25] Put another way, evangelicals are not above Scripture but are ever under its authority as the Spirit addresses them and calls them forth to the obedience of faith. If these kinds of discussions are taking place in the Baptist and Presbyterian churches, which can clearly trace their roots back to the rise of fundamentalism, what about those communities of faith that contain significant numbers of evangelicals, such as the Methodists, the Salvation Army, and the Mennonites, who have never had such a fundamentalist heritage? To be sure, it is the frank recognition of the plural nature of American evangelicalism as well as attentiveness to these "other" stories as part of a larger evangelical identity that should result in significant discussions of the authority of Scripture in the days ahead.

Though the beginning of the twenty-first century, in light of the preceding, has obviously been marked by a vigorous debate among American evangelicals about how best to express the full implications of the inspiration and the authority of the Bible, there is actually a level of considerable *unanimity* between the "Old Lights," who prefer the language of "inerrancy," and the

"New Lights," who embrace the language of "trustworthiness." Indeed, virtually all American evangelicals are united in affirming the unique authority of Scripture, that the Bible as the *Word of God* is in some respects unlike all other books. In other words, the Bible remains the *normata normans* for the evangelical community in a way that it has ceased to function for theological liberals. That is, evangelicals are and remain preeminently a biblical people, and their outlook, morals, hopes, and dreams all coalesce around Scripture. The Bible's idioms and cadences are found on their lips, its precepts are inscribed in their minds, and its promises, especially the good news of the gospel, are emblazoned on their hearts. The stories of the Bible are a constant friend and guide to evangelicals as they face all the challenges that living in an increasingly vulgar and post-Christian age brings. Yes, there is far more unanimity among evangelicals with respect to Scripture than appears at first glance. Indeed, the very energy and passion of their ongoing discussions demonstrate all the more clearly that they are nothing less than "a people of the book."

## The Atoning Work of Christ

One of the leading themes in Scripture is the passion and death of the Messiah, the sacrifice of the Suffering Servant. In fact, in some Gospel accounts, almost a quarter of the material is devoted to the careful telling of this historical event. Little wonder, then, that the cross of Jesus Christ, who is the one and only mediator between God and humanity, is at the center of evangelical faith and witness. Indeed, while other theological traditions such as Eastern Orthodoxy have preferred, by and large, to emphasize the incarnation, evangelicals, while not neglecting the importance of the Word made flesh in Jesus Christ, have stressed the cruciality of the cross for Christian life and practice. From Augustus Toplady's hymn "Rock of Ages, Cleft for Me" in the eighteenth century to Fanny Crosby's "Jesus, Keep Me Near the Cross" in the nineteenth century to the old beloved African American spiritual "Were You There (When They Crucified My Lord)?" revised in the twentieth, American evangelical churches have resounded with the songs of the death of Christ.

Recognizing that the atoning work of Jesus Christ, foreseen in the Old Testament and expressed in the New, is so rich in significance, evangelicals have an almost natural appreciation for the several theories of the atonement that have surfaced in the church throughout the ages. Each theory of the atonement, of course, *as a theory* is a human construct, an artfully conceived creation put forth in order to best explore the witness of Scripture to the full range of meaning concerning the death of Christ. Five major theories have emerged that illustrate this range.

First of all, the ransom theory, held by Origen and Augustine and designated the classic theory in Gustaf Aulen's work *Christus Victor*,[26] maintains that humanity was enslaved to Satan, as the ruler of this world, and therefore needed to be delivered from this bondage by the ransom of the death of Christ. But when the question, "To whom was this ransom paid?" was posed and seriously considered, difficulties with this theory began to emerge. By the time of the Middle Ages, for instance, several scholars, Anselm among them, criticized the notion that Satan has any rights with respect to humanity or redemption, a troubling notion that could possibly be deduced from the classic view.[27]

Second, the Latin theory championed by Anselm, archbishop of Canterbury, during the eleventh century was promulgated in his groundbreaking text *Cur Deus Homo* (Why God Became Human), and this work constitutes perhaps the best expression of the satisfaction theory of the atonement. In this view, the death of Christ, in some sense, satisfied the offended honor of God. Here the "Godward" aspects of the atonement, the elements that pertain to the satisfaction of divine justice, are amply treated, but some have suggested, even in Anselm's own age, that the "humanward" aspects of a *mediated* relation, that is, how human rebellion and resistance to God can be overcome, are left largely unexplored.

Third, the weakness of the satisfaction theory, interestingly enough, became the strength of the moral influence theory or the subjective view of the atonement. Advanced in a thoroughgoing way in the twelfth century by Abelard, French scholastic and rival of Bernard of Clairvaux, the moral influence theory sees the grounds for the necessity of the atonement not in God but in humanity. In other words, human sin, rebellion, and even outright hatred of God must be overcome *in the human heart* by a magnificent display of the humble, sacrificial love of God so evident at Calvary. But as Anselm had his critics, so too did Abelard. The chief complaint was not only that divine justice and holiness in this setting are hardly addressed but also that if the atonement were indeed "subjective," could not an easier, less costly way have been found by an omniscient God to demonstrate divine love other than the humiliating and wrenchingly painful death of Christ?

Fourth, the governmental theory expounded by Jacobus Arminius in the sixteenth century and by Hugo Grotius, a Dutch jurist, in the seventeenth focuses on the integrity of the moral order, which is vigorously maintained by God through a public demonstration of the punishment of sin, a demonstration that also serves to deter the ongoing practice of evil. This view, though centuries old, is sometimes expressed even today among Wesleyan Arminian evangelicals as they reflect on the full significance of the death of Christ.

Finally, the atoning work of Christ considered chiefly as a penal substitution, a variation on Anselm's satisfaction theory, whereby Christ was not only our substitute at Calvary but also the bearer of our just and righteous penalty, can be found in the writings of Luther and Calvin as well as Wesley. In this view, Christ is one with the Father ("God was in Christ reconciling the world to himself, not counting their trespasses against them" [2 Cor. 5:19]) and yet as the sole and unsurpassed mediator is one with sinners ("He made him who knew no sin to be sin on our behalf, so that we might become the righteousness of God in him" [2 Cor. 5:21]).

Though the evangelical faith as proclaimed in America today resonates with several of the theories of the atonement just outlined, some key leaders have insisted that the substitutionary atonement theory lies at the heart of the evangelical faith and witness. J. I. Packer, for example, affirms that substitutionary atonement is "a distinguishing mark of the world-wide evangelical fraternity (even though it often gets misunderstood and caricatured by its critics); it takes us to the very heart of the Christian gospel."[28] Moreover, Alister McGrath observes, "Evangelicalism places a special emphasis on the centrality of the cross of Christ. The cross is the unique and perfect sacrifice that covers and shields us from the righteous anger of God against sin."[29] And the *Cambridge Declaration,* which emerged out of a seminal conference of evangelical pastors, teachers, and leaders in Cambridge, Massachusetts, in 1996, declares, "We deny that the gospel is preached if Christ's substitutionary work is not declared and faith in Christ and his work is not solicited."[30]

Many theological liberals (and even some younger evangelicals) find the language of substitution remarkably troubling, especially as it highlights both the *penalty* of the death of Christ as well as the *wrath* of God. Indeed, according to John Stott, acclaimed British evangelical, "No two words in the theological vocabulary of the cross arouse more criticism than 'satisfaction' and 'substitution.'"[31] In its most stereotypical and exaggerated form, penal substitution supposedly embraces such troubling assertions as "God abuses his Son, glorifies suffering and encourages victims to be subservient."[32] Richard Mouw, scholar, churchman, and president of Fuller Theological Seminary, points out that "liberals would accuse [evangelicals] of adhering to a slaughterhouse religion in which a primitive deity could get over his anger only if he smelled the blood of his enemies—or a fitting sacrificial substitute."[33]

Two prominent evangelical scholars, drawn from both the Reformed and the Wesleyan communities, who have done more to lay aside some of the stereotypes, half-truths, and outright muddled thinking that have at times informed the criticism of a penal substitutionary doctrine of the atonement are John Stott and Richard Taylor. Stott, for instance, in his classic work *The Cross of Christ,* first of all notes that the "Bible everywhere views human death not as a natural but as a *penal* event. It is an intrusion into God's good world and not a part of his original intention for humankind."[34] Second, Stott explores the historical reality of the Passover in terms of not only its Old Testament setting but also its New Testament significance. He demonstrates how this sacrifice, the death of the Passover lamb with all its typological meaning, richly informs the death of Christ. This evangelical scholar also carefully draws a relation between the Suffering Servant of Isaiah 53—in which the theme of penal substitution is strong—and the person and work of Christ. "It seems to be definite beyond doubt, then, that Jesus applied Isaiah 53 to himself," Stott observes, "and that he understood his death in the light of it as a sin-bearing death."[35] Beyond this, Stott suggests that it is only when the sacrifice of the Passover lamb and the Suffering Servant of Isaiah 53 are separated from their New Testament explication that criticism of the substitutionary atonement can take root.[36] In fact, contemporary views that repudiate penal substitution have little basis on which to draw the appropriate connections between the Old Testament and the New with respect to a crucified Lord who is sacrificed on the altar of a cross. Thus, the temple offerings, the Levitical priesthood, the Passover lamb, and even the Pentateuch, in a sense, are all left dangling in their Old Testament context with little significance for Christian believers. But Stott draws the proper balance, explores the typological relations, and demonstrates the continuity of the two covenants in his pithy statement:

> For the essence of sin is man substituting himself for God, while the essence of salvation is God substituting himself for man. Man asserts himself against God and puts himself where only God deserves to be; God sacrifices himself for man and puts himself where only man deserves to be. Man claims prerogatives which belong to God alone. God accepts penalties which belong to man alone.[37]

To clear up any lingering misunderstanding, Stott insists that the "Judge and Saviour are the same person." That is, "We must never characterize the Father as Judge and the Son as Saviour. It is one and the same God who through Christ saves us from himself."[38]

This last statement may prove to be a puzzle to some contemporary believers who have sentimentalized the love of God and thereby have mistaken it for a divine indulgence of sinners left in their sin or have assumed that the Most High does not take sin seriously. As Dietrich Bonhoeffer taught us so many years ago, just as there is such a thing as cheap grace, the kind of grace that entails "the justification of sin without the justification of the sinner,"[39] so too is there cheap love. It is the kind of love that lacks seriousness, pays no price, and in the end "tolerates" evil—all of this in the name of kindness, affability, and social grace.

As a corrective to these grievous misunderstandings, Richard Taylor, competent Nazarene scholar, affirms that God is holy as well as loving and that holiness governs the way love functions.[40] "It is never a love ungoverned by holiness," he cautions. "Holiness requires that sin be costly, [and] love bore the cost."[41] While making it clear that it is not his purpose to minimize the relation of the cross to the love of God but to "establish the relation of the cross to God's integrity,"[42] Taylor holds both the love as well as the holiness of God in a careful, well-nuanced tension, a tension that is expressive of the sophisticated biblical witness itself. Consequently, all sentimentalized versions of the atonement, which fail to take seriously the *holy* love that informs the integrity of God, ultimately falter in failing to recognize the God with whom we have to deal. In other words, the Most High is uncannily holy, distinct, set apart, the One whose eyes are too pure to behold evil, the One of whom the author of the book of Hebrews exclaims, "It is a terrifying thing to fall into the hands of the living God" (10:31).

For Taylor, then, precisely because God is holy, the Most High cannot simply wink at sin, for to do so would be to deny the beauty and the integrity of the divine nature itself. Instead, sin must be judged, and part of the richness of the good news of the gospel is that Christ as the unique mediator between God and humanity bore the judgment, suffered the curse, and paid the penalty that should have rightfully fallen on all humanity. To those evangelicals, especially in the Wesleyan communion of faith, who have basically denied that the death of Christ was indeed a penal substitution in their preference for a version of the governmental theory of the atonement, Taylor offers this caution:

> If Christ's blood was not primarily penal in nature and directly a means of satisfying the moral and legal claims against the sinner, but rather merely a means of proclaiming God's wrath against sin for the sake of upholding moral government, then the connection between Christ's death and the Old Testament breaks down.[43]

In a way remarkably similar to Stott, Taylor adds that in this setting "the continuity between [Christ's] blood and the shedding of blood in the Old Testament disappears."[44]

In light of the contributions of both Stott and Taylor, it is clear that many evangelicals see the cross at the center of their faith. Redemption, though free by God's grace, remains costly. Jesus Christ, despised and rejected by many, bore that cost in humble, obedient sacrifice precisely because a holy God so loved the world. Such truths are often found on evangelical lips as they proclaim the gospel; such truths are often cherished in their hearts as they minister to a hurting world. Again, the death of Christ is precious in evangelical eyes, for it is a death that removed the temple curtain to unveil a God of holy love, a love that is serious in its sacrifice and joyous in its forgiveness and embrace.

## Conversion

As one of their more prominent identifying traits, American evangelicals have stressed the importance of being regenerated or born again. This language is not new but is actually drawn from the pages of the New Testament in which Jesus declares to Nicodemus at a late-night meeting, "Truly, truly, I say to you, unless one is born again he cannot see the kingdom of God" (John 3:3). Some scholars translate the Greek phrase γεννηθῇ ἄνωθεν as "born from above," which is an option, while others prefer the translation "born again," especially since the context seems to suggest it. That is, in this well-known and often-cited passage, Nicodemus is actually pondering how difficult it would be for a person to go back into a mother's womb. At any rate, evangelicals employ this language to underscore the salient truth that being renewed and washed in the blood of the lamb, just as a bloody baby comes fresh out of its mother's womb, is not a superficial matter but affects a person thoroughly with respect to outlook, attitude, and purpose. Indeed, this work of grace as a sheer gift of God is nothing short of a new creation, and it is, therefore, hard to overestimate its importance for evangelicals.

When George Gallup, the popular American pollster, conducted a recent survey, he discovered that "nearly four in ten adults (39%) claim to be evangelical believers."[45] Three criteria were integral to this designation. People had to regard the Bible as the Word of God, "although belief in its inerrancy [was] not mandated";[46] they had to have experienced some form of personal conversion; and they had to have a desire to "lead nonbelievers to a point of conversion."[47] Though the percentage who maintain that they have had a born-again experience may seem high, especially given the depth of this work of grace, the numbers are even higher with respect to African Americans. "Black Americans exceed the national trends for evangelicalism,"

Gallup explains. "Fifty-eight percent of them described their spiritual lives as born again."[48] Moreover, though Protestants outdistance Roman Catholics in identifying a conversion experience by a ratio of greater than two to one, over 20 percent of American Roman Catholics attest to this reality today.[49] Such trends suggest that in the days ahead, white, Protestant, American evangelicals may come to a greater appreciation that they have more in common with their African American and Roman Catholic neighbors than perhaps they had initially imagined. The barriers of race and theological tradition that sometime divide may yet be transcended in the recognition of the one Spirit who is above us all.

Though the born-again experience is well attested in America, many misunderstandings still surround this evangelical emphasis on regeneration or conversion. For one thing, the new birth is not simply a sociological and demographic reality that can be tracked by pollsters. It is also at the heart of the New Testament witness to the *radical* transformation that occurs in the lives of believers who are rooted in Jesus Christ. Joanmarie Smith explains:

> Any belief is legitimately called radical when it strikes at the roots of our identity, belief system, and life style. To heat up any such belief and move it to the center stage is so dis-easing that the fact that it ever happens makes conversion seem like a supernatural event—an interference in the laws of inertia.[50]

This radical nature of conversion is sometimes missed, however, when critics of the evangelical emphasis on being born again deem this reality to be little more than a pious indulgence, a species of excessive individualism, or worse yet needless self-preoccupation in the face of a hurting world.[51] Indeed, theological liberals even today often set up a tension between the individual and the social dimensions of the gospel, and once they find the individual aspects problematic, even egocentric, they proceed almost exclusively on a social and political level, neglecting for the most part the precious life of the soul.

But all of this, of course, is to begin in the wrong place. American evangelicals are not championing the wonders of individualism when they underscore the necessity of being born again. Instead, they are highlighting the reality of the *personal* dimensions of the gospel, that saving faith in Jesus Christ is not a superficial work but a work of great depth in the life of the soul, one that touches believers deeply in terms of their hearts, dispositions, and affections. Richard Mouw elaborates:

> We present-day evangelicals, like the pietists of the past, insist that to be a Christian, properly understood, is to experience the regeneration of the inner self, so

that the claims of the gospel are appropriated in a very personal way. We want people to know Jesus as a living Savior.[52]

Like the atoning work of Jesus Christ, the reality of being born again is so rich in meaning and purpose that many frameworks are needed to express such richness. On a physical level, the new birth often leads to healing and better care of the body, now viewed as the temple of the Holy Spirit, as Pentecostal evangelicals have reminded us so well. On the psychological level, the new birth results in integration, the harmony of thoughts, loves, and passions now centered in a holy and loving God. On the spiritual level, the new birth is manifested in transcendence, a genuine going beyond the resources and limitations of the solitary, natural self to enjoy the grace of God as a sheer utter gift and life in the Spirit as an emblem of that grace. On a social level, the new birth arises out of and issues in fellowship and community, the oneness of the Spirit that unites brothers and sisters and that breaks down the artificial, humanly constructed barriers that often divide us. Finally, on a political level, the new birth is manifested in concern for the "other," especially for those who have the least of all, for the poor and the downtrodden across the globe. All this and more pertain to the reality of being born again. Little wonder, then, that American evangelicals have stressed its importance.

Sometimes, however, the cruciality of the new birth is neglected or even repudiated in a second way by those who appeal to a distinction developed by William James, early in the twentieth century, between healthy minded and sick souls, the former needing to be born only once, the latter needing to be born yet again.[53] But to deny that all people must be regenerated is not only to fail to recognize the depth and extent of original sin, in all its unbelief, alienation, and pride, the inordinate self-curvature out of which people cannot deliver themselves, but also to mistake some form of personal or social virtue for the very substance of redemption. But as Søren Kierkegaard demonstrated so ably in the nineteenth century, the opposite of sin is not virtue; the opposite of sin is faith.[54]

A slight variant of this view put forth by James is that one can know oneself as almost always having been a Christian. Since the time of one's baptism as an infant to the rigors of old age, there is never a need for what evangelicals call the new birth.[55] This conception presupposes that the new birth occurs *only* in infancy (as in some mainline Protestant understandings), and therefore no radical transformation needs to occur again throughout the course of one's life. Such a view looks remarkably similar in its outworking, though of course it is not identical, to the once born model of James. Observe, however, that the crucial question in this setting is not whether infants are regenerated (although that is an important issue in its own right) but whether there is any *further* need of change as moral accountability and spiritual responsibility are reached and as life progresses with all of its problems, challenges, and defeats.

To illuminate this important query, it is helpful to appeal to the life and thought of John Wesley, the father of Methodism and a principal leader of the eighteenth-century British revival. As a good Anglican, Wesley did not deny the reality of infant regeneration, though in a very evangelical way he stressed the importance of further renewal. Once born models and their variants in the Christian teaching of infant baptismal regeneration were simply not enough for this evangelical leader. Indeed, Wesley was painfully familiar with numerous instances of those who had been baptized in infancy (or in their later years) who yet had none of the marks of the new birth and who were instead steeped in sin: "How many are the baptized gluttons and drunkards, the baptized liars and common swearers, the baptized railers and evil-speakers, the baptized whoremongers, thieves, extortioners?"[56] he asked. "What think you? Are these now the children of God?"[57]

Such questions, of course, reveal that Wesley simply refused to comfort these open, flagrant sinners with the notion that they were still the sons and daughters of God, heirs of the kingdom of heaven, because they had been baptized in their youth. "Say not then in your heart," Wesley wrote, "I *was once* baptized; therefore I am *now* a child of God. Alas, that consequence will by no means hold."[58] And again, "Lean no more on the staff of that broken reed, that ye *were* born again in baptism."[59] Indeed, to the mistaken claim that there is no new birth beyond baptism, a claim inimical in so many ways to the evangelical emphasis on transformation and renewal, Wesley energetically responded in his *Farther Appeal:*

> I tell a sinner, "You must be born again." "No," say you, "He was born again in baptism. Therefore he cannot be born again now." Alas! What trifling is this? What if he was *then* a child of God? He is *now* manifestly a "child of the devil!" For the works of his father *he* doth. Therefore do not play upon words. He must go through an entire change of heart.[60]

Accordingly, to counsel these sinners that there is no new birth but in infant baptism, that they can no longer be renewed and cleansed after they have succumbed to the enslaving powers of sin, is cruel counsel indeed. It is, says Wesley, "to seal [them] all under damnation, to consign [them] to hell, without any help, without any hope."[61]

One last way in which the evangelical emphasis on being born again can be misunderstood is to maintain that the new birth must always be dramatic or that its exact time must always be known. Both assumptions are false. Though the apostle Paul, Augustine, Luther, Pascal, and Wesley all had dramatic and memorable conversions, many evangelicals chronicle a narrative that occurred over time, whereby the Holy Spirit slowly and patiently wooed the soul until it entered into the very heart of redemption. Nevertheless, if the supernatural and redeeming grace of God was *actualized* or *realized* in time and space, in the warp and woof of life, then there was indeed a moment, even if that moment cannot be recalled or even recognized. By way of analogy, can many people remember the exact day and hour that they first fell in love with their spouse? Few actually can, though many agree that a significant, not a superficial, modification of the heart actually occurred at some point in the past. Both truths, then, must be affirmed. There is process, to be sure, but also instantiation, an instantiation that highlights the significance of this life-changing grace. Billy Graham weaves these two themes remarkably well as he considered the conversion experience of his own wife, Ruth, in the following words: "My wife, for example, cannot remember the exact day or hour when she became a Christian, but she is certain that there was such a moment in her life, a moment when she actually crossed the line."[62]

Since the process of redemption must also be understood in terms of the actualization of grace, that process can never simply be open-ended. If one, for example, is taking a trip from New York to California, it cannot be all process, for there must finally come the point of actualization, of arrival in California. In the same way, ask evangelicals if they are saved, and they will likely respond enthusiastically, "Yes." They have the assurance, in some measure, that they are *now* the sons and daughters of God. Ask some Eastern Orthodox believers, on the other hand, the same question, and they may respond with not something as bold as that they are saved but that they are "being saved." Evangelicals, however, by and large, while genuinely appreciative of this Christian tradition, have found this response somewhat troubling because the process of redemption apparently does not eventuate in the instantiation of key graces (Christian assurance, for instance) where a line is crossed, to use the language of Ruth Graham, and all things become new.

Viewed in another way, the continuity of process must be matched by the discontinuity, the concluding work of actualization. That is, aspirants to God's grace, for many evangelicals, cannot simply evolve into the new birth; they cannot simply be nurtured into conversion as if it were an open-ended process of socialization, theological instruction, or better churchmanship. Why is this so? Because these significant works of grace are preceded by nothing less than the discontinuity of death. The new does not appear out of the reform or the nurturing of the old; rather, the old must die. Once more Bonhoeffer is both to the point and instructive: "When Christ calls a man . . . he bids him come and die."[63] And in a similar fashion, Donald Bloesch maintains that "the old man must die. He must be crucified and buried. He cannot evolve into the new."[64] All of this, then, highlights the significant truth that though conversion may not be dramatic or its exact time even remembered, it is nevertheless an actualized, instantiated change that is momentous, life-changing, and in its best sense a supernatural work of God's sovereign grace. American evangelicals, then, have been wonderfully appropriate and theologically astute in celebrating its importance.

## Evangelism

Motivated by an overwhelming spirit of thankfulness and gratitude, evangelicals are eager to proclaim the good news of the gospel, what God, through Christ and by means of the Holy Spirit, has done for their bodies and souls. Indeed, the work of an evangelist, as one who is a "publisher of glad tidings," and as reflected in the activity of Philip (Acts 21:8), has been so eagerly embraced by American evangelicals that in Protestant liberal, Roman Catholic, and even secular circles, "the words evangelical and evangelism are often used incorrectly to mean the same thing."[65] But as Richard Quebedeaux reminded us so many years ago, an "evangelical is something you *are*, evangelism is something you *do*."[66]

Today, the challenges of as well as the opportunities for spreading the gospel have never been greater. One especially troubling challenge arises out of postmodern thought, which contends that Christians, in professing the universality of the gospel (there is neither male nor female, slave nor free, Jew nor Gentile), not only are attempting to superimpose their own story or metanarrative on others by maintaining that Jesus Christ is the *only* way to salvation but also are failing to recognize the full extent of our radically pluralistic environment. In response to this criticism, Alister McGrath, in developing a distinction originally crafted by Lesslie Newbigin,[67] differentiates "descriptive pluralism," which takes full account of diversity and difference by acknowledging its reality, from "prescriptive pluralism," which seeks to impose a pluralistic paradigm in a normative way to the exclusion of any universal claims.[68] This British evangelical elaborates:

> Claims by any one group or individual to have any exclusive hold on "truth" are thus treated as the intellectual equivalent of Fascism. This form of pluralism

is strongly prescriptive, seeking to lay down what may be believed, rather than merely describing what is believed.[69]

The ironic nature of postmodern prescriptive pluralism, even its contradictory claims, should be obvious. In seeking to eliminate the "hegemony" and the "oppressive" nature of Christianity's universal claims, prescriptive pluralism, in a coercive fashion, has created its own hegemony of political correctness, one in which the inclusive, ethnocentric-transcending claims of the Christian faith are not tolerated but are actually silenced, and all of this in the name of pluralism!

While mainline denominations, influenced by postmodernism as a cultural movement and in an attempt to respect the dictates of prescriptive pluralism, have been and largely remain ambivalent about the evangelization of non-Christians,[70] evangelicals continue to maintain the "priority of evangelism and conversion"[71] in a way that is faithful to the narrative of the church. Not surprisingly, then, evangelicals dominate in the areas of both evangelism and mission. "Fifty years ago," Nathan Hatch and Michael Hamilton point out, "evangelical agencies sponsored 40 percent of all American missionaries; today the figure is over 90 percent."[72] Again, among theological liberals, evangelism and missions, in the sense of winning sinners to Christ to redeem them from eternal death, are considered merely "a secondary task of the church."[73] In some cases, these tasks are actually completely dissociated from the work of the community of faith. In fact, among mainline liberals, the historic language of "missions," which entailed conversion and the making of Christians in lands where there were few or none at all, has been replaced by the term *mission,* which refers to "everything the Church is sent into the world to do."[74] The former term underscores the importance of personal and social salvation and embodied transformation, and it is fleshed out in the practices of the church, especially in the means of grace. The later term, on the other hand, is far less focused and is often open to diverse understandings of redemption in which "justice" becomes the principal theme and is more often than not informed by secular political ideology, a script that is not the church's own—a story that, in a real sense, is alien to a kingdom ethic.

So determined have evangelicals been on reaching the world for Christ that they have overcome, in a very ecumenical way, national, denominational, and cultural boundaries in order to proclaim the gospel, and they have fostered international conferences on evangelism to that end. The first major International Congress on World Evangelism occurred in Lausanne, Switzerland, in 1974. The Second International Congress, known as Lausanne II, took place in Manila, the Philippines, in July 1989. The major theme of this second assembly was "the evangelization of the world under the catchword 'A.D. 2000.'"[75] Both conferences held together, in a sophisticated and earnest way, the importance of personal and social action and the depth of the good news of the gospel as well as its far-ranging extent. Indeed, as Richard Hutcheson points out, "The Lausanne combination of evangelicalism and social responsibility is probably much closer to the spirit of third world Christianity generally than is mainline American liberalism."[76] Moreover, one of the principal evangelical instruments to effectuate this combination on a global level is World Vision International, an organization whose purpose includes following Jesus Christ by working with the poor and oppressed, seeking justice as informed by the church's own story, and bearing witness to the good news of the gospel among the least of all.

Closer to home, American evangelicals have established a number of parachurch structures and organizations with the goal of fostering interdenominational cooperation (reminiscent of the voluntary societies of the nineteenth century), especially in the area of evangelism. For example, the National Association of Evangelicals, described in greater detail in the last chapter, brings together a host of denominations and groups that are genuinely concerned about inviting those beyond the walls of the church to enter in and thereby come to know the goodness, truth, and beauty that is Jesus Christ. However, much more focused in its evangelistic purpose is the Billy Graham Evangelistic Association, which for more than half a century has sought to win as many people to Christ as possible by conducting major crusades and evangelistic rallies both in North America and around the world.[77] Unfortunately, no corresponding group with such an evangelistic purpose exists among theological liberals. Billy Graham has the field almost by default.

Campus Crusade for Christ, founded in 1951 by the late Bill Bright and his wife, Vonette, as a ministry to students at UCLA, is a thriving evangelistic organization. Today, this parachurch structure empowers ministries in more than 190 countries and employs roughly 25,000 staff and more than half a million trained volunteers. Central to the message of Campus Crusade, of course, are the four spiritual laws (God loves us; humanity is sinful and separated from God; Jesus Christ is the only provision for sin; all must, therefore, receive Jesus Christ as Lord and Savior), laws that though often criticized by liberal evangelicals, whom Richard Quebedeaux in an earlier period called "the worldly evangelicals," nevertheless state the basic truths of the gospel in a way that most people, even those slow of understanding, can easily comprehend.

In a similar fashion, InterVarsity Christian Fellowship/USA is an evangelical and interdenominational campus ministry whose purpose is to raise up witnessing communities of students and faculty who follow Jesus Christ as

Savior and Lord. A special emphasis of this fellowship has been to demonstrate the universality of the gospel by transcending ethnic and cultural divisions. Unlike Campus Crusade, however, InterVarsity has British roots. Like Oxford Methodism in the eighteenth century, InterVarsity began in 1877 at the University of Cambridge, where a group of students began to meet together to pray and study the Bible and to witness to others, despite the disapproval of some university officials. Today, InterVarsity is active on more than 560 college and university campuses in the United States. It employs more than 1,000 people in a variety of positions, and 34,000 students and faculty participate in its ministries. Beyond this, its publishing house, InterVarsity Press, is well known for excellence in Christian literature.

Add to these evangelistic ministries the efforts of World Vision International, which labors on six continents on behalf of the poor; the Navigators, which emphasizes one-to-one relationships and small group studies and has been especially effective among military personnel (though its ministry is by no means limited to them); and Evangelism Explosion International, which was founded by D. James Kennedy in Florida but currently ministers in over two hundred countries, and the picture that begins to emerge is one in which the evangelistic activity of American evangelicalism is and remains nothing less than prodigious.

## The Value of Distinctives

Because evangelicals take Scripture so seriously as the lodestar of their lives, they are suitably equipped to undertake the difficult task of reform with respect to those Christians who have allowed current political movements, philosophical trends, or even popular ideologies to redefine or in some cases to replace the truth of the gospel. Because evangelicals greatly value the atoning, sacrificial work of Jesus Christ, knowing at what terrible cost salvation comes, they are properly directed toward the joyous and at times exuberant worship of God in both Word and sacrament. Because evangelicals underscore the significance and necessity of the new birth, they can foster the healing work of renewal in those communions of faith whose theologies and practices so easily spawn nominal Christianity or who mistake docility, good churchmanship, or even the formal elements of religion for the very highest graces. And because evangelicals are so thankful, indeed, eternally grateful, for the sheer utter gift of salvation, the result of divine grace *alone,* they are galvanized to proclaim the good news of the gospel both near and far with an energy and an enthusiasm that are contagious.

All these distinctives, then, not only empower evangelicals to pursue their prophetic high calling as they proclaim the essential and perennial truths of the Christian faith but also render them suitable dialogue partners with those both inside and outside the church who are eager to go deeper into the very heart of the Christian faith. To be sure, the clear and uncomplicated focus on the basics of salvation, for which evangelicals are well known and at times smugly criticized, and the avoidance of the unduly speculative and the inane allow this godly people to have both an intensity and a direction in their many conversations that befit the wonder and the beauty of the gospel and that in the end are of inordinate value to the church.

# 3

# The Wesleyan Leavening
# of Evangelicalism

To describe the richness of American evangelicalism properly, cultural observers must be aware of the diversity of stories that represent different church traditions, polities, and even theological understandings. In the twentieth century, however, one story or paradigm dominated the discussion to the virtual exclusion of other key voices. Indeed, ever since Harold Ockenga took on the label "neoevangelical," the Reformed or Presbyterian wing of the movement has often presented itself as if it were virtually equivalent to American evangelicalism.[1] This identification is especially troubling when the theological preferences of a particular tradition, in this case some form of Calvinism, are mistakenly identified with the very substance of American evangelicalism. Indeed, when such judgments are made, Wesleyan Arminianism can only emerge as a "liberal" departure from the basic evangelical (read Reformed) way.

# The Dayton/Marsden Debate Revisited

During the latter part of the twentieth century, the scholar who did more than anyone else to gain a basic hearing for the theological and sociological contributions of the Wesleyan and Pentecostal communities of faith to broader American evangelicalism was Donald Dayton. Indeed, the historiographical observations of this leading Wesleyan scholar sparked a lively debate with George Marsden, the dean of American evangelical historians. In this ongoing dialogue, which lasted several years, Dayton distinguished what he termed a "presbyterian paradigm" from a "pentecostal" one. He described the former in the following way:

> By the "presbyterian paradigm" I mean *any* understanding of "evangelicalism" that interprets the phenomenon as a "conservative" or "traditional" or "orthodox" response to the Enlightenment—any position that interprets "evangelicalism" primarily in terms of a "conservative/liberal" spectrum on which "evangelicalism" is a point just to the left of fundamentalism and just to the right of conservative, neoorthodoxy, no matter what the denominational tradition in question (whether Presbyterian, Methodist, Catholic, or whatever).[2]

In this pointed observation, Dayton questioned whether the maintenance of doctrinal orthodoxy, displayed along a conservative/liberal axis, best describes American evangelicalism. Are evangelicals, for instance, principally concerned about issues pertaining to truth, epistemology, and doctrinal articulation? Such a judgment, he contended, is plausible only if one makes the fundamentalist controversy and the neoevangelicalism that followed in its wake the very heart of the tradition.

To counter the effects of this "reigning" model, especially when it operates in a coercive way, muting or even distorting the voices of other key stories, Dayton offered his "pentecostal" paradigm. The term *pentecostal* in this setting is employed in a specialized way. It does not refer specifically to any one theological tradition or even to a distinct mode of worship.[3] Rather, the term *pentecostal,* so employed, underscores sociological and cultural considerations, as revealed in Dayton's following observation:

> By this [the pentecostal paradigm] I mean that "evangelicalism" is related to the rest of Christianity more as the Pentecostal or Charismatic movements—that is as a specific and modern form of Christianity that disrupts the "traditional" and "conservative" churches—and less as the "orthodoxy" from which the "mainstream churches have departed in their supposed rush to 'liberalism.'"[4]

Put another way, the pentecostal paradigm entails "the pulling off of the 'underchurch' of the mainline denominations in response to a wedding to the middle class."[5] Here the axis is not the doctrinal one of conservative/liberal that highlights orthodoxy and is so prominent in the presbyterian paradigm but the sociological (and political) axis of radical/bourgeois that highlights social reform. In defining evangelicalism this way, Dayton chose a different period of American religious history to inform his preferences. Instead of the fundamentalism of the twentieth century, socially conservative and at times reactionary, Dayton lifted up the great evangelical reforms of the nineteenth century in terms of the revivalism and perfectionist tendencies that fed into them and that galvanized the causes of abolitionism and the rights of women.

This radical/bourgeois axis is in some sense descriptive of the nineteenth-century Holiness movement and the British Methodism that preceded it in that it underscores the salient truth that both movements were principally, though not exclusively, soteriologically rather than epistemologically oriented. To be sure, both John Wesley in England and Orange Scott and B. T. Roberts in America assumed that doctrinal orthodoxy, for the most part, was *already* in place, with the notable *exceptions* of the doctrines of entire sanctification and Christian assurance.[6] Accordingly, their ministries (as well as their occasional criticisms) proceeded in the largely pietistic fashion of reforming the broader, acculturated church. That is, all three men were chiefly concerned about the specter of nominal Christianity in which self-identified Christians were seen as simply having the form of religion but not its power.[7] Again, Wesley, Scott, and Roberts all tried to inculcate both personal and social holiness in their respective settings, whereby the love of God reigning in the human heart would ever issue in reform of both the church and the broader society, a gracious movement that in its full outworking was a fine instance of the love of God and neighbor. In all of this, Dayton's analysis was very much on target.

But in another sense, Dayton's radical/bourgeois axis was not descriptive of Wesley's well-nuanced and carefully articulated doctrine of salvation and social action, nor was it expressive of the reformist concerns of nineteenth-century leaders such as Theodore Weld or Charles Finney. Growing up in the wake of 1960s radicalism, Dayton apparently assumed that the reforming impulses of this period and its aftermath were remarkably similar to Wesley's work among the poor and to the radicalism of antebellum American Christianity, Oberlin College and the Lane rebels in particular. However, the analysis of Dayton moves much too easily from the language of contemporary leftist thought, with all its politically correct agendas, "preferential options," and Marxist readings of society—a clear throwback to the sixties—to the reformist movements of the nineteenth and eighteenth centuries, where they simply do not belong. In short, the problem of anachronism here is simply insuperable. Differing social, theological, and historical locations do indeed make a difference.

Pointing out that he is "more comfortable with certain (perhaps post-Marxist) themes concerning the way in which theological ideas often mask ideological concerns and class interests,"[8] Dayton pursued this class-attentive analysis as he considered the work of Wesley: "One aspect of pietism and its related currents was a profound commitment to a 'preferential option for the poor,' flowing in the nineteenth century [*sic*] in John Wesley's work among the neglected working classes of England."[9] Though the father of Methodism greatly loved the poor and humbly ministered to their needs in a way almost without parallel in Christian history,[10] his ministry was informed principally by what is best termed a "kingdom ethic," the universal love of God and neighbor, not by the requisites of an ideological theory such as Marxism (and post-Marxist themes) or any other class-driven analysis that gives the maintenance needs of the poor or their social condition an ultimacy that they simply cannot bear. Moreover, though some liberation theologians have balked at calling the poor "sinners" (and I am not suggesting that Dayton did this) simply because they have placed class and economic interests at the soteriological center, Wesley, on the other hand, had no such reservations. Indeed, to call the poor "sinners," in the British leader's estimation, was nothing less than a high honor. That is, such a designation ever held before the oppressed, in a kind and gracious way, that the most important and determinative thing about them was not their economic status, no matter how severe, but that they were beings made for a relationship with no one less than a holy God of love.

Furthermore, though Wesley was concerned about the harmful effects of wealth on the Methodists, which could strip them of the very power of religion,[11] his salvific concern was transmuted, at least to some extent, in Dayton's theme of "embourgeoisement," a term that often plays out in Marxist and other leftist class analyses of religion with all their confused and at times ill-advised deprecation of the middle class.[12] To be sure, Wesley's fear was that the Methodists would become rich; Dayton's fear, however, was that they would become middle class. Eighteenth-century British Methodism, according to Henry Rack, ministered for the most part to the "middling" sort, those tradesmen who were down on their luck.[13] Dayton, on the other hand, maintained that both Wesley and the Holiness movement ministered to the lower class, the truly marginalized, the very least of all.

Just how far down the economic scale Wesley and the Holiness movement actually reached may surprise some readers, especially given some of the reigning myths. To be sure, eighteenth-century British Methodism, the nineteenth-century American Holiness movement, as well as twentieth-century Pentecostalism all generally ministered to people of the lower middle class and beyond. The truly marginalized, on the other hand, the very least of all in these respective societies, were hardly reached by the church then as now. In other words, what sociologists call the lower class as well as the more impoverished underclass have ever remained a stubborn part of the unchurched,[14] those whom respective ministries continually fail to reach, despite all the rhetoric, or to bring into the church. In light of this, Joel Carpenter is much closer to the truth of the matter, the actual demographics, when he points out that "evangelical congregations and movements may involve blue-collar and lower-middle class people to a greater extent than other American Christian groups do, but only slightly more."[15] Moreover, Peter Oblinger astutely observes that those men and women of the Methodist Episcopal Church in Illinois who participated in Holiness associations during the nineteenth century were only somewhat poorer than non-Holiness Methodists.[16] And this pattern was repeated again and again.

Though Dayton is Wesleyan-Arminian in theological orientation, a tradition that places a premium on gracious liberty for response to the leading of God, his depiction of the process of embourgeoisement, that is, the transition to middle-class status, is marked by an overarching determinism typical of analyses informed by materialist, secular ideologies but one that is hardly descriptive of historic Methodism and Pentecostalism, especially in terms of their celebration of the freedom of the Spirit. In Dayton's reading, on the other hand, class participation, belonging to a particular economic group, is apparently determinative and largely identity defining, a reading that fails to appreciate in a serious way the broader catholicity and ecumenical power of much of American evangelicalism. For one thing, the body of Christ embraces a diversity of classes and peoples and transcends the ways the politically correct often divide things up with their "in groups" and "out groups," class opposition, unswerving preferences, and the like, all of which can issue in an incipient form of tribalism that is no less troubling even though it is often touted amid calls for justice and social concern. In light of all this, it must be affirmed by both moderate and conservative evangelicals, and for the sake of clarity and balance, that it is no more sinful to be middle class than to be lower class. To be rich, however, as Wesley pointed out, is "dangerous beyond expression."[17] Economic status, in other words, does not immediately and unproblematically translate into soteriological status.

Furthermore, few can read any of Dayton's works without quickly realizing that this process of embourgeoisement is largely a negative thing, one of declension, a process supposedly against which Wesley, the Holiness movement, and Pentecostals all railed in a "prophetic" way. And just what are some of the elements that make up embourgeoisement? Apparently such things as industry, frugality, and placing a premium on education. Dayton explains:

> But I also see the founding of many "evangelical" seminaries (the Nazarene Seminary, the Alliance Theological Seminary, Trinity Evangelical Divinity School, Gordon Divinity School—now Gordon-Conwell—and so on) that are better described in terms of the *embourgeoisement* of their constituencies.[18]

Even more emphatically, Dayton describes the work of his own father in moving to Asbury Theological Seminary in 1957 and establishing a foundation for the Wesleyan church that, to use his own words, "marked one of the clearest signs of the *embourgeoisement* of our denomination."[19] But is education a negative thing? Does the acquisition of knowledge characterize the declension of the bourgeoisie?[20] Is repentance in order here? Just what values are being affirmed in such judgments, and perhaps more important, will these judgments lead to a real and lasting amelioration of the plight of the poor? Indeed, in deprecating the middle class in his description of embourgeoisement, a subtext of much of what Dayton writes, he may also be criticizing, even if indirectly, the constellation of values (such as patience, delayed gratification, sacrifice, discipline, keeping commitments, self-respect, valuing education, etc.) that can actually do the poor the most good along with, of course, generous and vigorous social reform.[21]

In the end, the explanatory power of Dayton's pentecostal paradigm can be called into question, especially when he writes about its major task of disrupting "the traditional and 'conservative churches'"[22] and when he contends that "lower class churches in the nineteenth century [rose] in opposition to the middle-class churches of the mainstream."[23] However, the task of criticizing doctrinally conservative churches was not really a part of the agenda of Wesley, Orange Scott, or B. T. Roberts. On the contrary, these ecclesiastical leaders took exception to *liberalizing,* culturally accommodated churches that epitomized their respective social orders and that therefore looked askance at the "fanatical" *doctrines* of both entire sanctification and Christian assurance. Indeed, neither the eighteenth-century Church of England nor the nineteenth-century Methodist Episcopal Church were as doctrinally "conservative" as Dayton would have us believe, for key theological teachings were being neglected (the exceptions to their orthodoxy noted earlier) and were in danger of outright extinction in these communions of faith. Therefore, conserving some important elements of a rich and vibrant tradition, entire sanctification and Christian assurance among them, for which the pentecostal paradigm does not make room in its inattentiveness to doctrinal preservation, was also very much a part of the historical mix. For this crucial task, elements from the presbyterian paradigm, so neglected by Dayton, are indeed required.

Therefore, in reacting to a perceived hegemony on the part of Reformed evangelicals, of which there is unfortunately some evidence, Dayton essentially calls for replacing one paradigm with another. "Much of what constitutes evangelicalism today," he observes, "is, historically and theologically, illumi-nated more by the 'pentecostal' paradigm than the 'presbyterian' paradigm."[24] However, is class analysis, chronicling the movement of evangelicals into the central regions of the middle class (from their earlier lower-middle-class status, not lower-class or underclass status as Dayton would have it) the lodestar of all? Does the process of embourgeoisement, with all its apparent anti-intel-lectualism, epitomize the concerns of Wesleyan, Pentecostal, and Reformed evangelicals today? Does such a process allow generous room for attentiveness to inward religion and the inculcation of holiness in both persons and com-munities? Does it grapple seriously with the ongoing threats of theological confusion and dissolution in our postmodern, relativistic age?

Representing a Reformed evangelical view, George Marsden was quick to respond to this interpretive move and maintained that in his alternative paradigm Dayton had gone to "an opposite extreme where concerns about defending orthodoxy against theological liberalism virtually disappear."[25] Much clarity would be lost, Marsden added, by "lumping together fundamental-ist and holiness movements in such a 'pentecostal paradigm.'"[26] Even more emphatically, Joel Carpenter, a leading scholar of American fundamentalism, observed, "But alas, it seems that Dayton's grudge against the neoevangelicals is so great that he does not want even to hear about them. Nothing will do but to rewrite the story so that it downplays the significance of fundamental-ism and neo-evangelicalism altogether."[27] What sense would it make for the broader evangelical community, as it faces the complicated challenges of the twenty-first century, if one hegemony were simply replaced by another?

The story of American evangelicalism is so rich and multifaceted that many paradigms are required for an accurate assessment to emerge. The pentecostal paradigm, properly understood and critically analyzed, and the presbyterian paradigm do indeed illuminate important aspects of the complex phenomenon that is American evangelicalism. The holders of each must, therefore, make room for the "other," for evangelical brothers and sisters, variously defined, have a host of concerns, not simply a proffered or privileged one: both social reform *and* doctrinal conservation, both heart *and* mind, both soteriology *and* epistemology. Clearly, in making room for the "other," American evangelicalism will be strengthened; it will be empowered to participate in a much larger conversation than any one tradition or paradigm can provide. And the Wesleyan communion will undoubtedly have a few salient contributions to make to its Reformed brothers and sisters. But they are not what Dayton would have them to be. In fact, ever since the time of Carl F. H. Henry's classic work *The Uneasy Conscience of Fundamentalism,* Reformed evangelicals, among others, have been concerned by and large with both personal *and* social reform, the cruciality of conversion as well as social justice, a truth that will be more clearly and fully articulated in a subsequent chapter. The present focus, therefore, will devolve upon the contributions of the Wesleyan paradigm[28] to broader American evangelicalism with respect to the salient matters of both Scripture and conversion, two of the basic elements integral to evangelical identity itself.

## Wesleyan Evangelicals and Scripture

The preceding chapter demonstrated how the Princeton theology of Charles Hodge and B. B. Warfield, in the hands of twentieth-century antimodernists, issued in a doctrine of inerrancy that soon became a litmus test of evangelical identity in some corners of American religion. Accordingly, both Harold Lindsell and Francis Schaeffer painted a picture of theological dissolution once this "key" article of the faith was abandoned. Such claims, however, have most often been disbelieved if not outright rejected by many Wesleyan evangelicals, especially since they have not only understood but also continue to see the authority of Scripture much differently but no less seriously.

John Wesley, the father of Methodism and the theological mentor of a large number of American evangelicals, began to read and study the Bible as "the one, the only standard of truth, and the only model of pure religion"[29] in 1729, that is, nine years before his conversion to the proper Christian faith at Aldersgate on May 24, 1738.[30] Several years after this crucial experience of the redemptive and sustaining grace of God, Wesley indicated something of the normative value of Scripture in a letter to John Smith penned in September 1745: "I receive the written Word as the whole and sole rule of my faith."[31] Elsewhere, in a missive to William Law, Wesley's onetime theological mentor, the Methodist leader exclaimed in 1756, "In matters of religion I regard no writings but the inspired. . . . In every point I appeal 'to the law and the testimony,' and value no authority but this."[32] But perhaps the best window on

Wesley's overall estimation of the authority of Scripture is found in his preface to *Sermons on Several Occasions,* in which he observed:

> I have thought, I am a creature of a day, passing through life as an arrow through the air. I am a spirit come from God, and returning to God: Just hovering over the great gulf; till, a few moments hence, I am no more seen; I drop into an unchangeable eternity! I want to know one thing—the way to heaven; how to land safe on that happy shore. God himself has condescended to teach the way: For this very end he came from heaven. He hath written it down in a book. O give me that book! At any price, give me the book of God! I have it: Here is knowledge enough for me. Let me be homo unius libri.[33]

This excerpt clearly indicates not only the normative value of Scripture for Wesley, that it was the "touchstone" of his faith, but also that the Bible was preeminently understood not in an epistemological way but in a soteriological one. In other words, the main purpose of Scripture is not to answer all the speculative questions that we can bring to it from a diversity of human disciplines. Nor does the Bible attempt to integrate all human knowledge, however worthy that design may be. Rather, its purpose is to show, as Wesley puts it, "the way to heaven; how to land safe on that happy shore." This more limited focus is by no means a deficit but is actually a strength in that the Bible, unique in this power, carefully illuminates and guides sinful men and women in an unswerving way, and in the midst of a cacophony of stories in a fallen world, to the justifying and sanctifying grace of the Savior, Jesus Christ.

Though Wesley appealed to "four grand and powerful arguments" (miracles, prophecies, the goodness of the doctrine, and the moral character of the writers) that "induce us to believe that the Bible must be from God,"[34] his strongest appeal concerned the work of the Holy Spirit, who not only inspired the authors of Scripture in the past but also continues to inspire contemporary readers so that they may approach the Bible salvifically. "Serious and earnest prayer should be constantly used before we consult the oracles of God," Wesley cautions, "seeing Scripture can only be understood through the same Spirit whereby it was given."[35] In fact, the Holy Spirit, mediated through the Word, appears to be Wesley's overall emphasis with respect to the authority of Scripture. That is, the Spirit of the living Christ is ultimately authoritative, an estimation that avoids the shoals of bibliolatry. Moreover, with his focus on the *testimonium spiritus sancti* and being well versed in Koine Greek, Wesley was not adverse to engaging in textual criticism when warranted in order to ascertain the best text available. In fact, the British evangelical at times even corrected the Authorized Version.[36]

But there is another side to Wesley. The same evangelist who engaged in textual criticism also exclaimed, "Nay, if there be any mistakes in the Bible there may as well be a thousand. If there be one falsehood in that book, it did not come from the God of truth."[37] Beyond this, Wesley offered a facile and often-quoted argument for the divine inspiration of the Holy Scriptures as follows:

> The Bible must be the invention either of good men or angels, bad men or devils, or of God.
> 1. It could not be the invention of good men or angels; for they neither would nor could make a book, and tell lies all the time they were writing it, saying, "Thus saith the Lord," when it was their own invention.
> 2. It could not be the invention of bad men or devils; for they would not make a book which commands all duty, forbids all sin, and condemns their souls to hell to all eternity.
> 3. Therefore, I draw this conclusion that the Bible must be given by divine inspiration.[38]

Though these and other statements have led some Wesleyan evangelicals to claim that Wesley was an "inerrantist," this judgment not only is inaccurate but also constitutes the bane of all historians, that is, anachronism. First of all, "neither the word 'inerrancy' or 'infallibility' ever occurs in the index to *Wesley's Works*."[39] This is the language of a later era, with all its epistemological judgments, that has been superimposed on the Methodist leader.[40] The nineteenth and twentieth centuries, with all their concerns, preferences, and agendas, however, must not be placed atop the eighteenth.

Second, and perhaps more important, Wesley, deeply influenced by the piety of the Salzburgers Bolthius and Gronau and of course by the Moravian Peter Böhler, approached Scripture "sacramentally" and with a deep sense of expectancy. Put another way, Wesley believed that the Holy Spirit, once again mediated through the Word, would call into account not simply his theoretical, cogitating reason but also his entire person (body, soul, and spirit) as Scripture was read and interpreted *within* the community of faith.[41] Therefore, it is not so much that Wesley would apprehend (though this movement also is important), whereby his own reason would ever be in control at the very center of things in making various judgments. Rather, the Methodist leader would be apprehended and "decentered," so to speak, by no one less than a holy, transcendent, and evoking God, so evident in Scripture, who would call him into account and thereby bring greater clarity and illumination with respect to a diversity of judgments, cognitive and theoretical ones among them. In fact, in his sermon "The Case of Reason Impartially Considered," produced in 1781, Wesley demonstrates that though theoretical reason is often adept at articulating certain kinds of truths, a necessary endeavor in the life of the church ("When therefore you despise or depreciate reason you must not imagine you are doing God service."),[42] it nevertheless is utterly powerless to produce the *salvific,* relational, and theological virtues of faith, hope, and love in the hearts of believers within the community of faith. Wesley elaborates:

> Let reason do all that reason can: employ it as far as it will go. But at the same time acknowledge it is utterly incapable of giving either faith, or hope, or love; and consequently of producing either real virtue or substantial happiness. Expect these from a higher source, even from the Father of the spirits of all flesh. Seek and receive them not as your own acquisition, but as the gift of God.[43]

Simply put, the sacramental, ecclesial, and soteriological dimensions of Wesley's reading of Scripture, some of which hail from the Anglican Reformation,[44] must not be missed—nor misprized.

Unfortunately, what Wesley held in a well-balanced tension, kept in place by carefully drawn nuances, was misconstrued by not a few of his theological heirs, especially those in the Holiness movement in America. For example, although H. Horton Wiley tried to construct a "third alternative" between liberalism and fundamentalism,[45] many Holiness adherents were nevertheless caught up in a fundamentalist reading of Scripture, at least for a time, during the early part of the twentieth century. As Joel Carpenter points out, "Many holiness Wesleyans came to accept the doctrine of biblical inerrancy even though that belief is not a Wesleyan way of understanding the Bible's inspiration and authority."[46] In fact, the Article of Faith on Scripture, as found in the 1928 edition of the Church of the Nazarene Manual, is indicative of such acceptance:

> We believe in the *plenary inspiration of the Holy Scriptures* by which we understand the sixty-six books of the Old and New Testaments, given by divine inspiration, *inerrantly* revealing the will of God concerning us in all things necessary to our salvation; so that whatever is not contained therein is not enjoined as an article of faith.[47]

Noted Nazarene scholar J. Kenneth Grider, however, maintains that even this language does not constitute a full embrace of a fundamentalist view of Scripture since inerrancy, as specifically defined in this article, is limited to matters "necessary to salvation."[48]

During the 1930s and 1940s, the Church of the Nazarene by and large continued in its fundamentalist reading of Scripture and often augmented its case by an appeal to the arguments of A. M. Hills. In the meantime, Wiley tried to revive the historic Wesleyan arguments of the *testimonium spiritus sancti* but with little consequence. Indeed, a "conservative" ethos and spirit now pervaded the Holiness movement (which Dayton's paradigm, by the way, once again failed to take into account), such that the Wesleyan church, a historic Holiness body, combined both soteriological and epistemological concerns in its revised statement on Scripture in 1955 in a way similar to what the Church of the Nazarene had already done. As noted Wesleyan scholar Leon Hynson observes, the new definition affirmed the Old and New Testaments to be "the inspired and infallibly written Word of God, fully inerrant in their original manuscripts and superior to all human authority."[49]

Moreover, a few years later the power of the Reformed paradigm in American evangelicalism had grown so strong, especially in terms of its well-known judgments on Scripture, that the Wesleyan Theological Society, founded in 1965 in some sense as a counterpoise to the Evangelical Theological Society, took on the doctrine of biblical inerrancy as if it had always been a part of the historic Wesleyan witness. Subsequent generations of Wesleyans caught this error, chaffed under it, and therefore modified the statement on the Bible by putting aside the society's earlier construction and reproducing the doctrinal statement of the Christian Holiness Partnership, of which the Wesleyan Theological Society is an important component as its scholarly arm. The newly acquired statement, still in use, reads as follows:

> [We believe] in the inspiration and infallibility of sacred Scripture and evangelical doctrine that pertains to divine revelation, the incarnation, the resurrection, the second coming of Christ, the Holy Spirit, and the Church as affirmed in the historic creeds.[50]

Beyond these changes, there is a growing sense among younger members of the Wesleyan Theological Society that "the tradition is not well stated in the logic and ethos of the fundamentalist tradition,"[51] though it apparently once was. This means, of course, that although the "fundamentalist leavening," of which Paul Bassett wrote, is still evident in pockets of the society, especially among the older generation, it is being quietly though resolutely eased out in favor of views of the Bible more in keeping with the historic Wesleyan witness.

The scholar who perhaps has done more than anyone else to reacquaint Wesleyan evangelicals with their own rich tradition in terms of the authority and normative power of Scripture is William Abraham. In his most recent work, *Canon and Criterion in Christian Theology,* Abraham contends that it is a serious mistake to approach the canon of Scripture as if it were an epistemological norm (as many Reformed evangelicals have done), as if it constituted the criteria through which difficult questions with respect to human knowledge, some of which hail from the Enlightenment, would all be resolved. "The fundamental problems which arise in treatments of authority in the Christian faith," Abraham observes, "stem from a long-standing misinterpretation of ecclesial canons as epistemic criteria."[52] Put another way, it is problematic to offer Scripture as an answer to all the kinds of questions that the methodologies of rationalism or scientific empiricism suggest, a process through which the truth of the Bible can only be misconstrued and diminished by shifting the context, however subtly, from soteriology to epistemology. In fact, according to Abraham, the broad heritage of the church, which includes Scripture, liturgy, iconography, the fathers, and the sacraments, was "systematically dismantled in the Western Church before, during, and after the Reformation."[53] This rich deposit of the church was reconceived, in a defensive move and as part of an ongoing apologetic task, "to fit the primacy of epistemology," such that how one knew that one knew "overshadowed knowing God."[54] That is, a second-order task edged out a primary one—and all of this to the diminishment of the body of Christ.

The corrective to this kind of inevitable reductionism whereby the truth of Scripture is construed to fit the tastes and preferences of Enlightenment empiricism or some other privileged epistemology is to acquire a renewed appreciation of Scripture as an ecclesial canon, that is, as a conduit through which the salvific strength of the Most High can be communicated within the church as a community of *faith*. Simply put, Scripture is perhaps best understood as a means of grace that communicates the favors and powers of the redeemed life.[55] Such a judgment is remarkably similar to that of Wesley, who, in defining the means of grace in the larger life of the church and with respect to Christian discipleship in particular, observed, "By 'means of grace' I understand outward signs, words, or actions ordained of God, and appointed for this end—to be the *ordinary* channels whereby he might convey to men preventing, justifying, or sanctifying grace."[56] Accordingly, understanding Scripture as the canon of the church instead of as an epistemic norm underscores the ecclesial, formative setting in which Scripture is to be read, understood, and actualized in the warp and woof of life—and all of this to the holy purpose of nothing less than redemption.

Remarkably enough, the carefully constructed arguments of Abraham on the topic of canon and criterion not only have served to reacquaint many Wesleyans with the soundness of their own theological traditions, having been deflected from this earlier deposit by the fearful appeals of fundamentalism, but also have been congruent, in harmony, with many of the contributions of leading contemporary evangelical scholars who represent a diversity of traditions, Wesleyan and Reformed included. All of this has come as a surprise to the older generation of Reformed neoevangelicals who believed that the doctrinal articulations pertaining to Scripture, informed by the nineteenth-century Princeton theology of Hodge and Warfield and hammered out in the fundamentalist controversy in the early twentieth century, would be perennial, an enduring legacy for all subsequent ages. And failure to take into account in a serious and forthright way the social location of this earlier period, its limited and at times insular view on a range of theological constructions, is very much a part of the problem that critical evangelicals discern today. If anything, the passage of time is slowly revealing not the endurance of all this theology but that change is in order, at least in some respects, a change called for by evangelical leaders themselves.

What William Abraham has done for the Wesleyan evangelical world, in helping it to see Scripture principally in its ecclesial setting as a means of grace rather than in the context of the world's agenda or script, Stanley Grenz has done, although in a somewhat different way, for the Reformed evangelical world. Ever careful in his scholarship, this leading evangelical scholar reminds us not only that the Bible is "God's Word to us in the form of human words" but also that as a consequence we must not "idolize the Bible itself."[57] In a way similar to Abraham, Grenz affirms that the Bible is nothing less than a means of grace, and it is authoritative "in that it is the *vehicle* through which the Spirit speaks."[58] In his work *Beyond Foundationalism,* coauthored with John Franke, Grenz elaborates:

> The declaration that the Spirit speaking in or through Scripture is our final authority means that Christian belief and practice cannot be determined merely by appeal to either the exegesis of Scripture carried out apart from the life of the believer and the believing community or to any supposedly private (or corporate) "word from the Spirit" that stands in contradiction to biblical exegesis.[59]

This full-orbed understanding of Scripture, whereby the Spirit addresses believers through its words and within the context of the church, moves away from a *mere* propositional understanding of the truth of Scripture in order to appreciate the relational nature of much of what the Spirit seeks to communicate. Again, while affirming the reality and importance of the propositional dimension of the truth of Scripture, Grenz wisely does not leave it there, certainly not in any reductionist or diminished sort of way, but suggests an interpretative framework that allows some of the larger, relational, and ecclesial truths of Scripture, incapable of being properly discerned by a scientific, empiricist methodology, to appear on the photographic plate, so to speak. Here the methodological hegemony of empiricism is broken so that some of the deepest truths of Scripture, especially as the "grand story" relates to the narrative outworking of our own lives, are fully and wonderfully embraced. In the past, however, neoevangelicals routinely assumed that the "task of the theologian was to apply the scientific method, assisted by the canons of logic, to the deposit of revelation found in Scripture."[60] Such an approach, if it constitutes the entirety of evangelical methodology, leaves one's own theoretical reason at the center of things, in a way typical of the Enlightenment project, and its emphasis on autonomy, but one in which the larger personal and relational truths of Scripture remain virtually unexplored.

Beyond this, Donald Bloesch contends that the final authority is not Scripture but the living God. "Jesus Christ and the message about him," he notes, "constitute the material norm for our faith just as the Bible is the formal norm."[61] Much earlier, John Stott had already distinguished an evangelical from a fundamentalist reading of Holy Writ by making the following distinction: "The fundamentalist emphasizes so strongly the divine origin of Scripture that he tends to forget that it also had human authors."[62] And for his part, Alister McGrath maintains that contemporary evangelicals are expressing increasing misgivings with respect to approaches to biblical authority associated with the Old Princeton School, "seeing the continuing use of the ideas of this school as contributing to the lingering bondage of evangelicalism to the ideas and outlooks of Enlightenment rationalism."[63] More to the point, this British evangelical observes that "to allow one's ideas and values to become controlled by anything or anyone other than the self-revelation of God in Scripture is to adopt an ideology rather than a theology."[64] In light of all of this, it can surely be asked, Does one have to be a modernist in order to be an evangelical? Does one have to genuflect before Enlightenment understandings in order to express the truth of the gospel? Is "objective," universal truth, the truth of facts, data, and "things," *though clearly important,* the highest form of truth that is manifested in the life and ministry of Jesus Christ?

At any rate, it should be evident by now that both Wesleyan and Reformed evangelicals are united in acknowledging some of the last remains of the fundamentalist mind-set that have at times distorted evangelical theology, especially during the contentious twentieth century, by making it captive to philosophies and other ideational structures that were subtly imbedded in privileged theological methods and preferred biblical hermeneutics. The distinct Wesleyan contribution to this reforming process, then, is not so much in terms of specific arguments and reasoning—for the Reformed evangelical contribution on this score is already considerable—but in having a history, an evangelical tradition, of a faithful witness to the integrity and saving power of the gospel apart from a doctrine of biblical inerrancy, a doctrine held in place for the most part by various epistemological preferences. Simply put, "the slippery slope" argument is false. Indeed, the evangelical tradition, especially as it underscores the grace and truth that is Jesus Christ, does not unravel, nor does it lose its purpose apart from a fundamentalist reading of the authority of Scripture. Accordingly, the fundamentalist leavening of the Holiness movement that marked an earlier age is now viewed by many Wesleyans as having been an alien accretion, a humanly constructed overlay that dampened the Wesleyan soteriological vision and that never characterized *all* evangelicalism throughout the ages, despite protests to the contrary. The Wesleyan witness, then, offers encouragement to its Reformed evangelical brothers and sisters that at the beginning of the twenty-first century, as we prepare for a broader evangelical future, it is time to throw off the last vestiges of fundamentalism, not simply in terms of its militancy, ongoing social and cultural irrelevance, and even anti-intellectualism, but also in terms of its all-too-human constructed view of Scripture. The way ahead, therefore, in a typically evangelical fashion, calls for ongoing reform. More important, perhaps, it calls for courage.

## Wesleyan Evangelicals and Conversion

Because Reformed and Wesleyan evangelicals each have their own distinct traditions and rarely engage in serious theological dialogue with each other, they are both open to misunderstandings, sometimes quite serious, with respect to each other. In 1994, for example, Mark Noll published *The Scandal of the Evangelical Mind* and laid the burden of that scandal on the backs of Holiness adherents, Pentecostals, and dispensationalists.[65] Never once did Noll, the otherwise careful historian, consider what the purpose, the historic mission, of the Holiness movement and broader Wesleyanism was. Is it fair, for instance, to judge one tradition by the purposes and standards of another? Is it accurate to judge a decidedly soteriological tradition by the epistemological and cognitive standards of another and then to conclude that the former tradition is not simply inadequate intellectually speaking but actually anti-intellectual?

The fact that Noll failed to comprehend the basic ethos of the Holiness and Wesleyan movements is revealed in a couple of his more troubling observations. First of all, apart from much substantiating evidence, he contends that "the movements that seemed to do such damage to evangelical thought—Holiness, Pentecostalism, dispensationalism—hid the most important thing behind a veil of secondary concerns."[66] Beyond this, and in a similar vein, Noll argues that the distinctive teachings of the Holiness movement (as with dispensationalists and Pentecostals) are "not essential to the Christian faith."[67] He concludes, therefore, that the "intellectual consequences of these theologies [are] damaging."[68]

But are the central concerns of the Holiness movement "secondary" and "not essential to the Christian faith," as Noll maintains? Is holiness as that qualitative change in the human heart that arises in the new birth secondary to the Christian life? Is actual, participatory change at its highest levels peripheral to what it means to be a Christian? In a real sense, no one less than John Wesley is the ongoing theological mentor, if not the father, of the later Holiness movement. And Wesley's burden for eighteenth-century England (as it later became for the nineteenth-century American Holiness movement) was to spread "scriptural holiness over the land,"[69] a holiness that he deemed integral to the good news of the gospel. In other words, the Methodist leader's overarching purpose, in good pietistic fashion, was "not to form any new sect; but to reform the nation, particularly the Church."[70] Put another way, the chief dialogue partner for Wesley (and the later Holiness movement) was the church itself, an institution that had grown quite comfortable with and had been compromised by broader cultural trends. The particular form that this declension took, as seen through a *soteriological* lens, was that the precious promises of the gospel in terms of liberty and holiness, the very staples of redemption, were being obscured, rendered virtually opaque, by a pessimism of unbelief. Such pessimism could, of course, be found on the lips of unbelievers, but it was also found, remarkably enough, on the lips of those who ascended pulpits. To be sure, Wesley in his own age was well acquainted with articulate and well-constructed theologies that, despite a display of "learning," basically left men and women in their sins under some of the most grievous bondages. Accordingly, neither Wesley nor the subsequent Holiness movement were preoccupied by secondary concerns, as Noll contends. The inculcation of holiness from its inception at the new birth through its maturation by the gracious agency of the Holy Spirit is a teaching that belongs not simply to Holiness adherents or Methodists but to the entire church.

From their vantage point, when Wesleyans, Methodists, and Pentecostals look out upon the American church today, especially in its evangelical manifestations, they are often saddened to learn how the good news of the holy love of God reigning in the hearts of believers is often washed out in a message marked more by the pessimism of nature than by the optimism of grace. To illustrate, as Francis Schaeffer pointed out more than a decade ago, "There is now easy divorce and remarriage. What the Bible clearly teaches about the limitations placed upon divorce and remarriage is now put by some evangelicals in the area of cultural orientation."[71] In fact, the current divorce rates among American evangelicals are not very different from those of the broader culture and demonstrate that the ways of the world have unfortunately become a part of the church.[72] The sad fact is that, as Harold Lindsell reminds us, "adultery is common, and conjugal faithfulness, even among some who call themselves evangelicals, is dying out."[73] To counter these disturbing trends, no doubt one of the legacies of the sexual revolution of the sixties, the sixteen-million-member Southern Baptist Convention recently adopted a resolution encouraging newlyweds to make a marital "covenant" to seek help if their marriage sours.

But there are other problems as well. Evangelical congregations are repeatedly taught from the pulpit and in the classroom that they are "only sinners saved by God's grace" (which in some sense is true, rightly understood), that they "sin in thought, word, and deed every day," and that in the end they are "only human." Moreover, the conflict, the divided will of Romans 7, not only is made the major script of the Christian life but also constitutes for some the highest reaches of Christian maturity and discipleship—and all of this with troubling consequences for the liberties of the gospel. This division, this wrenching double mindedness (which is hardly a prescription for peace or joy), is actually situated within the mature Christian soul according to some evangelical leaders such that it has now virtually become a house divided against itself. James Sire, for instance, observes that all of us are really sinners: "Our lives are split; our souls have two allegiances," he insists. Thus, in his work *Habits of the Mind,* Sire elaborates on how he sees this "dynamic" playing out in Christian life and practice:

> Take a simple, gut-level example. Jesus makes an essentially ethical equation; ethically, lust is adultery. . . . Moreover, I say that I believe this equation is true. Nonetheless, I still experience lust. If belief requires obedience, then how can I believe and not obey? Do I know that lust is adultery if I do not act as if I do?[74]

If by this observation Sire means that Christians, those washed and renewed by the blood of the lamb, still sense the carnal nature within, a contrary principle (in this case in the form of lust), then we are in full agreement. If, however, Sire understands this division as one in which the carnal nature repeatedly breaks out, dominates, and enslaves believers such that they succumb to the filth of lust on an ongoing or even intermittent basis, then we must sharply disagree. Indeed, Christ clearly expressed the graciousness of the gospel in terms of sin, bondage, and liberty in the following well-chosen words: "Truly, truly, I say to you, everyone who commits sin is the slave of sin. The slave does not remain in the house forever; the son does remain forever. So if the Son makes you free, you will be free indeed" (John 8:34–36).

Concerning this important matter of deliverance from the slavery or dominion of sin, John Wesley made a helpful distinction that was passed on to the Holiness movement and that fully acknowledged the ongoing drag of the carnal nature while at the same time upheld the standards of redemption that kept the liberties, the precious freedoms of the gospel, very much in place. Wesley reasoned, "We readily acknowledge, 'he that believeth is born of God,' and 'he that is born of God doth not commit sin,' yet we cannot allow that he does not feel it within: It does not *reign,* but it does *remain.*"[75] In this more restricted sense, in terms of the carnal nature that remains, a Christian is rightly described as *simul justus et peccator.* But this division or twofold sense is different from that of Romans 7, which entails disobedience, rebellion, and open sin. That is, the former distinction highlights the truth that *original* sin remains as a contrary principle within the hearts of believers, where one may sense a propensity toward pride or lust without yielding to it. The latter distinction, on the other hand, describes in painful detail the dynamics "of those who know the law," as verse 1 clearly states, a pre-Christian state properly speaking, and who apart from sanctifying, regenerating grace unfortunately live under the bondage of the ongoing practice of *actual* sin.

Some evangelical leaders today will undoubtedly claim that no Christian, or perhaps only a very few, a spiritual elite, can realize the graces of the gospel that Wesley both taught and proclaimed as the *common* privilege of the sons and daughters of God. To be sure, even in his own day Wesley faced critics within the Anglican Church who claimed that believers could not be free from the power or dominion of sin (sin defined as a "willful transgression against a known law of God")[76] but could be free only to the extent that they would not commit sin "continually." Wesley, however, always found the logic here both troubling and, more important, unscriptural. Indeed, in 1756, he responded to his detractors by considering the example of a drunkard who argued that the state of his soul was "well" since he was not drunk *continually.* In a letter to William Dodd, Wesley reasons:

> I tell my neighbour here, "William, you are a child of the devil; for you *commit sin:* you was drunk yesterday." "No, sir," says the man, "I do not *live or continue in sin*" (which Mr. Dodd says is the true meaning of the text), "I am not drunk

*continually,* but only now and then, once in a fortnight or a month." Shall I tell him he is in the way to heaven or to hell? I think he is in the high road to destruction, and that if I tell him otherwise his blood will be upon my head.[77]

For Wesley, then, orthodoxy or correct belief, though clearly important, is never enough. There must also be a transformation, a reform of the heart, what Gregory Clapper calls "orthokardia."[78] In this view, Jesus Christ is a Redeemer in so many different ways—so great and sufficient is his atoning work. He saves his people not only from the *guilt* of sin in justification but also from its *power* in regeneration—a truth that has at times been obscured even in the church, *especially among Protestants.* And it is Wesley's estimation of things (especially his definition of sin) that allows the precious truths and liberties of 1 John to be taken at face value and not explained away, in a hermeneutics of unbelief, as in some other theologies.

One way to underestimate the precious promises of the gospel, of the graces that should be actualized in conversion, is to overwork the forensic theme of redemption, that is, justification and the forgiveness of sins, to the virtual neglect of the participatory theme of sanctification or holiness. Anthony Hoekema, for instance, writes:

> Sanctification further effects a renewal of our nature—that is, it brings about a change of direction rather than a change in substance. In sanctifying us, God does not equip us with powers or capacities that are totally different from those we had before; rather, He enables us to use the gifts he gave us in the right way instead of in sinful ways.[79]

However, the renewal that sanctification, in the form of the new birth, brings about must be seen as a *qualitative* change in the lives of believers such that they have now become, through divine redeeming grace, what they had never been before, namely, *holy.* In other words, the *presence* of the Holy Spirit in their hearts in this first movement of a larger process of sanctification cleanses, renews, and empowers believers. Grace is not simply imputed; it is also imparted. Again, not only has our (forensic) relation to God been restored through the ministrations of Jesus Christ through justification, but our very nature (participatory theme) has been transformed through regeneration, that is, through the presence of the Holy Spirit *in* us.

Looking simply to the magisterial Reformation for spiritual guidance, however, many American evangelicals may once again run the risk of emphasizing justification to the relative neglect of the "catholic" theme of sanctification. Thus, if salvation is presented as principally entailing the forgiveness of sins without also a concomitant change in nature, then salvation so construed may appear as a cruel joke being played upon believers, for if their natures have not been transformed at least in some sense as a result of God's enabling, empowering grace, then after receiving the forgiveness of sins they will likely soon commit the very sins for which they had asked forgiveness in the first place! For some evangelicals, however, this cycle of falling, repenting, only to fall yet again constitutes the normal Christian experience, is all that can ever be hoped for in this life, and is precisely what they mean by the phrase *simul justus et peccator.* From a Wesleyan perspective, however, this is a serious misunderstanding of both this Latin phrase and the gospel, as revealed in the comments of Theodore Jennings, a leading Methodist theologian:

> *Simul Justus et peccator,* as normally understood, is fancy Latin for open defiance of God. To say that justification leaves sinners still in the grasp of sin as before is like saying that resurrection leaves the dead in their graves. If God's declaration of us as justified does not result in our really being just, then God is a liar and faith is illusion.[80]

Elsewhere in his writings, Jennings targets those evangelicals who, though they use the words *gospel, grace,* and *redemption* and make a fine show of it all, essentially preach half a gospel: "These pseudo-evangelicals preach a forgiveness of sins that leaves us still enslaved to the power of sin, removing the guilt without touching the reality of sin, thus making their savior a collaborator in the dominion of Satan."[81] Though the comments of Jennings are to the point, even trenchant, their meaning is not far from that of Wesley, who in his own age warned against "gospel preachers" who left their hearers steeped in their sins. Wesley observed:

> Let but a pert, self-sufficient animal, that has neither sense nor grace, bawl out something about Christ, or his blood, or justification by faith, and his hearers cry out, "What a fine Gospel sermon!" Surely the Methodists have not so learned Christ! We know no Gospel without salvation from sin.[82]

In light of these observations, is it not time for many evangelicals to question their overly pessimistic theologies (which are, after all, human constructions) that make undue allowances for sin? Is it not time to move toward Christian maturity? Indeed, though American evangelicals are well known for leading sinners to Christ, and the altar call in some churches has virtually become a sacrament, many are less adept at leading Christians into serious and costly discipleship, the kind of discipleship that is marked by patient suffering and sacrifice over time as men and women are led into the fullness that is Christ. Again, it is simply not enough to become a Christian, as marvelous as this work of grace is. One must also grow, thrive, and mature as a Christian. However, some theological models of the Christian life present in American evangelical-ism today never allow for such serious maturation. Instead, by means of them, believers remain in effect baby Christians, ever repeating the first works of repentance and renewal (Heb. 6:1), never entering into the deeper things of the Lord. In this spiritual roller-coaster ride with all of its ups and downs, it is not actually holy love that is being habituated over time but rather the *cycle* of sin and repentance. The repeated confessions of the same sin, the resolutions that are *always* broken ("I'll stop; I promise."), and the lingering division of the will should all be indicators that something is terribly wrong here. Jesus Christ as a risen Savior died for more than this, for far more than to leave American evangelicals comfortable in their ongoing sins, cosseted by theolo-gies that mistakenly tell them that all is well simply because they have *already* responded to an altar call or were baptized and converted in their youth. "Say not in your heart," Wesley cautions, "I was once baptized; therefore I *am now* a child of God. Alas, that consequence will by no means hold,"[83] an observation made in the previous chapter but now repeated for emphasis.

Moreover, though American evangelicalism often claims that it is in conti-nuity with New Testament Christianity, maintaining a faithful witness to the apostolic testimony, neither Christ nor the early church ever took sin so lightly. The dire warnings of Jesus that "if your eye causes you to stumble, pluck it out and throw it from you. It is better for you to enter life with one eye, than to have two eyes and be cast into the fiery hell" (Matt. 18:9) are reinterpreted and often quickly put aside by evangelicals amid chorus after chorus of the gospel truth that God is love. But what the verses of some of these newfangled hymns have left out is clearly found in the Bible, that is, God is not simply love (and certainly not in a sentimental or self-indulgent way). Rather, God is *holy* love, the One whose eyes are too pure to behold evil (Hab. 1:13). Salvation, then, encompasses both grace *and* standards, forgiveness *and* renewal, love *and* holiness. Moreover, the thought that Constantine would actually delay his baptism until just prior to his death (a practice not uncommon at the time) is virtually unintelligible to some evangelicals who have grown so accustomed to the reality of ongoing post-baptismal sin.

The Holiness movement, on the other hand (as well as some pockets of evangelical Methodism), has kept the focus on these important truths. To be redeemed is not only to be forgiven but also to become—and remain—holy, where willfully and stubbornly committing sin is not the rule of the Christian life but rather its faith-breaking exception.[84] That is, redemption is an invitation not simply to know *about* God, certainly not merely in a cognitive or intellectual way, but also to know and enjoy in an intimate way the divine *presence* in all its wondrous, satisfying, and sustaining beauty. It is precisely this soteriological *truth,* this aesthetics of redemption, so to speak, hardly discerned by methodologies oriented to rationalism or scientific empiricism, that Wesleyans and some Pentecostals have championed before evangelicalism and the broader American church.

In light of all this, perhaps the pungent gospel truths that Wesley boldly held before eighteenth-century England can help to reawaken us American evangelicals from our soteriological slumbers and thereby lead us to genuine renewal in order to appreciate in a thoroughgoing way not only the scriptural truth that "without holiness no one will see the Lord" (Heb. 12:14 NIV) but also that God's grace is sufficient for all our need. Cautioning his readers, some who were doubting the efficacy of divine grace, Wesley wrote:

> No, it cannot be; none shall live with God, but he that now lives to God; none shall enjoy the glory of God in heaven, but he that bears the image of God on earth; none that is not saved from sin here can be saved from hell hereafter; none can see the kingdom of God above, unless the kingdom of God be in him below. Whosoever will reign with Christ in heaven, must have Christ reigning in him on earth. He must have "that mind in him which was in Christ," enabling him "to walk as Christ also walked."[85]

So, then, if there has been a scandal of the evangelical mind, as Noll has claimed, has there also been a scandal of the evangelical soul? One wonders.

# 4

# The Promise
# of Evangelical Theology

The theological task for American evangelicals today, as they face an increasingly complex and challenging world, is to examine the most basic questions pertaining to the knowledge of God and humanity in light of Christian resources, especially in terms of Scripture and the interpretive community (theological tradition) in which they participate. Viewed another way, theology is a second-order activity as it reflects on the primary revelation that has already occurred in the decisive and liberating acts of God in the history of Israel and in the life, death, and resurrection of Jesus Christ. Revelation, then, embraces both historical event and revealed Word, elements that factor into any serious theological reflection.

In terms of an appropriate theological method, it is important to stress at the outset, and in a way that Karl Barth did in the twentieth century,[1] that theology is an activity not of a speculative, "objective," uninvolved community but of the church, of the believing, participatory, and engaged community. Indeed, the Swiss theologian's designation of his major theological work as *Church Dogmatics* was no mere accident. It underscored that theological reflection is appropriately associated with the presuppositions and perspectives of *faith*, perspectives that were misprized in the Enlightenment in its demand that all truth must conform to its own preferred script of "objectivity," that is, the truth of an impartial, supposedly universal observer.

In the past, the "apologetic" aspect of the larger theological enterprise was overly stressed such that theology itself was defined, in its most basic form, as the task of communicating the genius of the Christian faith to the world or as the endeavor of forging a conversation between the truths of Christianity and the leading thought forms of the day. While both of these elements are vital in sound theological reflection, the principal community for whom theology is done is neither the world nor the articulators of the leading thought forms of the day. To be sure, when a particular kind of apologetics is made the *principal* purpose of theology, to the relative neglect of the life of the believing community, that is, when theologians seek to please not a risen Lord but the halls of unbelief, then theological dissolution is not far behind, the kind of dissolution that marked twentieth-century liberalism in its accommodating tendencies, which were often foisted upon the church in the name of "critical thought." In fact, the ongoing liberal embrace of homosexual practices, as an indifferent private matter (surely an Enlightenment script), as well as the championing of the cause of ordaining avowed, practicing homosexuals, an issue that is currently dividing mainline denominations, is a clear indication that theological liberals have forgotten that the gospel is irreducibly about holiness, about the holy love of God reigning in the community of faith, a reign that is the very substance of redemption.

At any rate, the fact that theology is rightfully an activity of the church means that the social location of the community of faith, its perspective and vantage point, must ever be taken seriously. Here the story of the church has its own integrity, coherence, and purpose. This means, of course, that this narrative can no longer be excluded out of hand as a result of the dominance or the privileging of some other story. More to the point, though the claim of the church that God has been revealed in the history of Israel and preeminently in Jesus Christ cannot be fully substantiated—in a way that would preclude faith—at the bar of autonomous empirical reason, it is no less true. Indeed, the larger, full-orbed truth of the gospel *disrupts* the self-referential perspective of Enlightenment autonomy and calls it into account. Put another way, truth and knowing, in accordance with the life of the church, are ever participatory and are mediated principally as the community of faith is addressed by the Spirit through Scripture, its ever-present norm, and as it participates in both Word and sacrament.

# The Nature of Evangelical Theology

One of the major concerns of evangelical theology, given that its historic dialogue partner has been modernistic liberalism, is to maintain a faithful witness to the apostolic testimony that has been passed down from the disciples of Jesus through the corridors of history and on to the contemporary church. As such, American evangelicalism sees its story, its own narrative outworking, as part of a much larger script that is coursing its way through time and eternity, through the life and witness of the church militant and through the completed labors of the church triumphant. Key expressions of that faithful witness for evangelicals can be found not only in the great creedal epoch of the fourth and fifth centuries (from the Council of Nicea to Chalcedon, for example) but also in the reforming creedal epoch of the sixteenth century, which produced the Augsburg Confession, the Westminster Confession of Faith, and the Thirty-nine Articles of Religion, creeds that continue to express the life and faith of the contemporary evangelical community.

It is precisely because twentieth-century evangelicalism strove to maintain doctrinal integrity in the aftermath of the fundamentalist-modernist controversy that it placed a premium on *orthodoxy*, on preserving correct teaching with respect to the saving efficacy of the Christian faith. So understood, orthodoxy, ever a crucial characteristic of the proper Christian faith, is like the signet that holds the precious jewel of the gospel in place and where the reality of the Holy Spirit, the Spirit of truth, in the midst of the worshiping, believing community, can be both properly affirmed and celebrated. Without the signet of orthodoxy and attentiveness to the facts of the Christian faith, the community would be left to the direction of other scripts, humanly constructed "gospels" that would masquerade as the truth for a season but would be unable to bear the test of time. However, in this noble even heroic process, as evangelicals courageously maintained a faithful witness in the midst of smug criticism and condescending disfavor, they unwittingly employed the theoretical and methodological wherewithal of their "cultured" despisers. Put another way, the methodological preference for rationalistic empiricism, found among several Enlightenment thinkers, was duplicated, ironically enough, in the apologetics of the evangelical community. Stanley Grenz explains:

> The understanding of the relationship between theology and science that reigned from the seventeenth century to the 1970s, and hence that cradled the evangelical movement since its genesis, look[ed] to science for the methodological model for all intellectual endeavor, including theological construction.[2]

This methodological preference among several leading evangelicals caused them to see certain aspects of the truth of the gospel clearly (its cognitive elements), whereas other aspects were largely neglected, especially those truths that could not easily be objectified through a rational, empiricist lens. This observation, once again, does not deny the importance of propositional truth or the correspondence theory, but it does call for a diversity of methodological frameworks to explicate the richness of the gospel of Jesus Christ.

To be sure, some of the deepest truths of the gospel cannot be empirically discerned through the five senses, nor are they the kinds of "objects" that an autonomous reason can master and thereby control. Instead, they are truths indicative of the divine being as effulgent, outgoing, value-creating love and of human beings created in that image. In this setting, the truth of relations, of persons, and of the rich and abiding love between God and humanity must be factored into the methodological equation. Indeed, such engaging truths will not fare well when brought under a method ruled by the subject/object antithesis or by an overweening rationalism because these truths are not "objects" available to a universal, unbelieving, and largely indifferent reason. On the contrary, these truths are participatory and are received as the *gifts* of grace known only through engagement and a process of transformation. Put another way, knowing God as manifested in Jesus Christ through the Holy Spirit, not simply in a cognitive way but in a full-orbed salvific way, is a different kind of knowing than ascertaining the atomic weight of gold or the precise hour when John F. Kennedy was shot. It is a knowing that is wonderfully transformative, that never leaves us where we are—the kind of knowing that evangelicals have celebrated repeatedly in the life-changing event called conversion.

Such observations do not deny the importance of the intellect in the Christian faith or the immense value of orthodoxy in our relativistic age. But if the *imago Dei* is understood principally in terms of reason (a legacy from Hellenistic thought), and if revelation itself is seen for the most part as rational communication in conceptual-verbal form,[3] then some of the richest wisdom of the gospel will be left unappreciated. To be sure, the image of God, in which humanity has been created, is not exhausted in a rational capacity. On the contrary, that image is perhaps best explored in terms of the relations and other-directedness that characterize the Christian understanding of God. In other words, human beings reflect the *imago Dei* as they go beyond themselves in love and transcend the inhibiting, isolating, and self-referential perspective to realize the *imago Dei* corporately and communally. Accordingly, the individualism of the Enlightenment, modernist paradigm should hold little place in the church precisely as it sees itself as the body of Christ. Human beings are not simply cogitating intellects, nor are they merely developed capacities that make their own judgments ever the referential center. Instead, it is the very addressability of men and women, the power to be evoked and called forth to participate in the divine life of loving *relations,* that is so indicative of the image of God. And that image, marked by holy love, is perhaps most resplendent in the doxological response to the prior gracious and redeeming activity of the Most High, an activity that calls forth not simply our intellects but our entire being in worshipful adoration in the midst of the faithful community.

A second major element that holds promise for evangelical theology, beyond its concern for orthodoxy, is "orthokardia,"[4] a term that was introduced in the previous chapter. In other words, evangelicals have historically been concerned about not only carefully articulating the doctrines of the Christian faith (orthodoxy) but also embracing the truths of the gospel within the depths of the human heart (orthokardia) in a profound, meaningful, and life-transforming way. This first emphasis, apart from the second, could easily result in a stale and rigid faith, the kind of "scholastic" faith and theology against which the Pietists of the seventeenth century reacted in their celebration of inward, personal religion. Moreover, modulations of this pietist, convertive theology can be found throughout evangelical history, as exemplified in John Wesley's stress on inward religion and what he called real, true, proper, scriptural Christianity as he ministered in eighteenth-century England. These same emphases can be found in some of the most recent expressions of American evangelicalism, in particular in Roger Olson's explication of "conversional piety."[5] That is, because evangelicals then as now have been concerned with the reality of conversion, with knowing Jesus Christ in the depths of one's soul in a profound, not a superficial, way, they have insisted that theology should not only be practical and thereby foster ongoing serious Christian discipleship but should also empower the redemptive witness of the church in the face of a hurting world.

Surprisingly enough, evangelicalism's celebration of "conversional piety" in its basic theological orientation has not always been appreciated by others within the broader institutional church, especially by theological liberals. Indeed, as noted in chapter 2, such an emphasis has often been looked down upon as a "pious indulgence," as rampant "individualism,"[6] or worse yet as "spiritual narcissism." But this is to misunderstand crucial elements that inform the practical theology of American evangelicals. For one thing, the usual charge of individualism (in which individualism is played against social justice) is seriously misdirected. Evangelical religion, in its best sense, is not individualistic. Rather, it is personal. That is, the proper Christian faith must ever engage the throne room of our being, the very depths of the human soul. It is precisely the recognition of the confusion of these two terms, the substituting of one for the other, that goes a long way in impugning such misdirected criticism. Beyond this, the evangelical community might rightly realize in the face of such objections that if faith in Jesus Christ does not touch believers at their depths, then such a faith—probably largely informed by ideological commitments—may be far too superficial to deliver from the kinds of wrenching evils, dispositionally understood, that enslave sinners and from which they must find deliverance and redemption. In short, theology must not only be practical but must also express what it means to set the captives free.

A second misunderstanding of "conversional piety," a piety that informs much of evangelical theology in its celebration of the lordship of Jesus Christ reigning in the heart, is to maintain that such a perspective gives undue weight to "feelings" that are fleeting, ephemeral, and therefore of little consequence. As in the first example, this second criticism is largely based on a confusion and a substitution of terms. Indeed, American evangelicals are not preoccupied with feelings, despite protests to the contrary. Rather, they are concerned with the *dispositions* of their hearts, the proper orientation and direction of their wills toward God and neighbor. Again, dispositions, unlike feelings, are not fleeting. They are long-lived, ongoing orientations to what we love. Since they are habituated over time, as a consequence of God's grace, dispositions are not easily shaken. Indeed, they constitute some of the elements of serious Christian discipleship, the kind that goes beyond the first things to enjoy the deeper things of Christ. For example, a woman may be tired and run down through the work required for her doctoral studies, and though she may not feel very well at the moment, she yet loves her husband and is disposed and oriented toward him in a way distinct from all others. In the same fashion, dispositions, the entirety of which constitutes the human will, must be properly oriented in love toward God and neighbor through divine, sustaining grace. Given this ongoing emphasis, evangelical theology is eminently practical because one of its salient concerns is the transformation of human existence in conversion itself and in ongoing Christian discipleship. Moreover, it is precisely because evangelicals have remained open to genuine spiritual experience—an openness, by the way, that was not always appreciated during the philosophically materialistic twentieth century—that their theological inclinations continue to resonate quite well with the contemporary interest in spirituality. As Bernard Ramm noted much earlier, "The evangelical believes that the real touchstone of a theology is its spiritual power not necessarily its intellectual shrewdness, or sophistication, or learning."[7]

## The Context of Contemporary Theology

The nature of evangelical theology, especially in its concern for *both* orthodoxy *and* conversional piety, has been refracted in various cultural manifestations given the different social and theological settings of evangelicalism through the ages. More to the point, careful observation reveals that the exigencies of the twenty-first century, especially in terms of its approach to questions of knowledge, are remarkably different from earlier periods. Accordingly, as the evangelical community remains faithful to the integrity of its own story, which is ever oriented toward the good news of the gospel, it will likely encounter new dialogue partners and thereby display the genius of the evangelical faith in a slightly different but no less serious fashion. In fact, the recent philosophical trends of nonfoundationalism, postliberalism, and postmodernism all suggest that evangelicals may be able to "plunder the Egyptians" in the service of the Lord if such plundering is done in a critical fashion and with an eye on what remain the nonnegotiables of gospel witness. But to understand both the promise as well as the challenge that these philosophical movements pose for American evangelicalism, it will be helpful, first of all, to explore what is meant by foundationalism.

## Foundationalism

To raise the question of a foundational approach to knowledge is to bring into view many of the presuppositions that inform both practical and professional theology. Often unnoticed, these epistemological presuppositions are simply assumed as men and women go about the task of theological reflection. These very structures of thought, preferred ways of thinking, in this case some form of foundationalism, may be just as tightly held as the content of the faith itself, the one concern flowing almost imperceptibly into the other.

Just what is foundationalism? It is the epistemological orientation that holds that some beliefs are more basic than others. In other words, certain beliefs constitute the foundation for others that are rightly held. To illustrate this dynamic, consider a ten-story building with a foundation. In a real sense, the foundation "holds up" the building in a way that the tenth floor does not. Again, the ninth floor is "foundational" to the tenth but not to all the preceding floors. Consequently, if the ninth floor is lost, it takes with it the tenth but not neccessarily the others. If the foundation is lost, however, the entire building collapses. According to foundationalism, the same dynamic holds in terms of human knowing. Some beliefs are more basic and therefore anchor others.[8] Indeed, the closer one gets to foundational beliefs, the more weight or value is attached to them.

There is a certain sense in which a foundational approach operates in the many kinds of knowing that occur in daily life. But as this basic philosophical orientation played out during the Enlightenment and into modernity, often in academic circles, it was associated with the desire for *certainty*, as had been the case in the earlier writings of Descartes. Indeed, this quest for indubitable foundations on which to construct much of human knowledge, a part of the project of modernity, had the unfortunate result of rendering religious belief (that God exists, for example) an inappropriate foundation for knowledge and therefore, in the eyes of many, quite suspect. Many theologians naturally took issue with these negative judgments with respect to God, but at the same time they quietly acceded to these structures of thought and the foundationalist assumptions that held these judgments in place. As a result, as Nancey Murphy points out, not only did foundationalism set theologians on a quest for an indubitable starting point for theology, but it also directed them to only two suitable possibilities: "Scripture or a special sort of religious experience."[9] The former was developed by fundamentalists and neoevangelicals, the latter by theological liberals, but both groups were united in preferring this particular way, structurally speaking, of substantiating knowledge.

Another approach to this dilemma would have been to insist that religious beliefs can count as foundational or be properly basic. Such a view, however, would have been subject to unending criticism by lingering post-Cartesian modernists. Religious *beliefs*, it could be argued, do not give *certain* knowledge and therefore cannot be foundational. At their best, religious beliefs can be posited and assumed to be true, and a functional structure of knowledge could, therefore, emerge, but it would lack certainty, the very element on which Enlightenment approaches insisted. Simply put, religious *beliefs* would remain *beliefs* whose truth cannot be ascertained with exactitude. But some theologians could no doubt respond to this line of criticism by pointing out that the demand to prove first principles is itself problematic because not only must human knowing have a starting point, but if that starting point were confirmed by something else, then that something else—whatever it was—would be properly foundational, and on and on it would go, a true epistemological house of mirrors. The problem here, then, consists in the demand for an "external" corroboration of the veracity of first principles or beliefs, a demand that actually undermines foundationalism itself.

A foundationalist way of proceeding theologically, however, can survive the aforementioned criticisms if the demand for certainty is dropped and if its first principles are carefully chosen and constitute truly "open" questions whose truth or falsity cannot be conclusively ascertained by some sort of external test. Interestingly enough, the premise that "God exists" would qualify. Indeed, the truth of this statement can be neither conclusively affirmed nor denied on the basis of any external tests; that is, it walks an epistemological gauntlet whose clubs hit "nothing." Therefore, "God exists" is a basic and fundamental assertion that can function as a first principle and thereby anchor other beliefs, but it is an assertion that nevertheless leaves generous room for both doubt and faith. But is the statement "God exists" and others like it best situated in a rational epistemological structure whose truths are implicatorily related as the floors are to the foundation of a house?[10] Simply put, is human reason being made the final arbiter here?

## Nonfoundationalism

Given these and other concerns with foundationalism, an increasing number of evangelicals are calling for a nonfoundational approach to theology that they judge to be far more appropriate to the truth of the Christian faith. These theologians, which include both British and American evangelicals, realize that the Christian faith has been so wedded to foundationalism, especially since the time of the Enlightenment, that it will be difficult, at least initially, to gain a serious hearing for a new direction in theology. Part of the "apologetic" task of these theologians is to convince the faithful not only that the truth of the gospel does not rise or fall with foundationalism, a difficult task for any theologian, but also that its truth is perhaps best understood in a nonfoundational way. To this end, Alister McGrath has issued a clarion call to his evangelical colleagues:

> The time has come for evangelicalism to purge itself of the remaining foundational influences of the Enlightenment, not simply because the Enlightenment is over, but because of the danger of allowing ideas whose origins and legitimation lie outside the Christian gospel to exercise a decisive influence on that gospel.[11]

In a similar fashion, McGrath sees the collapse of foundationalism as a liberation of evangelical theology from the dominance of philosophical rationalism. He observes:

> We have been liberated from the rationalist demand to set out "logical" and "rational" grounds for our beliefs. Belief systems possess their own integrities, which may not be evaluated by others as if there were some privileged position from which all may be judged.[12]

As such, the ultimate substantiating authority of the truth of the gospel is not theoretical reason, an approach that would simply be another way of placing all-too-human thinking on the throne, so to speak. Indeed, the gospel has its own integrity that is best explored in terms of the canon of Scripture, by means of which the living Spirit of God calls forth the believing community for obedience, not for impartial, objective distance, in relation to Jesus Christ. As such, many of the truths of the Christian faith that are wonderfully transformative are best understood in terms of *vocatio* and addressability. That is, the Father of our Lord Jesus Christ, who transcends humanity in beauty, power, and love, is an evoking, calling God who invites us by means of the Holy Spirit through the proclamation of the Word to participate in the divine life, to have, in other words, the mind that was in Christ Jesus our Lord (1 Cor. 2:16). However, to force these deep and rich truths through a self-referential rationalistic sieve in which God is no longer an evoking subject but largely the *object* of discursive thought can result only in reductionism. Put another way, the church does not have to kneel before the canons of modernity to be secure in its identity, and its wisdom is by no means a mundane wisdom but remains foolishness in the eyes of the world, as Paul taught the Corinthian community in the first century. Such a judgment does not preclude a rational explication and defense of the faith, especially in the area of apologetics; it simply affirms that the ultimate substantiating grounds of the Christian faith lie elsewhere. In one sense, a God that could be "proved" (like a differential equation) through impartial and objective reason by *sinners* is not the God who redeems nor the Lord worshiped by the church. As Pascal perceptively noted in his own age, "Not the God of the philosophers, but the God of Abraham, Isaac, and Jacob."

## POSTLIBERALISM

In light of the difficulties with foundationalism, two principal nonfoundationalist approaches to doing theology in the twenty-first century are suggested by both postliberalism and postmodernism. The former movement was initially associated with Yale Divinity School and the work of Hans Frei and George Lindbeck. It emerged in the aftermath of the general disillusionment with liberal theology since the 1960s[13] and has sought to chart a course that does not make the fictive "universal experience" of liberalism the center of theological reflection.

Rejecting the totalizing projects of modernity and emphasizing the role of narrative, Lindbeck distinguishes three ways of doing theology in his work *The Nature of Doctrine:* (1) cognitive propositionalist, (2) experiential expressive, and (3) cultural-linguistic. This Lutheran scholar repudiates the first approach, often found among fundamentalists and neoevangelicals, because in its emphasis on cognition and intellectual products, it unwittingly carries on the dominating script of modernity in its postulation of universal reason, the application of which is often coercive. Moreover, Lindbeck finds the second approach, often found among theological liberals, troubling for similar reasons, though its hegemonic script is not universal reason but universal experience—a postulated, indeed artificial, experience that fails to take into account, ironically enough, the particularities of a diversity of stories.

In light of these criticisms, this Yale scholar proposes, in a creative and constructive fashion, what he calls a cultural-linguistic approach in which the experiential foundationalism of theological liberalism is turned on its head. In other words, instead of inward subjective experience, which supposedly gives rise to doctrinal formation, the linguistic and cultural products of the community fashion inward experience. Put another way, a religion is above all "an eternal word, a *verbum externum,* that molds and shapes the self and its world rather than an expression or thematization of a preexisting self or of preconceptual experience."[14] In short, the richer the cultural and linguistic system in which we participate, the more subtle and differentiated can be our experience.[15]

Given Lindbeck's premises, religious change must be conceived not as issuing from new experiences, and certainly not in the sense of Schleiermacher's *Das Gefühl,* but as issuing from the "interactions of a cultural-linguistic system with changing situations."[16] Again, first come the "objectivities" of religion, in terms of its language, doctrine, rituals, and ethics, and then the passions and "subjectivities" that are shaped into various *forms* of religious experience arise. The role of the community is crucial in the sense that it gives life to and fosters the linguistic dimension, a dimension that knows no private vocabularies (as Wittgenstein himself pointed out) and hence no private religious experience. Indeed, what personal religious experiences do emerge must be understood as a function of the interaction with the communal, linguistic structures that engender them.

In postliberalism, then, we encounter the primacy of narrative over human experience (and over historical events for that matter), and the world that emerges from the biblical narratives is the chief hermeneutical referent. As such, Lindbeck's proposal is akin to the hope and promise of literary criticism in that the world of the biblical text itself is given primacy over not only the ancient social and cultural conditions that gave rise to it (historical criticism) but also the contemporary social location of the community of interpreters (theological criticism) that must actualize its meaning. As Lindbeck so aptly puts it, "It is the text, so to speak, which absorbs the world, rather than the world the text."[17]

Though postliberalism correctly highlights the ongoing weaknesses of both fundamentalism and theological liberalism (dependent as they both are on the basic assumptions of modernistic foundationalism), it nevertheless falters in the eyes of many evangelicals in terms of the primacy that is given to the text. Theological doctrines are deemed to be the "grammar" of the community, and their truth is assessed not in light of any external appeal but simply in terms of their internal coherence. This results in a "flat" or "horizontal" reading of the truths of Scripture in which the reality of linguistic constructs and their communal nature are clearly affirmed, but the reality of the divine being outside the text, as Lord of history, for example, is not. As McGrath puts it, "The most fundamental evangelical critique of post-liberalism concerns the inadequacy of its commitment to extralinguistic and extrasystemic realities."[18] More to the point, this British scholar exclaims, "At least in the writings of Holmer and Lindbeck, the postliberal emphasis on Scripture runs the risk of suggesting that Christianity focuses on a text, rather than a person."[19] In other words, postliberalism is unable to take into account some of the elements that are crucial to understanding the evangelical concern with "conversional piety," a concern through which the evoking nature of God as well as the addressability of persons is clearly affirmed. Moreover, if Lindbeck is correct in his assertion that it is the cultural-linguistic dimension that gives rise to personal religious experience, and not the other way around, then a *humanly* created communal and linguistic construct is responsible for the diversity of religious experiences, conversion among them, that occur in the Christian community—an assertion that will be problematic for the idea of revelation.

## POSTMODERNISM

A second nonfoundationalist approach can be found in the cultural and philosophical movement known as postmodernism. The term *postmodern,* which makes modernity in some sense a dialogue partner, may have been first coined in the 1930s as a description for particular developments in the artistic world, but it did not gain widespread attention until the 1970s when it described a novel style of architecture.[20] As the term made its way into other venues, especially academic circles, English and philosophy departments in particular, it began to take on new meanings as the heritage of the Enlightenment, expressed in the paradigm of modernity, was rigorously critiqued. Whereas the eighteenth century had called for universal, impartial, and timeless knowledge in its celebration of reason, a call that supposedly laid aside the bondages of authority and tradition, the twentieth century witnessed the rise of thought that championed the particular, the indigenous, the timely, the peculiar—perspectives that had been washed away in the modernistic quest for universality.

Though several elements make up a variety of postmodern approaches, it is perhaps best for the larger purpose at hand and for the sake of clarity to focus on three major motifs: (1) the rejection of metanarratives, (2) the social construction of reality, and (3) the loss of transcendence. Concerning the first of these elements, the French scholar Jean François Lyotard epitomized the spirit of this new movement in his pithy statement, "I define postmodern as incredulity toward metanarratives."[21] Just what does this mean? A metanarrative is an all-inclusive, universal script that in the eyes of its postmodern detractors, such as Lyotard, Foucault, and Derrida, is inevitably "oppressive" in that it silences all other stories. Indeed, its predominance is held in place by cultural elites through the *pretense* of universality. Viewed another way, and as Dave Tomlinson puts it, "Postmodernity is what happens when marginalized peoples refuse to keep quiet anymore,"[22] when they demand that their stories be heard. Thus, in this view, the larger narrative of Enlightenment modernity was never as impartial or universal as it was reputed to be. Indeed, its chief articulators, such as Locke and Kant, were not sufficiently aware, according to some postmodern critics, that the narrative they told through their philosophical works was neither inclusive nor objective but actually an account that they preferred as a function and reflection of their own privileged social location. In other words, some of the writings that helped to carve out the modern worldview can no longer be taken at face value or in light of their own claims for universality. Instead, they must be seen in terms of "the cultural forces and paradigms of power that [they] represent."[23] In short, a hermeneutics of suspicion has set in.

Second, it should be apparent by now that the incredulity toward metanarratives has undoubtedly grown out of, at least in some respects, a greater appreciation for the social location out of which various intellectual and cultural products have emerged over time. From this new vantage point, the claim that the employment of reason constitutes impartiality and therefore marks the way toward progress, a view held by Montesquieu and Voltaire, is now by and large seriously doubted. It is precisely attentiveness to social location that has unmasked reason, so to speak, that has shown it to be not an objective faculty, an unbiased window on reality, but the expression in discursive form of underlying interests that are once again a function of various social and cultural forces. Stanley Grenz elaborates:

> Postmoderns denounce the pretense of those who claim to view the world from a transcendent vantage point from which they are able to speak imperiously to and on behalf of all humankind. Postmoderns have replaced this Enlighten-

ment ideal with the belief that all claims to truth—and ultimately even truth itself—are socially conditioned.[24]

Moreover, informed by the social thought of Marx, who maintained that the culture of any given society is a function of its more basic and determining socioeconomic environment (the relation of the means and mode of production), and fed by insights from the sociology of knowledge, the work of Peter Berger and Thomas Luckman in particular,[25] postmodernism suggests that the various realities that surface in the human community are but reflections of the underlying social forces that give rise to them. These constructions of reality may be useful, even expedient, as a society pursues any number of goods, but these constructions are not objectively true; they are instead relative to their own social location. Simply put, what is "true" in one culture may not be true in another.

But if as postmodernism maintains all truth is relative to social location and therefore absolute truth of a universalizing perspective does not exist (claims that most evangelicals reject), then this premise must also be socially derived and therefore simply perspectival and relative—only true for those communities in which it emerges.[26] Moreover, how is it that postmodern thinkers deny the universality of reason, on the one hand, and yet employ arguments that evidence all the tools of reason, on the other? Given this perplexing situation, J. Richard Middleton and Brian Walsh perceptively ask, "How is it possible to judge the worldview of another person or group of people to be wrong when we realize that we have no privileged, universal access to truth and so can only pass judgment from the perspective of our own worldview?"[27] Moreover, if we cannot step outside the constructions of our own reality to discern or judge the truth and wisdom of other distinct groups, then the pursuit of knowledge may become exceedingly narcissistic, even tribal, as we are left simply to talk to ourselves. Again, if there is no objective, universal basis beyond the preferences of conflicting groups to *communicate* their truth claims, then the pursuit of truth itself may very well be undermined, and it will likely devolve into the vagaries of political maneuvers and power machinations.

In light of these difficulties, it may be best for evangelicals not to take the postmodern claims at face value. For one thing, though the premise of universality is denied in cultural, ideational life, that is, on the level of the superstructure of societies, it nevertheless reemerges with respect to the infrastructure of these same societies in the assertion that *all* cultural realities are socially constructed, even determined. This basic premise of postmodern thought functions as a universal, a truism, operative in *any given* culture and one that would, therefore, rival the hegemonic tendencies of either Descartes or Kant. It is precisely because postmodernism posits a determinism from below (where the ethics or religious truth of any given culture is merely a function of social *forces*) that it has vigorously denied the ontological reality of anything beyond this determinism, whether it be a transcendent self or almighty God. Put another way, the same kind of reductionism that was evident in modernistic philosophical materialism is present here as well, though it is well masked. However, the mistake of postmodern reductionists, as in Derrida's nihilistic critique of ontotheology, is to conclude that since the religious and spiritual dimensions of life must be grounded in either the constructions of language or broader social forces, then such dimensions are nothing but complex manifestations of these forces. Again, an appreciation of anything that could possibly be transcendent (that though rooted in physical and social realities nevertheless cannot be fully explained by them) is swept aside *methodologically* from the outset. This methodological sweep, so to speak, so characteristic of modernity, means that the works of Derrida and other nihilists are best described as "ultramodern" rather than postmodern.[28] That is, they take some of the prominent themes of modernity to their ultimate, radical conclusion without going beyond them to transcendence.[29]

One way out of this dilemma is not only to realize that a diversity of postmodernisms exist, not all of which deny a "metaphysics of presence," as in the work of Derrida, but also to recognize that writing has some extralinguistic referent. Indeed, an alternative *constructive* postmodern project is articulated in Jerry Gill's engaging work *Mediated Transcendence: A Postmodern Reflection.* Mindful that transcendence has been dismissed by modern and ultramodern epistemologies, Gill offers a corrective in the following thesis, which is developed throughout his work:

> The intangible reality mediated by means of tangible reality neither exists nor is known independently of the particulars of the tangible, but at the same time it cannot be reduced to an account of those particulars.[30]

In this view, then, a number of simultaneously interpenetrating dimensions exist and are experienced as "mediated in and through one another rather than being juxtaposed to each other."[31] For example, the transcendent dimension of beauty is mediated through the sounds, the very notes, of Beethoven's Ninth Symphony. Here beauty transcends the notes and is by no means reducible to them, and yet beauty is dependent on these very same notes for its mediation, its concrescence into being. In this case, the "higher" dimension of beauty is dependent on the "lower" dimension of notes or sounds but is not reducible to or fully explained by it. In a similar fashion, Gill reasons, "The mind is transcendent of the brain without being separate from it; it is known in and through the brain,"[32] an understanding that clearly breaks out of Cartesian dualism.

Though Gill's offering is marked by many strengths and provides some of the philosophical wherewithal through which the evangelical community can give expression to a broader expanse of knowledge, of what it knows but what it cannot empirically prove, it nevertheless suffers significant difficulties, especially in the eyes of hard-nosed empiricist types, in that the reality of the "transcendent," whether it be spirit, beauty, or even God, is a knowledge that is not universally replicable. "There is, of course, no guarantee," Gill observes, "that a person will be able to experience the dimension of reality to which another person seeks to introduce him."[33] It is precisely this issue of not being able to replicate this knowledge universally that has led some to conclude that nothing is actually mediated through the lower dimensions other than various forms of human consciousness that are fully explicable in terms of brain states without any appeal to a touted notion of transcendence.

But there are far more serious problems with Gill's postmodern reflection, especially when he states that intangible reality (the presence of God?) does not exist independently of the particulars of the tangible:

> The notion of mediated dimensions speaks to this dualistic difficulty by affirming the reality of a transcendent dimension that exists and is known in and through the natural dimension or dimensions of human existence. This transcendent reality is nevertheless more or other than that through which it is mediated, yet without being independent of it.[34]

In this setting, both transcendence and immanence are affirmed, but evangelical theologians such as Donald Bloesch and Thomas Oden actually conceive the transcendence of God somewhat differently.[35] That is, the Most High is revealed sacramentally through event and word, to be sure, but is not dependent on them in terms of the divine being itself. Gill's effort, then, marks an important beginning, but much more work needs to be done.

# The Promise and Challenges of Evangelical Theology

Given this larger environment in which contemporary evangelical theology is articulated and received, what then is the best way forward? First of all, several critical and progressive evangelicals have not only moved beyond the modernistic commitments of theological liberals but have also, for the most part, welcomed the rise of postmodernism since they had struggled for so long with the restrictions, exclusions, and outright prejudices of Enlightenment modernity, especially in its demand for scientific "objectivity." Today, American evangelicals, as a distinct cultural and linguistic group, have a place at the table, so to speak. Since the reasons for excluding their stories are no longer viable, their voices can at least be heard. While such a turn of events may in the eyes of some constitute a reason for rejoicing, upon further reflection, there is far less reason to celebrate.

For one thing, the shift from modernity to postmodernity in American culture is only gradually occurring and is by no means complete. Therefore, the old, worn-out modernist critique that has excluded Christian voices in the past, almost out of hand, can unfortunately still be found in the academy. "The idea of scientific objectivity as an obtainable standard for the larger questions of life is generally considered passé," George Marsden writes. "Yet when the subject of religion is mentioned [in the academy], the categories of Enlightenment skepticism seem to be miraculously resuscitated."[36] Again, this leading Reformed historian observes, "If postmodernists who denounce scientific objectivism as an illusion are well accepted in the contemporary academy, there is little justification for the same academy to continue to suppress religious perspectives because they are 'unscientific.'"[37] Yet such suppression continues, and it belies the hope and promise of not only postmodern tolerance but also a true "liberal" education in which a rich diversity of views should be expressed for the sake of approaching knowledge in both a critical and a fair-minded manner.

Second, though some evangelicals are now clearly at the table, no longer relegated to the halls of the uninvited, their voices are nevertheless diminished from the outset due to the cacophony of voices that are in the mix. That is, the evangelical story is deemed to be simply just one story among many caught up in a context that in its denial of universality necessarily relativizes all stories as simply expressions of particular cultural and linguistic locations. Accordingly, the premise that there are no metanarratives, the staple of the postmodern perspective, is inimical with respect to those larger stories, such as the gospel, that "transcend" the usual group divisions of postmodern life. This premise also constitutes, ironically enough, a metanarrative whose outworking is just as oppressive as Enlightenment modernity ever was—a truth alluded to earlier. Middleton and Walsh state:

> Do postmodernists consider their own worldview as simply one option among many? Not at all. Postmodernity, as the master discourse which guides our

understanding that all stories are mere human constructs, does not appear on the table. . . . Postmodernity thus functions as the larger interpretive frame that relativizes all other worldviews as simply local stories with no legitimate claims to reality or universality.[38]

Simply put, the postmodern view is all the more problematic precisely because it is a metanarrative that claims it is not one.

Again, postmodernism as a philosophical and cultural movement has not made a clean break with modernity, as is so often claimed, since a lingering commitment to philosophical naturalism, a staple of modernity that has and continues to repudiate a transcendent dimension, is evident in so many postmodern works. Add to this the postmodern habit of parsing all truth claims as simply one among many and the employment of an ongoing hermeneutics of suspicion in which knowledge is reduced to its cultural and linguistic sources, and it can be readily seen that much of postmodern life has unfortunately been reduced to its political elements. In other words, in the end what has value or meaning are groups, representing different social locations, and the power that they can wield vis-à-vis *others*. Each group, at least on some level, is at odds with every other group since there is no transcendent or universal basis in the postmodern void that can possibly unite them. And so if individuals are inordinately self-referential, then such a tendency is only compounded on the group level, as Reinhold Niebuhr has taught us so well,[39] where the specter of a divisive ethnocentrism is ever in the offing. In a real sense, postmodernism attempts to cut the gospel story down to size to make it the narrative of just another group that bears the badge of "Christian." Simply put, the underside of diversity is tribalism, the underside of tolerance is meaninglessness, and truth is reduced to a show of hands.

In light of these trends, evangelicals must approach postmodernism both forthrightly and critically. For instance, evangelical theologians, for the sake of both honesty and integrity, cannot pretend for a moment that the gospel is simply one story among many. Using the newly found cultural space afforded by some strands of postmodernism, evangelicals must proclaim, teach, and embody the gospel story as a witness to those both in and outside the church and provide the occasion whereby the Word and the Holy Spirit can work their "magic," their "enchantment," so to speak, on the hearts and minds of suffering sinners. To illustrate, in his own day, Martin Luther wrote about the power of the Word, its efficacy as an instrument of illumination and truth:

All that I have done is to farther, preach and teach God's Word; otherwise I have done nothing. So it happened that while I slept or while I drank a glass of Wittenberg beer with my friend Philip [Melanchthon] and with Amsdorf, the papacy was weakened as it never was before by the action of any prince or emperor. I have done nothing; the Word has done and accomplished everything. . . . I let the Word do its work!"[40]

This description of the power of the Word is by no means a call for inaction or quietism, but it is an honest recognition that the gospel story is unique, uncanny, and nothing less than the greatest story that has ever been (or can be) told, despite the postmodern protests to the contrary. Indeed, even through the most gifted and creative use of human imagination, one still cannot fathom a greater narrative, a more captivating story, than that the Most High, the Holy Lord, the One whose eyes are too pure to behold evil, comes and dwells among us. This truth by itself would be wonderful enough, but the Christian community maintains that there is much more. Not only did God come in a movement of deep lowliness and self-forgetfulness, but the Lord also descended to the lowest depths of human existence as he was mocked by religious leaders, deserted by his friends, derided by a common criminal, tortured mercilessly by soldiers, and finally executed. It is precisely this descent, this kenotic movement that placed the divine on a despicable cross, that reveals that there is not a man or a woman, elder or child, no matter how despised or oppressed, that this One cannot touch. His coming and descent, then, his life and death, distinct among all others, changed everything. Christ alone bridged the gap, the wretched alienation between God and sinners. It is none other than this grief-stricken, rejected, and crucified person who rose from the dead, a rising that reveals that hatred and mocking, shame and death are not the last words. God has the last word, and it is one of holy love, a love that is sacrificial, embracing, and far stronger than death.

In light of all this, the unavoidable question must be asked of postmodern philosophers and literary critics alike: Is there a greater story than this, more poignant in its details, more glorious in its outworking and conclusion? In the face of all the evil and suffering of a very troubled world, can *anyone* worship a God who has not come to us or who has not so thoroughly identified with the human condition? And if the Christian community is wrong in its teaching of the incarnation, that the Word became flesh, then it must be affirmed that God, precisely to be God, a being of which a greater cannot be conceived, *should* have come.

Evangelical theologians, evangelists, and missionaries, then, should be encouraged by all of this (though some difficult days lie ahead), since the postmodern distaste for metanarratives is virtually powerless to prevent the gospel from being heard for what it actually is, namely, the greatest of all narratives, the story-encompassing story, the one that in the context of the community of faith holds enormous transformative power as the ongoing paradigm in light of which people live their lives. The gospel is a story that invites but does not coerce, embraces but does not force. However, in thinking that all narratives simply speak of the socially determining forces that gave rise to them, the horizontal reading referred to earlier, postmodern thinkers inevitably miss "the strange new world within the Bible,"[41] to borrow a phrase from Barth, and therefore fail to realize the kind of story that is now at the table, especially as it will be taught and proclaimed by American evangelicals in the twenty-first century. That is, the gospel refuses to remain "flat" but introduces a vertical dimension, an axis that includes the transcendent God "above," to draw from Gill's insights, as well as the depths of the human soul below. By reading the Word and hearing it proclaimed, believers find themselves addressed by a gracious God, experience a sense of something "more" not simply reducible to the individual words, and therefore respond with their whole being to such a *personal* call. Again, knowing God, through the ministrations of Word and Spirit, reveals a depth of the heart in terms of its dispositions, affections, and loves, a depth hitherto not fully explored. It is the awakening of these "vertical" dimensions in human experience, the acquaintance with mystery and enchantment, that will help believers well beyond modern and postmodern reductionism to enjoy the enduring fruits of faith. Moreover, it is precisely the ongoing mistake of the postmodern worldview, in its "flat" reading of narrative as simply a linguistic and social construction, that holds such promise for a vigorous proclamation of the gospel, whose telling will inevitably prove to be *not* just another story. In this way, evangelicals can "plunder the Egyptians."

# 5

# Evangelicals and Politics

olitical thought in America today, whether from the right or the left,
ever assumes a context of presuppositions, first principles, and judgments, many of which are often unstated. Given this situation, the
politically naive among us, in hearing the words *justice, rights,* and *equality,*
championed both by national leaders and sometimes even by demagogues,
immediately conclude that all is well because they have heard favorable speech
and the larger values with which they can identify. It is only the more discerning among us, who in their attempts to think critically, realize that the pleasant
language of "justice" in all its various forms may actually be caught up in a
larger script in which justice is hardly in the offing and significant segments
of the population will be denied their basic rights as human beings, all for the
sake of some social utility.

To be sure, the political dimension of American society embraces any number of scripts in which the terms *good, right,* and *fair* are defined differently
by liberals, conservatives, libertarians, and socialists. It is therefore imperative
for cultural and political analysts to explore the various *contexts* in which such
speech emerges in order to discern its appropriate meaning. But even when
this arduous task is done fairly and accurately, one must also realize that any
contemporary American political movement has a history, a story, that is itself marked by changes over time. In other words, the political liberalism of

the twenty-first century, for example, is not the same as "classic" liberalism, which emphasized limited government and laissez-faire economics, as in the thought of John Locke, nor is it to be confused with the liberalism of John F. Kennedy's vaunted "New Frontier." Both liberalisms have been transformed through time and circumstance and the latter, in particular, by a crucial epoch in American history.

## American Politics and the Heirs of the 1960s

It is neither desirable nor possible to explore contemporary evangelical political thought apart from the numerous social, cultural, and political changes that occurred during the 1960s. In many ways, this was not only a crucial decade but also one of many contrasts: On the one hand, Congress passed civil rights legislation that guaranteed the freedoms of African Americans, freedoms that had been neglected or outright repudiated under the laws of several states. On the other hand, the counterculture during this period, which ironically enough eventually became the establishment, challenged the sexual mores of American society in a thoroughgoing way, staged "love ins" across the country, and in the end spawned a rise in the rate of illegitimacy that by the turn of the century became nothing less than catastrophic. For example, around the middle of the decade, when Senator Moynihan conducted his famous study on poverty, he learned, among other things, that the out-of-wedlock birthrate was 3 percent for whites and nearly 24 percent for blacks. "A little more than thirty years later," as Ron Sider points out, "33 percent of all our children are born to unmarried women. The white illegitimacy rate is now 25 percent and the black rate 70 percent."[1]

Again, on the one hand, in 1965, Congress not only abolished the earlier immigration quota system that harkened back to 1921 and had preferred Europeans over Asians and Africans but also passed new legislation that allowed for greater diversity, the kind of diversity that strengthens a nation. On the other hand, this was also a decade of hedonism, narcissism, and outright vulgarity that entailed what Roger Kimball calls "the institutionalization of immoralist radicalism." This took the form of "drugs, pseudo-spirituality, promiscuous sex, virulent anti-Americanism, naive anti-capitalism, and the precipitous decline of artistic and intellectual standards."[2] And while women demanded and received an increasing number of rights, throwing off their 1950s second-class status with its limited and stifling roles, this was also a decade of searing violence:

From the war in Vietnam to the police brutality at the Chicago Democratic Convention, from the murder of civil rights workers, both black and white, Christian and Jewish, to the assassinations of the Kennedy brothers and Martin Luther King Jr., all in all this was a decade of blood.

In the midst of the chants of protest marches, in the wake of the smell of tear gas, and in the aftermath of the cries for justice, the nation was actually spared the class revolution that Marx had predicted, but it "succumbed to the cultural revolution,"[3] whereby the nation's sense of justice was dramatically altered as was its very understanding of moral authority. As James Davison Hunter points out, "Different formulations and sources of moral authority"[4] emerged during this period, some of which are still with us today. To illustrate, many veins of anti-authoritarianism developed among the ranks of the New Left, whose animus was directed against the state, the church, and the family. In many instances, it was the morally irresolute, who fornicated freely and often, who not only claimed the mantle of moral authority in the name of liberation from sexual oppression—to the delight of Freudians and neo-Freudians alike—but also virulently attacked the peace and stability of the nuclear family as a species of the "bourgeois" mentality they so loathed. Indeed, as Irving Kristol observes, "The identifying marks of the New Left was its refusal to think economically and its contempt for bourgeois society precisely because this is a society that does think economically."[5] The moral reversal, a vital part of the cultural revolution, was unmistakable and without precedent in American history. The counterculture that had championed sexual responsibility as passé, a drag on personal freedom, was oddly enough actually carving out the nation's newfangled ethic.

Though the American political scene may upon first glance appear to be a confusing, incomprehensible welter of competing voices, further reflection reveals stable and enduring political alignments in terms of two key ideas: liberty and equality. Indeed, though both liberals and conservatives hold each of these ideas as integral to a just and orderly society, how they understand these terms and what weight they assign to them make all the difference. American liberals, for instance, have stressed "freedom from the constraints on personal liberty imposed by religion, morality, law, family, and community"[6] in a way that continues the anti-authoritarianism of the 1960s. Though some claim that this move constitutes the development of a "radical individualism,"[7] what is actually affirmed here is not individualism per se (since liberalism often stresses the group *above* the rights of individuals) but liberty understood essentially as "hedonistic freedom," echoing in some sense the voice of John Stuart Mill, a liberty that should be restricted only in the name of the prevention of harm to others or in terms of some other form of social expediency. Accordingly, for American liberals, sexual relations among unmarried couples is no longer a moral problem to be adjudicated in terms of an overarching standard or norm. Instead, it is deemed by and large a *medical* problem whereby "safe sex," condom distribution, and disease prevention make up much if not the entirety of their concern.

But this hedonistic freedom, almost a moral anomie, apparently does not extend to the free and unfettered pursuit of wealth, for it is at this point that the left calls on the authority and force of the state to redistribute property—all, of course, in the name of justice and *equality*. As one scholar observes, "Liberals today have . . . [given] the government ever increasing powers in economic affairs while endowing the individual with ever greater autonomy in moral affairs."[8] In short, freedom, so defined, is largely social and not economic. Moreover, in this setting, equality entails a redistribution of the various goods of society (entrance to schools, jobs, funding, etc.), not in terms of sheer achievement, indicative of a meritocracy, but often in terms of a predetermined social ideal, usually along the lines of a class, race, and gender grid. The inequalities that are allowed to emerge from this social engineering are justified not only in terms of past discrimination but also in terms, once again, of their purported social usefulness.

Political conservatives, on the other hand, in articulating a transcendent moral order (often expressed in the form of natural law), accept "the constraints that a clear view of reality, including a recognition of the nature of human beings, places upon the main thrusts of liberalism."[9] That is, conservatives eschew many of the social freedoms entailed in hedonistic freedom and see them as undermining not only human dignity but also the orders of society, such as church and family, that keep a community stable. As such, conservatives are often willing to call on the powers of the state to enforce a "social morality" through law (restricting nearly unlimited access to abortion, for example, or the "right" to pornography) and through an appeal to *tradition* (reinstating prayer in schools, for instance). Indeed, neoconservatives such as Himmelfarb, Kristol, and Wanniski (who were awakened from their liberal slumbers partly as a result of the rise of the New Left) seem to be far more concerned about economic than social freedom. Their writings demonstrate by and large the conviction that the prosperity of any civilization requires a differentiation of orders and classes that emerges in the wake of significant personal and economic achievement. Of the rise of neoconservatism, Irving Kristol writes:

> We regarded ourselves originally as dissident liberals—dissident because we were skeptical of many of Lyndon Johnson's Great Society initiatives and increasingly

disbelieving of the liberal metaphysics, the view of human nature and of social and economic realities, on which those programs were based.[10]

In short, in this context, freedom is largely economic and not social. Equality is understood chiefly in terms of the dignity of a human being (theologically understood in terms of the image of God), of having the same rights before "the law," and of being afforded an equality of opportunity (to succeed or fail in accordance with one's talents) though not an equality of results.

Although these two political philosophies are both clearly represented in broader American culture, the nature of their representation is decidedly different. That is, a distinction must be made between the sheer numbers or the demographics of these political groups and their ongoing cultural influence, for though political conservatives currently constitute the majority of both the Senate and the House of Representatives, liberal political influence nevertheless dominates the broader cultural arena with but a few exceptions. Sociologists explore this surprising dominance by appeal to the "new class" or the "knowledge class," postindustrial workers who make their living principally through the manufacture and distribution of knowledge, such as university professors, church bureaucrats, newspaper publishers, editors, judges, journalists, and health care workers. The difference in cultural power, for example, can be clearly seen in the churchgoing habits of the majority of Americans when compared to those of the media. According to George Gallup, "In a typical week during 1998, two in five adults (40%) attended church or synagogue, a figure that has remained remarkably constant since the early 1960s."[11] Compare this with a study of the Washington press corps that found that "86 percent seldom or never attended religious services."[12] Indeed, it is not so much that the new class controls the media but that "they are the media, just as they are our educational system, our public health and welfare system, and much else."[13]

Other differences can be seen in terms of the distaste among the new class for referring to America as a "Christian" nation, though according to Gallup, 87 percent of Americans identify themselves as either Protestant, Catholic, or Eastern Orthodox.[14] Differences can also be seen in terms of the reluctance of the *New York Times,* emblem of the knowledge class, to acknowledge that its latest offering on the best-seller list is actually wrong. It is the Bible, not some latest political exposé, that continues to outsell all other nonfiction books when long-term trends are considered. Again, this dissonance between cultural power and demographics, between perception and reality, suggests that some of the well-worn mirrors of the American nation that are held up to the public often distort and in the worst instances hide images of American life that clearly warrant a viewing. In short, these guides fail to describe the reality of American life accurately and fairly and in terms of numbers that do not lie.

Not surprisingly, then, new class ideals in terms of social liberty and equality clearly predominate among mainline Protestant leaders who look to this class for both legitimization and approval, which they apparently "cannot win through their merits as religionists, but only through their political attitudes and political usefulness."[15] Put another way, some Protestant leaders, seminary professors among them, have concluded that the way to cultural influence is through the translation of the gospel into the political idiom of the left. To illustrate, Stephen Carter, an African American and noted Yale law professor, recounts the "sermon" he heard from an energetic divinity student who among other things admonished the congregation that it was "our Christian duty to support the good (left wing) terrorists in their holy struggle to massacre the bad (right wing) terrorists."[16] Devout in his Christian faith, Carter was stunned with the realization that this student "had no conception of the possibility of a faith not guided by her prior political commitments." For her, as he puts it, "politics should lead faith, rather than the other way around."[17] And I recall sitting in a United Methodist church during the late 1980s and reading a denominational insert that proclaimed that the "astute observer" will realize that the kingdom of God is emerging through the Sandinista revolution. Having read my share of the writings of both Karl Barth and Reinhold Niebuhr, I deemed all such pronouncements, then as now, thoroughly naive and incredibly mistaken.

At any rate, the influence of the new class, a class that carries many of the ideas of the political left (though it is, of course, not equivalent to the left, since there are quite a few conservative knowledge workers), is so extensive, culturally speaking, that it has affected even the attitudes and outlook of many American evangelicals. An important study of this phenomenon was conducted during the early 1990s by John Schmalzbauer. His careful research demonstrated that evangelical knowledge workers as a whole are "more liberal than working-class people on every attitude scale."[18] Moreover, though evangelicals in this social context "seem to resist new-class liberalism on sexual mores," they nevertheless are increasingly accommodating "to its liberal ethos on gender roles, abortion and civil liberties."[19] Though this cultural influence is clearly real and pervasive, it nevertheless must be brought into a proper perspective through the realization that these same workers, no doubt as a consequence of their evangelical faith, do indeed "resist the liberalizing effects of the new class variable more than other knowledge workers."[20]

In light of the liberalizing influence of the new class on American culture, such that it often frames many of the leading issues of the day and even suggests at times the very language of the discussion, it will be helpful to explore such influence in terms of the following three areas: (1) religion, (2) ethics, and (3) education, all of which are the concerns not simply of American evangelicals but of the broader American public as well.

## Religion and Politics: Do They Mix?

Many of the founding fathers of the American nation, such as Thomas Jefferson and James Madison, were keenly aware that the preference of the state for a particular religion could easily result in tyranny. Indeed, Voltaire, a key leader of the Enlightenment, quipped at the time, "A Nation with one religion has oppression, a nation with two has civil war, and a nation with a hundred has peace."[21] Remarkably enough, several Baptist leaders, such as Isaac Backus and John Leland (and Roger Williams of an earlier age), added their voices to the call for religious liberty because they feared that an encroaching state, as had appeared in England, could easily stifle religious opposition, demand conformity in matters of conscience, and thereby squelch dissent. "Government has no more to do with the religious opinions of men than it has with the principles of mathematics,"[22] Leland declared. And many of his co-religionists agreed.

Therefore, the fact that James Madison proposed a series of amendments to the Constitution (which make up the Bill of Rights), the first of which pertained to the issues of freedom of speech, press, assembly, and religion, should not lead us to conclude, as so often happens today, that this founding father had an utterly secular interest in mind. As Stephen Carter points out, "The metaphorical separation of church and state originated in an effort to protect religion from the state, not the state from religion."[23] Part of the problem no doubt is that the first amendment articulates two key principles with respect to religion that because of their general nature have been variously interpreted. Terse in its composition, the First Amendment states quite simply, "Congress shall make no law respecting an establishment of religion or prohibiting the free exercise thereof."[24] This amendment, along with nine others, formally became a part of the Constitution in 1791, and it was only a few years later, in 1802, that Jefferson, in his famous letter to the Baptists of Danbury, began to surmise that a "wall" now existed between church and state.

Though many Christians, especially evangelicals, are quick to point out that the Constitution does not contain the language of a "wall of separation between church and state," the Supreme Court picked up this Jeffersonian language and *interpreted* the Constitution precisely in this way. In 1947, for example, in the case *Everson v. The Board of Education,* the Court not only employed the language of a wall of separation but also insisted that the wall "must be kept high and impregnable."[25] According to what has become known as the "Lemon Test," first articulated by Chief Justice Warren Burger in 1971 in the case *Lemon v. Kurtzman,* for a statute or law to pass constitutional muster, it must meet three criteria: "First, the statute must have a secular legislative purpose; second, its principal or primary effect must be one that neither advances nor inhibits religion; finally, the statute must not foster 'an excessive entanglement with religion.'"[26] Despite these precepts, Carter maintains that "the embarrassing truth is that the Establishment Clause has no theory; that is, the Supreme Court has not really offered guidance on how to tell when the clause is violated."[27] To be sure, when the intellectually curious examine the numerous Supreme Court decisions made in the last century that affect religion, they have difficulty determining what is actually the guiding and enduring principle being expressed in a number of cases.

Moreover, some of the sharpest critics of the Court's decisions on religion suggest that what is carefully being "exegeted" is not the First Amendment but a cultural ethos that has offered itself as "the American way" and therefore serves, in some subtle forms, as the basic presupposition of many who have sat on the bench. From *Engel v. Vitale* in 1962, which banned prayer in public schools, to *School District of Abington v. Schempp* the following year, which extended the ban to include Bible reading, to *Wallace v. Jaffree* in 1985, which declared that Alabama's "moment of silence" in public school classrooms was a violation of the First Amendment, Judge Robert Bork and others have viewed these "activist" judgments as "the judicial adoption of the tenets of modern liberalism [which] has produced a crisis of legitimacy."[28]

It is one thing to call for a separation of church and state, a call to which even some evangelical leaders such as Cal Thomas and Ed Dobson would assent in the interest of protecting the integrity of religious faith.[29] It is quite another thing to call for the separation of church and *culture* and to demand that the religious life of Americans be virtually ignored or trivialized in the press, on television, on the radio, and in films and that religious people transform their moral reasoning so that their specifically religious language or motivations do not appear at the national level when discussing the leading issues of the day. Put another way, secularists, atheists, and agnostics are all allowed, in this approach, to bring their own preferred ways of moral reasoning intact into the public area; religious people are not. This demand for a naked public square, however, to use an expression coined by Richard John Neuhaus,[30] is not required by the Constitution, though many Americans mistakenly think that it is. Indeed, various factions of the political left have successfully portrayed their own provincial and limited interests, especially *their* preference for the privatization of religion, as if these interests represented the common will, the very ethos of the nation. They do not.

Given the mistaken judgments and the outright shoddy thinking surrounding the topic of church and culture, the religious rights of Americans, which should be protected by the second clause of the First Amendment's treatment of religion, are often up for grabs, so to speak, to be decided by the vagaries, the whims, of a local high school principal, a textbook editor, or a newly composed school board. In fact, a public school teacher in Colorado was required by his superiors to remove his Bible from his desk, "where students might see it."[31] And as if this were not enough, the teacher was then forbidden "to read it silently when his students were involved in other activities."[32] For one thing, the moral soundness of the nation can be questioned when one of the most radical acts that high school students can do today, an instance of sheer rebellion against the powers that be, is to refuse to obey a court order and to pray publicly and voluntarily at a high school football game. Where is that old liberal principle of "I strongly disagree with what you say, but I affirm your right to say it" when you need it?

Viewed in yet another way, the struggle in this country over religion and culture is simply a matter of truth telling. For example, many people of faith have been disheartened to learn that the high school textbooks of their sons and daughters often tell the story of the American nation with little awareness of the role that religion has played in national life. Thus, students are rarely invited to learn *why* the pilgrims came to the New World in the first place or what their purpose was once they got here. It is no surprise, then, that Winthrop's classic speech aboard the *Arabella,* "We shall be as a city on a hill" (a good window, by the way, on the self-consciousness of the future nation, cited even by American presidents, Ronald Reagan among them) is not mentioned at all. Its theme is apparently too offensive for the politically correct among us who much prefer past events that illustrate their own contemporary scripts. Beyond this, students are often left in the dark with respect to the significant role that the black church played in the civil rights movement. And though Martin Luther King Jr. is, of course, prominently mentioned in textbooks, some leave more of the impression that he was a Hindu carrying out the philosophy of Ghandi than the Baptist minister that he actually was. Indeed, as one black scholar points out, "Liberal philosophy's distaste for explicit religious argument in the public square cannot accommodate the open and unashamed rhetoric of the nonviolent civil rights movement of the 1950s and 1960s."[33]

If we cannot tell the story of America fairly and accurately, if religious elements are repeatedly removed from the narrative, greatly minimized, or reinterpreted, then we are no longer telling the story of the American nation but of a fictional country that has never existed. When this occurs, it is clear that Christians, Jews, Muslims, Hindus, and other people of faith will become second-class citizens. Their story, their voice, will be lost in judgments that find religion by and large superstitious, a throwback to an earlier age, oppressive, or in the worst instances simply offensive.[34] If this is the case, how will Christians, evangelicals in particular, participate in the political life of the nation? How will their voices be heard on the leading issues of the day? Apparently, they will do so only with great difficulty simply because many cultural hurdles have been placed in their way, hurdles that not only deny an entire class of people some of their basic human rights but also undermine the hope and promise of democratic freedom.

## Ethics and Public Life

Hannah Arendt, a German intellectual who made her way to America as the Nazis were invading France, remarked in 1966, before the cultural revolution was in full force, that the Enlightenment "meant nothing more or less than that from then on Man, and not God's command or the customs of history, should be the source of law."[35] At first thinkers such as Locke and Jefferson appealed to a notion of natural law expressed in the form of inalienable rights, even if that law was understood largely in a humanistic way. In time, however, the objectivity of a standard transcendent to the common will of the people was rejected by subsequent philosophers. By the time of the twentieth century, the postmodern critique of the Enlightenment had been so thorough that even the lingering legal traditions that had appealed to natural law, even if implicitly, were quickly brushed aside. In their work *The Betrayal of Liberalism,* Hilton Kramer and Roger Kimball describe the current situation in the following way:

> The notion of natural law has been treated with derision in our own time, by jurists and lawyers on the right as well as the left, even though, at every turn, they keep backing into its logic and drawing on its language. After all, the very appeal to "first principles" as the ground of a constitution or as a guide to its content, is itself a move into natural law.[36]

In the absence of an objective standard through which moral and legal conflicts can be adjudicated, both political liberals and conservatives are often left with a legal positivism that is grounded simply in the force of the law itself, where legal documents are viewed not as an expression of larger transcendent principles but as ends in themselves. Such views invite a legal subjectivism whereby the politics of the day can easily become enmeshed in the interpretation of a document such as the Constitution. Thus, for example, partial birth abortion has been considered to be "the exercise of a constitutional right even by judges who acknowledge the difficulty in distinguishing it from infanticide."[37]

Beyond this, the collapse of natural law reasoning, championed by the postmodern outlook, has resulted in the crass politicalization of both the moral and the legal dimensions of American society, where right and wrong, legal and illegal are often decided in light of political pressure and will. Nevertheless, it would be a mistake to conclude that the contemporary American cultural scene, wary as it is about "absolutes," is without its own norm or standard of judgment. To be sure, something has filled the vacuum left by the collapse of traditional legal and moral reasoning. It is the principle not of a basic equality, which most people would favor, but of something far different: a radical, aggressive egalitarianism that grew out of—in a very idealized form—the earlier counterculture's Marxist and post-Marxist vision of a "classless" society in which Trotsky was a prophet and Marcuse a saint.

For one thing, the new class, which trades on the average person's favorable estimation of equality, has radicalized and politicized the notion to require, through the coercive powers of the state, the enforcement of its own preferred vision of justice, which quickly moves beyond equality of opportunity to demand equality of results. Some societies, historically speaking, such as many of the old European aristocracies, were based primarily on blood and on being "well born," while others, such as French bourgeois society before the revolution, elevated the ownership of property above all. Still others, American democracy among them, stressed the importance of achievement as the principal avenue to social and economic betterment.[38] In the past, as America embraced a frontier, its values included among other things achievement, rugged individualism, meritocracy, as well as the importance of private property as a reward—blending two of the earlier historic types. But this cultural and political amalgam is now clearly out of vogue and is deemed "hostile to the egalitarianism impulse."[39]

In handling the tension between liberty and equality, a concern of both liberals and conservatives, radical egalitarianism tips the balance decidedly toward the latter. Indeed, hierarchies of achievement and merit that emerge, in part, as a result of different values, abilities, and talents are all judged in a simplistic fashion to be the consequence of class privilege and are therefore found to be both distasteful and "undemocratic." But in this vision of justice the centralized powers of the state, as even D'Toqueville forewarned, are invariably called upon to "level" the differences, to break down any lingering hierarchies, all in the name of equality. But in the pursuit of this artificial, even contrived, equality, the liberty to succeed as well as to fail is clearly lost. This is precisely what this brand of political thinking is all about. In fact, an issue of *Newsweek* reported that political correctness is "Marxist in origin, in the broad sense of attempting to redistribute power from the privileged class . . . to the oppressed masses."[40] In other words, talent and the fruits of achievement are just like capital in that they can be redistributed by an overarching and guiding authority so that none has too much and none has too little.

The consequences of this coercive political vision are startling, and they undermine the hard-fought freedoms articulated in the civil rights legislation of the 1960s that effectively made it illegal to discriminate on the basis of race, color, religion, sex, or national origin. Simply put, people should be judged on the content of their character, not on the basis of those groups into which they have been born. Now, however, discrimination in terms of these memberships is actually encouraged if it advances the causes of those groups that were the objects of discrimination in the past. In other words, a policy of discrimination has been put in place (in which belonging to a particular race or gender is sufficient warrant for different treatment) in the name of "democratic" equality, a discriminatory policy that is supposed to solve, ironically enough, the problem of discrimination itself. Though the logic here is odd and clearly faulty, it nevertheless has convinced no one less than the U.S. Supreme Court, which once again has apparently confused the self-interested political platform of a number of radicals for the American way. Myron Magnet, author of *The Dream and the Nightmare*, explains the loss of freedom entailed in these judicial decisions through the political activism of others: "With affirmative action, a bureaucracy staffed with committed partisans of blacks and women's causes overturned the nondiscriminatory principles of the 1964 Civil Rights Act and won sweeping endorsement from the Supreme Court."[41] Therefore, "in the case of civil rights," as the evangelical leader Ralph Reed notes, "the initial goal of equal protection under the law . . . became transformed into quotas and set-asides that actually institutionalized inequality."[42]

What holds this public policy in place is not reasoned argument, carefully weighing the rights of people, but a well-touted moral and political force, often expressed in intolerant ways, that is employed against all of those who for whatever reason disagree. For example, a Berkeley anthropology professor who tried to get a conversation going for the sake of critical thinking wrote in the alumni magazine that the university's affirmative action program discriminates against Asian and white applicants, with the result that his class was "disrupted and shouted down by seventy-five student protesters chanting, 'Bullshit.'"[43] Elsewhere a number of psychologists created the new category of "symbolic racist," confusing their own political preferences for sound, reasoned argument, and maintained that one fell under this undesirable category if "he voted against black candidates for office, opposed social *quotas* in hiring or admission and opposed school busing to achieve integration."[44]

In each instance, the merits of the issue at hand were never discussed much less debated. Instead, those who claimed the mantle of a dubious moral authority had already made up their minds and therefore felt more than entitled to engage in shouting, name-calling, or some other form of *ad hominem* argument to carry the day. It is precisely the fear of being labeled in a negative way that constitutes much of the force of the "argument" here. But Ron Sider in his book *Just Generosity* calls for a far more balanced approach, especially among Christians. He reasons, "Do I think you are morally degenerate or un-Christian if you disagree with my specific proposals? Not at all. But please don't call me names. Just explain clearly to me how the normative biblical framework I spell out is not adequately scriptural."[45] Beyond this, Jim Wallis reveals that the political correctness offered on behalf of the poor often reflects "the values of liberal elites more than the authentic voice of the powerless."[46]

## Education

In an institution that was established out of a commitment to the Western principles of free and at times difficult dialogue for the sake of truth, the American university has likewise fallen under the politicizing influences of the knowledge class. As Arthur Schlesinger, the dean of American historians, observes, "A peculiarly ugly mood seems to have settled over the one arena where freedom of inquiry and expression should be most unconstrained and civility most respected—our colleges and universities."[47] To illustrate, Robert Hughes, noted art and culture critic, recounts the incident that occurred at Cooper Union in New York when the topic "Can a Liberal Be Pro-Life" was broached. "A gang of pro-abortion protesters," he writes, "some wearing buttons that read F— Free Speech, took over the hall and prevented any speaker being heard, so that the debate itself was aborted."[48]

That the politicalization of the academy is well under way is evident in the comments of professors such as the Berkeley activist Annette Kolodny, who became the dean of the humanities faculty at the University of Arizona. "I see my scholarship," she told *U.S. News & World Report*, "as an extension of my political activism."[49] Such a move, repeated in numerous instances, turns university education on its head and constitutes what Allan Bloom has identified as the closing of the American mind.[50] Since reasoned argument and the weighing of evidence place a barrier to the labeling and glib moralism of the politically correct, then so much the worse for reason. Impatient with the intricacies and supposed Western orientation of logic, some university professors have turned to "the rhetoric of hectoring dogmatism."[51] And the attempt to reintroduce professional standards of academic inquiry and excellence, in terms of fair-minded, critical thinking, for instance, have been met with utter disdain. Indeed, "to apply strict canons of objectivity and evidence in academic publishing today," Hughes contends, "would be comparable to the American economy's returning to the gold standard. The effect would be the collapse of the system."[52]

The earlier, far more sophisticated vision of American education as reasoned inquiry that is challenging, at times disruptive (in terms of undermining prejudice and narrow thinking), and in the end transformational has been displaced by a vision that is more akin to therapy than anything else. In other words, such a politicized outlook ever seeks to affirm the group identities of students (though evangelicals and other theists are often excluded), and it never wants them to hear a discouraging word, that is, some expression they might find offensive to their well-cosseted sense of self. To this end, several universities have actually established speech codes under the "Orwellian rubric of diversity"[53] precisely to set the boundaries with respect to what speech will be tolerated. James Davison Hunter, the noted sociologist, explains the outworking of this agenda at one of America's leading educational institutions. He explains:

> The University of Michigan, for example, adopted a six-page "anti-bias code" (later found to be unconstitutional) that allowed for the punishment of students whose behavior [including speech] stigmatizes or victimizes an individual on the basis of race, ethnicity, religion, sex, sexual orientation, creed, national origin, ancestry, age, marital status, handicap, or Vietnam era veteran students.[54]

In a similar fashion, at the University of Buffalo, the law school faculty voted unanimously to adopt "a 'Statement Regarding Intellectual Freedom, Tolerance and Political Harassment' that says that free speech must be limited by 'the responsibility to promote equality and justice.'"[55] In other words, speech must be restricted for political ends with the result that once again freedom is lost. Beyond this, and in a truly chilling move, Stanford professor Robert Rabin, who is the chairperson of the Student Conduct Legislative Committee, championed the notion that free speech rights "extend only to victimized minorities, since the white majority does not need such protections."[56] Here American education has been utterly politicized; that is, the only speech permitted is that which affirms well-chosen political ends. This is not education but indoctrination.

Dinesh D'Souza, in his book *Illiberal Education,* offers an egregious example of just how illiberal speech codes can be and what a stifling effect politically justified censorship has on the enterprise of developing young minds in America today. In this work, he describes the episode that involved a university professor who felt "challenged" and no doubt offended when a curious student asked for the source for her claim that "lesbians could raise children better than married couples."[57] Instead of as an invitation for dialogue, the professor took this question and the conversation that ensued as an attack. The following day, the young man, who was ever polite and respectful in his demeanor, was nevertheless banned from class and labeled as a "chauvinist —— bastard."[58] The teacher, as D'Souza relates, "had two campus police officers waiting in the hall to escort him away."[59] David Riesmann, professor emeritus of sociology at Harvard, reflected on this national trend and made the following telling observation:

> It is very sad for me to see so many people from the sixties cohort become enemies of true diversity. What we have now in universities is a kind of liberal closed-mindedness, a leading impulse. Everyone is supposed to go along with the so-called virtuous position.[60]

But censorship and the name-calling hate speech that follows in its wake are especially troubling when they are directed against people of faith, especially evangelical Christians. As one scholar points out, "On America's elite campuses today, it is perfectly acceptable for professors to use their classrooms to attack religion, to mock it, to trivialize it, and to refer to those to whom faith truly matters as dupes, and dangerous fanatics on top of it."[61] To illustrate, A. Bartlett Giamatti, former president of Yale University, addressed the incoming freshmen in a speech that warned against those "politically active Evangelical Christians and their 'client groups' [those] 'peddlers of coercion.'"[62] Indeed, according to the American Civil Liberties Union, there are more than a hundred educational institutions that now have policies that prohibit speech, that stifle the public expression of thought.[63] But such policies obviously do not prevent American evangelicals from being held up to scorn. If evangelicals are going to be criticized on an ongoing basis, however, then let them also be given ample opportunity to reply to the likes of Giammati and others. Again, whatever became of the old liberal way of leaving speech open and free, of offering the right of rebuttal as a courtesy, even if it is offensive to certain individuals or groups, and fighting racist, sexist speech not with censorship but with more speech?

## Evangelical Participation in Politics

Due to some of the broad cultural shifts that have occurred in America since the 1960s in the areas of religion, ethics, and education, it will be difficult for evangelical thinking to be heard, much less welcomed, on the political level. With well-worked stereotypes and half-truths substituting for facts, the reality of American evangelicalism often floats by the knowledge class like a blur, especially as it has politicized one area after another. For example, in 1993, a front-page story in the *Washington Post* described the "Gospel Lobby" (meaning followers of evangelical religious broadcasters such as Pat Robertson) as "poor, uneducated, and easy to command."[64] Once again, a difference emerges between well-worked public perceptions (often the result of "spin") and the actual demographics, the facts, of American evangelicalism. For one thing, evangelicals are "more highly educated than those calling themselves either religious liberals or secularists and only slightly less likely to have had a graduate education than mainline Protestants."[65] But the myths die hard.

One common misunderstanding among journalists is to lump fundamentalists, evangelicals, Pentecostals, and Holiness people into a vast right-wing conglomerate known as the religious right. But careful research reveals not only that there is a political difference between fundamentalists and evangelicals but also that the "majority of evangelicals and fundamentalists are not affiliated with religious right groups."[66] In fact, during every national election for the past fifty years, significant numbers of evangelicals have continued to vote for the Democratic Party.[67] Furthermore, such blurring by the media, keeping American evangelicalism continually out of focus, is unable to explain why Pat Robertson, for instance, in his 1988 presidential campaign, ran *less well* among "white voters attending fundamentalist churches than among whites as a whole."[68] Stephen Carter, no doubt frustrated with some of these national trends, maintains that the phrase "Christian Coalition" has now become something like the "great liberal bugaboo" and that the much discussed and ballyhooed "monolithic Religious Right" is, in short, "a media invention."[69] Again, American evangelicalism is far more diverse and sophisticated than the *Washington Post* and other media moguls have imagined. It's time to tell the truth.

One step in the right direction would be for cultural commentators to recognize that the evangelicalism of the twenty-first century is a chastened movement. For one thing, it has received and profited from criticism within its own ranks, offered by Carl F. H. Henry, for example, as well as by theological liberals who maintained that evangelicalism was weak on social justice and preoccupied with personal salvation. Sider elaborates:

> The bitter battle between conservative Christians who emphasize evangelicalism and liberal Christians who stress social action that weakened the church for much of this century has largely ended. Increasingly, most agree that Christians should combine the Good News with good works and imitate Jesus' special concern for the poor.[70]

Contrary to some of the public images touted by the media, one of the chief reasons that more Christians are identifying with evangelicalism today is because it is both soteriologically oriented (focusing on redemption) and politically diverse.[71] From the time that Richard Quebedeaux began tracking the "Young" Evangelicals back in 1974 to Robert Webber's popular work *The Younger Evangelicals* today, the evangelical left has been the subject of much scholarly discussion and interest. From *Sojourners Magazine* to the *Other Side*, from Jim Wallis to Clark Pinnock, from Tony Campolo to Ron Sider, both progressive institutions and leaders have always felt at home in the broader evangelical arena. Indeed, Evangelicals for Social Action, a politically leftist leaning group, was established more than thirty years ago when about forty evangelical leaders gathered in Chicago to discuss "the need for more social concern in the churches."[72] Its members, Rufus Jones and Ron Sider among them, called on all Christians, not simply evangelicals, to "work for structural changes to combat poverty and redistribute wealth, [and] to oppose discrimination of any sort."[73] Even Martin Marty, that ever winsome bow-tie liberal, acknowledges that "many of the evangelical congregations have programs that outstrip those of the mainstream when it comes to care for the environment, the poor, and the victims of injustice."[74]

However, unlike many who make up the secular political left, evangelicals as *theists* recognize that ideology or philosophical materialism will not meet the pressing needs of the poor today, that the problems in this new century are far too complex for such simplistic and rigid solutions. Again, unlike the secular political left, progressive evangelicals are in dialogue (sometimes heated but always illuminating) with their conservative and moderate counterparts in which free speech flows and all are reassured in knowing that evangelicals of whatever political persuasion are united in their zeal for the lordship of Jesus Christ. To be sure, it is the transcendent unity of participating in something greater than themselves that reminds evangelicals that the bonds of the gospel are far stronger and much more important than whatever political differences remain. And evangelical thought and action, precisely because they are dialogical, hold great promise for American political life, especially in terms of the amelioration of poverty.

## Evangelical Responses to Poverty

Recent statistics indicate that the poverty level for a family of four in America today is roughly just under twenty thousand dollars. According to Ron Sider, about thirty-six million people fall under this definition, and an even larger number (forty-three million) have no medical insurance to stave off possible economic catastrophe.[75] In the past, the politically liberal approach to these social ills was to focus, almost in a post-Marxist way, on the "sinful structures" of society. As Cal Thomas and Ed Dobson, former members of the Moral Majority, point out, "The liberal has an unshakable religious faith that given sufficient money, the right program, the right education system and sufficient power to coerce, then human ills can be eliminated and a paradise on earth can be created."[76] Marvin Olasky, evangelical political activist who has advised George W. Bush on occasion, contends that liberals have "re-interpreted compassion (which literally means 'suffering together') to mean acceptance of self-destructive behavior and postponement of pressure to change until all [are] in a good environment."[77]

Though many evangelical leaders would not go so far as the neoconservative Irving Kristol in calling the very notion of social justice into question ("Social justice is a loaded phrase. . . . This assumption is now so common that few people realize how controversial its implications are."),[78] nevertheless, they are increasingly troubled by a structural social analysis that is unswerving in its commitments and therefore functions largely in an ideological way, oblivious to other key elements in a complex social problem such as poverty. That is, not only are other classes, such as middle-income people and the rich, often deemed the principal cause of poverty in this "zero sum" world, but also, and more important, the question of what *values* and choices may actually result in a life of poverty is never seriously entertained. Myron Magnet points out that modern theories of social justice are "impersonal and economic, rather than intimate and moral like the Victorian notions . . . [and they] hold the prosperous, as a class, responsible for the condition of the poor, as a class."[79] Simply put, "If I have too little, it must be because you have too much."

In such a view, social justice principally entails the coercive redistribution of the wealth of a nation by a burgeoning state in a way that is oblivious to the realm of moral valuation. Accordingly, the National Council of Churches offered a proposal in 1968 for a "guaranteed income for everyone, regardless of conduct."[80] You could drink this money away or shoot it up your arm; the NCC simply did not care. As a result, this body failed to make a distinction between the respectable poor, those people who are simply down on their luck largely because of the circumstances of life, and the irresponsible poor, who stubbornly live in an antisocial way and who will, therefore, continue to waste whatever resources they acquire. The dynamic here would be interesting if it were not so pathetic. In championing hedonistic freedom, a throwback to the 1960s counterculture, the secular political left today often advocates many of the counterproductive behaviors found among the poor (sexual promiscuity and out-of-wedlock births, for instance) that lead to a life of imprisoning poverty. It then rushes in with all the moral authority it can muster (but based on what?) to solve the very social problems it helped to create in the first place.[81] Through its skillful and ideological use of the notion of "social sin," the cause of poverty is carefully laid on the backs of others (usually the middle class and the rich) since they have now been *labeled* in a political way as "oppressors." The hypocrisy of this move, however, becomes all too evident on Sunday mornings as priests and ministers repeatedly deride the middle class from the pulpit after they have just carefully collected their money and sung a doxology to the glory of God.

Far more promising and balanced analyses are found among key evangelical leaders today. Ron Sider, for example, realizing the dangers of simplistic, ideologically driven thinking in this area, affirms the multiple causes of poverty that therefore call for diverse, costly, and engaging approaches. "Structural causes; personal decisions and misguided behavior patterns; sudden catastrophes; and permanent disabilities,"[82] he notes, can *all* lead to economic malaise. In a similar vein, Olasky reveals that the war on poverty of the 1960s was a disaster largely because of a bureaucratic "emphasis on entitlement rather than need. Opportunities to give aid with discretion disappeared."[83] Moral behaviors and the discerning judgments based on them in giving appropriate and responsible aid were swept aside by the political left as they "victimized" the poor of the nation all in the name of social justice. In 1971, William Ryan published the justification for such a move in his *Blaming the Victim*, a work that championed the notion that the status of "victim" entailed the privilege of not being held accountable for one's choices.[84] Accordingly, for Ryan and other radicals, having the status of a "victim" meant "never having to say you're sorry or suffering the consequences of your misdeeds."[85] Indeed, even in the case of shiftless men, those who fathered and then abandoned their children, "there was *always* someone else to blame."[86]

In a climate of victimization in which the social system itself is deemed the chief culprit, the poor, both the worthy and the irresponsible, are stripped of those values that would actually do the most good in alleviating their plight. As society's victims, the indigent are taught to be "passive, hopeless, resentful,"[87] up against potent, even deterministic, forces far beyond their control. Olasky, on the other hand, rightly recognizes that poverty is both a material *and* a spiritual problem, a truth that the secular left is often loathe to recognize much less fully integrate into its analyses of key social ills. Describing a group brought together by Howard Ahmanson, a devout Christian leader, to consider the problems of third-world relief and development, Olasky explains, "Most poor people don't have the faith that they and their situations can change. The group concluded that economic redistribution by itself cannot fight poverty effectively because it does not affect the attitudes that frequently undergird poverty."[88] Moreover, Jim Wallis points out that "liberalism is unable to articulate or demonstrate the kind of moral values that must undergird any serious movement of social transformation." Again, why is this so? It is because, as Wallis explains, "the critical link between personal responsibility and societal change is missing on the left."[89]

It is one thing to advocate the values of hedonistic freedom that will do the most harm to those just on the margins; it is quite another thing to deprecate those positive "bourgeois" values such as sacrifice, delayed gratification, the dignity of work, and so on that will actually help the poor in most instances to a better life. Again, Olasky perceptively discerns the cruel dynamic that is often played out on the backs of the needy by many well-to-do cultural leaders:

> Today, the United States needs to recover from the social civil war that has raged since the 1960s. On the one side are those who scorn words like responsibility, discipline, and maturity; some are affluent enough to act foolishly and not be out on the streets, but the poor who imbibe the propaganda of a radical elite have no such margin for error.[90]

Indeed, in American society, the key to rising out of poverty, according to some observers, is relatively straightforward though perhaps nonetheless difficult for some: "finish high school, get and keep *any* full-time, full-year job (even at minimum wage), get married as an adult and stay married, even if it takes more than one try."[91] According to Charles Murray, completing high school alone is almost a "sufficient antidote to poverty itself."[92] In fact, according to one study, "only 0.6 percent of adult men with four years of high school and only 2 percent of women fall below the poverty line."[93]

Furthermore, several studies reveal that the single best indicator as to who will become poor in America today is marital status.[94] Indeed, the scenario of unwed mothers raising children whom fathers have abandoned is a veritable engine for poverty as well as for a host of other social ills, crime among them. As John Naisbitt and Patricia Aburdene point out in their book *Megatrends 2000,* "Welfare is a direct result of couples not marrying, of fathers failing to support their offspring. Thus 90 percent of adults on welfare are mothers with dependent children."[95] Here the law of unintended consequences comes into play with some very cruel results. Though many government programs are well intentioned, they nevertheless have been disruptive of both personal relationships and family life by cutting off support if the father ever enters the picture. Equally disturbing, as one analyst notes, "The welfare system . . . by subsidizing out-of-wedlock births, implicitly legitimizes such births."[96] "The war on poverty of recent years," Olasky maintains, "has been in many ways a war on the family."[97]

Though fathers are often made fun of in TV sitcoms, if you remove a father from the home, all sorts of terrible things happen. According to research conducted by the National Father Initiative, children living without fathers are more likely to "be suspended from school, drop out, be treated for an emotional or behavioral problem, commit suicide as adolescents and experience child abuse or neglect."[98] Even more chilling evidence reveals that "almost two thirds of rapists, three quarters of adolescent murderers, and the same percentage of long term prison inmates are young males who grew up without fathers in the house."[99] However, because the new class took up the sexual "freedom" advocated by the counterculture during the 1960s, it has—to borrow a phrase from Moynihan's classic study cited earlier—"defined deviancy down."[100] That is, what was once considered deviant is now accepted, what was once beyond the pale is now mainstream. And the social consequences of this sexual and moral revolution of hedonistic freedom have, unfortunately, fleeced the poor.

Evangelical leader Sider points out, "In 1960 unmarried moms gave birth to only 5 percent of all children born that year. In 1980, it was 18 percent. [And by] 1994, it was 33 percent—almost a third of all children."[101] In light of these facts, we must realize that this situation is part of a larger cultural problem, a thing of values and choices, and not *merely* the consequences of an unjust economic system. By way of contrast, Japanese culture so frowns upon these deviant sexual practices that out-of-wedlock births are rare and constitute only a fraction of that of the United States. Thus, in Japan today, only 1 percent of all births fall under this category.[102] Contrary to what American culture often teaches, this is *not* a problem endemic to the human condition ("Boys will be boys," and "Girls will be girls") but a cultural one, a matter of learned behavior that is passed along, even approved, by various cultural norms, choices, and values. Therefore, part of what it will take to get back to balance and sanity is for American society to learn from the experience of its Asian neighbors, to draw on traditional sexual and cultural wisdom spurned by the Abbie Hoffmans and Allen Ginsbergs of the 1960s, and then begin to inculcate, teach, and affirm those values that lead to solid, enduring relationships between fathers and mothers such as fidelity, honesty, and painstaking commitment. These are precisely the values that can provide for a healthy environment for raising children. In other words, being pro-family is not "a conservative agenda." As Sider observes, "It is a crucial component of a rational search for justice for the poor."[103] It strikes at the very root of the problem.

## Going Further

It should be evident by now that evangelical Christians can be of enormous service to the nation if they bring their gifts, graces, and talents to the public issues of the day. At this time of pressing need and near cultural crisis, evangelicals cannot hide their light under a bushel and pretend that all is well, nor should they be deterred by those who would like to stifle or eliminate their voice for political ends and in a way that undermines the promise of democracy. Graced by the beauty of the gospel, empowered by the love of God, evangelicals know a liberty, a freedom of heart and soul, that those outside the church can hardly contemplate. The values of the evangelical community in terms of disciplined, responsible living can be of enormous value to those who have been taught otherwise by a culture that is adrift with alluring though enslaving pleasure and that therefore lacks real, solid wisdom.

For one thing, evangelicals can help Americans think through the issue of liberty, real liberty, not the phony kind of liberty that the 1960s generation offered that left one more a slave of self after the "liberation" than before, that mistook self-will for happiness and moral licentiousness for freedom. Indeed, many evangelical Christians know all too well that though hedonistic freedom may be enticing and even satisfy in the short term, it nevertheless pays its bitter wage in the end in bondage, disintegration, and shattered relationships, as the life of the rock star Jim Morrison, champion of the counterculture, demonstrated all so well. Real liberty entails not simply "freedom to" but also "freedom from."

Second, evangelicals can help Americans reconsider the issue of equality in a way that will not only preserve the fruits of democracy but will also protect the rights of all. Granted, evangelicals were shamefully slow in defending the civil rights of African Americans, but they have subsequently repented of this egregious sin as demonstrated in the public confessions of the Southern Baptist Convention, a denomination that contains numerous evangelicals, and of the men's group Promise Keepers. Chastened by their confession, humbled in the admission of their guilt, American evangelicals now understand that the ideal of equality must respect the dignity and rights of all individuals, whether they be black, brown, yellow, red, or white, and that such equality must be employed in a judicious way that honors the freedom to succeed as well as to fail, a way that leads to self-respect, integrity, and satisfaction, the very elements that edify a people. Beyond this, many evangelical leaders have cautioned that equality must not be made an absolute value in an idolatrous way such that it is allowed to undermine the fruits of freedom that mark one as a child of God and that are necessary for any stable democracy.

Finally, the frank recognition among several American evangelical leaders that many of the social and political ills of the nation, such as wrenching poverty, have both structural causes and cultural ones puts the movement as a whole in a good position to counsel the nation, beyond the ideology of overly self-interested groups, as to how best to alleviate and possibly eliminate this social malaise. Indeed, mindful of some of the social and structural causes of poverty, evangelical leaders such as Wallis, Sider, Olasky, and Pinnock call for a more inclusive and generous approach—one that takes into account those personal values that not only are a real means of grace to all who receive them but also can empower the poor to a better way of life. In addition, these evangelical leaders have the boldness and the courage, despite ongoing criticism, to speak these truths to a culture that is often heedless.

Though seldom mentioned in the American media, by far the most generous charitable organization in the United States today is not the parachurch arm of any liberal, mainline denomination, nor is it the agency of a newfangled political activist group. It is none other than that old evangelical stalwart the Salvation Army, which has a budget of over two billion dollars. This evangelical impulse for service and reform is described by Michael Hamilton as a "unique combination of holiness denomination and parachurch agency devoted to human services."[104] In many respects, the Salvation Army epitomizes the balance and good sense of evangelical social concern, and its unflagging "soldiers" can be found *among* the very poorest of the nation, ministering to people who have a *diversity* of needs.

Beyond this, of the nine largest parachurch organizations in America today that are dedicated to spreading the gospel in both its personal and social dimensions, fully eight of them are evangelical.[105] These born-again believers, who love the risen Christ, are both gospel equipped and socially engaged. Their ministry among the poor, then, is multifaceted and therefore poised to do the most good to both body *and* soul. Indeed, the ground has clearly shifted in American religion, and the old clichés and stereotypes do not apply. American evangelicals, through careful and critical analyses of the social problems of the day, in their balanced concern for both freedom *and* equality, and in their energetic service to the poor are finally getting back to the kind of balance that was so typical of the religion of a much earlier period: Everywhere the gospel is preached, there must also be reform.

# 6

# Evangelicals and Feminism

Though Christian women make up the majority of church members, whether Protestant, Roman Catholic, or Eastern Orthodox, and though they tend to be "more religious in their beliefs and practices than men,"[1] they nevertheless continue to struggle for equality in the church and in broader American society as well.

In the past, two waves of mass mobilization for the political, social, economic, and ecclesiastical equality of women emerged, the first between 1880 and 1914 and the second between 1963 and 1980.[2] Though progressive evangelicals such as Luther Lee and B. T. Roberts championed the cause of the equality of women during much of the nineteenth century, the following century witnessed the deflection of this generous impulse among some evangelicals as they confronted the challenges to Christian orthodoxy by modernists early in the century and by in-your-face radicalism much later. Indeed, during the second period of mobilization, a different narrative for the liberation of women arose among the New Left that not only employed some of the resources that hailed from the Enlightenment, mixed with some Marxist ideology, but also expressed the hope of what some cultural critics called a radical egalitarianism.

Interestingly enough, as American evangelicals struggled to reflect on the rights of women during the twentieth century, they often became the targets of radical, secular feminist critiques. Lori Beaman, for instance, in failing to discern the complex and at times baffling nature of American evangelicalism referred to it quite simply as "an ideology rooted in patriarchy or sexist gender relations."[3] Mary Daly, who now describes herself as a post-Christian feminist, maintained that "a woman's asking for equality between men and women in the church would be comparable to a black person's demanding equality in the Ku Klux Klan."[4] Beyond this, some feminist leaders deemed evangelicals to be Christians of the worst sort: "narrow-minded bigots who prefer the wives at home, submissive, pious and pregnant."[5] Once again American evangelicals were slapped with the well-worn *"Kinder, Küche, und Kirche"* argument, the stuff of which stereotypes are made.

Other troubling elements of radical, secular feminism for American evangelicals can be found in the following: (1) the teaching that religion is an illusion concocted by men to control women,[6] (2) the rejection of Feminists for Life by the National Organization of Women as embodying an "irrelevant philosophy"[7] of pro-life, and (3) the claim that there are five genders, bisexuality among them, all of which are socially constructed.[8] Add to this the preoccupation of the American media with some of the more divisive, sensational elements of feminism, as, for example, when it reported that female students at the University of Maryland posted the names of random, innocent male students as "potential rapists,"[9] and the picture that emerges is that although evangelicals do indeed have a rich heritage of supporting many of the goals of feminism, they nevertheless remain deeply offended at some of its current and more radical expressions.

Given the welter of voices in American culture today calling for reform in terms of the status of women, it is crucial that American evangelicals recognize that radical, secular feminism, in many ways inimical to the values of the church, does *not* constitute the entirety or even perhaps the most representative part of feminism. To be sure, evangelical feminists, both women and men, have been seeking the equality of women for more than a century. But these gifted Christian leaders have done so in terms of a much different narrative, a story that embraces not power politics in a zero sum world, with winners and losers among any number of divisive polarities, but nothing less than the universal love of God manifested in Jesus Christ. Again, the fact that the story of feminism has and can be told by means of other scripts should not inhibit or dissuade evangelicals from considering the status and roles of women in terms of their own broader and more inclusive narrative—one that remains, despite postmodern objections to the contrary, the greatest and most liberating story ever told.

# Evangelical Views on Women

Contrary to some of the ongoing critiques from radical, secular feminists, American evangelicals remain quite diverse with respect to their thinking about women. No single viewpoint, therefore, should be used to paint the movement in a broad stroke and thus largely inaccurate fashion. Accordingly, to explore this variety of viewpoints, this chapter offers four categories that will help to explain the different kinds of thinking found among evangelicals on this salient issue.

First of all, there are indeed some *traditionalists* or *hierarchicalists* who object to the full participation of women in the labor force, especially in those fields that have traditionally been dominated by men (such as firefighting and police work). In addition, traditionalists reject a leadership role for women in the church, especially in terms of ordination to the office of elder, and also affirm a hierarchical arrangement of the family in which the husband is the literal head of the household and therefore the wife (as well as the children) has an obligation to submit. However, even here a number of researchers have suggested that significant variance exists between the public pronouncements of traditionalists and their actual practice. Beaman, for example, notes that "even though evangelical traditionalists espouse submission, translated and mediated, this acceptance is practiced as equality within their marital relationships. Traditionalists [women] are not mousy doormats."[10]

Second, there are a number of *neotraditionalists* among evangelicals who tolerate, though they hardly support, a leadership role for women beyond the walls of the church but clearly not *within* those same walls. Thus, they will sit under the lectures of a female university professor, for example, but not if she steps behind a pulpit. Beyond this, neotraditionalists by and large support a Christian patriarchal family (in theory at least) in a way similar to the traditionalists, but they strongly reject "any notion of women as inferior."[11] According to this view, women are equal but different from men, a difference that is employed to support complementary, though not the same, roles for women when compared to those of men. The chief "sin" in this perspective consists of "attempting to obliterate the distinctions between males and females" and of women asserting "their own autonomy in defiance to God's plan."[12] But as Daymon Johnson aptly points out, neotraditionalists have a tendency not only to overstate the differences between the sexes but to fail "to seriously consider in what ways men and women are similar, not withstanding a few occasional qualifications."[13]

Third, *feminist evangelicals,* or to use the broader term *biblical egalitarians,* include both women and men who argue for a scriptural equality (rather than for a particular ideology, as with the secular left) as the basis for the affirmations that women and men are equal in their nature and that such equality must be reflected, with but a few exceptions, in their roles as well.[14] One area of difference concerns human sexuality, and Rebecca Groothuis, an evangelical feminist, is careful to point out, in contradistinction to many secular feminists, that "obviously, male and female are not identical, nor are male and female sexual roles interchangeable. Sexually differentiated roles follow from the differences that exist between men and women."[15] Therefore, Groothuis avoids the weaknesses of the complementarian argument by observing that difference does not justify distinct roles for women, with the exception, of course, of human sexuality itself.

To take this a step further, biblical egalitarians are broad enough as a group to embrace difference with respect to the roles of father and mother in the home (equality does not mean absolute sameness), especially in terms of what each gives to children, a difference that can be understood once again principally in terms of human sexuality. This difference of motherly love or fatherly discipline, however, does not become the basis on which to set up a hierarchy whereby the father arises as a patriarch, as he does in the traditionalist and neotraditionalist views.

Fourth, *quasi-egalitarians* are in basic agreement with biblical egalitarians in terms of the leadership roles of women both in society and in the church, thereby affirming a basic equality, though they contend vigorously for a "traditional" patriarchy in the home. Put another way, quasi-egalitarians support women entering the professions, even the ministry, and champion M.Div. programs for both males and females. Nevertheless, quasi-egalitarians maintain that the husband is the head of the home and require as a consequence the submission of wives to their husbands with all the elements of a reemergent hierarchy, elements that were previously put aside in terms of both the church and society.

To sum up, unlike traditionalists, feminist evangelicals not only support the full participation of women in the labor force and in the church, in accordance with their gifts and talents, but also reject the hierarchical (Victorian) family structure whereby the father governs "his flock" as a patriarch. Unlike neotraditionalists, feminist evangelicals repudiate the complementarian argument as specious, an argument that applies an "equal but different" standard not simply to human sexuality, which is appropriate, but also to roles within the church, which is not. To be sure, "equal but different" was a principle employed to keep African Americans in substandard schools; this same principle must not be used to keep women in diminished and unequal roles, especially within the body of Christ. Finally, unlike quasi-egalitarians, feminist evangelicals reject all forms of patriarchy, even if they are confined to the home. The different views are displayed in the following chart:

## Leadership Roles for Women in Various Sectors

|  | Society | Church | Home |
|---|---|---|---|
| Traditionalists (Hierarchicalists) |  |  |  |
| Neotraditionalists | X |  |  |
| Feminist Evangelicals (Biblical Egalitarians) | X | X | X |
| Quasi-egalitarians | X | X |  |

But if feminist evangelicals can be distinguished from traditionalists, neotraditionalists, and quasi-egalitarians, then they can also be distinguished from radical secular feminists. And this distinction may be the most important of all. For one thing, feminist evangelicals are obviously people of faith. Contrary to their critics, these evangelical leaders seek above all, in ideal if not always in practice, to glorify not themselves but the Most High in all that they do. They know the dangers, in other words, of ideological self-interested narrowness, whether on a personal or a group level, that is dismissive not only of the reality of God but also of the *other*, however that other is defined. Beyond this, many feminist evangelicals would not pass the test, so to speak, with respect to many of the principles of radical secular feminism, such as abortion on demand and aspects of gay and lesbian rights.[16] These and other differences have led evangelical feminist scholars such as Groothuis to declare, "I offer a clear and careful definition of evangelical feminism (or biblical equality) and explain how its premises, goals, theology, and history differ fundamentally from that of other types of feminism today."[17]

Despite these careful distinctions, as evangelical feminists undertake the arduous task of calling the sinful and reluctant among us to a greater, more inclusive vision of the love of God and neighbor, they often find themselves, oddly enough, the objects of criticism from diverse quarters. On the one hand, radical secular feminists such as Mary Daly denounce all Christian feminists, evangelical or otherwise, as "roboticized tokens who play into the hands of phallocentric male supremacists."[18] Moreover, she contends that "only lesbian radical feminists can rise above the normal way of life of the patriarchal male and 'spin deeper into the listening deep.'"[19]

On the other hand, many traditionalists or hierarchicalists fail to make the proper distinctions between evangelical feminists and feminists in general. As a result, evangelical feminists can hardly be seen under the multiple layers of a generic, one-size-fits-all feminism.[20] Feminism is rarely parsed in terms of its great variety, and therefore, even if it is found among evangelicals, it must be bad. Here the negatives of radical secular feminism are allowed to define the totality of the movement apart from the works of leading evangelical feminists. Moreover, once this move is made, feminism, broadly and negatively defined, is tied to the radical left and to the ongoing culture wars in America. As a result, evangelical feminism evokes a negative reaction among even evangelical women. Thus, despite the rich legacy of evangelical participation in the feminist movement of an earlier age, carefully chronicled by Donald Dayton, "evangelical women are not entirely comfortable with present-day feminism."[21] When nonevangelical women are placed in the mix, the picture is not much better. Katherine Kersten, for example, observes:

> Clearly feminism, traditionally defined as equal rights for women, has played a major role in bringing women into full and equal citizenship. But while most women share feminism's traditional goals, today fully two-thirds refuse to call themselves feminists.[22]

Indeed, with the blurring of the lines among different feminist movements, it is difficult for evangelical feminists to be properly heard much less understood.

With these various positions concerning the role of women in mind, it will be helpful to consider the ordination of women as well as the matter of marriage and the family in order to grapple more seriously with evangelical diversity.

## The Ordination of Women

For much of the twentieth century, only a fraction of women were among those formally ordained by their denominations. This trend began to change somewhat after 1970, and Mark Chaves, in an important study on ordination, cites the statistics:

> Since 1970 women in the United States have become clergy in increasing numbers. According to the 1970 U.S. census, approximately 3 percent of clergy were female. That number rose to approximately 10 percent by 1990 and is likely to

climb further. Today over 30 percent of students enrolled in theological schools are female. In some denominations the figure is 50 percent or higher.[23]

Though these trends are somewhat encouraging, several American churches remain reluctant to ordain women. In fact, even today "only about half of U.S. denominations grant full clergy rights to women."[24] And even if a woman becomes ordained, her chance of being placed in a church that will actually *accept* her is much less than it is for men. Indeed, a recent study determined that on average it takes twice as long for female master of divinity graduates (225 days in comparison to 104 days) to be placed in their first congregation as it does for men.[25] Such data have led some scholars to conclude that "formal gender inequality in the West could not be sustained on a large scale in the late twentieth century except by an institutional subworld organized around religious authority."[26]

Though gender inequality and religious authority are mutually reinforcing in some American denominations, held in place, in part, by the fear of liberalism, Chaves suggests that in the day-to-day religious life of many churches, "loose coupling" occurs. Take the Roman Catholic Church, for example. Though this communion of faith formally repudiates the ordination of women, "most of the priestless Roman Catholic parishes in the United States are pastored by women."[27] In this setting, women function in virtually every pastoral role with the exception, of course, of consecrating the host, an act that is tied to all sorts of gender considerations. Or consider the conservative Missouri Synod Lutheran Church, which maintained a symbolic difference between men and women who did precisely the same work: "Male teachers held a 'Diploma of Vocation'; female teachers held a 'Solemn Agreement.'"[28] Though some communions are currently experiencing a clergy shortage, this consideration does not make the ordination of women any more likely. Again, as Chaves observes, "Although denominations with a clergy shortage are more likely to draft women to do the necessary work of the church, these results show that such drafting of women does not necessarily translate into granting them official status and recognition."[29] As the *New York Times* once quipped, "Churches are one of the few important institutions that still elevate discrimination against women to the level of principle."[30] This is an old script: Women do much of the work but get little of the credit.

## *Sacramental Traditions*

Religious authority, especially in terms of the ordination of women, is often informed by the maintenance of gender inequality, which is held in place by a differentiation of roles. Such inequality can be found in two broad groups of Christians: *sacramentarians,* such as Roman Catholics and Eastern Orthodox, and *inerrantists,* which include some evangelicals and many fundamentalists. Interestingly enough, Roman Catholics and evangelicals have been finding common cause of late, at least on an informal level, as reflected in the discussions (about evangelical and Catholic relations in Latin America) that took place in September 1992, talks that eventually led to the promulgation of Evangelicals and Catholics Together, a topic that will be explored more fully in the following chapter. During these talks, many of the participants came to an important realization that was duly noted in a later book:

> In the course of our conversation, it dawned upon a number of participants, almost simultaneously, as though by the prompting of the Holy Spirit: "Here is the Church. Here around this table. Christ is here, his gospel is being spoken, and therefore his Church is here. How do we make that simple but wondrous truth clear to our fellow believers? What does that truth mean for us and our ministries?"[31]

Though I do not doubt for a moment that both the church and Christ were present at this historic meeting, it is highly ironic that when these two theological traditions sat around the table with an ecumenical and inclusive purpose in mind, there was not a single woman among them. From Charles Colson to Cardinal Avery Dulles S.J., from Richard John Neuhaus to Jesse Miranda, from Archbishop Francis Stafford to George Weigel, there was not a woman to be found. And though the exclusion of women in this instance was not likely intentional, it nevertheless apparently emerged out of what was comfortable, familiar, near at hand—as is so often the case.

Because evangelicals have been working more closely with Roman Catholics of late, sharing common cause in many social and political concerns, and because Catholicism under John Paul II has basically ruled out any further discussion on the question of women's ordination (in the important encyclical *Ordinatio Sacerdotalis*), it is important to explore the reasoning of what appears to be the *permanent* denial of women's ordination in this sacramental tradition.

A decade after the Second Vatican Council, in October 1976, Pope Paul VI and the Vatican Congregation for the Doctrine of Faith brought forth a document titled *Inter Insignores* that considered the question of admitting women to the priesthood.[32] This work argued for the exclusion of women from the priestly office on two grounds: The first one concerned the supposed unbroken tradition of restricting priesthood to men. Much later, in July 1995, John Paul II reiterated the logic of this claim in his "Letter to Women":

If Christ, by his free and sovereign choice, clearly attested to by the Gospel and by the church's constant tradition—entrusted only to men the task of being an "icon" of his countenance as "shepherd" and "bridegroom" of the church through the exercise of the ministerial priesthood, this in no way detracts from the role of women.[33]

Although on the surface this argument may at first seem plausible, on closer examination it becomes increasingly clear that it contains a number of assumptions that can be called into question. For one thing, what the Roman Catholic Church in the twentieth century meant by the office of priesthood can easily be distinguished from what Christ and his disciples understood by this. Committing the basic historical error of anachronism (reading later historical products into earlier times), Rome has not only conflated the sequential development of charismatic and administrative ministries in the early church into one simple movement but also, perhaps more important, read back into the first century, placing its own judgments on the very lips of Jesus, conceptions of the priesthood that took literally centuries to develop. Accordingly, not even Peter, James, and John were ever priests in the way that Rome would have it, a construction that is then used to exclude half the human race. But the fact that these three disciples as well as several women, Junia the Apostle among them, served the early church in distinct ministries, empowered by the Holy Spirit, is abundantly clear.

Second, if only males can be an "icon" of Christ's countenance through the exercise of the priesthood, that is, if women are incapable of acting "in persona Christi" at the consecration of the elements during the Mass,[34] then women are necessarily adjudged to be soteriologically less than men, at least in the sense that females in their *essential* being are not and cannot be an image of Christ. This move not only fails to recognize the fullness and splendor of the *imago Dei* in all females but also gives "maleness" an ultimate significance that it simply cannot bear. Such a view is contrary to the clear teaching of Jesus that in heaven the redeemed shall be as the angels (Matt. 22:30) and also fails to reckon with, in a careful and judicious way, the affirmation of Paul in his letter to the Galatians, where he exclaims, "There is neither Jew nor Greek, there is neither slave nor free man, there is neither male nor female; for you are all one in Christ Jesus" (3:28).

In a somewhat different way, Cornelius Plantinga, Reformed theologian and philosopher, has taken issue with the gender-excluding reasoning of the sacramental traditions in his observation: "How does it follow in any way that Jesus' maleness is basic to his role as our incarnate Savior? One might as well argue that because God incarnate was Jewish, single, and an inhabitant of a pastoral setting, that Jewishness, bachelorhood, and thorough knowledge of sheep are all basic to Jesus' saving us."[35] But does Rome, by implication, in its fixation on maleness really wish to claim something like this? Along these lines, Sandra Schneiders, noted Roman Catholic biblical scholar, has questioned the Vatican's unending emphasis on all things male in terms of both salvation in general and the priesthood in particular. She observes:

> We are talking about whether the god of Judaeo-Christian revelation is the true God or just men-writ-large to legitimate their domination; whether Jesus, an historical male, is or can be messiah and savior for those who are not male; whether what the church has called sacraments are really encounters with Christ or tools of male ritual abuse of women [private confession, for example]; whether what we have called church is a community of salvation or simply a male power structure.[36]

Furthermore, appeal to the "church's constant tradition" to justify the ongoing exclusion of women from the priesthood is also problematic when one considers the troubled views that some of the early church fathers held with respect to females that may have colored their judgments. Clement of Alexandria, for instance, once observed that "a woman should properly be shamed when she thinks 'of what nature she is.'"[37] Augustine, who was sexually dissolute before becoming a Christian, exclaimed that "the good Christian likes what is human, loathes what is feminine."[38] In a similar way, Jerome viewed women more often than not as temptations to male lust and therefore advised his brothers to associate principally with one another and only with those women who had lost the seductive, female form and looked more like men through rigorous fasting. "Let your companions," this Latin father cautioned, "be women pale and thin with fasting, and approved by their years of conduct."[39] Beyond this, Jerome revealed his estimation of women as he championed the cause of "continent" marriage in his observation, "You have with you one who was once your partner in the flesh but is now your partner in the spirit; once your wife but now your sister; once a woman but now a man; once an inferior but now an equal."[40] Add to this the views of Aquinas, who wrote that a woman is "defective and misbegotten," and it is readily apparent that several key theologians of the church, even some early church fathers, held a distorted view of women that helped to foster a far more limited role for women in the church than they had enjoyed in charity and grace during the first century.

Finally, the very form of the Vatican's argument is specious as it subtly detracts from the God-given dignity of women, especially in terms of the fullness of the *imago Dei* in denying that women can image or be an "icon" of Christ. As if this denial were not bad enough, the argument then goes on, quite oddly, to conclude that "this in no way detracts from the role of women." In actual practice, however, the basic elements of the Vatican's argument are indeed employed in the Roman Catholic Church today to do precisely that, to deny various leadership roles to women, especially in terms of the priesthood. This is yet another instance of having your cake and eating it too—of hoping that people, especially women, will focus on the concluding affirmation without paying much attention to the details of the earlier denials.

Given this history, some traditionalists in the Roman Catholic Church have been emboldened, even invigorated, by Pope John Paul II's pronouncements on women. To illustrate, Austin B. Vaughan, an auxiliary bishop from New York City, remarked, "In the year 2000, 20,000, or 2,000,000 there will still be a Catholic church and it will still have an all male clergy. *A woman priest is as impossible as for me to have a baby.*"[41] But the old Vatican proverb "*Roma locuta, causa finita* ('Rome has spoken; the case is closed')," as Thomas Fox aptly points out, "no longer seems to carry much weight in some Catholic circles."[42] In fact, in the American Roman Catholic Church today, a full 65 percent of those who sit in the pews on Sunday mornings favor the ordination of women.[43] But the hierarchy is evidently not listening to those whom Vatican II, with a greater degree of inclusiveness, referred to as the "people of God."

A similar sort of argument for the exclusion of women from the priesthood can be found in those traditions that look to Rome for guidance in the area of church polity, especially in terms of the priesthood and apostolic succession. Nevertheless, not a few progressive evangelicals were surprised in 1991 when J. I. Packer, an evangelical leader, argued in a very neo-Catholic way in *Christianity Today* that an all-male presbytery was called for in light of the theological consideration that a woman cannot represent God to the church. Such representatives, so Packer contends, ought to be male simply because Christ was male, a variation on an old, worn-out logic.[44] Packer elaborates:

> The creation pattern, as biblically set forth, is: man to lead, woman to support; man to initiate, woman to enable; man to take responsibility for the well-being of woman, woman to take responsibility for helping man. . . . But this role [of a presbyter] is for manly men rather than womanly women.[45]

In a way remarkably similar to Rome, Packer gives "maleness" an ultimacy that flies in the face not only of the biblical record itself but also of the genius of the Christian faith, as will be demonstrated shortly. He mistakes his own social location, as his language of "manly man" clearly suggests, for the graciousness of the created order.

## *Inerrantists*

Michael Novak, a Roman Catholic intellectual and winner of the Temple-ton Prize, maintains that those who reject the Catholic view of the priesthood "have no theological reason to object to the ordination of women."[46] With-out "a theological defense," he continues, "the only grounds for opposition are custom, habit, and psychological resistance to change."[47] Though most American evangelicals and fundamentalists do indeed repudiate the Roman Catholic notion of priesthood and recognize it to be a historical construct, a human institution that evolved over time, some among their number never-theless refuse the pastoral office to women. For example, the Southern Baptist Convention, which contains many members who would fit most definitions of an evangelical, passed a resolution in 1984 prohibiting female clergy. Years later, in June 2000, the Southern Baptists brought forth a policy that declared, "While both men and women are gifted for service in the church, the office of pastor is limited to men as qualified."[48] The intervening step in this logic is not the inability of women to image Christ, as it is in sacramental traditions, but rather "the [supposed] biblically mandated submission of women to men."[49]

The judgments of Southern Baptists and others come out of a particular way of reading Scripture, a distinct hermeneutic that is tied in, accurate or not, with the authority of the Bible. Discerning what she terms a "gender inerrancy," Nancy Nason-Clark maintains that conservative Protestants are less willing to "compromise" on the issues of gender and women's roles in the church because these issues are rarely considered by themselves. They are seen instead as yet another illustration of the larger concern of the authority of Scripture.[50] Since it is *this* authority that is actually at stake in any discussion of the role of women in the church, the larger script of the liberal/fundamental-ist controversy (and all the antimodernism that flowed in its wake) is always lurking in the background. Indeed, this historic controversy, in a real sense, becomes the chief interpretive guide, and women in pastoral, leadership roles can be seen only as an instance of liberalism, a sellout to the contemporary Zeitgeist. Chaves succinctly describes the dynamics entailed:

> The answer to this question [of women's roles] lies in the construction of an inerrantist institutional world defining itself in opposition to the world of liberal religion. Support for women's ordination became increasingly difficult to har-monize with biblical inerrancy within Protestantism because the fundamentalist movement took on antimodernity as its central defining identity, and made inerrancy and opposition to women's ordination, among other issues, symbols of that antimodern stance.[51]

But the research of Michael Hamilton, in an important study on women, public ministry, and fundamentalism, also needs to be factored into the equation. Indeed, this work suggests that the "loose coupling" that was noted earlier in terms of the actual leadership roles of women in the Roman Catholic Church, that is, a difference between theory and practice, has also been present virtually from the beginning among many inerrantists and fundamentalists. To be sure, despite the public pronouncements of male fundamentalist leaders, many organizations in this movement allowed for "female entrepreneurs exercising authority over male subordinates."[52] Part of the problem, then, as Hamilton sees it, has to do with the depiction of fundamentalism by scholars in the past. "Scholars have elbowed women to the margins of the histories of Fundamentalism," he points out, "far more thoroughly than men ever pushed women to the margins of the movement itself."[53] Therefore, even in terms of fundamentalism, in which a doctrine of inerrancy has dominated, the picture is far more complicated than it initially appears based on the movement's public proclamations of gender hierarchy.

## Evangelicals and Holiness Adherents

Even though many American evangelicals are careful to distinguish themselves from fundamentalists, especially in terms of the necessity of social action and a more irenic spirit, the "third plank" of fundamentalism, that is, a doctrine of inerrancy, remains. This doctrine, especially when seen in the light of the historic fundamentalist-modernist controversy, became one of the principal ways that both fundamentalists and later neoevangelicals defended orthodoxy against the inroads of liberalism and the modernistic spirit. This defensive posture of the movement, throughout much of the first half of the twentieth century, issued in a sharp contrast when compared to the reforming spirit of the nineteenth century, especially in terms of the roles of women. Thus, for example, Wheaton College had "no women on its board of trustees between 1896 and 1975."[54] Moreover, it was not until 1969 that Moody Bible Institute finally placed a woman on its board.[55] Even the National Association of Evangelicals, that flagship institution, back in the heyday of its founding in 1941, was constituted "entirely of men, with women segregated into a women's auxiliary."[56]

Compare this with the far more gracious understanding of women in the nineteenth century found among evangelicals in general and Holiness folk in particular.[57] Indeed, according to the Wesleyan historian Donald Dayton, the roots of American feminism can be traced back to "the revivalism of Charles G.

Finney and the reform movements it spawned."[58] For example, one of Finney's much criticized "new measures" was to permit women to pray in "promiscuous or mixed assemblies."[59] His fellow preacher, Theodore Weld, likewise encouraged women to proclaim publicly what Christ had done for their souls. Weld's sister-in-law, Sarah Grimke, published her *Letters on the Equality of the Sexes* in 1837 in which she made a comparison between "the state of the slave and the condition of women."[60]

In a way similar to their "radical" evangelical cousins, the Holiness denominations that emerged in the nineteenth century and looked to John Wesley as a theological mentor also championed the cause of women as a consequence of their optimistic, reformist, and perfectionist tendencies. Donald Dayton and Lucille Dayton observe:

> We should notice the Holiness perfectionist impulse that emphasized the power of grace to restore *in this world* the pre-fallen Edenic state. Opponents of both abolitionism and feminism were more oriented to the prevalence of sin in this world than to the power of redemption. . . . Such fatalism and pessimism were anathema to the Holiness "utopian" vision grounded in an affirmation of the power of God to work out the Divine will for this world.[61]

In terms of Donald Dayton's own denomination, the Wesleyan Methodists hosted the first Women's Rights Convention in the Wesleyan chapel in Seneca Falls, New York, in 1848.[62] Luther Lee, one of the founders of the church, delivered a sermon on the occasion of his own ordination titled "Woman's Right to Preach the Gospel."[63] As with many other Holiness believers, Lee had likely read Adam Clarke's commentary on the Bible, which called for a vigorous employment of women in ministry, for they have "equal *rights,* equal *privileges,* and equal *blessings,* and let me add, they are equally *useful.*"[64]

A spirit of biblical equality that grew out of the recognition of the sanctification of both men and women surfaced in the Free Methodist Church, an institution that was established on reformist, abolitionist grounds just prior to the Civil War. Accordingly, Free Methodist bishop W. A. Sellew in his work *Why Not?* maintained that "women the world over have been patiently waiting . . . for the glorious gospel of love, as taught by Jesus Christ and its attendant civilization, to restore to her those rights which have been taken from her by force."[65] B. T. Roberts, the principal founder of this church, brought forth his case for the elevation of a woman's role in his *Ordaining Women.* In this work, Roberts appealed not to any sort of radical egalitarian *ideology* but once again to the basic principle of biblical equality as seen in the context of holy love.

Later in the century, in 1894, the founding constitution of the Church of the Nazarene articulated the right of women to preach the gospel. As with other denominations that placed a premium on the sanctity of heart and life (such as the Church of God, the Pillar of Fire, and the Salvation Army), the Church of the Nazarene graciously granted women full equality from the outset.[66] To be sure, Dayton contends that it was precisely because these churches underscored the experience of the Holy Spirit that they gave a greater role to women. They recognized "the autonomy of the Spirit to use persons apart from usual patterns of ecclesiastical ordination, theological training, and other types of certification."[67] One of the best examples of this dynamic can be found in the life and ministry of Phoebe Palmer, who, though unordained, nevertheless played a significant role in the Holiness movement as editor, along with her husband, of the enormously influential *Guide to Holiness*. Moreover, Palmer's personal testimony and preaching, along with such writings as *The Way of Holiness, Entire Devotion to God*, and *Faith and Its Effects*, helped not only to galvanize the movement but also to sustain its theological direction. Later in life, Palmer wrote *The Promise of the Father; or, a Neglected Specialty of the Last Days*, in which she argued specifically for a woman's right to preach the gospel and for an evangelical egalitarian piety. A little more than a decade after Palmer's death, W. B. Godbey, who had been deeply influenced by the ministry of this saintly woman and was closely associated with Asbury College, composed a pamphlet in 1891 titled "Woman Preacher," in which he affirmed, "It is a God-given, blood-brought privilege, and bounden duty of the women as well as the men, to preach the gospel."[68]

In light of this rich heritage of equality found in many of the Holiness churches, Susie Stanley, leading Wesleyan/Holiness historian, offers the following reflection about her own childhood: "I grew up hearing women preach. I was sixteen before encountering Christians outside my denomination who believed women had no place in church leadership."[69] Though, as we have seen, Holiness churches initially fostered the ministry of women, Stanley believes that they now "often discourage women from engaging in professional ministry."[70] To correct this problem and to reacquaint Holiness adherents with some of their own rich heritage, Stanley has carefully examined more than thirty spiritual autobiographies of women (those of Phoebe Palmer, Mary Lee Cagle, Julia Foote, Jarena Lee, Amanda Smith, and Julia Shellhamer among them) to demonstrate in considerable detail the role of the "sanctified self" in terms of the ministry of women.

Just what is the "sanctified self," and what difference did it make in the lives of women in Holiness denominations? For one thing, this cleansing of the heart goes beyond freedom from the guilt of sin (justification) and its power or dominion (regeneration) to nothing less than the purity of holy love whereby the twofold great commandment of Jesus is actualized in the warp and woof of life. Simply put, entire sanctification is the holy love of God reigning in the soul and displacing sin. As the first letter of John states, "Perfect love casts out fear" (4:18). It was this experience of the cleansing of the carnal nature as well as freedom from the fear of men that ushered in a new reality for these women by richly empowering them for service. Put another way, the sanctified self of these women was a foretaste of the world to come, where there is neither male nor female. It was therefore in sharp contrast to the "gendered self" that was constructed by powerful males in order to preserve their own privileges to the detriment of women, effective ministry, and the larger good of the church. Stanley elaborates:

> When Wesleyan/Holiness women encountered gendered constructions of self, they abruptly dismissed them by asserting their spiritual authority. Women overthrew the restrictions of a gendered self by drawing on their experience as sanctified Christians and by claiming the power of the Holy Spirit in a religious atmosphere whose polity was characterized by egalitarian primitivism.[71]

These Holiness women, then, not only knew themselves as "the beloved" of the Lord in a deep and intimate way but also realized that they had been wonderfully "gifted" by God in an abundance of grace. These women, therefore, simply could not remain within the confines of a private and obscure Victorian domesticity. They were compelled to bless the body of Christ by proclaiming such gifts among all for whom Christ had died. "It was the empowerment of the Holy Spirit," Stanley notes, "that enabled Wesleyan/Holiness women to possess a self that successfully countered the weak, dependent self society sought to impose on them."[72] Total consecration to the will of God, which these women judged to be integral to the experience of entire sanctification, meant that "women answered to God and not to the men who sought to silence them."[73]

During a good part of the twentieth century, many women were unable to gain admission to bachelor of divinity programs (the title later changed to master of divinity), and they were often routed to "traditional" female fields such as Christian education. Today, however, leading American evangelical educational institutions such as Fuller Theological Seminary and Asbury Theological Seminary welcome women to all of their programs. Such contemporary openness must be seen in part in terms of the labors of nineteenth-century evangelicals and Holiness leaders who helped to prepare the way. As more women begin to realize that several progressive evangelical institutions often take great pains to affirm the leadership role of women in the church, the percentage of women at these same institutions will likely only increase.

## Evangelicals and the Family

Though many quasi-egalitarian evangelicals today fully recognize the call of women to all forms of ministry, ranging from elder to bishop, some nevertheless publicly balk at the notion of biblical equality when it is applied to the family. Current research suggests that some of the most outspoken defenders of the patriarchal family, in which the husband rules the roost, so to speak, are evangelical Protestants. According to John Bartkowski, "Rank-and-file evangelicals disproportionately support a patriarchal family structure."[74] The Southern Baptist Convention, for example, in its national meeting in 1998 amended its basic statement of beliefs (*The Baptist Faith and Message Statement*) to declare that "a woman 'should submit herself' to her husband's leadership, and that a husband should 'provide for, protect, and love his family.'"[75] Promise Keepers, an evangelical men's movement launched in the mid-1990s, urged men to reassume their roles as leaders of the family. One of the movement's promoters, for instance, counseled men to take charge and to put their house in order: "I'm not suggesting that you *ask* for your role back. I'm urging you to *take it back*."[76]

Beyond this, James Davison Hunter's research suggests that many of these hierarchical views are held by the "coming generation" of evangelicals who are assuming leadership roles now. "The majority of Evangelical students (collegians, 58%; seminarians, 62%) did agree that 'the husband has the "final say" in the family's decision making' compared with only a minority (12%) of the public university students."[77] In terms of spiritual authority in particular, Hunter discovered that "the majority (collegians, 61%; seminarians, 76%) accepted the notion that 'the husband is primarily responsible for the spiritual well-being of the family.'"[78] These results are similar to what Christian Smith found in his more recent study of American evangelicals:

> Most of the evangelicals we interviewed who spoke in support of headship said that the husband should have the "final say" in decision-making. Thus, with regard to arriving at decisions, most evangelicals clearly affirmed, in theory, a nonegalitarian, patriarchal model of marriage.[79]

Both Hunter and Smith recognize, however, that a measure of dissonance exists between evangelical public pronouncements on gender construction, specifically in terms of the family, and actual practice. For example, Hunter maintains that a good number of evangelicals are actually abandoning a patriarchal model in favor of a more "androgynous/quasi-androgynous" one.[80] For his part, Smith observes that many evangelicals "construed 'headship' in ways that explicitly undermined male domination and privilege,"[81] and he also points out that though evangelicals did not want to abandon outright the language of male headship, they nevertheless were more than happy to "embrace the soft rhetoric of mutuality and equality."[82] Finding their marriages shaped by an array of social forces, some of which promote egalitarian practices, evangelicals "negotiate their lives," Smith writes, "with cultural tool kits containing a mix of tools that do not necessarily all work neatly together."[83] Put another way, whether they fully recognize it or not, many evangelicals are currently trying to combine the language of male headship with egalitarian practice.[84]

Interviews with evangelical women, whether traditionalist, neotraditionalist, or quasi-egalitarian, support these findings. Researchers have discovered that though some evangelical women employ the language of submission, they nevertheless interpret such submission so as "to preserve and enhance their own agency."[85] In other words, these women emphasize "partnership and mutuality in their relationships with their husbands, [and] not the familial patriarchy that seems to the outsider to be explicit in the call to submit."[86] All of this has led one evangelical feminist scholar to conclude:

> Other researchers have noted the apparently comfortable coexistence of the mutually contradictory concepts of equality and hierarchy in much evangelical thinking on marriage. Giving lip service to male leadership and female submission while living out a functional egalitarianism seems to have become the default mode of coping with the present uncertainty over gender relations.[87]

When the views of evangelical feminists, both male and female, are factored in, it becomes increasingly clear that evangelical perspectives on gender relations within the family are not as "monolithically hierarchical"[88] as public perceptions seem to suggest.

In a real sense, the differences between personal practice and public pronouncements with respect to the family is a function, as with ordination, of a larger cultural struggle in which the denial of male headship is often seen as a concession, once again, to radical, secular feminism. "The slippery slope argument," Groothuis contends, "brands evangelical feminism secular and ultimately heretical. As a result, an idea that *is* justifiable on biblical grounds tends to be dismissed before it is even fairly examined."[89] In other words, the fear evoked by radicals, many of whom are dismissive of the Christian faith, feeds into this dissonance between evangelical theory and actual practice and keeps it very much in place. Evangelicals, then, both men and women, may be quite comfortable at home; they are, however, ill at ease when they enter the public square.

## The Importance of Biblical Interpretation

Reflecting on the different ways that hierarchalists and feminist evangelicals interpret Scripture, we are reminded of the words of one of America's most humble and gracious leaders, Abraham Lincoln, who in his *Second Inaugural Address* uttered the following words: "Both read the same Bible and pray to the same God, and each invokes His aid against the other. . . . The prayers of both could not be answered. That of neither has been answered fully. The Almighty has His own purposes."[90] In a similar way, evangelicals who hold a deep commitment to the inspiration and authority of the Bible can be found among both hierarchalists *and* biblical egalitarians. As Ronald Pierce maintains, "Both camps have representatives who understand the passage as being in some way normative for the Church today."[91] Therefore, failing to affirm the full authority of Scripture as the *normata normans* is *not* the dividing line, despite protests to the contrary, between these evangelical groups. Rather, it consists chiefly in how they interpret the same passages for the community of faith.

In her own work, Susie Stanley has demonstrated how Wesleyan/Holiness women broke out of unequal and restrictive gender roles precisely through a careful interpretation of Scripture. "They saw," Stanley notes, "that the Bible documented women's leadership and public ministry in the early church."[92] Moreover, recognizing that the Bible was a primary resource for some who constructed a "gendered self" that limited the roles of females both in the church and in the family, Holiness women appropriated "the same authority and quoted liberating texts from the Bible to refute the opposition."[93] Moreover, Groothuis underscores the difference between a biblical egalitarianism, which arises from a careful interpretation of the sacred text, and radical, secular egalitarianism, which exegetes a much different text. "The idea of gender equality," she writes, "came not from society, but from the gospel of Jesus Christ."[94] In summarizing the purpose of one of her major books, this evangelical feminist highlights the importance of biblical interpretation, what scholars call "hermeneutics." She writes, "The purpose of this book is to show that the broad sweep of biblical thought aligns more readily with gender equality than gender hierarchy, and that the biblical proof texts used to support traditionalist gender roles fail to present an open-and-shut case for the position."[95]

Compare the basic interpretive approach to Scripture of these leading evangelical feminists to how their work is often portrayed in terms of, and then subsumed under, the catchall phrase "feminist theologians." Jim Leffel and Dennis McCallum, for example, exclaim:

> Therefore, feminist theologians call for a "liberation from the text." Liberation from the text means identifying sexist passages and rejecting or reinterpreting them. . . . We see here the discounting of reason in favor of the authority of the oppressed interpretive community. Whether these interpreters call themselves postmodern or not, their reliance on the postmodern method is unmistakable.[96]

Even more forcefully and in a way that fails to discern the nuances of the hermeneutic of both evangelical feminists and the group Christians for Biblical Equality, these authors declare:

> Feminists raise their experience as women above Scripture as the standard of truth and authority. For many feminists, the Bible is simply a pragmatic tool to further a highly politicized ideological agenda. When Scripture and ideology conflict, Scripture is either radically reinterpreted or rejected outright.[97]

Discounting reason, raising women's experience above Scripture, and treating the Bible simply as a pragmatic tool are all serious charges. Such judgments, however, fail to grasp in an accurate way the sophisticated views and careful interpretation of many evangelical feminists. In light of this, a far more helpful analysis may consist of discerning the presuppositions and assumptions that inform how reason is being used as a cognitive tool in *any* interpretation. Reason is, after all, not as neutral as some would have it. It is always in some sense "interested," an interest that can be understood at least in part in terms of the proclivity to self-referential claims and favored, well-grooved opinions. Indeed, the deeper commitments, the "cherished" ways of viewing things, can inform both the use of reason and the substance of a particular hermeneutic (How, for instance, will "conflicting" passages be weighted and understood?) and can lead to much different readings of a text. One does not have to be thoroughly postmodern to realize the importance of this analysis. As Reinhold Niebuhr supposedly once quipped, "Men use reason as kings use princes and courtiers in order to get what they want." We cannot go back, therefore, to a relatively naive understanding of reason and claim all its power for views that are often held and substantiated on remarkably different grounds.

# Two Passages That Make a Difference

Two significant passages that will help to depict some of the basic principles of Scripture with respect to gender and therefore should be a part of the interpretation of any subsequent material are Genesis 1:26–27 and Galatians 3:26–28. The first passage reads as follows:

> Then God said, "Let us make humankind in our image, according to our likeness; and let them have dominion over the fish of the sea, and over the birds of the air, and over the cattle, and over all the wild animals of the earth, and over every creeping thing that creeps upon the earth." So God created humankind in his image, in the image of God he created them; male and female he created them. (NRSV)

Observe in this context two key things: First of all, humanity, both male and female, is created in the image and likeness of God.[98] But just what does it mean to be created in the *imago Dei*? For one thing, it signifies that all who bear a human face are beings created for a relationship *with* and for the glorification *of* a personal God of holy love. That is, the persons of the Father, Son, and Holy Spirit, out of their other-directed holy love, brought forth the sons and daughters of the earth to communicate boundless and effulgent love to them. Therefore, as beings made for no one less than the Most High and for fellowship with one another as *one* flesh, males and females *participate* in the image of God in their personhood (as subjects, not as objects or things), in their other-directedness, and in their relationality and love. So understood, the *imago Dei* is an active term, not a passive one. It bespeaks of a calling, evoking, inviting, and overwhelmingly generous God. It does not, therefore, chiefly consist of a *capacity* of the solitary self such as the faculty of reason, for this "candle of the Lord," though precious, can leave the sinful self very much at the center of its own life, cut off from the very heart of the divine being and purpose. On the contrary, the image of God is active and participatory, going beyond the isolation of the autonomous self, and it also underscores the importance of personhood, mutuality, community, and love. Accordingly, just as the Son is not less divine than the Father, and as the Holy Spirit is not less than either, so too are males and females created equally in their *essential* being, that is, in terms of the resplendent image of the Most High.[99]

Second, in this Genesis account, both male and female are given dominion, not simply males. Women and men are equally afforded the authority to govern in a God-given created order, and such a rule must be understood as a clear expression of the divine will, what the Most High had purposed in an innocent, good, and unspoiled creation. Only after sin erupted in all its distorting and debilitating effects, especially in terms of *relationships,* did the curse upon women state, "Yet your desire will be for your husband, and he will rule over you" (Gen. 3:16). Viewed from a Christian perspective, the curse represents the effects of sin, and the joint rule of male and female represents the reality of a restored order in Christ.

The other significant passage that helps us to understand the nature and roles of men and women is Galatians 3:26–28:

> For in Christ Jesus you are all children of God through faith. As many of you as were baptized into Christ have clothed yourselves with Christ. There is no longer Jew or Greek, there is no longer slave or free, there is no longer male and female; for all of you are one in Christ Jesus. (NRSV)

In this text, Paul is underscoring the unity that the children of God have in Christ through faith. As there is one Lord, one faith, and one baptism, so too there is one communion, one body of Christ, which is the church. Paul explores the *universality* of the Christian faith in terms of three basic social distinctions: ethnicity (Jew or Greek), social order (slave or free), and gender (male and female). Put another way, the Christian faith, precisely because it is universal and inclusive, *transcends* the distinctions, divisions, and even polarizations that often play out in sinful society. In other words, its encompassing value, in a truly monotheistic way, is not Jewishness, as if the Christian faith were simply another Jewish sect; it is not the preference of one class to the diminishment or exclusion of another, whereby the faith would almost immediately take a "tribal" turn; and it is not patriarchy, as if maleness defined the very substance of the Christian faith or gave one a soteriological privilege or advantage. On the contrary, the Christian faith goes beyond all these lesser values to find its unity in nothing less than the God who transcends us all in goodness, power, being, mercy, and love. Simply put, the Christian faith lets God be God; it does not take what is penultimate or provincial (ethnicity, social order, and gender) and make it ultimate, giving it a significance that teeters on both idolatry and heedless self-love.

Moreover, it should not go unnoticed that Paul considers the genius of the Christian faith precisely in his letter to the Galatians, a letter in which he not only distinguishes the new covenant from the old, the gospel from the law, but also underscores the immense liberty, the gracious freedom, that all believers have in Christ. Consequently, those elements over which we have little or no control, having been born into them, do not preclude the enjoyment of the richness of grace manifested in Jesus Christ. Such elements may lead to diminishment in other world religions whose embrace is not as broad and whose vision is not as wide as the faith that Paul describes in Galatians. But these same elements, remarkably enough, may also lead to diminishment in the Christian faith when in fear its proponents shy away from the very heights of transcendence and universality to wallow in the valley of provincialism and discrimination, which in the end divide the very body of Jesus Christ. Therefore, as the Genesis passage casts light on the nature of men and women created in the image and likeness of God, the Galatians passage casts light on the nature of the Christian faith itself in its inclusive embrace.

In exploring the biblical equality of men and women as a key interpretive orientation, I am not suggesting that men and women are the same. Created differences in terms of sex, not gender or cultural roles, must indeed be taken into account. The created, not ascribed, sexual differences between men and women that have consequence for intimacy, coupling, and marriage support the appropriateness and goodness of heterosexual unions as indicative of a God-given created order. So understood, the Most High created humanity not as androgynous beings interchangeable in every respect (that is, even in terms of human sexuality) but as both male and female.[100]

## The Hermeneutic Applied

Several passages from the New Testament are often cited by traditionalists, neotraditionalists, and quasi-egalitarians in order to limit the roles of women in a programmatic way. The first does so in terms of society, church, and home; the second in terms of church and home; and the third simply in terms of the home. Though several passages are employed in this way (1 Cor. 11:3–8; 14:34–37; Eph. 5:22–24; 1 Tim. 2:12–14), due to space limitations, only one of the most difficult ones, 1 Timothy 2:12–14, will be considered here.

Since the style of 1 Timothy is in general agreement with what the apostle Paul employed elsewhere (especially in terms of its hortatory and authoritative statements), and since several historians now contend that the polity of the church revealed in this letter is not as late as earlier critics maintained, there are indeed considerable grounds for affirming the plausibility of Pauline authorship of this letter, as both church tradition and contemporary evangelical (and other) scholarship have so often maintained.[101] Paul most likely wrote this missive from Macedonia as he was making his way to Nicopolis. In this letter, the apostle gives some much needed advice to his associate, Timothy, who was left in charge of the work in Ephesus and Asia Minor. In the crucial passage at hand, 1 Timothy 2:12–14, Paul counsels his co-laborer as follows:

But I do not allow a woman to teach or exercise authority over a man, but to remain quiet. For it was Adam who was first created, and then Eve. And it was not Adam who was deceived, but the woman being deceived, fell into transgression.

First of all, if verse 12 is taken literally, apart from its historical context in which Paul and Timothy confronted incipient forms of Gnosticism in the early church, and if this same verse is then universalized and applied to all times and all places, the interpretation would fly in the face of Paul's other writings. For example, Paul not only knew of the leadership of such Old Testament women as Miriam, Deborah, Huldah, and Esther but was also appreciative of the efforts and initiatives of Phoebe, Priscilla, Euodia, Lois, Eunice, Syntyche, Junia the Apostle, and others in his own age. In fact, Gregory Boyd and Paul Eddy cite ten examples of women exercising spiritual authority over men, including the instance of Priscilla explaining to Apollos the way of God more accurately (Acts 18:26), and women serving as the first evangelists as they announced the resurrection of the Lord (John 20:16–18).[102] Moreover, J. Lee Grady, Pentecostal leader, points out that "in 2 Timothy 1:5 Paul commends Lois and Eunice for teaching the Scriptures to young Timothy."[103] Add to this Richard and Catherine Kroeger's observations that "other Pauline material contains commandments that women as well as men should teach [1 Cor. 14:26, 31; Col. 3:16, for example]"[104] and that "women were specifically granted permission to prophesy,"[105] and it becomes remarkably evident that women did all sorts of speaking, teaching, and prophesying in the early church—even when men were present. Therefore, any interpretation of this admittedly difficult passage must be in harmony with this basic scriptural truth.

Second, traditionalists contend that they are justified in universalizing Paul's counsel in verse 12 in light of the appeal he makes to the first two chapters of Genesis in verses 13 and 14. There he specifically refers to Adam and Eve and an implied created order. In other words, Paul is supposedly grounding the prohibition of women's speech in an order established by God, and such a prohibition is therefore deemed universal. A distinction must be made, however, between grounding a principle in a created order, thereby rendering it universal, and illustrating a principle from that same order, thereby not implying a notion of universality.[106] Accordingly, the first interpretive approach by and large fails to take into account the specific, historical, and social context of the passage in 1 Timothy and therefore champions the wrong universal principle based on its literal, analytical reading of verse 12. The second approach, on the other hand, is mindful of the particular cultural context (both Jewish and Greek) that Paul is addressing, out of which a universal principle emerges that is indirectly illustrated by the creation account. But it is not the principle of men lording it over women; rather, it is that in the church, as Paul affirms elsewhere, things must be done decently and in order, given the prevailing social customs, just as there is an order in creation.

To be sure, both Jewish and Greek cultural sensibilities of the period made it difficult for a woman to be heard. In Jewish morning prayer, for instance, a man thanked God that he had not been made "a Gentile, a slave, or a woman."[107] In the Hellenized culture of Asia Minor, respectable women lived very circumscribed lives: They could neither appear on the street alone nor engage in public assemblies, lest they be thought to be of loose morals.[108] Given these social customs, it was a considerable advance for the church to foster the assembly of men and women. The "quietness" that Paul counsels must therefore be understood as a remedy in this particular setting so that the gospel could be embraced in the context of some difficult, even prejudicial, social customs. As with the troubling practice of slavery, Paul's views on women in this passage are not an endorsement of a social custom. Rather, they suggest a temporary solution until the liberty of the gospel is allowed to have its transformative effect in hearts, towns, cities, nations, and the world. As Boyd and Eddy point out:

> We are guilty of idolizing fallen culture and quenching the Spirit if we canonize first-century restrictions against women and construe them as part of God's ideal for all time. It is no different than certain Christians in the past trying to use the Bible's acceptance of slavery as a justification for its ongoing practice.[109]

Beyond this, two interpretive principles must be brought to bear on any text: First, women, no less than men, are equally created in the image and likeness of God, and second, the Christian faith is a universal one that transcends the petty provincialisms (ethnicity, class, and gender) that often preoccupy sinful human cultures. Accordingly, and in a way similar to the reasoning of Augustine in his *De Doctrina Christiana* with respect to proper hermeneutics,[110] if any interpretation of a particular passage violates these two basic truths of Scripture, it is, quite simply, in error. Again, these affirmations, especially as they pertain to women, are not peripheral to but are at the very heart of what the Christian faith is all about.

Traditionalist interpretations, therefore, have faltered with respect to 1 Timothy 2 and other passages. They have been beset with numerous unresolved tensions, even contradictions, simply because they have failed to appreciate that Paul is not advocating a universal ban on female speech or leadership, a ban that would actually undermine the divine will clearly expressed in the first chapter of Genesis. Indeed, the Creator had purposed a joint rule and dominion of both males and females, which sin disrupted and largely destroyed. Moreover, the Christian faith, in its redeeming efficacy and grace, announces a restoration of that good created order grounded in the will of the Holy One who transcends us all and in whom we have, as brothers and sisters in Christ, equality, love, and life itself.

Second, in our own age, a cacophony of voices clamors to be heard, and not all of them acknowledge much less celebrate the lordship of Jesus Christ. Should the name of Christ, then, be less glorified? Should women who are equally created in the image and likeness of God be barred from proclaiming the glad tidings of salvation, what God has done for their souls? Who will stifle and ultimately censor this naturally thankful, grateful, and joyous speech? Is this the will of God? Is this how the body of Christ can be built up and edified? On the contrary, is it not sin for one to know the good and yet fail to do it, to watch the harvest rot on the ground, so to speak, because of a refusal to send willing and capable laborers? Again, should saintly women be limited in their leadership roles when they have been obviously blessed by an abundance of grace and talents? Should these gifts be buried so that the *single* talent of male leadership can be returned to the Master? Finally, should the Christian faith itself retreat from its universality and transcendence, so amply displayed in Galatians 3:28? Should it take the "tribal turn" in which the polarizing distinction of male and female will likely be understood in a script that is not the church's own, part of a cultural war, with the result that a generous and inclusive unity in Christ is lost?

These and similar questions must be addressed by the evangelical community in the days ahead. Yet neither these questions nor the analyses detailed above resolve all the issues of the debate currently taking place among evangelicals with respect to the roles of women in society, church, and home. The goal here has been much more modest. It has been simply to suggest that in light of significant biblical, ecclesiastical, historical, and sociological data, both biblical egalitarians and quasi-egalitarians will likely win the debate, so to speak, and give increasingly convincing answers to the majority of evangelicals in the days ahead, especially in terms of the role of women in the church. When the context of the evangelical home is considered, however, the dissonance with respect to theory and practice may linger much longer, but even here a basic equality is likely to be practiced, even if it is not fully admitted. Therefore, these emerging evangelical views, inclusive and marked by the grace of holy love, will likely transform American evangelicalism, preparing it for a much larger leadership role in the twenty-first century. Such work will no doubt require courage; it will also require an abundance of wisdom and grace.

# The Ecumenical Promise
# of Evangelicalism

Throughout the course of church history, several diverse theological traditions have emerged. As early as the third century, for example, Eastern, Greek ways of doing theology, as found in the work of Origen, could easily be distinguished from the Western, Latin ways of a writer such as Tertullian. In terms of content, Latin authors tended to be more practical, concerned principally with ethics and polity, whereas their Eastern counterparts were far more speculative and philosophical. It is little wonder, then, that in the early church, when it was governed in a conciliar way, as by the ecumenical councils of Nicea (325), Constantinople (381), Ephesus (431), and Chalcedon (451), the Eastern theologians provided most of the resources and virtually all the leadership to grapple with the intricate and difficult theological problems with respect to both Christology and the doctrine of the Trinity.

Over time the differences between East and West were compounded by cultural factors and distinct social locations. The differences between the traditions became so great that in 1054, the catholicity of the church was undermined by the mutual excommunications of the pope and the Eastern patriarch. What scholars call "the old catholic church," however, had already been long gone. The papal bull posted on the altar of St. Sophia in Constantinople simply made it official. What remained, then, was the *Roman* Catholic Church and the *Greek* Catholic or Orthodox Church, and each tradition, interestingly enough, continued to claim that it was the center of catholicity.

Further division of the once unified church took place during the sixteenth century when the Holy Spirit raised up the Protestant Reformers, Luther, Calvin, and Cranmer among them, to bear witness to the clarity and the truth of the gospel, which had been obscured in the Latin West by all-too-human practices and some very obscure traditions. As these reforms were resisted by some, the Roman Catholic Church broke up into communions led by theological reformers and those who wanted to keep the innovations crafted by scholastic theologians during the Middle Ages, some of which helped to render the gospel opaque. With such crucial issues at stake, the Western church, unlike her Eastern counterpart, was divided yet again, and the medieval synthesis was hopelessly lost.

In a real sense, the unity or catholicity of the church and its vocation as the bearer of the truth of the gospel are ever in a delicate tension. Accordingly, when theological novelties emerge that detract from the apostolic witness, unity may be lost, if the issue is important enough, as reformers rise up to call the church, in a prophetic way, back to its first love. In this context, the matter of the truth of the gospel is paramount—a truth that should not be lost or obscured for subsequent generations. Nevertheless, the gracious and God-given unity of the church should not be disrupted by any matter that is not *essential* to maintaining the integrity of the faith once delivered to the saints. Unfortunately, Luther's careful distinction between *diaphora* (essential things) and *adiaphora* (unessential things) pertaining to matters of the Christian faith was apparently not valued by fellow Protestants from his own and other theological traditions. Today, the "plague" of Protestantism is and remains divisiveness and separation. In fact, according to one estimate, there are currently over twenty thousand Christian denominations and independent churches in the world.[1] It seems that whenever you bring two Protestants together, you have three different opinions, and Baptist churches form almost at will. Surely something vital has been lost, and this is one of the reasons why the stability and unity of Roman Catholicism and Eastern Orthodoxy have proven to be so attractive to earnest Christians, Protestants and evangelicals among them.

Embarrassed by Christian disunity and seeking a greater arena for their views, theological liberals of the early twentieth century helped to create the ecumenical infrastructure that is still in existence today. In 1908, for example, the Federal Council of Churches of Christ in America was established to give a common voice to the religious life of the nation. Other ecumenical institutions include the National Council of Churches of Christ in the U.S.A. founded in 1950 and the Consultation on Church Union created a decade later. The largest and most inclusive component of the ecumenical matrix, however, is the World Council of Churches, which was constituted in 1948 in a meeting in Amsterdam and is today a broad fellowship of over 340 churches in 120 nations.

Though the goals of these ecumenical structures are worthy and call for serious attention on the part of committed Christians of all ranks, the reality of the ecumenical movement, especially as it played out after the 1960s, has been far less promising. Riven by ideologies that masqueraded as the gospel, both the Federal and the World Council of Churches quickly became partisan in their prescriptions. Leftist politics, exclusive and divisive in so many ways, substituted for the universal love of God manifested in Christ Jesus. Moderating voices that called for a sophisticated and well-thought-out balance and the real unity of holy love were quickly swept aside as "irrelevant in the face of a hurting world." Thomas Oden describes the odd, ironic, and regrettable decline:

> Sadly, not all claims and attempts at manifesting the unity of the church do indeed rightly express that unity in Christ. Too many pretentious pseudo-ecumenical efforts have been themselves divisive, intolerant, ultra political, misconceived, utopian, abusive, nationalistic, and culturally imperialistic. All of this has occurred under the banner of modern bulldozer ecumenism.[2]

To be sure, one of the greatest shortcomings of the modern ecumenical movement is that it has often, oddly enough, undermined the mission of the church by exchanging this noble purpose for a "mess of political pottage."[3] Thus, many church bureaucrats, removed from the realities of common parish life, mimicked the language of Marx in a polarizing way, with all its in-groups and out-groups, oppressors and oppressed. These same leaders were then surprised to learn that the ecumenical movement was actually breeding factionalism. For one thing, many devout and earnest believers felt alienated from this movement during much of the twentieth century. They knew that the universal love of God manifested in Christ Jesus was something far greater than WCC pronouncements. Moreover, in the modern ecumenical movement, as Oden points out, "secular humanistic moral teachings [were] baptized as Christian teaching and moral standards of church membership lowered to the lowest common denominator."[4] But the "oneness" of the church must from the outset have a proper focus, one that is significant enough to be genuinely inclusive and will embrace, not divide, those for whom Christ died. Simply put, alienation should have no place in the fellowship of the church, especially among those who continue to maintain a faithful witness with respect to the historic truths of the Christian faith.

But Oden is clearly not alone in his criticisms. Jon Stone reveals the evangelical quandary as evangelicalism looks toward the modern ecumenical movement and asks, "How does one maintain Christian unity without forcing either the ecclesiastical regimentation of liberalism or the doctrinal regimentation of fundamentalism?"[5] Indeed, early supporters of the NAE believed that the ecumenical movement "blurred, if not altogether erased, the line between the church and the world, between sacred and profane."[6] "Cooperation without Compromise" and "Unity amid Diversity," therefore, became two of the more popular slogans as evangelicalism confronted liberal "hegemonic" ecumenism, demonstrating once again evangelicalism's prophetic commitment to truth.[7]

It would be a mistake, however, to associate modern liberalism with the ecumenical movement in an almost exclusive fashion, as is often done today, for this judgment would fail to take into account that though liberal ecumenism has indeed influenced the outlook of contemporary evangelicalism, the interest of American evangelicals in the unity of the church has much earlier origins. For example, with roots that go back to the nineteenth century, the World Evangelical Alliance in the following century reaffirmed its vision for unity in an important meeting held in Holland in 1951. At this time, over ninety men and women from twenty-one countries established a global administrative body to further its ministry. Today, the WEA is a global network of 120 national and regional church alliances serving the worldwide church. In light of these trends, Martien Brinkman aptly observes, "I cannot but conclude that the more or less 'classical' contrast between Ecumenicals and Evangelicals, which manifested itself in different attentions for sanctification of life and a politico-social stand, has faded more and more into the background during the [nineteen] nineties."[8] Indeed, today evangelicals are as ecumenically oriented and socially concerned as their liberal counterparts.

As a reforming movement par excellence, American evangelicalism naturally welcomes conversations that will further the life of the church in terms of unity, doctrinal integrity, and contagious witness. Because of its ecclesiology and high ideals, evangelicalism—while not neglecting the importance of conversations among confessional bodies—nevertheless generally "concentrates on believers, in keeping with its focus on the invisible church."[9] Two principal dialogue partners for evangelicals, historically speaking, have been theological liberals, going back to some unfinished business of the early twentieth century, and Roman Catholics, harkening back to the much-needed calls for reform in the sixteenth century—both important windows on what contemporary evangelicalism is all about. Indeed, ongoing conversations with these two communions, even if only on an informal or personal level, will continue to map the genius and identity of the evangelical witness.[10]

## Conversations with Theological Liberalism

Modern theological liberalism was so tied to its social location at the turn of the twentieth century that it attempted to bring its modernizing project forward to subsequent ages without realizing that the historical, ideational, and cultural ground had drastically shifted. Indeed, the reinterpretation of the Christian message in accordance with the modern scientific outlook (various demythologizing projects come to mind) and the nearly exclusive demand for objectivity and nonparticipatory kinds of knowing, the elements of a supposed "critical" perspective, are now considered methodologically naive, even imperialistic, by postliberals and postmoderns alike. If a person's faith is his or her most valuable "possession," then the academic and ecclesiological institutionalization of theological liberalism's cultural accommodation to the Enlightenment can only be considered tragic, for many young people entered liberal seminaries during the twentieth century with faith but left with painful unbelief. The truly sad part is that this loss of faith was unnecessary, a sheer waste of God's greatest gift.

But not all students lost their faith in liberal dominated classrooms. Some intellectually gifted evangelicals (who were often well schooled in logic, critical thinking, and philosophy by the time they entered seminary) were busy critiquing the methodology of their teachers—an element that often goes unnoticed—with respect to assumptions, presuppositions, and basic judgments. Once this genuinely critical work was done, these students could only conclude that their professors had claimed to know, in a very un-Socratic way, far more than they actually did.[11] Moreover, much of the debunking of the truths of the Christian faith represented an accommodation to a particular set of judgments, a way of viewing the world, that could never be proved.

Though the intellectual capital of American theological liberalism was already largely spent by the 1970s, a good effort was put forth to maintain the facade of "cutting-edge" learning, "critical" studies, and intellectual prowess through two chief means. First of all, because theological liberals were deeply committed to the hegemony of the Enlightenment project, especially because they had already made so many accommodations to it, they often became increasingly dogmatic, in a fearful and defensive manner, as the more astute among them began to realize that rigorous, open, and honest investigations did not support several of their often-touted claims. The mantle of free and genuinely dialogical inquiry, ironically enough, had fallen from their shoulders. As Alister McGrath observes, "The new dogmatism within liberalism is itself a sure indication of a deep sense of unease and insecurity, and an awareness of its growing isolation and marginalization within mainline Christianity."[12]

Second, many theological liberals polarized what discussions were taking place in both the church and the academy by maintaining that any significant disagreement with their views constituted "fundamentalism." In this setting, the term was not used in a historical sense and certainly not in an accurate way. It simply served to label quite negatively all competing judgments. That is, it sought to route both thoughts and emotions down well-traveled corridors, the stuff of which prejudices are made.[13] If theological liberals by this time could no longer distinguish the form of *modus ponens* from *modus tollens,* and if they were unwilling to engage in give-and-take discussions with their critics, then ad hominem approaches would simply have to do. Indeed, the ongoing failure of liberalism to distinguish evangelicals from fundamentalists (especially since the former took such great care during the latter part of the twentieth century to differentiate themselves from the latter) is nothing less than intellectually dishonest.[14] As Roger Olson notes, "Many fine, well intentioned mainline-liberal theologians of my acquaintance continue to stereotype all evangelicals as obscurantists who are committed to strictly pre-critical paradigms of thought."[15]

Because of these inaccurate judgments, theological liberals missed the rise of critical evangelicalism, a movement that embraces evangelical leaders such as Stanley Grenz, Alvin Plantinga, Nicolas Wolterstorff, William Abraham, Kevin Vanhoozer, and Michael Peterson who are not precritical in their judgments but postcritical.[16] In other words, these intellectually gifted evangelical leaders have thought their way through the modern project and have found it *intellectually* wanting. Their rejection, then, of some of the major elements of modernity is much different from that of a "reactionary" fundamentalist. As McGrath points out, "One of the most important developments within evangelicalism since World War II is an outbreak of confidence in its own intellectual credentials."[17] It is high time to mark this difference.

By now, many thinkers both inside and outside the church realize that what has held American theological liberalism in place during the past forty years has not been a comprehensive, coherent, and intellectually defensible vision but, remarkably enough, a putative moral force. In other words, theological liberals, borrowing from the moral and ethical wherewithal of the New Left and the knowledge class, especially in terms of their radical egalitarian tendencies, claim the moral high ground as they champion their various "agendas." Here their very partisan and sometimes divisive outlooks, which are always offered as "the common good," are wrapped in the mantle of justice, in the way things ought to be. Indeed, a favorite move of theological liberals is to identify their pet projects, state control of the economy, for instance, with the fate of hungry children, such that to be opposed to their vision is to be labeled a moral pariah. When this is done, the conversation about the merits of particular policies abruptly ends before it has even begun.

The strong ethical tone of theological liberalism, which has empowered and institutionalized the movement, giving it a legitimacy it could not otherwise attain, has led some of its chief proponents down a path that is much less mindful of doctrine and matters of truth. Christianity is "life and not doctrine,"[18] so they told us both in the classroom and in the pulpit. This second major methodological emphasis of liberalism does not fit in well with the earlier commitment to scientific objectivity and (higher) critical studies. Reflecting on this unmistakable trend, Robert Webber elaborates, "Liberals, having rejected doctrine as the touchstone of Christianity, moved toward a more pragmatic position which interpreted Christianity in terms of action. Truth was not what you thought but what you did."[19] Moreover, even the bureaucrats on the World Council of Churches, American theological liberals among them, insisted in an overbearing and coercive way that "doctrine divides; service unites."[20]

This minimizing of distinctively Christian doctrine, what William Abraham calls "doctrinal amnesia,"[21] in the face of overriding ethical and social concerns has apparently had a malign effect on those who grew up in homes where they learned how to parse the word *praxis* in virtually any context but failed to learn the basic theological significance of the term *incarnation*. Richard Hutcheson chronicles this dynamic now operative in many liberal households:

> He now discovers, however, that his own children brought up in an atmosphere of intense concern for the social requirements of the gospel, have inherited the social concern but not the gospel. They have left the church and wandered off into the secular left.[22]

Richard Mouw, reflecting on these same issues, suggests a corrective that can bring the church back to a much-needed balance. He observes:

> I read extensively in "social gospel" and "radical discipleship" literature. I learned much in and through all of this—but I found little to satisfy me in the deep

places of my soul. I had some new moral convictions, but I wanted to *ground* them in a larger understanding of the way things are.[23]

This "grounding" of which Mouw writes must be a theological one, deeply rooted in the story of the gospel rather than in one suggested by partisan American political culture. Clearly, the church has the right to expect its leaders in their moral deliberations, whether personal or social, to be richly informed by the values, motivations, and goals consonant with the gospel. Put another way, the communion of faith is more than justified in its expectation that its leaders think theologically, as difficult as this task can be at times, and in a way that will glorify the name of Jesus Christ among the nations. Doctrine and serious theological reflection are not optional, such that they can quickly be discarded for the sake of getting on with the "real business" of service. Instead, these salient elements of the life of the church are nothing less than prerequisites in order that service, now graciously undertaken, may become the genuine gift of ministry. Indeed, not to see the importance of both theological and spiritual preparation prior to works of mercy and the like is to neglect some of the greatest resources of the church and what constitutes its distinct witness in both thought *and* action.

In light of the preceding, the dialogue that will take place between theological liberals and evangelicals in the days ahead will undoubtedly embrace the issue of doctrinal integrity, especially as it relates to praxis. But as was already indicated in chapter 5, it will not be a matter of encouraging evangelicals to engage in social ministry, for they are already quite active in this area. In fact, according to some cultural observers, evangelicals undertake far more social ministries than do their liberal counterparts.[24] Instead, the conversations will likely devolve upon the relation of doctrine to ethics, how Christian *truth* must rightly inform the Christian *good*. Accordingly, the following discussion considers two of the more prominent approaches to these ecumenical discussions by leading evangelicals. Through this examination we should be able to assess the best way for evangelicalism to go forward as it embraces genuine dialogue with others, even some of its detractors, and as it maintains the integrity of its historic witness.

The first approach to dialogue is suggested by Henry Knight, well-known Wesleyan evangelical, and Don Saliers, "an ecumenically committed sacramental Methodist,"[25] in their book *The Conversation Matters: Why United Methodists Should Talk with One Another*. In this work, the authors attempt to bridge the broad divide that is now a part of Methodist life, as is the case in so many other old-line denominations, by addressing both "liberal and conservative viewpoints."[26]

Both authors are well aware that theological liberals and radicals in this historically evangelical church (which has its roots in the great revival of eighteenth-century Britain) have, as they put it, "[drunk] deeply of the waters of modernity and embrace theological innovation."[27] Moreover, the liberal party of the church, which often presents its views as if they constituted the very substance of United Methodism, underscores the importance of remaining faithful to the "new knowledge God is revealing in our day that corrects the culture-bound understanding of the biblical writers."[28] However, if this "new knowledge" is being employed in a normative way, that is, as a correction of the biblical writers, then how do we know, as it is so vigorously claimed, that God Almighty has revealed it?

What then is the authority that grounds the liberal claim of "new revelation," as expressed in Knight and Saliers's book, especially if it contradicts Scripture? The innovators "see themselves," the authors note, "in continuity with Christians in the past in that they claim the same faith *experience*,"[29] a historically liberal claim going back to the time of Schleiermacher. If one questions the theological variance or "doctrinal diversity" of liberals and radicals, then Knight and Saliers have a ready reply (no doubt in line with their ecumenical purpose): "Calling them heretics will not make them disappear."[30] Granted, on the one hand, name-calling and labeling, especially if done in an unloving and self-righteous spirit, will do little to move the dialogue forward between evangelicals and liberals. That much, at least, is clear. On the other hand, the church must not only be truthful in its judgments, rightly distinguishing heterodoxy from orthodoxy, but must also not accede to the requirement that the dialogue always be "civil" (in other words, that no one should "feel" offended by what is said). Such a demand may undermine a critical and open inquiry by privileging from the outset the normative value that liberals attach to personal *experience*, especially the experience of never having to feel offended or challenged.

A key window on the ecumenical approach offered in this book can perhaps be found in a conversation that occurred between one of its authors and a colleague who works at the same school of theology. Reflecting on the current doctrinal controversy in United Methodism, the woman observed, "I don't see why this is so important. . . . For instance, you believe Christ is divine but I do not. That doesn't make me any less a Christian, nor does it affect my faith in God."[31] The author's response to this claim (we don't know whether it was Knight or Saliers) was simply that "it certainly did not affect our being in effective ministry together."[32]

If this colleague is indeed a member, perhaps even a minister, of the United Methodist Church, then the reply of either Knight or Saliers is exceedingly troubling and constitutes part of the old-line theological drift that is so apparent in many denominations across America today. I make this claim because entering the Methodist Church entails either the recognition of a prior baptismal covenant (from Roman Catholicism, for instance) or entering upon one. In continuity with the historic witness of the church, all four forms of the sacrament of baptism as found in the *United Methodist Hymnal* employ the language of the Apostles' Creed in its articulation of a lively faith in Jesus Christ, the only Son of God.[33] Beyond this, the Methodist Articles of Religion, which were derived from the historic Anglican Thirty-nine Articles and also may not be altered according to the first restrictive rule of the United Methodist Church, affirm the divinity of Jesus Christ in an unequivocal way. Article 2, for example, states:

> The Son, who is the Word of the Father, the very and eternal God, of one substance with the Father, took man's nature in the womb of the blessed Virgin; so that two whole and perfect natures, that is to say, the Godhead and Manhood, were joined together in one person, never to be divided; whereof is one Christ, very God and very Man.[34]

In light of these observations, Knight or Saliers should have informed this colleague, much like a good doctor would inform patients that they are seriously ill, that her beliefs, as presently held, exclude her from the catholic witness of the United Methodist Church, a witness that this Protestant denomination shares in historic continuity with all other members of the body of Christ. Rejecting the divinity of Christ, this *divinity* school professor has little ground to presume she is Christian or that she knows some of the deeper, more gracious forms of efficacious ministry.

But there are other problems with this "sentimental" ecumenical approach as well. That is, as it acquiesces to the disingenuousness, indeed, the duplicity, of the colleague, it also becomes involved, in some sense, in undermining not only the sacredness of the baptismal covenant but also the integrity of the community of faith as expressed in its Articles, which should be affirmed by all clergy. In this context, truthfulness is crucial and can be easily lost in approaches that place an undue premium on "getting along" or "being nice." Clearly, this is the wrong kind of ecumenism, for it entails unity not for the sake of but at the expense of truth. For one thing, what group can embrace members who make it clear that they will lie when they feel justified (always, of course, in the name of some lofty goal), that they will privately (and perhaps idiosyncratically) deny what the community publicly affirms, indeed, celebrates? The dishonesty entailed in this approach is simply insuperable and undermines the institutional life of the church as well as its basic witness. Accordingly, if we can no longer be honest with one another, if mental reservation and exceptions rule the day, if members flout the very standards they are supposed to uphold publicly as ministers of the gospel, then the very basis for genuine ecumenicity is not even present.

A kind, gracious, and redemptive approach to this dilemma that the contemporary church faces can be found in part in a reappropriation of the distinction of groups found in historic Methodism, the "penitents," for example, or in the early life of the church, that is, in terms of the catechumens. Thus, when members have lost the faith or if they in a self-referential and stubborn way insist on denying the very essentials of what the community so purposefully upholds in its doctrinal standards and corporate worship, then they should be excluded from both communion and voting rights in the church, though not from the life of the community itself. In this way, the grace, holy love, and truthfulness of the community of faith can be made evident in careful redemptive concern as these unbelievers are placed in a group of "penitents" where they can receive ongoing guidance on the beauty of the witness of the church and the integrity of her historic witness. In the end, the Holy Spirit must be known in the church, not as a spirit of accommodation, acculturation, or duplicity but as nothing less than the Spirit of truth.

A far more promising approach to ecumenical dialogue between theological liberals and evangelicals can be found in the discussion that took place more than a decade ago between the British ecclesiastics David Edwards and John Stott, a discussion that has much to say to their American counterparts. As these two leaders explored such vital matters as the authority of Scripture, the cross of Christ, the miracles of the New Testament, and evangelism, the frankness of the exchange led Stott to the following observation:

> Does this not mean that in the end you accord supremacy to your reason rather than to Scripture? We are back in the conflict between the Reformation and the Renaissance. As Luther said to Erasmus, "The difference between you and me, Erasmus, is that you sit above Scripture and judge it, while I sit under Scripture and let it judge me."[35]

Indeed, Edwards had rejected traditional Christian teachings in several areas, not because they were not an accurate reflection of Scripture and the history of the church but because they proved to be, in *his* estimation, intellectually unacceptable according to the received wisdom of the day—a familiar theme by now. The final authority for Edwards, therefore, was and remains human reason, a self-legislating capacity and criterion that cannot bear the voice of revelation, of the calling, evoking God who addresses all things, even sinful human reason (especially in its self-interestedness, bias, and prejudices), and calls them into account. Reflecting on the authority of reason in its autonomous role as the ultimate authority that displaces revelation and transcendence, Stott developed a graphic image to communicate what is at the heart of this approach.

> The liberal seems to me to resemble (no offence meant!) a gas-filled balloon, which takes off and rises into the air, buoyant, free, directed only by its own built-in navigational responses to wind and pressure, but entirely unrestrained from earth. For the liberal mind has no anchorage; it is accountable only to itself.[36]

Viewed from yet another perspective, the dialogue between Edwards and Stott is valuable in that it demonstrates that after each "side" has had its say, the matter finally comes down to differing conceptions of authority. But who or what adjudicates this difference? In the long run, as liberals and evangelicals continue to converse, the truth of Scripture as it is exemplified in the corporate witness of the church and in the demonstration of the power of the Holy Spirit liberating human lives should remain attractive for those who are seeking the more excellent way. The power of the gospel is unleashed in part through proper orthodox belief. That is, orthodoxy is absolutely necessary for the vibrant Christian life, though correct belief by itself is never sufficient. To this must be added, of course, the transformation of heart and life that graciously occurs through the ministrations of the Holy Spirit. Though the theological acumen of liberalism has largely faded through evangelical, postliberal, and postmodern critiques, it nevertheless continues to hold significant institutional power, both in the church and in the academy, which remains perhaps its greatest strength and, in the eyes of some, its best argument.

## Conversations with Roman Catholicism

In the midst of what some have called a cultural war in America, evangelical Christians and Roman Catholics have often found themselves arm in arm at demonstrations, marches, and sit-ins designed to protect the basic rights of the least of all or to protest the latest vulgarity. Being pro-life in a full-orbed way (not simply anti-abortion, the prejudicial description given by the media moguls) comes easily for Roman Catholics who have been schooled in natural law theory and for evangelicals who understand what being created in the image of God, the *imago Dei*, entails.

Relations between these two large and burgeoning groups (over one billion Roman Catholics and nearly four hundred million evangelicals in the world)[37] have clearly improved since Vatican II, a council at which Pope John XXIII and his bishops had the courage to "update" the Roman communion and to look more favorably upon Protestants, now seen not as "heretics" but far more graciously as "separated brethren." Prior to this historic council, bad blood had existed on both sides, especially during the nineteenth and early twentieth centuries, as Protestants became increasingly fearful as wave after wave of Roman Catholic immigrants from Ireland, Germany, and Italy landed on American shores. Moreover, in the twentieth century, what some took to be misdirected criticism against Roman Catholics could just as easily be found among theological liberals as evangelicals. For instance, when President Truman in 1946 assigned a formal diplomatic representative to the Vatican, one of the loudest voices raised in opposition was by the liberal paladin G. Bromley Oxnam, bishop of the Methodist Church in New York and president of the Federal Council of Churches. Reflecting the mood of many of his colleagues, he criticized this appointment as "encouraging the un-American policy of a union of church and state."[38]

Today, the theological and ecclesiastical climate for genuine ecumenism exists among those communions of faith that have painstakingly remained doctrinally orthodox, in tune with the historic witness of the church, especially as it was articulated in the first four ecumenical councils. Indeed, evangelical Presbyterians today often have far more in common with their conservative Roman Catholic counterparts (and with their evangelical Methodist cousins) than with liberals from their own denomination. Moreover, as Colleen Carroll points out, "Conservative Catholics, too, are finding that they often have more in common with evangelicals on campus than with liberal Catholics."[39] According to some observers, these new alliances, which not only cut across Protestant denominations but also bridge the heretofore broad Protestant/Roman Catholic divide, are what the future of American religion is all about.

## Evangelicals and Catholics Together

The prospects of ecumenical fellowship, perhaps even reconciliation, have been embraced by both key evangelical leaders and prominent Roman Catholics. For example, Charles Colson, former Nixon aide and well-known evangelical leader, and Richard John Neuhaus, onetime Lutheran pastor turned Roman Catholic priest, met with several other ecumenically minded people in 1992 and took note of the common spirit among them. Through its many labors and discussions, this seminal group finally brought forth a public document for reflection by its constituencies titled "Evangelicals and Catholics Together: The Christian Mission in the Third Millennium," or more popularly known as ECT I. As Neuhaus considered the relationship between various Christian communities, he chartered a course of five stages leading to ever greater unity: from (1) hostility to (2) coexistence to (3) cooperation to (4) sharing to (5) full communion.[40]

The document "Evangelicals and Catholics Together" is fairly straightforward and acknowledges that "the one Christ and one mission includes many other Christians notably the Eastern Orthodox and those Protestants not commonly identified as Evangelical."[41] Though not an official statement of any major Christian body, ECT I, in noting that "the scandal of conflict between Christians obscures the scandal of the cross,"[42] rightfully calls for collegial exchange and when possible the undertaking of a common mission. As J. I. Packer points out, "ECT applied what was once called the 'Lund principle' . . . that ecclesiastically divided Christians should try not to do separately what their consciences allow them to do together."[43] However, the greater good and unity of one Lord, one faith, one baptism manifested so resplendently as Christians from different traditions participate in the Lord's Supper remains a vision, a possibility, that awaits actualization. In the meantime, the authors of ECT I are well aware that calls for unity must also be matched by adherence to the truth of the gospel. "We reject any appearance of harmony," they declare, "that is purchased at the price of truth."[44]

When evangelical leaders such as the late Bill Bright of Campus Crusade for Christ; Richard Mouw, president of Fuller Theological Seminary; and J. I. Packer of Regent College publicly endorsed ECT I, some of them were immediately criticized by their fellow evangelicals for having compromised on important matters of doctrine. Packer took this criticism so seriously that he participated in the drafting of a document titled "Resolutions for Roman Catholic and Evangelical Dialogue," which identified seven confessional theses from the evangelical side of the equation (justification by faith alone being one of them) "as agenda items for study, discussion, and prayer."[45] Packer hoped that this declaration, which is also known as the "CURE Statement of August 1994," would remove "all doubt as to whether support for ECT implied any minimizing of the theological difficulties with self-defined Catholicism that classic Protestantism has felt for over four centuries."[46]

Along these same lines, Packer's essay "Crosscurrents among Evangelicals" in the volume *Evangelicals and Catholics Together: Toward a Common Mission* raises a number of troubling issues that yet divide evangelicals and Roman

Catholics. Such matters include the doctrines of transubstantiation (that the bread is no longer bread but simply appears as such; it is essentially and substantively the very body of Christ), the un-bloody *sacrifice* of the Mass, the doctrine of justification by faith alone, the correlation between conversion and the new birth, the question of baptismal regeneration, and the sacramental structure of grace among others.[47] Some of Packer's most cogent and perceptive observations regarding Roman Catholicism, however, concern ecclesiology, the doctrine of the church. He exclaims:

> First, Rome's claim to be the only institution that can without qualification be called the Church of Christ seems to me theologically flawed, for it misconceives the nature of the church as the New Testament writers explain it. In the New Testament the Church is not a sacramental and juridical organization sustained by priests channeling divine life through set rituals, but it is a worldwide fellowship of believers who share in the resurrection life of the Lord Jesus Christ.[48]

This observation not only gets to the heart of the matter but also illuminates one of the crucial differences between the unofficial work of ECT I and the official teaching of the magisterium of the Roman Catholic Church. Neuhaus touches on the doctrine of the church assumed by many who endorsed ECT I when he points out:

> In the words of ECT, those who have been converted must be given full freedom and respect as they discern and decide the community in which they will live their new life in Christ. In such discernment and decision, they are ultimately responsible to God, and we dare not interfere with the exercise of that responsibility.[49]

Such a view appears to affirm freedom of religion as a basic human right (an implication of the freedom entailed in the *imago Dei*) that must be respected by different Christian bodies. In other words, if one is born and raised in a Lutheran home and then follows the leading of conscience by converting to Roman Catholicism, as Neuhaus himself did, then that decision must be respected by all. The Roman Catholic Church, however, apparently does not return the favor in kind, for when it becomes a matter of converting from Roman Catholicism to a Protestant "sect" (the favorite devaluating term of some Roman Catholics for a Protestant communion), all sorts of problems emerge. Indeed, in such a case, not only is official recognition found wanting, but Rome is also compelled to respond with rejection and condemnation since its often-touted claims to catholicity, that the church of Jesus Christ properly subsists in it and it alone, is not recognized by such a conversion. For example, the *Catechism of the Catholic Church,* in a very unecumenical way, declares with respect to these Protestant converts who have humbly and obediently followed the gentle leading of conscience and the Holy Spirit, "Hence they could not be saved who, knowing that the Catholic Church was founded as necessary by God through Christ, would refuse either to enter it or to remain in it."[50]

The problem here on the part of the Roman Catholic Church is to mistake its own particular tradition (remember Eastern Orthodoxy) for the genuine universality of the church, which embraces the entire family of Christians around the world united in faith in Jesus Christ. Clearly, there are many *real* Christians who are not members of the Roman communion who yet worship God in Spirit and in truth, who are doctrinally sound, and who participate in the apostolic testimony in a full and rich way. These orthodox Christian believers who belong to communions that are not "defective," as Cardinal Ratzinger would have it, have been forgiven and made holy, having been washed by nothing less than the blood of the Lamb.

Oddly enough, even wordplay is sometimes employed to support the Roman claim that its communion, its *particular* theological tradition, constitutes the very substance of the church, a claim that flies in the face of much of church history. In fact, the term *catholic,* which means "universal," is used unswervingly in the *Catechism* to refer specifically to the *Roman* Catholic Church, but careful historical analysis reveals that this institution is but a particular expression of that catholicity. Eastern Orthodoxy has as much a claim to catholicity as does Rome, perhaps even more so, though both claims in the end are specious, since the ancient or old catholic church, as noted earlier, broke up well before 1054. Again, the Roman communion, though important, is not at the center. Christ is—and should be—at the center. The catholic church, properly understood and in a way that embraces genuine ecumenical charity, rightfully subsists in all those communions of faith that are united in the apostolic witness that Jesus Christ is the Son of God (Mark 8:29).

## *"The Gift of Salvation"*

Unofficial ecumenical discussions—which seem far more promising—continued apace among the original Roman Catholic and evangelical drafters of ECT I. Finally, in 1997, another document was promulgated titled "The Gift of Salvation," which has become known simply as ECT II. Timothy George of Beeson Divinity School, who was not only actively involved in these discussions but also offered an "evangelical assessment" for his colleagues, made the following observation in terms of the concerns that led to this second major initiative:

> "The Gift of Salvation" has been made possible by a major realignment in ecumenical discourse: the coalescence of believing Roman Catholics and faithful evangelicals who both affirm the substance of historic Christian orthodoxy against the ideology of theological pluralism that marks much mainline Protestant thought as well as avant-garde Catholic theology.[51]

Though this second ecumenical document again did not reflect the official teaching of any religious body, it nevertheless tackled one of the more difficult issues that continues to separate evangelicals from Roman Catholics, namely, the doctrine of justification by faith. Well aware that the Protestant Reformers had deemed justification to be the doctrinal criterion by which some of the medieval practices of Rome had been found wanting, the drafters of ECT II were courageous to explore this doctrine at considerable length. Among its many observations, all of which seem to imply knowledge of historic Protestant critiques, were the following:

- "We agree that justification is not earned by any good works or merits of our own; it is entirely God's gift, conferred through the Father's sheer graciousness."
- "In justification, God, on the basis of Christ's righteousness alone, declares us to be no longer his rebellious enemies but his forgiven friends, and by virtue of his declaration it is so."
- "Thus it is that as justified sinners we have been saved, we are being saved, and we will be saved. All this is the gift of God."[52]

The drafters of this theological statement realized, of course, that other significant matters pertaining to justification by faith had yet to be addressed, namely, "the historic uses of the language of justification as it relates to imputed and transformative righteousness [and] the normative status of justification in relation to all Christian doctrine"[53] among other things. Despite these omissions, "The Gift of Salvation" indeed evidences some progress with respect to this potentially divisive doctrine. In light of this, the committee members who composed ECT II must have been surprised that some of their sharpest critics were not Roman Catholics but evangelical Protestants. For example, in an essay published in *Christianity Today*, Arthur Moore noted that this ecumenical contribution does not "use either the term *imputed* or *infused*, causing [some] to view the document as 'dangerously ambiguous.'"[54] Developing this point even further, Moore reasoned:

> The Protestant Reformers held that God justifies believers by imputing Christ's righteousness to them. But Catholic doctrine, formulated in response to the Reformation, taught that God saves the faithful by infusing them with Christ's righteousness through a process that requires human cooperation.[55]

Suggesting that the Protestant influences on the declarations of ECT II may actually have been less than initially supposed, this evangelical scholar subsequently pointed out that the Jesuit leader Avery Dulles, now cardinal, who signed the document, stated quite clearly that the Roman Catholic members of the committee "were careful to follow Trent."[56]

Moreover, in an essay titled "'The Gift of Salvation': Its Failure to Address the Crux of Justification," Mark Seifrid raised an issue that Luther himself considered, namely, is justifying faith formed by love, or does faith inform love? In his own day, the historic German Reformer had clearly maintained:

> We must conclude with Paul: By faith alone, not by faith formed by love, are we justified. We must not attribute the power of justifying to a "form" that makes a man pleasing to God; we must attribute it to faith, which takes hold of Christ the Savior Himself and possesses Him in the heart. This faith justifies without love and before love.[57]

The principal question for Luther in the past and for Seifrid in the present is not whether justifying faith issues in lively works, for all agree that "faith without works is dead" (James 2:26), but whether justifying faith must be formed by an infusion of love in order to be rightly justifying. Put another way, must justifying faith "be supplemented by charity in order to effect justification?"[58]

Some of the strongest and most systemic criticism of ECT II, however, came from John Armstrong, who contended that this work "accepts the actual slogans of the Reformation without agreeing on the actual content of the slogans."[59] Indicating why "The Gift of Salvation" was warmly accepted by so many evangelicals, Armstrong criticized his own colleagues in claiming, "The reason evangelicals are now prepared to listen is because they are actually closer to the theological beliefs of Rome than they are to those of their Protestant forefathers."[60] Whether this statement is accurate will likely be revealed in the days ahead. In the meantime, the drafters of both ECT I and II are to be commended by Roman Catholics and evangelicals alike for undertaking the difficult and courageous work of forging these conversations, for in the end, dialogue is better than silence.

## The Joint Declaration on the Doctrine of Justification

More serious and formal ecumenical talks took place between the Lutheran World Federation and the Roman Catholic Church, resulting in the solemn confirmation *The Joint Declaration on the Doctrine of Justification,* which was signed by both parties in the historic city of Augsburg in October 1999. Mindful of the importance of the Reformation as well as of the Council of Trent, the *Joint Declaration* declares that there now exists a basis for a common understanding of justification by faith by Lutherans and Roman Catholics:

> The present *Joint Declaration* has this intuition: namely, to show that on the basis of their dialogue the subscribing Lutheran churches and the Roman Catholic Church are now able to articulate a common understanding of our justification by God's grace through faith in Christ. It does not cover all that either church teaches about justification; it does encompass a consensus on basic truths of the doctrine of justification and shows that the remaining differences in its explication are no longer the occasion for doctrinal condemnations.[61]

The central argument of the *Joint Declaration* is that since there now exists a consensus on some basic truths with respect to the doctrine of justification, the remaining differences between these two traditions are no longer the occasion for doctrinal condemnations. This claim is undermined at least in part by the recognition that the consensus achieved is perhaps being improperly employed as a warrant for an area in which consensus has not been achieved, that is, in terms of the differences that remain, differences that may yet call for theological censure. That is, what has been accomplished in one area does not hold consequence for the next. Indeed, given this form of argumentation in which the areas of consensus are employed to repudiate, even obviate, criticism of remaining differences, it is crucial for scholars to ascertain not only whether the consensus constitutes a *sufficient* doctrine of justification by faith, one faithful to the apostolic witness revealed in Scripture, but also whether the theological differences beyond that consensus actually matter.

In light of these and other problems, upon its promulgation in 1999, the *Joint Declaration* was greeted with mixed reviews. Though several church leaders in both the Lutheran World Federation and the Roman Catholic Church believed that a theological breakthrough had been made, others were not as convinced. In fact, more than 165 of Germany's leading theologians and historians, such as Jürgen Moltmann, Gerhard Ebling, and Eberhard Jüngel, criticized the new Lutheran-Catholic statement along several lines.[62] In America, Robert Preus, a well-respected Lutheran scholar, though he had died in 1995, was nevertheless aware of the language that would later be published in the *Joint Declaration*. His largely negative judgment is revealed in the following pointed observation:

> For the Lutheran churches to accept [the] *Joint Declaration* as a consensus on the doctrine of justification will not only compromise their witness to the evangelical Lutheran doctrine on justification; but will compromise the confessional principal itself.[63]

In his observations, Preus not only pointed to the different cultural, religious, and intellectual climates of the sixteenth century as compared to the nineteenth and twentieth but also suggested that both Lutherans and Catholics, if they did not succumb to the contemporary Zeitgeist, were at least at times heavily influenced by it.[64]

As a Methodist theologian well acquainted with the Anglican Reformation and with the theological power and cogency of John Wesley's evangelical theology, I find the *Joint Declaration* theologically problematic in a number of respects. With its omissions as well as with its ambiguities, this document is apparently incapable of communicating the fullness of the apostolic testimony pertaining to justification. Three major elements illustrate this claim.

First of all, reflecting the theological preference of Rome at the Council of Trent (Session VI, Canon 10), the *Joint Declaration* "says nothing about the imputation of Christ's righteousness."[65] In fact, as McGrath points out, the entire post-Tridentine Catholic tradition "continued to regard justification as a *process* in which man was made righteous involving the actualization rather than the imputation of righteousness."[66] Therefore, perhaps out of deference to the teaching of Rome at Trent that justification is intimately associated with *infused* grace, the Lutheran representatives during the 1990s simply let the matter of the imputation of the righteousness of Christ drop, what Luther in several contexts referred to as "the alien righteousness of God."[67] If the imputation of the righteousness of Christ is not affirmed, however, whereby sinners, not those who are already righteous, are declared righteous, then a basis of justification is being offered other than the life and death of Christ or the basic Pauline truth that *sinners*, not saints, are justified is subtly being denied in favor of the teaching that only those who have the infused grace (which makes them righteous and holy) are justified. Simply put, infused grace, in a real sense, becomes the *basis* of justification in this teaching so that this crucial doctrine does not become a supposed "legal fiction."[68] R. C. Sproul, prolific evangelical writer, expresses the remaining differences between these two traditions in the following observation: "For Rome the declaration of justice *follows* the making inwardly *just* of the regenerate sinner. For the Reformation the declaration of justice follows the imputation of Christ's righteousness to the regenerated sinner."[69] This difference is vital and cannot be ignored in the name of ecumenical interest and endeavor.

Second, in failing to develop or even to acknowledge the importance of the imputation of the righteousness of Christ in its doctrine of justification, the *Joint Declaration* quite naturally falls into yet another difficulty that undermines both the grace and the power of the gospel. It confounds the doctrines of justification and sanctification. More to the point, the failure to distinguish these doctrines in a proper and biblical way results in sanctification being made in some sense the basis for justification. In the following statement, the *Joint Declaration,* in portraying Roman differences, confuses these two senses:

> The Catholic understanding also sees faith as fundamental in justification. For without faith, no justification can take place. Persons are justified through baptism as hearers of the word and believers in it. The justification of sinners is forgiveness of sins and *being made righteous* by justifying grace, which makes us children of God.[70]

Moreover, under the heading "Biblical Message of Justification," both Lutherans and Catholics affirm that justification is "the forgiveness of sins . . . [and] liberation from the dominating power of sin and death."[71] What is this but to confuse, once again, justification with regeneration or the new birth? Contrary to this document, it must be reaffirmed for the sake of gospel clarity by both the Protestant community in general and evangelicals in particular that justification is not liberation from "the dominating power of sin and death." That is regeneration or initial sanctification. As John Wesley so clearly taught during the eighteenth century, justification, quite simply, is the forgiveness of those sins that are past. It is the work of grace that God does for us, not in us. Therefore, confusing these two senses, as the *Joint Declaration* does, allows sanctification to "bleed" into the doctrine of justification with the result that once again some measure of sanctification or holiness or infusion of grace and charity has been made the basis of justification. But it is no one less than the apostle Paul who reminds the church, "God demonstrates his own love toward us, in that while we were yet sinners, Christ died for us" (Rom. 5:8).

Third, though the Annex to the Official Common Statement on justification indicates that both Lutherans and Roman Catholics affirm that "justification takes place 'by grace alone' (*JD* nos. 15 and 16), [and] 'by faith alone,'"[72] the main body of the *Joint Declaration* restricts the usage of the phrase "by faith alone" to a Lutheran understanding of justification. For example, compare the following two excerpts from the *Joint Declaration:*

1. According to Lutheran understanding, God justifies sinners in faith alone (sola fide).
2. The Catholic understanding also sees faith as fundamental in justification. For without faith, no justification can take place.[73]

This omission of a key component of the doctrine of justification, the language of "by faith alone" in the Catholic statement, an element that preserves the excellence and utter sufficiency of the work of Christ on behalf of sinners, is not surprising given the reluctance of the Roman Catholic Church to pay much attention to the doctrine of justification prior to Vatican II.[74] Accordingly, the mere mention of the term *faith* in the context of justification should not be sufficient for Protestants, or for Roman Catholics for that matter, who seek to communicate the generous Pauline witness to the graciousness of the gospel. To be sure, the doctrine of faith must be affirmed and its implicatory relations demonstrated to illuminate this teaching as nothing less than, as Luther reminds us, the "rector et judex super omnia genera doctrinarum."[75]

In summary, since the *Joint Declaration* does not affirm the imputation of the righteousness of Christ in its common statements, since it repeatedly confuses the issues of justification and sanctification in these same statements, and since it relegates the language of *sola fide* simply to Lutheran differences and to the Annex, failing to include such language in terms of the Catholic articulation in particular, then surely American evangelicals have the right to ask, first of all, do the common statements on justification actually reveal a sufficient and full-bodied doctrine, one commensurate with the life and witness of the historic church, or is it a doctrine that unfortunately has been eviscerated due in some measure to the ecumenical enterprise itself? Furthermore, should some of the differences that remain, especially the vital matter of faith alone, become a part of the consensus rather than being relegated to the "periphery" Annex as the present declaration requires?

Even judged in a most charitable way and with great ecumenical sensitivity, the *Joint Declaration* does not clearly express the truths that were so precious to the early church, the apostle Paul in particular: "But to the one who does not work, but believes in him who justifies the *ungodly,* his faith is credited as righteousness" (Rom. 4:5, emphasis added). Since this is the case, evangelicals, as with others, must still undertake the labors of reform, a mark of their identity, and not be dissuaded from this vital task in the least. Empowered by grace and led by the rich ministrations of the Holy Spirit, they must in an ongoing prophetic way call the broader church to a clarity and a witness with respect to both grace and faith, which alone justify. In the past, evangelicalism sacrificed unity in the name of truth. In the future, it must seek unity for the sake of truth. In an ecumenical age, nothing less is warranted; in an age that seeks for wisdom, nothing less will do.

# 8

# Looking Back
# and Going Forward

The history of American religion is filled with ironies, unintended consequences, and even a few surprises. Who would have guessed back in the
1920s that conservative religion would bypass its liberal cousins in so
many ways by the turn of the twenty-first century? And yet it is so. As Alister
McGrath points out, "There is every indication that it [evangelicalism] will
soon become—if it is not already—the dominant form of Protestant Christianity in North America."[1] Indeed, the statistics now tell a story that can no
longer be denied: Of the five hundred most rapidly growing congregations in
the United States today, "89 percent were found to be evangelical."[2] According
to Mark Shibley, "Slightly more than half of all white Protestants (54 percent)
identify with evangelical churches. That figure is 66 percent in the South and 46
percent outside the South."[3] Beyond this, the strength of the evangelical faith
in terms of its institutional practices, an important measure by any standard,
is blossoming. For example, a relatively recent survey revealed that "a much
higher proportion of adherents to evangelical denominations practice their faith
actively than either Catholics or mainline Protestants."[4] In fact, as Christian
Smith notes, "Fully 80 percent of evangelicals attend church services once a
week or more. Comparatively, only 67 percent of fundamentalists, 63 percent of

mainliners, 47 percent of liberals, and 65 percent of Roman Catholics do so."[5] By the year 2025, various forms of evangelicalism will virtually displace Roman Catholicism as the numerically dominant form of faith in Latin America.[6] The outsiders have become insiders; the marginalized are now mainstream.

Yet as strong and vital as American evangelicalism is, there have been some important "defections" to the traditions of Roman Catholicism (Thomas Howard) and Eastern Orthodoxy (Franky Schaeffer)[7]—communions of faith that have placed a premium on liturgy, ecclesiology, and doctrine.

## The Lure of the Liturgical Traditions

Remarkably enough, it is the very strengths of evangelicalism that are perceived as weaknesses by others, even by some evangelicals who have left the fold. As Stanley Grenz points out, evangelicals generally prefer "the simple Christianity of the Hutterite . . . to the pomp and ceremony of St. Peter's Cathedral"—even to the point of distrusting "institutional, liturgical Christianity."[8] In light of these preferences, contemporary American evangelicalism, informed by the rich and vital streams of the Reformation, has quite naturally placed a premium on the public proclamation of the gospel, to the dismay of rigid sacramentarians, a premium that is consonant with nothing less than the witness of the early church. For the apostle Paul, for example, the Holy Spirit was not *initially* received in justifying and regenerating richness by sinners at a communion table—indeed, they were barred from such participation—but through the proclamation of the glad tidings of salvation by apostles, elders, and evangelists: "This is the only thing I want to find out from you: did you receive the Spirit by the works of the Law, or by *hearing with faith*?" (Gal. 3:2, emphasis added). When the apostle considered the missionary purpose of the church, the drive to reach others for Christ, he could only conclude, "How then will they call on him in whom they have not believed? How will they believe in him whom they have not heard? And how will they hear without a preacher?" (Rom. 10:14).

To be sure, the very orality of preaching as one of the principal means of grace suggests something of the "addressability" of sinners who are called forth in their entire being for a relationship with a God of holy love. Put another way, the proclamation of the gospel, a means that is itself wonderfully discerned by bodily senses, though invisible, places hearers in a kerygmatic setting wherein the evoking, calling God is not likely to be misunderstood as an object or a thing as could easily be the case if sight were given preeminence. It is this knowing of God through Word and Spirit, a verbally mediated transcendence, that is in accordance with the Christian understanding of the Most High as revealed in Jesus Christ through the Holy Spirit. Why is this so? Because this knowing appreciates the cruciality of relationality and love with respect to the divine being, as well as the salience of the invisible and intangible, that are communicated so wonderfully and appropriately through the public, oral proclamation of the Word. This is preaching at its best whereby the words of the preacher, as Karl Barth has reminded us, become the very Word of God. Through the miracle of grace, the words of the minister demonstrate both aesthetic and spiritual power as the presence of the Holy Spirit is discerned in the midst of the community of faith and in the mysterious invisibility of the tabernacle of the human heart.

But contemporary evangelical preaching has clearly fallen from such lofty heights. Instead of understanding the preached word in an aesthetic and sacramental way, as capable of communicating the very Word of God through the ministration of the Holy Spirit, many American evangelicals view the preached word through the lens of a theory of language that actually stifles the larger liturgical purposes of the church. In other words, as modern evangelicals engaged in apologetics in the wake of the liberal deconstruction of some of the basic truths of the Christian faith, they took on a theory of language that ironically enough was carved out of modernistic materials—with all of its reductionism and annoying limitations. Equipped with a "scientific" propositionalist understanding of language that had worked well to defend some of the truths of the Christian faith, evangelicals by and large reduced the power of language to a correspondence theory of truth in general and the ascertaining of facts in particular. This move proved to be disastrous when it was brought to the pulpit, where sermons became little more than lectures and where God was presented more often than not as the highest *object* of thought. Given these trends, it is small wonder that the onetime evangelical leader Thomas Howard offered a true *cri de coeur* as he made his way out of evangelicalism and into the Roman Catholic Church: "To prohibit ceremony, or even to distrust it, and to reduce the worship of God . . . to the meager resources available to verbalism, is surely to have dealt Christendom a dolorous blow."[9]

One way in which to avoid the verbalism of which Howard writes, while at the same time maintaining the centrality of the Word in corporate worship (in a way he does not) and without neglecting the importance of the Lord's Supper, is to recognize that languages are capable of being variously understood and employed. Like the notes of a symphony, language is evocative and in its best sense can reveal something of the presence and beauty of God, even if it is fleeting. Its metaphors, similes, and even rhythms can invite the *hearer,* body, soul, and spirit, to participate in something more—the uncanny, the numinous, even the mysterious. Logocentric approaches, on the other hand, that often make the self's own theoretical reason the final arbiter of virtually everything must therefore be cracked open with approaches that allow the voice of the beautiful Other to be heard, even the voice of God. Once again, it is no one less than the apostle Paul who understood that the almost ineluctable power of language in terms of the proclamation of the gospel is not a human power but a divine one: "And my message and my preaching were not in persuasive words of wisdom, but in demonstration of the Spirit and of power, so that your faith would not rest on the wisdom of men, but on the power of God" (1 Cor. 2:4–5). Can American evangelicals recover from their preoccupation with apologetics (a discipline that remains important) and its associated language preferences and become more liturgically sensitive such that the miracle of preaching can once again flower in their midst?[10]

## Ecclesiology

One of the ongoing strengths of American evangelicalism is that it is a trans-denominational movement for reform.[11] Though there are indeed evangelical denominations such as the Free Methodist Church, the Evangelical Presbyterian Church, and the Church of the Nazarene, many evangelicals belong either to independent churches or to mainline denominations in which they are a distinct yet growing minority. Given the understanding of evangelicalism as a reforming movement with key dialogue partners, this transdenominational flavor means that evangelicals will be actively engaged in a number of conversations simply because they are situated in so many different ecclesiastical contexts. Though good for dialogue and for the possibilities of reform, the *plurality* of ecclesiastical settings in which evangelicals find themselves also gives the movement a fissiparous flavor such that once again a strength can quickly turn into a weakness. Given this environment, the unity and stability of the Catholic *traditions,* in this case Roman Catholicism and Eastern Orthodoxy, can easily appear attractive.[12]

In light of these developments, some former evangelicals, such as Scott Hahn, have found the doctrine of the church articulated by Rome to be thoroughly convincing. Though such converts are clearly a minority (and many Roman Catholics, by the way, are making their way into evangelical churches as well), it will be helpful nevertheless to consider, even if only in a cursory way, some of the basic claims that make Rome's (and Eastern Orthodoxy's) doctrine of the church so inviting for some erstwhile evangelicals. The *Catechism of the Catholic Church,* for instance, makes the case not only for a particular kind of ecclesiology but also for Roman supremacy, a supremacy that remains even after Vatican II and that gives some believers a much desired sense of security and order. The *Catechism* develops three basic themes, the first having to do with the catholicity of the church itself:

> First, the Church is catholic because Christ is present in her. "Where there is Christ Jesus, there is the Catholic Church." In her subsists the fullness of Christ's body united with its head; this implies that she receives from him "the fullness of the means of salvation which he has willed: correct and complete confession of faith, full sacramental life, and ordained ministry in apostolic succession."[13]

Beyond the wordplay of implying Roman Catholic every time the phase "the Catholic Church" is used, as noted in the previous chapter, this statement also fails to consider in a careful and judicious way the catholicity of Eastern Orthodoxy, whose traditions and graces are as ancient as those of Rome. Indeed, as Hans Küng points out, "Around the middle of the fourth century Latin Christianity still appeared largely to be no more than an appendix to Eastern Roman, Byzantine Christianity, which was *the* spiritual leader."[14] Moreover, the statement that the church has received from Christ the "apostolic succession" is historically inaccurate and places at the hands of Jesus what is actually a later historical development. Along these same lines, Küng once again observes, "It cannot be verified that the bishops are successors of the apostles in the direct and exclusive sense. It is historically impossible to find in the initial phase of Christianity an unbroken chain of laying on of hands from the apostles to the present-day bishops."[15]

Second, the Roman Catholic Church believes that Christ instituted a *divine society* while on earth and that redemption, therefore, consists chiefly in uniting with "Holy Mother Church," especially in terms of her authority and sacramental life. The *Catechism* elaborates:

> Fully incorporated into the society of the Church are those who, possessing the Spirit of Christ, accept all the means of salvation given to the Church together with her entire organization, and who—by the bonds constituted by the profession of faith, the sacraments, ecclesiastical government, and communion—are joined in the visible structure of the Church of Christ, who rules her through the Supreme Pontiff and the bishops.[16]

In other words, full membership in the *society* of the church entails the acceptance of those later historical developments, especially in terms of organization and government, even to the point of acceding to the authority of the bishop of Rome. Indeed, at one point, Pope Boniface VIII made the claim—for which he was rightly criticized later by Eastern Orthodox and Protestants alike—that "it is absolutely necessary for every human creature for salvation to be subject to the Roman pontiff."[17] Though the first-century church knew nothing of a monarchical bishop (the bishop "above" the elder), the preeminence of Rome, or a pope for that matter (many historians consider Leo I of the fifth century or Gregory I of the sixth to be the first pope), these developments in *polity* are nonetheless legitimized by an appeal to tradition, given virtually equal weight with the teaching of Scripture, and are thereby required to be affirmed by all the faithful—a requirement that will be examined more carefully below.

Finally, the Roman Catholic Church questions the authority and legitimacy of other communions of faith beyond its own particular expression and fails in the eyes of some to discern in a faithful way the fullness of the presence of the Holy Spirit within the entirety of the blessed and holy body of Christ, especially in its claim that:

> Particular Churches are fully catholic through their communion with one of them, the Church of Rome "which presides in charity." "For with this church, by reason of its pre-eminence, the whole Church, that is the faithful everywhere, must necessarily be in accord."[18]

Such a claim not only once again fails to take into account the reality of Eastern Orthodoxy as a "catholic" communion but also flies in the face of much of early church history. To be sure, the preeminence of Rome as a discrete tradition was a later historical development. In its earliest days, the church quite naturally looked not to Rome but to Jerusalem, a city intimately tied to the Savior and the birth of the church. Later on, the faithful looked to Antioch, where the communion of the saints were first known as Christians.

But some evangelicals today are drawn not simply to the many claims made by Rome about the identity of the "true" church but also to those offered by "Constantinople." Indeed, for the Orthodox, their community is not a denomination at all; "it is quite simply the Church of Christ—the same church that the apostles founded."[19] Eastern Orthodoxy, in the eyes of its adherents and in a way similar to Rome, is deemed to be "the one true church of Christ on earth, which alone has guarded right belief and true worship in absolute identity and unbroken succession with the apostolic church."[20] More to the point, ever since the public and dramatic rending of the garment of catholicity in 1054, the Orthodox have maintained with force equal to that of Rome that the priesthood is effectively found only in its church.[21] Given such views, which mistake the particular for the universal, Protestant churches are quite naturally judged to be no churches at all. Furthermore, "their sacraments are no sacraments, and the Spirit is not received through them."[22] Moreover, when the evangelical theologian Daniel Clendenin, who has studied this tradition extensively, asked an Orthodox priest over coffee one day whether he might be considered a "true Christian," the cleric simply replied, "I don't know,"[23] revealing something of the extent of his ecumenical vision.

The doubt of some Orthodox priests about the soteriological status of believers in other branches of the Christian faith has no doubt caused undue pain for some genuine evangelical believers. Shaken by these broad and sweeping claims, disturbed by the subtle appeals to fear and eternal loss, not a few evangelicals have sought the security that results from acquiescing to such teaching and returning to "Holy Mother Church," though this time with the face of Eastern Orthodoxy. But even the most basic theological reflection about the life and history of the church should demonstrate that when two communions of faith such as Eastern Orthodoxy and Roman Catholicism *both* make claims about the catholicity of the church that ultimately devolve upon their *particular* historic expressions, something has gone terribly wrong.

Many Christians, however, both evangelical and nonevangelical alike, are realizing that the church of Jesus Christ is far greater, more inclusive and generous in its embrace, and more loving in its extent than to be restricted almost in an exclusive way to a particular communion, no matter how extensively or frequently the claims are made. Here the danger of a "churchy" ethnocentrism is great—and one that would belie the genius of the Christian faith in its transcending and universal dimensions. To be sure, part of the beauty of participating in the body of Christ comes from *koinonia*, the genuine fellowship and love that arise in the recognition of one Lord, who is the sole and unique head of the church universal, and of the gracious and salvific work of the Holy Spirit throughout the fullness of communions that bear testimony to the truth that Jesus is the Christ.

Yet part of the problem here is that American evangelicalism has not developed a significant and well-thought-out ecclesiology that can both inform and sustain its sons and daughters in their own self-understanding as they serve a risen Lord. Beyond some broad-stroke attempts at historiography, evangelicals by and large have not grappled sufficiently with the way in which their communions constitute the church. Stanley Grenz traces this development back to the Puritans, who in their desire for a church composed of visible saints allowed ecclesiology to be "eclipsed by soteriology."[24] Reacting perhaps to the Roman teaching that the institutional church is essentially a mediator to which one must be properly related in order to be redeemed (a not-so-subtle variation of Cyprian's earlier teaching that outside the church there is no salvation), many evangelicals have gone the other way, so to speak, and have minimized the agency of the church to the point that the body of Christ is seen as little more than a voluntary association of believers. Grenz notes this trend and observes:

> Our forebears forsook the view that the church is the dispenser of the grace of God. A person does not come to the church to receive salvation. Rather, a believer—one who has saving grace—joins the Christian community in order to participate with the people of God in the mandate given to the church.[25]

Sensing a need for a more developed and articulate theology of the church, Miroslav Volf (formerly of Fuller Theological Seminary and now a professor at Yale Divinity School) has explored these themes extensively in his masterful work *After Our Likeness: The Church as the Image of the Trinity*. Reflecting key elements of the reign of God, Volf's understanding of the body of Christ embraces both the universality and the transcendence of the Christian faith, as evident in his following definition:

> Every congregation that assembles around the one Jesus Christ as Savior and Lord in order to profess faith in him publicly in pluriform fashion, including through baptism and the Lord's Supper, and which is open to all churches of God and to all human beings, is a church in the full sense of the word, since Christ promised to be present in it through his Spirit as the first fruits of the gathering of the whole people of God in the eschatological reign of God. Such a congregation is holy, catholic, and apostolic.[26]

So understood, the church is not a mother that stands "*over against* individual Christians," as in the Roman definition; rather, "Christians *are* the mother church [which is] the communion of brothers and sisters."[27] Put another way, Volf can affirm, on the one hand, that faith comes to people from "the multidimensional confession of the faith of *others*," a view that embraces far more than a "voluntary association" can allow. Yet on the other hand, he insists that "the church is not the subject of salvific activity with Christ; rather, Christ is the *only* subject of such salvific activity."[28] That is, one does not receive faith *from* the church (since saving faith is a gift of the Most High) but *through* the church.[29] At each step along the way, then, believers are rightly directed not to the church itself but to the Father, through the Son and in the Holy Spirit.

In light of these basic though sometimes obscured truths of the church, Volf maintains that the "minimal requirement" for catholicity is the "*openness* of each church to all other churches."[30] The reality of the Holy Spirit in an abundance of salvific graces and evident in the faithful confession of the lordship of Christ by believers must be fully recognized with honesty and in charity by any communion that bears the name catholic. Volf elaborates:

> A church that closes itself off from other churches of God past or present, or a church that has no desire to turn to these churches in some fashion, is denying its own catholicity. A church cannot reflect the eschatological catholicity of the entire people of God and at the same time isolate itself from other churches.[31]

Even more emphatically, Volf reflects on the work of the Orthodox theologian John Zizioulas, considers the relation between catholicity and Eucharist, and concludes:

> Any church excluding Christians at a given place is not merely a bad church, but rather is no church at all, since a Eucharist to which not all the Christians at a given place might gather would not be merely a morally deficient Eucharist, but rather no Eucharist at all. That is, it could not be the body of him who encompasses *everyone* into "the ultimate criterion."[32]

In light of these observations, it will be important for the evangelical community in the days ahead to come to a better understanding of its own life and mission, its relation to various dialogue partners, and its witness to a rapidly changing, highly relativistic postmodern world by being deeply grounded in the story of the church. Though the evangelical faith is often expressed through parachurch structures, the instruments of a particular, timely, and appropriate witness, its vision must nevertheless be broad enough to embrace a rich understanding of the body of Christ in its most catholic extent, not only in terms of Christian communions of faith different from its own but also with respect to all those believers who have gone before, the church militant mindful and appreciative of the church triumphant. Indeed, failing to recognize that evangelicals, as with others, are members of the body of Christ, without defect or diminishment in terms of redemptive graces, and that they have a rich and long history is to be stripped of one's story, heritage, and even identity. Stripped and naked is no way in which to enter the twenty-first century.

# Doctrine

During the last quarter of the twentieth century, many old-line denominations erupted in heated debates as several outspoken advocates for various forms of heterodoxy championed their "agendas." These innovators came to the conclusion that modern thought was somehow "more relevant," "up-to-date," and "compassionate" than some of the historic truths of the church. From John Shelby Spong to Gene Robinson, the word *tolerance* took on new meanings and was offered as the justification for basically neglecting the church's historic teaching on creation, Christology, the Trinity, and human sexuality. Nevertheless, there is a far greater issue here than simply the assessment of the latest doctrinal fad. How does the church, the evangelical community in particular, preserve the integrity of its own story and yet remain open to the best of human knowledge? How does the community of faith go through time and pass on to its sons and daughters the substance of the faith unalloyed with foreign scripts? Simply put, how can the church be mindful of the past and yet prepared for the future?

## *Scripture, Tradition, and the Preservation of the* Kerygma

Evangelicals and other orthodox believers are certainly not alone in these concerns. In fact, the early church, in recognizing the immense value of the *kerygma,* the proclamation of the gospel, took great care to preserve this treasure intact for subsequent generations. In this context, *kerygma* refers both to the *act* of proclamation as well as to the *content* or message of that same proclamation. This Greek word, as employed in the New Testament, underscores the message of redemption (Mark 16), the power of deliverance (1 Cor. 1:21), as well as the resurrection of Christ (1 Cor. 15:14).[33] Moreover, in the book of Romans, Paul's gospel is presented as nothing less than "the preaching [*kerygma*] of Jesus" (Rom. 16:25).[34] This last usage, then, suggests that the *kerygma* of the early church entailed not only proper *preaching* but also correct *teaching*. In other words, the *kerygma* embraces both the events of the life of Christ (especially his incarnation, crucifixion, and resurrection) and the interpretation of these same events, soteriologically understood, that together make up the deposit of faith entrusted to the church.

Faced with their own contemporary dilemmas (as some leaders in mainline denominations attempt to move the church off its essential story), evangelicals can learn a good deal by considering how the early church protected the genius of the gospel, the *kerygma,* from being dissolved by the teachings of Ebionites, Gnostics, Arians, and other heterodox movements. Though, as Luther pointed out in his sixteenth-century setting, the gospel is best understood as an oral word, a *proclamation* of good news, the early church nevertheless quickly recognized that this same word had to be preserved in a written form lest the vagaries of oral transmission subtly distort or in the worst instances actually change the content of the message. Therefore, the gospel, which originally was proclaimed publicly, often in the open air, was also written down for the sake of subsequent generations in what we now have as the Gospels of Matthew, Mark, Luke, and John. Moreover, the primacy of Scripture as the Word of God, as revelation, was recognized in the church as early as the drafting of the Paschal letter of Athanasius in 367 and more formally at the Synod of Carthage in 397.

The early church preserved its witness not only by the recognition of the canon of Scripture but also by elevating the office of bishop such that it became a locus of order and authority in the face of heretical teaching. Ignatius of Antioch, for example, around the beginning of the second century, cautioned the Christian community as follows: "See that ye all follow the bishop, even as Jesus Christ does the Father, and the presbytery as ye would the apostles; and reverence the deacons, as being the institution of God."[35] In time, Tertullian and Irenaeus developed "rules of faith" that helped to express the basic truths of the *kerygma,* the substance of the apostolic testimony. This conserving movement later resulted in the promulgation of more extensive and formal *creeds* (from the Latin *credo,* "I believe") such as the Apostles', the Athanasian, and the Nicene-Constantinopolitan. Interestingly enough, this last creed is recited today at every Orthodox celebration of the Eucharist, and many Orthodox believers include it as part of their ongoing devotional life,[36] thereby demonstrating continuity with the old catholic church. Though some contemporary evangelicals are noncreedal as a matter of principle, not wanting to detract in the least from the supremacy of Scripture, they nevertheless affirm the basic truths of apostolic Christianity in both thought and practice—often through the singing of hymns.

Though the traditional move of elevating the office of bishop above that of elder, whereby the bishop became a virtual "monarch" in the midst of his flock, resulted in the preeminence of the Roman bishop (initially as "first among equals"), the early church was not only guided to a great degree by the gentle sway of Eastern theological reflection but was also, perhaps more importantly, governed in a conciliar fashion,[37] as noted in a previous chapter. For example, the early ecumenical councils such as Nicea (325), Constantinople (381), Ephesus (431), and Chalcedon (451) preserved the truth of the apostolic testimony *through time* and in the face of such heretical movements as Arianism, Apollinarianism, Pelagianism, and Eutychianism. Reflecting on these developments in the sixteenth century, John Calvin, the leading Reformed theologian, observed:

> Thus those ancient Councils of Nice, Constantinople, the first of Ephesus, Chalcedon, and the like, which were held for refuting errors, we willingly embrace, and reverence as sacred, in so far as relates to doctrines of faith, for they contain nothing but the pure and genuine interpretation of Scripture, which the holy Fathers with spiritual prudence adopted to crush the enemies of religion who had then arisen.[38]

Luther likewise affirmed the value of these early councils, but he also made it clear that they offered no new articles of faith. They offered only those that could already be found in Scripture, a truth affirmed by contemporary evangelicals as well. In other words, the councils made explicit what was implicit in Scripture. Accordingly, the German Reformer declared, "Well then, I think that my conscience is clear when I say that no council (as I said before) is authorized to initiate new articles of faith, because the four principal councils did not do that."[39] Such a judgment underscores the primacy of the *kerygma*, so intimately connected with Scripture, while acknowledging the value of those secondary "traditioning" instruments such as church councils that are integral to the preservation of the apostolic witness.

Beyond the authority of Scripture, bishops, rules of faith, creeds, and councils, the early church appealed to the teaching of several church fathers, both Eastern and Western, to maintain the truth of the "faith once delivered to the saints." Many of these church fathers, ranging from Gregory of Nyssa in the East to Augustine in the West, proved their value to the church essentially as biblical theologians, that is, as careful exegetes and expositors of Scripture. Their authority, therefore, was a derived one, and it remained intact *insofar as* it rightly reflected the light of Scripture. Once again Luther is instructive on this score as he comments on the views of Augustine:

> Furthermore, in the same section of the *Decretum* is St. Augustine's statement from the preface to his book *On the Trinity:* "My dear man, do not follow my writing as you do Holy Scripture. Instead, whatever you find in Holy Scripture that you would not have believed before, believe without doubt. But in my writings you should regard nothing as certain that you were uncertain about before, unless I have proved its truth."[40]

In terms of a proposal made in 1538 to publish his own collected works, Luther cautioned, "I'll never consent to this proposal of yours. I'd rather that all my books would disappear and the Holy Scriptures alone would be read. Otherwise we'll rely on such writings and let the Bible go."[41] Put another way, Scripture as the Word of God holds primacy among secondary elements employed by the church to preserve the substance and integrity of the *kerygma.*

Therefore, this "traditioning" process undertaken by the early church is clearly vital and takes into account that the fellowship of the saints will walk along the path of history as it awaits the return of its Lord. But a distinction must be made between tradition understood as the work of the early church in preserving the *kerygma,* the *revelation* of God (as manifested in Jesus Christ through the Holy Spirit), and subsequent traditions, the various teachings of men and women, that cannot be equated with the Word of God itself. Simply put, the words of Irenaeus, Chrysostom, or Augustine, important as they are, cannot be equated with the words of the apostle John or Paul. Here a *category* difference is at stake, one that is often lost in the Eastern Orthodox notion of tradition, which does not properly distinguish the Word of God from the words of subsequent, all-too-human traditions. However, to the extent that the doctrinal constructions of the later tradition express the truths of Scripture, they must be taken seriously.

## *Tradition and the Distortion of the* Kerygma

Though all the great communions of the orthodox Christian faith (Roman Catholicism, Eastern Orthodoxy, and Protestantism) agree that tradition as *paradosis* in the Pauline sense of having *received* this deposit of faith from the Lord (1 Cor. 11:23; 15:3) plays an important role in the life of the church, Protestants in particular have taken great pains to point out that from the perspective of the New Testament, tradition must also be understood in a second sense. Here the term is conceived in a largely negative way (see Matt. 15:1–9, for example) as a constellation of human ideas and practices that slowly emerges over time and that must be judged by the faithful community, guided by the gracious leading of the Holy Spirit, to be at variance in some important respects with the *kerygma* preserved in Scripture.

Remarkably enough, neither Roman Catholicism nor Eastern Orthodoxy has developed the implications of tradition understood in this second sense to any significant degree. Instead, they conceive tradition, for the most part, in a monological way on par with Scripture, and they therefore do not make the necessary distinction between the *paradosis,* which has been handed down in the

Bible, and the ongoing tradition of the church as it seeks to preserve the deposit of the faith. The *Catechism of the Catholic Church,* for example, states:

> As a result the Church, to whom the transmission and interpretation of Revelation is entrusted, "does not derive her certainty about all revealed truths from the holy Scriptures alone. Both Scripture and Tradition must be accepted and honored with equal sentiments of devotion and reverence."[42]

So understood, the Word of God comes to the church from both the Bible *and* tradition in what looks like a dual-source conception of revelation. For example, the *Catechism* once again declares, "The task of giving an authentic interpretation of the Word of God, *whether in its written form or in the form of Tradition,* has been entrusted to the living, teaching office of the Church alone."[43] Moreover, what gives added force to tradition, beyond its association with the Word of God, and what legitimizes it in the eyes of many is the full weight and authority of the magisterium, the teaching office of the Roman communion with the pope as its monarchical head. In this view, it is supposedly no one less than the Holy Spirit who guides the teaching office of the church and its pontiff throughout history. Cardinal Avery Dulles, representing the Roman view, elaborates:

> Catholics are convinced that the teaching and governing office of the apostles is perpetuated by the hierarchical magisterium, which enjoys the abiding assistance of the Holy Spirit, including its power to authenticate the canon of Scripture and to interpret the inspired text.[44]

This appeal to the Holy Spirit in terms of the ongoing judgments of the magisterium, however, has been questioned by many Protestants in that it may serve, oddly enough, to legitimize in an almost unquestioning and at times naive way *whatever* the magisterium teaches, *whatever* surfaces in the tradition. This would constitute, in the eyes of many, an improper relationship between the Holy Spirit and the *men* who make up this governing body. In other words, such an appeal may function as a "sacred canopy," to use Peter Berger's language, to affirm in every instance the rightness of institutional teaching and practice. Simply put, whatever is, is right. Others suggest, however, that the relationship of the Holy Spirit to the institutional church is far more complex than these judgments can allow. Indeed, room must be made for the roles of instructing, reproving, correcting, and convicting, all of which are commensurate with the larger ministry of the Holy Spirit to the institutional church composed as it is of sinful men and women.

In a similar fashion, Eastern Orthodoxy lacks any developed understanding of tradition in this second and negative sense of *human* customs, practices, and teaching that can distort the clear voice of the Word of God and thereby undermine the power of the *kerygma*. Nor does it have a rich appreciation of the sinfulness, often evident in political machinations and downright error, that can plague the church, composed as it is of both sinners and saints. Instead, Orthodoxy identifies holy tradition, again in a largely monological way, with those things that Christ passed on to his apostles that constitute revelation strictly speaking, *and* with Orthodox liturgy, the writings of the church fathers (Augustine, Chrysostom, and Gregory Nazianzus among them), *and* with the fruit of the seven ecumenical councils—among several other elements.

The weight that is ascribed to the ongoing tradition, as a second source of revelation, equating it with the status of the very words of Christ (and in a way similar to Rome) can be demonstrated by an appeal to the theology and use of icons in Orthodoxy, a church that liturgically celebrates the victory of the iconodules (who favored the use of icons) over the iconoclasts (who did not) each year in an event known more popularly as "the triumph of Orthodoxy." Though the use of icons cannot be traced back as far as the first-century church,[45] by the fourth century their employment was so common that Basil the Great, Cappadocian father, contended that "the honor that was paid to the image passed on to the prototype,"[46] opening up the way for all sorts of popular devotions, appropriate or not. But it was not until the eighth century, when the iconoclastic controversy was raging in the church, that John of Damascus, revered Eastern theologian, offered perhaps the most thorough theological defense of icons as a stimulus to Christian devotion. Eventually, the Seventh Ecumenical Council weighed in on the matter in 787 in what proved to be one of the more contentious and politicized councils ever with the Empress Irene exerting enormous influence on behalf of the iconodules. This assembly, also known as the Second Council of Nicea, declared that icons were not merely sacred art but were a *source* of revelation. That is, the council declared icons to be "of equal benefit as Scripture in presenting the gospel message. What Scripture proclaims by word, the icon proclaims by color."[47]

Though the appeal to the visual and the graphic has come to be quite popular within some corners of the contemporary church, influenced as they are by both tradition and postmodern tastes and sensibilities, many evangelicals have difficulty accepting the claim that icons are of equal benefit as Scripture. Mark Noll and Lyman Kellstedt, for example, representing the tradition, contend, "The turn from word-centered Christianity to image- or experience-centered Christianity does not bode well for nurturing the kind of faith that can be renewed by Scripture and Christian traditions."[48] Indeed, the Bible, which expresses the "still small voice" of the Most High, is an enormously costly book. It comes to the church through salvation history and out of the blood of the prophets and the Messiah himself. Its words, in many instances, were uttered by those who sealed their witness, their testimony, with their very lives. Its teaching, at times clear, distinct, and precise, offers the *promises* of God in a way not only unparalleled in any other form but also least likely to be misunderstood by the very least of all.[49]

Therefore, both Roman Catholicism and Eastern Orthodoxy, precisely because they fail to have a well-developed appreciation of tradition in this second sense, as a compilation of human innovations over time, lack the critical perspective as well as the institutional procedures necessary to discern when tradition has indeed departed from Scripture and the graciousness of the *kerygma* in significant ways. This deficit calls for both honesty and responsible action on the part of these communions and is one of the principal reasons that they should be in ongoing dialogue with Protestantism, evangelicals in particular. Though Eastern Orthodox theologians, for example, may take great comfort in the theological distinction between *latria,* which pertains to the worship given to God alone, and *doulia,* veneration that can properly be given to an icon, these distinctions are lost on the laity, who often commit outright idolatry by transgressing the very commandment of God. It is time, therefore, to take responsibility not simply for the theological subtleties and their *defense,* the delight of theologians, but also for the practice and abuses—especially among the laity.

## The Question of Evangelical Historiography

Because of its dialogue with the Catholic communions of faith, American evangelicalism has come to a greater appreciation of the role of tradition in the life of vibrant Christianity—not, of course, as a second source of revelation but as a vital instrument, a genuine means of grace, to preserve the substance of the *kerygma* throughout the ages. In a real sense, the "family history" of evangelicalism cannot be told apart from the story of the broader church expressed in orthodox belief. Not surprisingly, leading evangelical theologians such as Stanley Grenz and Robert Webber call for a renewed appreciation of the Christian past as relevant not only to contemporary theological understanding but also to evangelical identity. Grenz, for example, observes:

> Our revisioned theology must employ three norms: the biblical message, the theological heritage of the church, and the thought-forms and concerns of contemporary culture. Only in this way can our theology be at one and the same time, and in the best sense of these terms, biblicist, confessional and progressive.[50]

Robert Webber notes the refreshing turn that many younger evangelicals are taking as they face a twenty-first-century postmodern world. These young people are looking back through the theological family album, so to speak, precisely to go forward with integrity, theological propriety, and a sense of renewed purpose. Webber exclaims:

> The truth is that younger evangelicals are conservative in that they believe the road to the future runs through the past. They definitely are not returning to a fifties past. Instead, they are returning to the Wesleyan past, to the Reformers of the sixteenth century, and to the ancient past of the first three centuries of the church, for inspiration and wisdom.[51]

Though many Protestants are often accused of lacking the guiding value of tradition, this judgment is more often than not inaccurate. Indeed, the sixteenth-century Reformers did not repudiate tradition; instead, they called for its reform. Both Luther and Calvin, for example, appealed to the traditional resource of the church fathers, Augustine in particular, as they articulated the doctrinal reforms necessary for their own age. But they did so in a sophisticated and critical way. Calvin, for example, in his *Reply to Sadoleto,* insisted that "Fathers and Councils are of authority only in so far as they accord with the rule of the Word."[52] Many contemporary evangelicals likewise cherish the tradition of the ancient church as having a "*ministerial* rather than a *magisterial* function."[53] In other words, tradition, though clearly important, has a derivative or secondary authority.[54] Along these lines, Donald Bloesch cautions the evangelical community to "resist the temptation to interpret the Bible in the light of classical Christianity rather than vice versa."[55] In other words, a nostalgia for heritage, for all things "past" or "old," may "blind us to errors in the past that have crippled the Christian witness in various periods of church history."[56]

Again, Protestants are not without tradition. The late Reformation scholar Heiko Oberman indicated just how this is so by making a distinction between tradition one (single source) and tradition two (dual source).[57] Protestants participate in hermeneutical communities, distinct ways of interpreting Scripture (which is why they appreciate the early church fathers as biblical exegetes), that are passed on from generation to generation and therefore make up a broad tradition such as Lutheran Pietism, Calvinist Puritanism, or Wesleyan Arminianism. Oberman refers to this first understanding as tradition one because it underscores the truth that tradition is not itself revelatory. The Roman Catholic and Eastern Orthodox views, as should be evident by now, maintain a dual-source view (tradition two, even though Eastern Orthodoxy prefers to subsume both sources of revelation under the one "holy tradition"). Tradition itself is reputedly superintended by the Holy Spirit and is therefore revelatory in no less a sense than Scripture. It is precisely how each communion of faith handles this question of tradition and its relation to Scripture that goes a long way in explaining its respective differences—differences that are found not simply between Roman Catholics and Protestants but also between Roman Catholics and the Eastern Orthodox.[58]

The various understandings of tradition can now be summarized as follows:

- Tradition as *paradosis* in the Pauline sense of passing on the *kerygma* orally before the substance of it is inscribed and recognized as canon.
- Tradition as a second source of revelation guaranteed by an appeal to the ongoing activity of the Holy Spirit in the life of the church.
- Tradition as a divine/human phenomenon that is a genuine means of grace, a valuable secondary instrument, to preserve the substance of the gospel over time. Because of divine grace, it must be taken seriously; because of human sin, it must be reformed in those instances in which it departs from the canon of Scripture.
- Tradition as a hermeneutical community that preserves its readings of Scripture from generation to generation.

## Oden's Agenda for Theology

The two evangelical leaders who have done much to carve out an evangelical historiography, a way of viewing history and the broader tradition of the church, are Thomas Oden and William Abraham, both Wesleyan scholars. However, since Abraham's project of canonical theism is still being expressed (beyond its presentation in his work *Canon and Criterion*) in a number of writings,[59] scholars are still piecing together his position and are therefore yet preoccupied with the task of description (in order to be accurate and fair) rather than with evaluation and usefulness. On the other hand, Oden's "agenda" is already well known, and it offers counsel as to how American evangelicals can appropriate the past, the rich tradition of the church, to prepare for the future.

As one who had a noteworthy theological journey from an accommodation-alist, movement-driven, script-substituting liberalism to the serenity, integrity, and joy of Christian orthodoxy, Oden was finally awakened from his dogmatic slumbers, so to speak, as so many other Christian "new lefties" were, by the stated goals of the abortion-on-demand movement. "The climbing abortion statistics," Oden recounts, "made me movement-weary, movement-demoral-ized."[60] If there ever was a "theophanic" moment when this leading Wesleyan theologian came to a greater appreciation of the history of the church in the power of its tradition, it was when he was surveying his bookshelves to deter-mine which books he needed most: Hippolytus and Nicholas of Cusa among others made the cut, but the twentieth century did not.[61] Though clearly not all contemporary evangelicals would agree with this judgment, many have been impressed by Oden's call for a return to classical, consensual, orthodox Christianity as a way not only to avoid the shoals of drifting liberalism but also to form a sound basis for a vibrant Christian faith.

Oden's call for a return to classical Christianity entails embracing, to use his own words, "the Christian consensus of the first millennium."[62] Why focus on the first one thousand years of Christian history to the exclusion of others? This Drew University theologian explains:

> I am proposing in this agenda a return to the normative self-restrictions that prevailed in Christianity's first millennium. But why the first millennium? Not because this period was intrinsically more exciting than other eras, or its advo-cates more brilliant, but because of its close adherence to apostolic faith and because a more complete ecumenical consensus was achieved in that period than any period since, a consensus that in fact has been subsequently affirmed by Protestant, Catholic, and Orthodox traditions.[63]

Reacting to the "jaded Protestant myth that the earliest Christian commu-nities had the purest doctrine, and that soon afterward the church 'fell' into 'organizational rigidities' and 'catholic distortions,'"[64] Oden calls for a return to the past and for the elimination of theological novelty and innovation—a project that has been embraced by a number of evangelicals as one suitable for the church given the current culturally compromising tendencies of many of the old-line denominations.

Despite the merits of his carefully articulated argument, Oden's celebration of the first one thousand years of church history as well as his understanding of tradition is not without problems, historiographically speaking. First of all, where he finds consensus, other scholars find increasing diversity. In fact, from shortly before the year 500 to the end of the first millennium, the Eastern and

Western traditions of the church increasingly distinguished themselves in some important respects such that *before* the end of this period they had already emerged as separate and distinct traditions. Beyond the broad claims that each communion made for itself in terms of its own catholicity (Rome in 492 with the title of vicar of Christ for the pope; Constantinople in 518 with the title of ecumenical patriarch), the Latin church added the filioque clause ("and from the Son") to the Nicene-Constantinopolitan Creed at the Third Council of Toledo in 589, thus revealing its preference for a dual-source (Father and Son) understanding of the procession of the Holy Spirit. The Eastern church, on the other hand, could only greet such an interpolation as a dangerous *innovation,* one that not only detracted from the Father as the single source of the Holy Spirit but also undermined the *consensual* tradition of the church as expressed in her great ecumenical councils.

Relations between the two traditions deteriorated even further during the ninth century when Photius, the patriarch of Constantinople, publicly denied the procession of the Holy Spirit from the Son and opposed the filioque addition. By 879 the pope and the patriarch had already excommunicated each other, a mutually excluding action that was but a warm-up for the divisiveness and rancor of the great divide that broke out in 1054 otherwise known as the East-West schism or simply the Great Schism. But as was pointed out earlier and is now repeated for emphasis, the old catholic church, truly ecumenical in teaching and embrace, was already long gone before the end of the first millennium. Those Catholic and Eastern Orthodox theologians who criticize the Protestant and evangelical norm of *sola scriptura* (indicating that a plurality of interpretations will likely emerge in the wake of such a *soteriological* standard, and therefore a single tradition, the Catholic Church, is necessary to solve the plural interpretive "problem") must realize that the facts of church history, especially during the period from 500 to 1054, reveal quite clearly that the grounding of catholicity (and orthodoxy) in a single *tradition* ultimately failed. Though such a paradigm had served the church well in the past to fend off Arians and other heretics, by the ninth century it no longer worked in the same way. Henceforth, the Christian church would be composed of a diversity of traditions (in the beginning simply Roman Catholicism and Eastern Orthodoxy, later on, Protestantism as well) that were *orthodox* even though they were *diverse.* Simply put, the ecumenical consensus, of which each of these three great traditions drink, belongs to a much earlier period.

Moreover, the fact that Rome continues to maintain its claims of catholicity and universality, as if its own tradition were ever the center, despite the historical record and to the detriment of the Eastern Orthodox and Protestant communions, reveals a failure to acknowledge in a forthright way its own generous role in the Great Schism. Such an approach also applies a "paradigm of tradition," monologically conceived, that was originally meant to exclude the heterodox but is currently being employed against those who are very much orthodox, evangelical Protestants among them. For example, the *Catechism of the Catholic Church* states:

> The Church knows that she is joined in many ways to the baptized who are honored by the name Christian, but do not profess the [Roman?] Catholic faith in its entirety or have not preserved unity or communion with the successor of Peter. Those "who believe in Christ and have been properly baptized are put in a certain, although imperfect, communion with the [Roman?] Catholic Church."[65]

Are evangelical Protestants, in whom the soteriological efficaciousness of the Holy Spirit is so abundantly evident in a rich panoply of graces, *imperfect* or in some sense *defective* simply because they have not been subsumed under the head of a particular tradition that was not effectively distinguished until well after the year 500? Here "the immune system" of tradition, instead of targeting foreign elements, is now turning against the body itself. It is carrying out a purpose that was never meant to be. It fails to recognize that orthodoxy exists quite capably in other traditions as well.

Second, the virtual canonization of the first millennium is also problematic because the period between 500 and 1000, sometimes referred to as the Dark Ages, was one of doctrinal and liturgical innovation—innovations that detracted from the clarity of the *kerygma* as good news for all people. The period, therefore, warrants a Protestant critique. Indeed, in the wake of many deprecating comments with respect to women made by such church fathers as Ambrose, Augustine, and Jerome, even the office of deaconess disappeared throughout much of Europe during the sixth century.[66] But what the church took with one hand it apparently gave with the other. As the ministerial roles of women were further curtailed, the status of Mary, the mother of Jesus, was virtually idolized with doctrine after doctrine. Taking its cues in some sense from the church fathers as well as the broader culture, the council at Constantinople in 553 affirmed the perpetual virginity of Mary, though such a teaching contradicted Scripture. Beyond this, the doctrine of the bodily assumption of Mary into heaven, that the mother of Christ perhaps never died, made its way into church doctrine around the same time, though this teaching was not formally declared dogma until much later. The following century the notion that Mary was conceived immaculately, apart from original sin, was likewise judged to be the proper conclusion of the patristic teaching that the mother of Christ was the new Eve.[67]

Beyond this incipient and growing Mariology, well grounded in tradition, the liturgical practice of holding private Masses in which only the priest was present and not the *communion* of the saints began to emerge in the monasteries of northern Europe during the eighth century.[68] This innovation held consequence for how the Mass (as well as the gospel itself) was theologically understood, since it demonstrated quite graphically that the priest alone was sufficient "to have church." By the following century, priests were saying several private Masses a day—a practice that Luther himself rightly criticized much later. Also in the eighth century, communion in both kinds (both bread and wine) began to disappear such that the laity received only the bread. By the end of this period, at the turn of the millennium, then, there were more than enough reasons for reform. The first thousand years do not, therefore, unproblematically constitute the basis for consensus, especially when Protestants are considered a vital part of the body of Christ.

Though Oden's agenda clearly has its merits in terms of its preservation of orthodoxy and its focus on institutional maintenance, a different historiography can be offered that is more appropriate for evangelical Protestants in terms of their historic witness as a reforming movement within the broader catholic church. The tradition in the early church not only eventually broke up into a plurality of orthodox traditions, as noted earlier, but also gathered up many elements that over time helped to obscure the clear teaching of the gospel itself. Therefore, the proper response to Protestant theological liberalism is neither the tradition of Roman Catholicism nor Eastern Orthodoxy (and I am not maintaining that Oden is suggesting this) but evangelical Protestantism itself, a response that fully takes into account the clarity and wisdom of the Reformation.

## *A Modest Proposal*

In light of the foregoing, a historiography can be offered that can help contemporary evangelicals chart their way toward the future by being mindful of the past and appreciative of tradition properly understood and in which each of the three great communions of Eastern Orthodoxy, Roman Catholicism, and Protestantism can find a place at the table to affirm together the substance of the Christian faith. No period of the church is more suited for this ecumenical task than its first five centuries, which embraced the four great ecumenical councils (Nicea, Constantinople, Ephesus, and Chalcedon), three creeds (Apostles', Nicene, and Athanasian), two testaments (both Old and New), and one canon (Scripture as *the* soteriological norm). This, however, is by no means a new proposal. To be sure, such an understanding of how the orthodoxy of the church can be best sustained throughout the ages and in a way that is genuinely inclusive was evident in the writings of the Anglican Caroline divine Lancelot Andrews, who among other things was well known for his balance and good judgment.

Ecumenical evangelicals, however, recognize that this "Anglican" approach will not solve the "problem" of the diversity of orthodox traditions, but it nevertheless constitutes an important first step for ongoing dialogue. Again, these same evangelical leaders realize that each of the three great communions of the body of Christ will quite naturally bring its own understanding of tradition (and its relation to Scripture) to the table: Rome, a generous role for the magisterium and the pope; Eastern Orthodoxy, a single holy tradition that embraces both Scripture and a host of traditions, customs, and practices; Protestantism, a distinction between Scripture as revelation and the ongoing tradition of the church—especially valuable when critically understood. But what will *not* constitute a part of the consensus are many of the doctrinal and liturgical traditions that arose after the year 500.[69] Put another way, though the understanding of the Lord's Supper in terms of a real presence was clearly evident in the early church, the developed doctrine of transubstantiation was not; though icons were in use during this consensual period, a full-blown iconography was not. Here Protestantism appears to be at an advantage because its chief emphasis, the doctrine of justification by faith alone, was already well known in the early church, as Oden himself has so ably argued.[70] This emphasis in the sixteenth century, therefore, constitutes not a doctrinal development or innovation but a reform.[71]

Moreover, these different understandings of tradition by the three great communions of faith will also affect how the consensus itself is conceived. The Latin and Eastern traditions, for example, believe that the truth of the Christology of the early church was established by the *consensus* of church authority and councils. Protestants, on the other hand, though no less orthodox, believe that the truthfulness of this Christology was not grounded or substantiated by the consensual tradition itself (which is another way of making the judgment of sinful men and women ultimately normative) but was *recognized* by this same tradition. In short, the consensus *perceives* the truth, but it does not *establish* the truth. For many Protestants, the church's Christology is true precisely because it faithfully reflects the teaching of Scripture. The current proposal, then, for the sake of conversation, can embrace all these understandings of the consensus that each tradition brings to the table.

Can the universal church, then, be open, generous, and catholic enough to embrace this early consensus and yet allow for the diversity of traditions that eventually flowed from it? Will evangelical Protestants, for example, be willing to overcome their anti-Catholicism and their dislike of Eastern Orthodoxy, supposedly as an engine for narrow ethnicity and superstitious practice, in order to break bread with these traditions that affirm Scripture, the four great ecumenical councils, and the three creeds? Are Rome and Constantinople willing to do the same? Can the recognition of one Lord, one faith, and one baptism compel Christians of whatever stripe to live in holy love, breaking bread together as Christ commanded? Or have all traditions in some sense made their own subsequent history, beyond the early consensus, *the* deciding factor? Can one be a *real Christian* in recognizing and affirming the truths of the first five centuries, or is there yet a lack, an imperfection, that must be rectified by the subsequent traditions? Are the canon of Scripture, the creeds, and the early councils insufficient for the maintenance of orthodoxy? If so, then what does such a judgment say about the faith and life of the early church for nearly half a millennium?

On the other hand, one of the strengths of this proposal is not only its ecumenical promise but also its honesty. It recognizes, for example, in a forthright way, that the diversity of the three great orthodox traditions will likely continue until the Lord comes. In the interim, Protestant evangelicals will no doubt continue their reforming activities and urge the other communions to reappropriate the teaching of Scripture, as *the* sacred norm, and the first five centuries of the old catholic church, especially in terms of the doctrine of justification by grace through faith alone, a teaching that, though present in the early church, was eventually obscured by layer upon layer of medieval tradition and practice. Roman Catholicism, for its part, will continue to offer its own sacerdotal understanding of redemption, that the church and her full array of priests and sacramental life, especially the Eucharist, understood in terms of transubstantiation, are the very requisites of redemption. Eastern Orthodoxy, again out of resources drawn from the later tradition, in this case the council of 787, will continue to maintain that the gospel is presented as well through holy tradition, icons in particular, as through Scripture.

With all these ongoing differences, tension and even conflict will likely emerge. Nevertheless, Protestants will be free to highlight the second great creedal epoch of the church, the sixteenth century, and thereby underscore what value it holds in reforming the subsequent tradition of the church, in the name of gospel clarity, beyond the early consensus. In a similar fashion, Rome and Eastern Orthodoxy will likely offer a vigorous defense of the appropriateness of that very same tradition. The point, however, is that fellowship should not be broken nor the universal love of God manifested in Christ Jesus put aside, since each of these communions is already orthodox in several key respects in affirming the truth of Scripture, the early creeds, and the four great councils.

This irenic proposal, however, is also being brought forth for a second reason, not simply for its ecumenical value but also for its *didactic* and *soteriological* worth, especially for contemporary evangelicals. In other words, in the welter of voices that make up the postmodern mix of the twenty-first century, how will evangelicals stay the course and avoid the sirens of doctrinal dissolution? How will they maintain integrity and orthodoxy in the face of so many temptations for compromise—some suggested by the culture, some by a co-opted popular Christianity itself? Though many evangelicals belong to denominations that have articles, confessions, or creeds as a part of their doctrinal standards, some do not. What then of those free churches that champion the slogan "No creed but the Bible"? Will they be prepared for all that is coming in the days ahead? What of those evangelicals who spend much of their time in parachurch structures or in fellowships in which the words of the ancient church are displaced by wave after wave of choruses whose language never goes much beyond "I, me, mine" and the like? Just what will it take to get to "we" in the broadest sense possible?

As Robert Webber has so capably expressed, the evangelical community needs nothing less than an "ancient-future faith"[72] in order to be ecumenically responsible, theologically integrated, and prepared for the future. To be sure, the tradition of the early church can encourage and empower the present community of believers to remain faithful from age to age such that it will ever offer a living witness: mindful of the past and yet prepared for the future; informed by sound doctrine and yet ecumenically open; firm in its commitments and yet loving in its embrace.

# Conclusion

# The Evangelical Moment

The Greek language, rich in so many ways, has a number of words for the English term *time. Chronos,* for example, a term used by the ancient Athenians, has found its way into the modern English words *chronological* and *chronology,* which both depict clock time, that is, the clicking of seconds as time passes. But the Greeks had another word for time, *kairos,* and it is far more intriguing. Subtle in many respects, this term is not as easily translated into English, though a rough equivalent perhaps can be found in the word *season,* the time when all the necessary elements are finally in place. It is the kind of time a man discerns when he asks a woman to marry him. It is the time when a formerly agnostic woman steps forward to be baptized because she is responding to the healing love of God. It is the time when people who have been there all along (sometimes overlooked, at other times simply taken for granted) finally emerge as respected leaders of the community precisely because they have patiently borne obscurity, unreasonable criticism, suffering, and sometimes even abuse.

With this distinction in place, the "evangelical moment" we celebrate is not one of chronological time but of kairotic time.[1] Due to the flow of history, the maturation of evangelicals, and a few providential serendipities, most of the required elements are currently in place for a considerable leadership role for this movement throughout the twenty-first century. Indeed, many astute observers of culture and religion have not only marked this change of season but actually welcomed it. As in the words of the ambassadors of Mordecai to

Esther, spoken so long ago, American evangelicalism has been richly prepared and carefully chosen "for such a time as this" (Esther 4:14).

Growing more confident in its identity as a movement related to so many others for the sake of gospel witness, American evangelicalism, especially in terms of some of its key leaders, is currently reaching out in a generous way to bring understanding and healing where before there was none. For example, key leaders such as Thomas Oden, Stanley Grenz, William Abraham, Clark Pinnock, and Roger Olson, among many others, are breaking down the barriers of that great divide that hitherto existed between Reformed and Wesleyan evangelicals. With this important and necessary work comes the frank recognition that evangelicalism can, on the one hand, be quite diverse and yet, on the other hand, be wonderfully united. The two, after all, should go hand in hand in this transdenominational and engaging phenomenon. To be sure, these leaders seek to come together in the empowering love of Christ as they find common cause in ministering to a nation that is becoming increasingly heedless in its secularism and is therefore desperately in need of the grace of Jesus Christ.

Beyond its own household, evangelicals will continue to reach out to all those who bear the name of Christ and are marked in a characteristic way by the grace of the gospel. Accordingly, Roman Catholics and the Eastern Orthodox will remain important dialogue partners in the days ahead, and the evangelical community, composed as it is of Calvinists, Wesleyans, Pentecostals, and others, has much to learn from these ancient traditions, especially in terms of church order and unity, the dignity of ordained ministry, the beauty of corporate worship and liturgy, and the value of tradition, properly understood. In this relationship, evangelicals will naturally underscore some of the key elements of their historic witness, namely, the normative value of Scripture, the cruciality of the atoning work of Christ, the necessity of conversion for all, and the imperative of evangelism. But together, evangelicals, Roman Catholics, and Eastern Orthodox can stand up today for the rights of all God's children, even the very least of all. United they can enter the public arena and join hands so that the nation will come to know that Christians, of whatever community or tradition, are not second-class citizens. Joining hands, these great traditions can undertake the moral reforms necessary in the area of human sexuality for the sake of purity, beauty, and holiness. These same traditions can come together yet again, pool their resources, and minister to the poor, the neediest of all, in a way that not only honors the dignity and humanity of the marginalized but also brings great glory to a holy and loving God.

Intellectually equipped and socially engaged, the evangelical community now exudes a gracious confidence that has emerged out of earlier struggles, scars, and even a few defeats. With this confidence comes a new and refreshing openness, and far less defensiveness, especially in terms of the roles and dignity of women. Critical evangelical leaders are now setting the pace and leaving the sacramental traditions behind in some of the latter's more parochial understandings of women. Though not without opposition within their own ranks, key evangelical leaders are reaching out to women as never before. They are joining hands, uniting in song, and suffering in sacrificial service. Together evangelical men and women are becoming stronger, speaking more often with one voice, and are thereby demonstrating to the world the good news of the gospel, which is nothing less than the power of God unto salvation—a salvation that is rich, full, and satisfying.

In a similar fashion, it is only as American evangelicalism forgets itself and faces outward toward the broader church and the world in redemptive mission that it will truly find its lasting purpose and meaning. Set apart, evangelicalism runs the risk of becoming narrow, insular, and tribal, functioning more like a fraternity or a sorority, with sharp in-group/out-group distinctions and in which even fellow Christians are held at a distance, not included—much less embraced—in the circles of love. If it goes down this path, if it becomes preoccupied with the importance of separation for the sake of holiness or identity to the exclusion of sacrificial service for the sake of others, evangelicalism may lose its very soul. Great balance, along with wisdom and careful discernment, then, are needed at every step along the way. This movement of God's children has been called into being not for the sake of itself but for others. Without service, evangelicalism is empty; without mission, it is dead; and without love for others, especially the poor, it is lost.

Though many of the elements of the evangelical moment are in place, like a table well set, the question remains, Will there be a feast? Put another way, will the promise of a great and generous supper, marked by animated conversations, laughter, and joy, finally become a reality? One can at least wonder, for though evangelicalism has been chastened by its history, corrected in its dialogues with others, and equipped with significant intellectual, spiritual, and moral resources, all of this, as significant as it is, remains insufficient to meet the baffling challenges of a hurting world, oppressed in all sorts of ways. But just what more could possibly be lacking?

The answer once again can be found in Jesus Christ, who though he never wrote a book or traveled more than a few hundred miles from his home nevertheless touched human history in a way that no one else has—or ever will. The ancient church comprehended this considerable wisdom as well as the importance of the imitation of Christ (*imatio Christi*) in a way that was marked by a number of graces: courage, patient endurance, and the acceptance of suffering among them. Accordingly, the evangelical moment is present as both a promise and a gift, not in a triumphalistic, naive, or unrealistic way, as if cultural realignments, growing maturity, or institutional resources were simply enough, or as if the flowering of the movement itself would not be met by strong, determined, and unending opposition both within and outside the church. On the contrary, the evangelical moment is present principally by way of promise—a promise that will be realized, slowly and painfully, no doubt with setbacks along the way, as its people, marked by the grace of God and seasoned by love, follow the One who was despised, rejected, and richly acquainted with grief: "Remember the word that I said to you, 'A slave is not greater than his master.' If they persecuted me, they will also persecute you; if they kept my word, they will keep yours also" (John 15:20). There can be no other path to evangelical fulfillment; it can only come at great cost.

Therefore, the smooth and easy "success" stories that bear no burden, pay no price, and surface from time to time in evangelical pulpits represent a confusion of a well-worked cultural script masquerading as the church's own narrative. Congregations draped in their Sunday best are too often cosseted with the belief that they will not have to bear suffering in the days ahead, that their purpose can be achieved without much sacrifice or without wrenching, heartbreaking loss. Suffering, so it goes, is always for those *others*—a new twist on the ill-advised counsel of Job's friends now coming to a pulpit near you with a vengeance. It is difficult to imagine, however, a quicker and more effective way to stifle the evangelical moment, to put the church to sleep, and to induce a genuine spiritual stupor than to tell the community that it will not have to suffer, that its hopes can be realized easily and with comfortable, programmatic, and cushy success. The church militant, on the other hand, throughout her rich history has been spattered with the blood of persecution, attacked both physically and spiritually, and labeled with some of the most despicable epithets ever imagined—and yet it has endured. Let the evangelical community, then, not deceive itself into thinking that business and marketing strategies, the sirens of technological fixes, savvy communication prowess, or growing financial resources will usher in the kingdom of God, which is so bitterly opposed by nothing less than the principalities and powers themselves. The historical record is abundantly clear: The church of Jesus Christ lives by and through suffering. As with the Master so with the servant.

Therefore, only through humble obedience to the grace of God and with a hearty courage will the evangelical moment be realized, the kind of courage that realistically faces both internal fears and external dangers and resolutely moves forward. Only with patient endurance marked by fortitude will the evangelical moment break forth as its sons and daughters, young and old, rich and poor bear the painful cost of a faithful witness to the goodness, truth, and beauty that is Jesus Christ. And only with suffering, wide and deep, emulating a crucified Lord, will the evangelical moment blossom as it conquers all carnal means, not a conquering *over*, as Moses slew the Egyptian, but a conquering *through* humble sacrificial love, as the leader of the Hebrews himself eventually submitted to the One who alone can set the captives free. Empowered by faith, ennobled by hope, and invigorated by the love of God so richly manifested in Jesus Christ, the American evangelical community has already picked up the mantle of leadership and is poised for all that lies ahead. This is the evangelical moment. This is the evangelical promise.

# Notes

## Introduction

1. Jay Tolson, "The New Oldtime Religion," *U.S. News & World Report* 135, no. 20 (December 8, 2003): 38.

2. Ibid.

3. John Naisbitt and Patricia Aburdene, *Megatrends 2000: Ten New Directions for the 1990s* (New York: William Morrow, 1990), 278.

4. George Gallup Jr. and D. Michael Lindsay, *Surveying the Religious Landscape: Trends in U.S. Beliefs* (Harrisburg, Pa.: Morehouse, 1999), 40.

5. Colleen Carroll, *The New Faithful: Why Young Adults Are Embracing Christian Orthodoxy* (Chicago: Loyola, 2002), 83.

6. Christian Smith, *American Evangelicalism: Embattled and Thriving* (Chicago: University of Chicago Press, 1998), xi.

7. Christian Smith, *Christian America? What Evangelicals Really Want* (Berkeley: University of California Press, 2000), 10.

8. David Limbaugh, *Persecution: How Liberals Are Waging War against Christianity* (Washington, D.C.: Regnery Publishing, 2003), 111.

9. Smith, *Christian America?* 195.

10. Mark A. Noll, *American Evangelical Christianity* (Malden, Mass.: Blackwell, 2001), 14.

11. Ibid.

12. Ralph Reed, *Active Faith: How Christians Are Changing the Soul of American Politics* (New York: Free Press, 1996), 196.

13. John Telford, ed., *The Letters of John Wesley, A.M.,* 8 vols. (London: Epworth, 1931), 4:298.

## Chapter 1

1. James Davison Hunter, *Evangelicalism: The Coming Generation* (Chicago: University of Chicago Press, 1987), 6.

2. George M. Marsden, *Understanding Fundamentalism and Evangelicalism* (Grand Rapids: Eerdmans, 1991), 5. See also Martin Wellings, "What Is an Evangelical?" *Epworth Review* 21, no. 3 (September 1994): 45–53. Wellings maintains that there are roughly three hundred million evangelicals worldwide.

3. William J. Abraham, *The Coming Great Revival* (San Francisco: Harper & Row, 1984), 73; and Robert K. Johnston, "American Evangelicalism: An Extended Family," in *The Variety of American Evangelicalism,* ed. Donald W. Dayton and Robert K. Johnston, 252–72 (Downers Grove, Ill.: InterVarsity, 1991).

4. Timothy L. Smith, "The Evangelical Kaleidoscope and the Call to Unity," *Christian Scholar's Review* 15, no. 2 (1986): 128.

5. Jon R. Stone, *On the Boundaries of American Evangelicalism: The Postwar Evangelical Coalition* (New York: St. Martin's Press, 1997).

6. See Johnston, "American Evangelicalism," 255, 258.

7. Wellings, "What Is an Evangelical?" 47.

8. Donald Dayton, "Some Doubts about the Usefulness of the Category 'Evangelical,'" in *Variety of American Evangelicalism,* 245.

9. Ibid. Moreover, Dayton does not believe that one can establish a "family resemblance" that can tie all the diverse movements together.

10. Cf. Kenneth J. Collins, "Children of Neglect: American Methodist Evangelicals," *Christian Scholar's Review* 20, no. 1 (1990): 7–16.

11. Interestingly enough, these same four themes are reflected in Harold John Ockenga's presidential address on the occasion of the organization of the National Association of Evangelicals held at the LaSalle Hotel in Chicago. Cf. Garth M. Rosell, ed., *The Evangelical Landscape: Essays on the American Evangelical Tradition* (Grand Rapids: Baker, 1996), 7–12.

12. Donald G. Bloesch, *The Future of Evangelical Christianity* (Garden City, N.Y.: Doubleday, 1983), 12. And Robert Webber contends that the word *evangelical* can refer to "anyone who believes in the message that the death and resurrection of Jesus Christ is the good news of the forgiveness of sin, the inauguration of a new humanity" (Robert E. Webber, *Common Roots: A Call to Evangelical Maturity* [Grand Rapids: Zondervan, 1978], 33).

13. George Gallup Jr. and Jim Castelli, *The People's Religion: American Faith in the '90s* (New York: Macmillan, 1989), 93. Ronald Nash points out that "as many as four or five million Roman Catholics regard themselves as evangelical" (Ronald H. Nash, *Evangelicals in America: Who They Are, What They Believe* [Nashville: Abingdon, 1987], 21).

14. Along these lines, William Abraham maintains that "evangelicals are extremely reluctant to acknowledge the positive significance of tradition in theology and piety" (Abraham, *Coming Great Revival,* 1).

15. Martin Luther, *Luther's Works,* vol. 32, *Career of the Reformer II,* ed. Jaroslav Jan Pelikan, Hilton C. Oswald, and Helmut T. Lehmann (Philadelphia: Fortress, 1999), 112.

16. Mark Ellingsen, "Lutheranism," in *Variety of American Evangelicalism,* 222. Moreover, Ellingsen goes on to claim that "no North American Lutheran denomination . . . identifies with the evangelical family usually associated with the National Association of Evangelicals." Thus, when American Lutheran churches, following German and Scandinavian practice, place the word *evangelical* in their name, the substance of that designation should be understood in terms of the

Reformation of the sixteenth century. Cf. James Leo Garrett Jr., E. Glenn Hinson, and James E. Tull, *Are Southern Baptists Evangelicals?* (Macon, Ga.: Mercer University Press, 1983), 43.

17. For more on this recruitment of John Calvin, see T. H. L. Parker, *John Calvin: A Biography* (Philadelphia: Westminster, 1975), 52–53.

18. For an excellent study of the Anabaptist Reformation, see George Hunston Williams, *The Radical Reformation* (Philadelphia: Westminster, 1962). For Luther's relation to this movement, see W. R. Estep, ed., *The Reformation: Luther, the Anabaptist* (Nashville: Broadman, 1979); for Calvin's, see Willem Balke, *Calvin and the Anabaptist Radicals* (Grand Rapids: Eerdmans, 1981).

19. C. Norman Kraus, "Evangelicalism: A Mennonite Critique," in *Variety of American Evangelicalism*, 197.

20. Kenneth Hylson-Smith, *Christianity in England from Roman Times to the Reformation*, vol. 3, *From 1384–1558* (London: SCM, 2001), 198–235.

21. Diarmaid Macculloch, *The Boy King: Edward VI and the Protestant Reformation* (New York: Palgrave, 1999), 57–104.

22. Mark A. Noll, "The Evangelical Mind," in *The Evangelical Landscape*, ed. Garth M. Rosell (Grand Rapids: Baker, 1996), 13.

23. Johnston, "American Evangelicalism," 254.

24. Philip Jacob Spener, *Pia Desideria*, ed. Theodore G. Tappert (Philadelphia: Fortress, 1964), 87–122. It is remarkable, given the value of this work, that it did not appear in an English edition until this translation by Tappert in 1964! This work, important in many respects, can help to undermine some of the stereotypes of Pietism that continue to emerge even today, especially the charge of "individualism."

25. Gary R. Sattler, *God's Glory, Neighbor's Good* (Chicago: Covenant Press, 1982), 19.

26. K. James Stein, *Philipp Jakob Spener* (Chicago: Covenant Press, 1986), 132. The establishment of the brewery is interesting and indicates that the Pietists, like the evangelical Wesley, were *not* teetotalers. Both Francke and Wesley enjoyed alcohol; both, however, warned against the sin of drunkenness.

27. I am dependent on the distinction that William McLoughlin makes between awakenings and revivals, the former associated with "periods of cultural revitalization," the latter with "individual conversion." See William G. McLoughlin, *Revivals, Awakenings, and Reform* (Chicago: University of Chicago Press, 1978), xiii.

28. Reginald W. Ward and Richard P. Heitzenrater, eds., *The Works of John Wesley*, vol. 19, *Journals and Diaries II* (Nashville: Abingdon, 1988), 46.

29. Ibid. It is clear that Wesley's "churchmanship" was changing at this point. In time he would "violate parish boundaries" in his field preaching, a practice that roiled many of the Anglican clergy. For the best treatment of Wesley's relationship with the Church of England, see Frank Baker, *John Wesley and the Church of England* (Nashville: Abingdon, 1970).

30. Ward and Heitzenrater, *Works of John Wesley*, vol. 19, 46.

31. Frank Baker, ed., *The Works of John Wesley*, vol. 25, *The Letters* (New York: Oxford University Press, 1982), 616.

32. Perry Miller, *The Life of the Mind in America* (New York: Harcourt, Brace & World, 1965), 6.

33. Winthrop S. Hudson, *Religion in America: An Historical Account of the Development of American Religious Life* (New York: Charles Scribner's Sons, 1973), 143–44.

34. Mark A. Noll, "The Swelling Tide of Revivalism," in *Eerdmans' Handbook to Christianity in America*, ed. Mark A. Noll, Nathan O. Hatch, George M. Marsden, David F. Wells, and John D. Woodbridge (Grand Rapids: Eerdmans, 1983), 178.

35. Ibid., 177.

36. Cf. Michael Scott Horton, *Made in America: The Shaping of Modern American Evangelicalism* (Grand Rapids: Baker, 1991), 26–32. Horton, however, fails to distinguish "Wesleyan Arminianism" present in nineteenth-century America, with some modifications from its English roots, from the Continental Arminianism associated with the Synod of Dort.

37. Kenneth J. Collins, *John Wesley: A Theological Journey* (Nashville: Abingdon, 2003), 33, 114.

38. Gerald R. Cragg, ed., *The Works of John Wesley*, vol. 11, *The Appeals to Men of Reason and Religion* (New York: Oxford University Press, 1975), 47–48.

39. John Telford, ed., *The Letters of John Wesley, A.M.*, 8 vols. (London: Epworth, 1931), 6:287.

40. For a well-developed argument of the influence of American democracy on the churches, especially Protestant, see Nathan O. Hatch, *The Democratization of American Christianity* (New Haven: Yale University Press, 1989).

41. Cf. Charles G. Finney, *Lectures on Systematic Theology* (New York: D. H. Doran, 1878); and Asa Mahan, *The Baptism of the Holy Ghost* (Noblesville, Ind.: Newby Book Room, 1972).

42. Cheryl Johns contends that the Holiness and Pentecostal traditions are often marginalized even within broader American evangelicalism and have the dubious distinction of being "the 'embarrassing relatives'" (Cheryl Bridges Johns, "Partners in Scandal: Wesleyan and Pentecostal Scholarship," *Pneuma* 21, no. 2 [Fall 1999]: 183–97).

43. Donald W. Dayton, *The Theological Roots of Pentecostalism* (Grand Rapids: Francis Asbury Press, 1987), 18. Dayton indicates that the "exception" related to article 5, which reads as follows: "We believe that the full gospel includes holiness of heart and life, healing for the body and baptism in the Holy Spirit with the initial evidence of speaking in other tongues as the Spirit gives utterance."

44. Gallup and Castelli, *People's Religion*, 126–27. Gallup points out that roughly 4 percent of Roman Catholics call themselves charismatics. "While this percentage is low," he observes, "given the size of the Catholic population—28 percent of all Americans—this translates into approximately 2.5 million people" (126).

45. Hudson, *Religion in America*, 153.

46. Timothy P. Weber, "Premillennialism and the Branches of Evangelicalism," in *Variety of American Evangelicalism*, 5–21.

47. Martin E. Marty, "Tensions within Contemporary Evangelicalism: A Critical Appraisal," in *The Evangelicals: What They Believe, Who They Are, Where They Are Changing*, ed. David F. Wells and John D. Woodbridge (Nashville: Abingdon, 1975), 171–72.

48. Marsden, *Understanding Fundamentalism and Evangelicalism*, 38.

49. David Moberg, *The Great Reversal: Evangelism versus Social Concern* (New York: J. B. Lippincott, 1972), 30.

50. R. A. Torrey and A. C. Dixon, eds., *The Fundamentals: A Testimony to the Truth*, 4 vols. (Grand Rapids: Baker, 1980).

51. Cf. Marsden, *Understanding Fundamentalism and Evangelicalism*, 57.

52. J. Gresham Machen, *Christianity and Liberalism* (Grand Rapids: Eerdmans, 1990). Machen also contends that the "root of the movement" of theological liberalism consists in its

naturalism, "that is, in the denial of any entrance of the creative power of God (as distinguished from the ordinary course of nature)" (2).

53. Ernest Sandeen makes the case that premillennial dispensationalism, in conjunction with the theology developed at Princeton Seminary by Hodge and Warfield, goes a long way in explaining the reality of American fundamentalism. See Ernest R. Sandeen, *The Roots of Fundamentalism* (Grand Rapids: Baker, 1978).

54. Mark Ellingsen, *The Evangelical Movement: Growth, Impact, Controversy, Dialog* (Minneapolis: Augsburg, 1988), 87. Ellingsen also would like to include the Disciples of Christ, though I think the evidence for fundamentalism is less clear here and can be otherwise explained. Moreover, Marsden notes that "the Northern Baptist Convention and the (northern) Presbyterian Church in the U.S.A. were the centers of denominational controversy" (Marsden, *Understanding Fundamentalism and Evangelicalism*, 56).

55. Marsden, *Understanding Fundamentalism and Evangelicalism*, 70. See also Paul Bassett, "The Fundamentalist Leavening of the Holiness Movement: 1914–1940," *Wesleyan Theological Journal* 13 (Spring 1978): 65–91.

56. The founding of the National Association of Evangelicals is often described in terms of the meeting held in 1942 in St. Louis at the Hotel Coronado. Cf. Christian Smith, *American Evangelicalism: Embattled and Thriving* (Chicago: University of Chicago Press, 1998), 11.

57. George Marsden maintains that "an American fundamentalist is an evangelical who is militant in opposition to liberal theology in the churches and to changes in cultural values or mores" (Marsden, *Understanding Fundamentalism and Evangelicalism*, 1).

58. Donald Dayton claims that one-third of the member denominations of the National Association of Evangelicals are "holiness," and another third are "pentecostal." See Donald W. Dayton, "Yet Another Layer of the Onion: Or Opening the Ecumenical Door to Let the Riffraff In," *Ecumenical Review* 40 (January 1988): 99.

59. Abraham, *Coming Great Revival*, 17. Leonard Sweet points out the irony entailed as the neoevangelicals separated themselves from the fundamentalist separatists. See Leonard I. Sweet, "Wise as Serpents, Innocent as Doves: The New Evangelical Historiography," *Journal of the American Academy of Religion* 56, no. 3 (1988): 397–416.

60. Stone, *On the Boundaries of American Evangelicalism*, 130.

61. Carl F. H. Henry, *The Uneasy Conscience of Modern Fundamentalism* (Grand Rapids: Eerdmans, 1947).

62. Cf. Donald W. Dayton, *Discovering an Evangelical Heritage* (New York: Harper & Row, 1976).

63. Abraham, *Coming Great Revival*, 35, 52.

64. Marsden, *Understanding Fundamentalism and Evangelicalism*, 46.

65. William H. Bentley, "Bible Believers in the Black Community," in *Evangelicals*, 110.

66. Ibid., 111.

67. Cf. Gallup and Castelli, *People's Religion*, 30–42; and Hunter, *Evangelicalism*, 6.

68. Cf. Edward J. Larson, *Summer for the Gods: The Scopes Trial and America's Continuing Debate over Science and Religion* (New York: Basic Books, 1997), 239–42.

69. Bernard Goldberg, *Bias: A CBS Insider Exposes How the Media Distort the News* (Washington, D.C.: Regnery Publishing, 2002), 127.

## Chapter 2

1. This statement has been culled from the website of the Evangelical Theological Society. See http://www.etsjets.org.

2. See also the argument found in William J. Abraham, *The Coming Great Revival* (San Francisco: Harper & Row, 1984), 33–34. I am not claiming that the substance of an inerrant view cannot be found prior to the nineteenth century. I am making only the more modest claim that this setting is key to understanding the contemporary formulations of this teaching.

3. George M. Marsden, *The Soul of the American University* (New York: Oxford University Press, 1994), 92.

4. Charles Hodge, "Systematic Theology," in *Theology in America: The Major Protestant Voices from Puritanism to Neo-Orthodoxy*, ed. Sydney E. Ahlstrom (Indianapolis: Bobbs-Merrill Educational Publishing, 1967), 257.

5. Benjamin Breckinridge Warfield, Samuel G. Craig, and Cornelius Van Til, *The Inspiration and Authority of the Bible* (Philadelphia: Presbyterian & Reformed, 1948). Jack Rogers and Donald McKim contend that when science no longer supported Hodge's and Warfield's Scottish realist presuppositions, these theologians then argued, in a deductive way, from their preestablished doctrine rather than from empirical data. See Jack B. Rogers and Donald K. McKim, *The Authority and Interpretation of the Bible* (San Francisco: Harper & Row, 1979), 347–61.

6. Francis Turretin, George Musgrave Giger, and James T. Dennison, *Institutes of Elenctic Theology* (Phillipsburg, N.J.: Presbyterian & Reformed, 1992).

7. Ernest R. Sandeen, *The Roots of Fundamentalism: British and American Millenarianism, 1800–1930* (Grand Rapids: Baker, 1978), 103–31.

8. Stanley J. Grenz, *Renewing the Center: Evangelical Theology in a Post-theological Era* (Grand Rapids: Baker, 2000), 80.

9. R. A. Torrey and A. C. Dixon, eds., *The Fundamentals: A Testimony to the Truth*, 4 vols. (Grand Rapids: Baker, 1980).

10. J. I. Packer, *Fundamentalism and the Word of God* (Grand Rapids: Eerdmans, 1980), 19. Mark Noll refers to this work as "the most intelligent reassertion of biblical inerrancy since Warfield and Hodge" (Mark A. Noll, *Between Faith and Criticism* [Grand Rapids: Baker, 1991], 104).

11. Harold Lindsell, *The Battle for the Bible* (Grand Rapids: Zondervan, 1976), 120–21.

12. Ibid., 210. Carl F. H. Henry did not agree with Lindsell in making inerrancy a litmus test of being "a true evangelical." See Ronald H. Nash, *Evangelicals in America: Who They Are, What They Believe* (Nashville: Abingdon, 1987), 98.

13. Francis A. Schaeffer, *The Great Evangelical Disaster* (Westchester, Ill.: Crossway, 1984), 77.

14. Ibid., 51. Schaeffer, in an anachronistic way, uprooted the fundamentalist doctrine of inerrancy from its *American* context and attempted to read it back throughout much of Christian history, especially in his observation that "up until the last two hundred years or so virtually every Christian believed in the complete inerrancy of the Bible" (ibid., 45).

15. Ibid., 77.

16. Michael Scott Horton, "Recovering the Plumb Line," in *The Coming Evangelical Crisis: Current Challenges to the Authority of Scripture and the Gospel*, ed. John H. Armstrong (Chicago: Moody, 1996), 258.

17. R. Albert Mohler Jr., "Contending for Truth in an Age of Anti-Truth," in *Here We Stand: A Call from Confessing Evangelicals,* ed. James Montgomery Boice and Benjamin E. Sasse (Grand Rapids: Baker, 1996), 64.

18. Douglas Jacobsen, "The Rise of Evangelical Hermeneutical Pluralism," *Christian Scholar's Review* 16, no. 4 (1987): 328.

19. James Davison Hunter, *Evangelicalism: The Coming Generation* (Chicago: University of Chicago Press, 1987), 31.

20. Bernard Ramm, *The Evangelical Heritage: A Study in Historical Theology* (Grand Rapids: Baker, 2000), ix.

21. See David W. Bebbington, "Evangelicalism in Its Settings: The British and American Movements since 1940," in *Evangelicalism,* ed. Mark A. Noll, David W. Bebbington, and George A. Rawlyk (New York: Oxford University Press, 1994), 373.

22. See http://www.fuller.edu/provost/aboutfuller/sof.htm. Richard Mouw, the president of Fuller Theological Seminary, observes that "inerrant is not a term of choice for most of my Fuller colleagues; we much prefer infallible" (Richard J. Mouw, *The Smell of Sawdust: What Evangelicals Can Learn from Their Fundamentalist Heritage* [Grand Rapids: Zondervan, 2000], 138).

23. Alister McGrath, *A Passion for Truth: The Intellectual Coherence of Evangelicalism* (Downers Grove, Ill.: InterVarsity, 1996), 107.

24. Stanley J. Grenz, *Revisioning Evangelical Theology: A Fresh Agenda for the Twenty-first Century* (Downers Grove, Ill.: InterVarsity, 1993), 26.

25. Ibid., 136. Grenz elaborates on this theme in the following words: "Consequently, we must not idolize the Bible itself. . . . There is no other way of coming to know the divine reality except through an encounter with the living God. And this encounter is facilitated by the biblical message" (ibid., 133).

26. Gustaf Aulen, *Christus Victor: An Historical Study of the Three Main Types of the Idea of the Atonement,* trans. A. G. Herbert (New York: Macmillan, 1969).

27. J. N. D. Kelly, *Early Christian Doctrines* (San Francisco: Harper & Row, 1960), 183–88.

28. J. I. Packer, "What Did the Cross Achieve? The Logic of Penal Substitution," *Tyndale Bulletin* 25 (1974): 3.

29. Alister McGrath, *Evangelicalism and the Future of Christianity* (Downers Grove, Ill.: InterVarsity, 1995), 66.

30. Boice and Sasse, *Here We Stand,* 18.

31. John R. W. Stott, *The Cross of Christ* (Downers Grove, Ill.: InterVarsity, 1986), 127.

32. McGrath, *Evangelicalism and the Future of Christianity,* 62.

33. Mouw, *Smell of Sawdust,* 128. The American context is also complicated by the growing Muslim community, which contends that Christ did not die on the cross and that there is no need for a sin-bearing Savior.

34. Stott, *Cross of Christ,* 65.

35. Ibid., 147. Donald Bloesch points out, "Most objective scholars will agree that the theme of vicarious, substitutionary atonement runs through the entire Bible. The prophet Isaiah portrays Christ as 'an offering for sin' (53:10), as the one who 'has borne our griefs and carried our sorrows'" (Donald G. Bloesch, *Essentials of Evangelical Theology,* vol. 1 [San Francisco: HarperSanFrancisco, 1982], 148).

36. Stott, *Cross of Christ,* 149.

37. Ibid., 160. For two works that also illuminate the cross of Christ as an atoning, substitutionary sacrifice, see Samuel Chadwick, *The Gospel of the Cross* (Salem, Ohio: Schmul

Publishing Company, n.d.); and Leon Morris, *The Cross in the New Testament* (Grand Rapids: Eerdmans, 1965).

38. Stott, *Cross of Christ,* 140.

39. Dietrich Bonhoeffer, *The Cost of Discipleship,* 2nd ed. (New York: Macmillan, 1960), 46. In this work, Bonhoeffer also exclaims, "Cheap grace is not the kind of forgiveness of sin which frees us from the toils of sin. Cheap grace is the grace we bestow on ourselves" (47).

40. Richard S. Taylor, *God's Integrity and the Cross* (Nappanee, Ind.: Francis Asbury Press, 1999), 72.

41. Ibid. Moreover, Taylor states, "God does punish wrongdoers is taught so pervasively in the Bible that only rose-tinted glasses could so egregiously miss the obvious" (76).

42. Ibid., xiii.

43. Ibid., 96. Taylor notes that great stress in the New Testament is put on the manner of Christ's death as a criminal. This underscores the truth that Christ at Calvary was bearing the penalty for sin, "imposed by man unjustly, but imposed by God justly" (ibid., 67).

44. Ibid.

45. George Gallup Jr. and D. Michael Lindsay, *Surveying the Religious Landscape: Trends in U.S. Beliefs* (Harrisburg, Pa.: Morehouse, 1999), 65.

46. Ibid. This statement reflects good judgment on the part of Gallup and is indicative of his "objectivity" and fair-minded thinking, for it is clear that not all evangelicals affirm the doctrine of inerrancy, especially those from the Wesleyan household of faith.

47. Ibid. It is helpful to compare these recent trends with those from the 1990s. See George Gallup Jr. and Jim Castelli, *The People's Religion: American Faith in the 90s* (New York: Macmillan, 1989). Such a comparison reveals that American religion, especially in its evangelical manifestations, is healthy and strong.

48. Gallup and Lindsay, *Surveying the Religious Landscape,* 65–66. For a good window on African American religious experience, see William H. Bentley, "Bible Believers in the Black Community," in *The Evangelicals: What They Believe, Who They Are, Where They Are Changing,* ed. David F. Wells and John D. Woodbridge, 108–21 (Nashville: Abingdon, 1975).

49. Gallup and Lindsay, *Surveying the Religious Landscape,* 65–66. For two works that explore the rapprochement (at least on some levels) that is currently taking place between American evangelicals and Roman Catholics, see Timothy George, "Evangelicals and Catholics Together: A New Initiative," *Christianity Today* 41, no. 14 (December 8, 1997): 34–35; and S. M. Hutchens, "My Brother, Be He Ne'er So Vile? The Difficulty and Promise of Catholic-Evangelical Rapprochment: An Address to an Evangelical Congregation," *Touchstone (US)* 8 (Summer 1995): 13–16.

50. Joanmarie Smith, "Teaching toward Conversion," *Religious Education* 89, no. 1 (Winter 1994): 107. Alister McGrath correctly points out that evangelicalism is not tied to any one specific theory of conversion, where Reformed and Wesleyan perspectives are of particular importance in this regard, "but rather to a recognition of the *need* for personal conversion" (McGrath, *Evangelicalism and the Future of Christianity,* 58).

51. Theodore Jennings has been especially critical of the work of American evangelicals in general, converting people "stadium by stadium," as he puts it, and of Methodist evangelicals in particular. Indeed, Jennings is especially annoyed that some Methodist evangelicals continue to view John Wesley's Aldersgate experience as a conversion. Consequently, Jennings writes in language that is hardly balanced and fair, as is evidenced by the following: "What this means is that the conversionist myth of Aldersgate is a lie. It is unsupported by Wesley's own writings and depends upon a systematic distortion of these texts. To celebrate Aldersgate as . . . the

conversion of Wesley is to perpetrate an historical fraud. . . . But [Wesley] was not taken in by [this] phony evangelicalism that for all its talk of Christ, faith, and being born again, had no relation to that biblical faith that works by love to produce the holiness without which none shall see God" (Theodore W. Jennings Jr., "John Wesley against Aldersgate," *Quarterly Review* 8 [Fall 1988]: 20, 22).

52. Mouw, *Smell of Sawdust,* 21.

53. William James, *The Varieties of Religious Experience* (Harmondsworth: Penguin, 1982), 166.

54. See Søren Kierkegaard, *Stages on Life's Way,* trans. Howard V. Hong and Edna H. Hong (Princeton: Princeton University Press, 1988).

55. Compare this line of thinking with that of Horace Bushnell, *Christian Nurture* (New York: Charles Scribner's Sons, 1888). See also Ted Campbell's essay in which he distinguishes infant baptism as an "ordinary means" and conversion and renewal as an "extraordinary means" (Ted Campbell, "Conversion and Baptism in Wesleyan Spirituality," in *Conversion in the Wesleyan Tradition,* ed. Kenneth J. Collins and John H. Tyson, 160–74 (Nashville: Abingdon, 2001).

56. Albert C. Outler, ed., *The Works of John Wesley,* vols. 1–4, *The Sermons* (Nashville: Abingdon, 1984), 1:429.

57. Ibid. In a letter to William Green, Wesley maintains that "nine-tenths of men in England have no more religion than horses, and perish through the contempt of it." See John Telford, ed., *The Letters of John Wesley, A.M.,* 8 vols. (London: Epworth, 1931), 8:179.

58. Telford, *Letters of John Wesley,* 1:428–29.

59. Ibid., 1:429. Wesley's language here is strong: "Lean no more on the staff of that broken reed." Nevertheless, his point is to underscore the importance of real, vital, inward change, a change without which one would not be fit for the kingdom of heaven.

60. Gerald R. Cragg, ed., *The Works of John Wesley,* vol. 11, *The Appeals to Men of Reason and Religion* (New York: Oxford University Press, 1975), 107. See also Kenneth J. Collins, *John Wesley: A Theological Journey* (Nashville: Abingdon, 2003), 139–41.

61. Cragg, *Works of John Wesley,* 107.

62. John G. Stackhouse Jr., "Billy Graham and the Nature of Conversion: A Paradigm Case," *Studies in Religion* 21, no. 3 (1992): 340.

63. Bonhoeffer, *Cost of Discipleship,* 7. For a view that contends that some children have "never faced in any direction but in the direction of God," see William Barclay, *Turning to God: A Study of Conversion in the Book of Acts and Today* (London: Epworth, 1963), 93–94. See also Collins, *John Wesley,* 194–95.

64. Donald G. Bloesch, *Essentials of Evangelical Theology,* vol. 2 (San Francisco: Harper-SanFrancisco, 1982), 8–9.

65. Richard Quebedeaux, *The Worldly Evangelicals* (San Francisco: Harper & Row, 1978), 52.

66. Ibid. For a good description of American evangelicalism during the 1970s, see Richard Quebedeaux, *The Young Evangelicals* (New York: Harper & Row, 1974).

67. Lesslie Newbigin, *The Gospel in a Pluralist Society* (Grand Rapids: Eerdmans, 1989), 1–7. The terminology that Newbigin employs here concerns the difference between pluralism as a fact of life and pluralism as an ideology. It is the latter usage that is so troubling.

68. McGrath, *Passion for Truth,* 204.

69. Ibid., 206.

70. Richard G. Hutcheson, *Mainline Churches and the Evangelicals* (Atlanta: John Knox, 1981), 96.

71. Bloesch, *Essentials of Evangelical Theology*, vol. 2, 96.

72. Nathan O. Hatch and Michael S. Hamilton, "Can Evangelicalism Survive Its Success?" *Christianity Today* 36, no. 11 (October 5, 1992): 23.

73. Bloesch, *Essentials of Evangelical Theology*, vol. 2, 171.

74. Hutcheson, *Mainline Churches and the Evangelicals*, 83. Here Hutcheson is citing Lesslie Newbigin. Moreover, Hutcheson maintains that "because of its respect for other religions, it [liberalism] is at best ambivalent about evangelization of non-Christians. Its witness is necessarily unaggressive, and it is far more comfortable with social witness" (96).

75. Valdir R. Steuernagel, "Social Concern and Evangelization: The Journey of the Lausanne Movement," *International Bulletin of Missionary Research* 15 (April 1991): 55.

76. Hutcheson, *Mainline Churches and the Evangelicals*, 96.

77. For a helpful and informative exploration of the work of the Billy Graham Evangelistic Association, see Mark A. Noll, *American Evangelical Christianity* (Malden, Mass.: Blackwell, 2001), 58–63.

## Chapter 3

1. Robert Webber, for example, states, "The matrix out of which twentieth-century evangelicalism grew was the fundamentalist-modernist controversy in the first three decades of this century" (Robert E. Webber, *Common Roots: A Call to Evangelical Maturity* [Grand Rapids: Zondervan, 1978], 28).

2. Donald W. Dayton, "Rejoinder to Historiography Discussion," *Christian Scholar's Review* 23, no. 1 (1993): 67.

3. There are other levels of ambiguity in Dayton's pentecostal paradigm because not only do some Wesleyans want to distance themselves from Pentecostalism, however defined, but also, as William Kostlevy points out, some Pentecostals do not look to the Wesleyan but to the Reformed tradition for their guidance and self-understanding. See William Kostlevy, *Holiness Manuscripts: A Guide to Sources Documenting the Wesleyan Holiness Movement in the United States and Canada* (Metuchen, N.J.: Scarecrow Press, 1994), 36.

4. Donald W. Dayton, "The Search for the Historical Evangelicalism: George Marsden's History of Fuller Seminary as a Case Study," *Christian Scholar's Review* 23, no. 1 (1993): 18.

5. Donald W. Dayton, "Yet Another Layer of the Onion: Or Opening the Ecumenical Door to Let the Riffraff In," *Ecumenical Review* 40 (January 1988): 100.

6. To illustrate, both Roberts and Scott feared that the doctrine of Christian perfection was being lost in an accommodated Methodist Episcopal Church. See Benjamin Titus Roberts, *Pungent Truths: Being Extracts from the Writings of the Rev. Benjamin Titus Roberts, A.M.* (Salem, Ohio: Convention Book Store, 1973), 296.

7. According to Wesley, a Methodist is one, quite simply, who has not merely the *form* of religion but also its *power*, one who, to use the Methodist leader's own words, has "the love of God shed abroad in his heart by the Holy Ghost given unto him; one who loves the Lord his God with all his heart, and with all his soul, and with all his mind, and with all his strength." See Rupert E. Davies, *The Works of John Wesley*, vol. 9, *The Methodist Societies: History, Nature, and Design* (Nashville: Abingdon, 1989), 35.

8. Dayton, "Rejoinder to Historiography Discussion," 63.

9. Donald Dayton, "The Embourgeoisement of a Vision: Lament of a Radical Evangelical," *Other Side* 23, no. 8 (October 1987): 19.

10. See Kenneth J. Collins, *John Wesley: A Theological Journey* (Nashville: Abingdon, 2003).

11. See Wesley's sermons "The Danger of Riches" and "The Danger of Increasing Riches," in Albert C. Outler, ed., *The Works of John Wesley,* vols. 1–4, *The Sermons* (Nashville: Abingdon, 1984), 3:227–46; 4:177–86.

12. I have heard more than my share of sermons that criticize the middle class in an ideological, confused, and at times rambling sort of way, but these sermons always take place *after* the offertory, with the "preacher" often oblivious to the contradiction entailed.

13. Henry D. Rack, *Reasonable Enthusiast: John Wesley and the Rise of Methodism,* 2nd ed. (Nashville: Abingdon, 1993), 5–10.

14. Myron Magnet, *The Dream and the Nightmare: The Sixties' Legacy to the Underclass* (San Francisco: Encounter Books, 1993), 37–55.

15. Joel A. Carpenter, "The Scope of American Evangelicalism: Some Comments on the Dayton-Marsden Exchange," *Christian Scholar's Review* 23, no. 1 (1993): 57.

16. See Peter Oblinger, *Religious Mimesis: Social Bases for Holiness Schism in Late-Nineteenth-Century Methodism,* Monograph Studies, 1 (Evanston, Ill.: Institute for the Study of American Religion, 1973).

17. Outler, *Works of John Wesley,* 4:11. Moreover, Wesley does *not* affirm that the rich are by necessity evil. For example, in his journal of 17 November 1759, he notes, "It is well a few of the rich and noble are called." And he adds undoubtedly with hope and expectation, "Oh that God would increase their number!" Moreover, in his piece "The General Spread of the Gospel" produced in 1783, the Methodist leader exclaims, "Before the end even the rich shall enter into the kingdom of God," a truth not permitted even a hearing in so many class-driven contemporary analyses, but one affirmed by Wesley himself. See Outler, *Works of John Wesley,* 4:358; 2:494.

18. Dayton, "Search for the Historical Evangelicalism," 21.

19. Ibid. Dayton, apparently dissatisfied with current evangelical and historiographical trends, calls for an elimination of the use of the term *evangelical.* See Donald Dayton, "Some Doubts about the Usefulness of the Category 'Evangelical,'" in *The Variety of American Evangelicalism,* ed. Donald W. Dayton and Robert K. Johnston (Downers Grove, Ill.: InterVarsity, 1991), 245–51.

20. For a work that claims that Holiness adherents and Pentecostals (as well as dispensationalists) have been anti-intellectual, see Mark A. Noll, *The Scandal of the Evangelical Mind* (Grand Rapids: Eerdmans, 1994). For a Wesleyan and Pentecostal response, see Cheryl Bridges Johns, "Partners in Scandal: Wesleyan and Pentecostal Scholarship," *Pneuma* 21, no. 2 (Fall 1999): 183–97.

21. For an excellent discussion of how the politics and ideologies of sixties radicals have come to harm the poor in some important ways, see Magnet, *Dream and the Nightmare,* 11–22.

22. Dayton, "Search for the Historical Evangelicalism," 18. For a view that argues that Wesley in his ministry to the poor distinguished between bodies and souls, maintenance needs and higher-level needs, chronological priority and valuational priority in a way that contemporary liberation theology does not, see Kenneth J. Collins, "The Soteriological Orientation of John Wesley's Ministry to the Poor," *Asbury Theological Journal* 50, no. 1 (Spring 1995): 75–92.

23. Dayton, "Yet Another Layer of the Onion," 101. Dayton also writes about the "revivalist/pietist protest *against* 'orthodoxy,'" a phrase that is open to much misunderstanding, especially in a contemporary setting in which churches, such as many of the mainline denominations, are faced with doctrinal dissolution.

24. Donald Dayton, "The Limits of Evangelicalism: The Pentecostal Tradition," in *Variety of American Evangelicalism,* 51. Moreover, Marsden (as well as others) quite rightly took issue with Dayton's re-imagining of the history of Fuller Theological Seminary, a largely fictive account that emerged through the exclusive use of the lens of the pentecostal paradigm. "It is difficult to see," Marsden notes, "that Charles and Grace Fuller fit embourgeoisement very well" (George M. Marsden, "Response to Don Dayton," *Christian Scholar's Review* 23, no. 1 [1993]: 40).

25. Marsden, "Response to Don Dayton," 37.

26. Ibid., 40.

27. Carpenter, "Scope of American Evangelicalism," 55.

28. I am consciously dropping Dayton's pentecostal paradigm in favor of a Wesleyan one. Such a shift will embrace all those who look to John Wesley as a theological mentor, especially in the area of practical theology, and it will, therefore, embrace a rich diversity of peoples: mainline evangelicals, Holiness people, and some Pentecostals, among others.

29. Thomas Jackson, ed., *The Works of John Wesley,* 14 vols. (Grand Rapids: Baker, 1978), 11:367.

30. For treatments that continue to maintain the cruciality of Aldersgate for a proper understanding of the details of Wesley's spiritual journey, see Kenneth J. Collins, "Other Thoughts on Aldersgate: Has the Conversionist Paradigm Collapsed?" *Methodist History* 30, no. 1 (October 1991): 10–25; and Kenneth J. Collins, "The Motif of Real Christianity in the Writings of John Wesley," *Asbury Theological Journal* 49, no. 1 (Spring 1994): 49–62. For other treatments that attempt to "debunk" Wesley's Aldersgate experience, see Randy L. Maddox, *Aldersgate Reconsidered* (Nashville: Kingswood Books, 1990); and Theodore W. Jennings Jr., "John Wesley against Aldersgate," *Quarterly Review* 8 (Fall 1988): 3–22.

31. Frank Baker, ed., *The Works of John Wesley,* vol. 26, *The Letters II* (New York: Oxford University Press, 1982), 155.

32. John Telford, ed., *The Letters of John Wesley, A.M.,* 8 vols. (London: Epworth, 1931), 3:332.

33. Outler, *Works of John Wesley,* 1:105. Though Wesley clearly was a man of one book, this observation must be understood in a normative way. In other words, Wesley was not suggesting that Christians should read *only* the Bible, a counsel that would be a species of anti-intellectualism. Rather, the Methodist leader was indicating that in the many and varied readings undertaken by believers, the Bible should be the preeminent authority, especially pertaining to matters of salvation. Few people, then or now, have read as much or as widely as John Wesley.

34. Jackson, *Works of John Wesley,* 11:478.

35. Ibid., 14:253. See also Wesley's notes on 2 Timothy 3:16, where he observes, "All Scripture is inspired of God—The Spirit of God not only once inspired those who wrote it, but continually inspires, supernaturally assists those that read it with earnest prayer" (John Wesley, *Explanatory Notes upon the New Testament* [Salem, Ohio: Schmul Publishers], 554).

36. Duncan S. Ferguson, "John Wesley on Scripture: The Hermeneutics of Pietism," *Methodist History* 22, no. 4 (July 1984): 243.

37. Reginald W. Ward and Richard P. Heitzenrater, eds., *The Works of John Wesley,* vol. 23, *Journals and Diaries VI* (Nashville: Abingdon, 1995), 25.

38. Jackson, *Works of John Wesley,* 11:484.

39. Wilbur T. Dayton, "The Bible in the Wesleyan Tradition," *Asbury Seminary Journal* 40, no. 1 (Spring 1985): 23.

40. R. Larry Shelton, "John Wesley's Approach to Scripture in Historical Perspective," *Wesleyan Theological Journal* 16, no. 1 (Spring 1981): 36.

41. See Ferguson, "John Wesley on Scripture," 238.

42. Outler, *Works of John Wesley,* 2:599.

43. Ibid., 2:600. It is also clear that Wesley rejected a doctrine of divine "dictation," and as William Abraham points out, "The doctrine of inerrancy is intimately related to a doctrine of divine dictation that is now gone forever" (William J. Abraham, *The Coming Great Revival* [San Francisco: Harper & Row, 1984], 34).

44. Leon Hynson, for example, indicates that Archbishop Cranmer expressed the confessional position of the Church of England in soteriological language through which the value of Scripture was conceived in terms of its power "to bring men and women into a saving relationship with Christ" (Leon Hynson, "The Inerrancy Question: A Misplaced Debate," *Evangelical Journal* 5 [Spring 1987]: 30).

45. Paul Bassett, "The Fundamentalist Leavening of the Holiness Movement: 1914–1940," *Wesleyan Theological Journal* 13 (Spring 1978): 67.

46. Joel A. Carpenter, *Revive Us Again: The Reawakening of American Fundamentalism* (New York: Oxford University Press, 1997), 83.

47. As cited in Bassett, "Fundamentalist Leavening of the Holiness Movement," 74. Observe that this exact language remains in the current Nazarene *Manual.* See E. LeBron Fairbanks, Roger Hahn, Frank M. Moore, Jack Stone, and J. K. Warrick, eds., *Manual: Church of the Nazarene* (Kansas City: Nazarene Publishing House, 2001), 27 (article IV).

48. J. Kenneth Grider, "Wesleyanism and the Inerrancy Issue," *Wesleyan Theological Journal* 19, no. 2 (Fall 1984): 58.

49. Hynson, "Inerrancy Question," 32.

50. See "Purpose and Doctrinal Basis," *Wesleyan Theological Journal* 30, no. 2 (Fall 1995): 224.

51. Donald W. Dayton, "The Use of Scripture in the Wesleyan Tradition," in *The Use of the Bible in Theology: Evangelical Options,* ed. Robert K. Johnston (Eugene, Ore.: Wipf & Stock, 1997), 130.

52. William J. Abraham, *Canon and Criterion in Christian Theology* (Oxford: Oxford University Press, 1998), 1.

53. Ibid., 21. For a Wesleyan biblical scholar who maintains that the language of inerrancy is ill suited to express the truth of Scripture, see Joel B. Green, "Reconstructing the Authority of Scripture for Christian Formation and Mission," in *The Wesleyan Tradition: A Paradigm for Renewal,* ed. Paul W. Chilcote (Nashville: Abingdon, 2002), 40–41.

54. Abraham, *Canon and Criterion in Christian Theology,* 471. See also Abraham's earlier work in which he distinguished between inspiration and divine speaking: William J. Abraham, *The Divine Inspiration of Holy Scripture* (New York: Oxford University Press, 1981), 71, 78.

55. Abraham, *Canon and Criterion in Christian Theology,* 27.

56. Outler, *Works of John Wesley,* 1:381. For an excellent treatment of Wesley's understanding of the means of grace as a part of his overall theology, see Henry H. Knight, *The Presence of God in the Christian Life: John Wesley and the Means of Grace* (Metuchen, N.J.: Scarecrow Press, 1992).

57. Stanley J. Grenz, *Revisioning Evangelical Theology: A Fresh Agenda for the Twenty-first Century* (Downers Grove, Ill.: InterVarsity, 1993), 111, 133.

58. Stanley J. Grenz and John R. Franke, *Beyond Foundationalism: Shaping Theology in a Postmodern Context* (Louisville: Westminster John Knox, 2001), 65, emphasis added.

59. Ibid., 65. Grenz and Franke point out that "the Protestant principle means the Bible is authoritative in that it is the vehicle through which the Spirit speaks. Taking the idea a step

further, the authority of the Bible is in the end the authority of the Spirit whose instrumentality it is" (ibid., 65).

60. Stanley J. Grenz, *Renewing the Center: Evangelical Theology in a Post-theological Era* (Grand Rapids: Baker, 2000), 77.

61. Donald G. Bloesch, *Essentials of Evangelical Theology*, vol. 1 (San Francisco: Harper-SanFrancisco, 1982), 67.

62. John R. W. Stott, "Are Evangelicals Fundamentalists?" *Christianity Today* 22 (September 8, 1978): 44–46.

63. Alister McGrath, *A Passion for Truth: The Intellectual Coherence of Evangelicalism* (Downers Grove, Ill.: InterVarsity, 1996), 116–17.

64. Alister McGrath, *Evangelicalism and the Future of Christianity* (Downers Grove, Ill.: InterVarsity, 1995), 62.

65. Mark A. Noll, *The Scandal of the Evangelical Mind* (Grand Rapids: Eerdmans, 1994), 227.

66. Ibid., 249. For a different take on the problems of anti-intellectualism, see Preston Jones, "More Scandals of the Evangelical Mind," *First Things* 84 (June–July 1998): 16–18.

67. Noll, *Scandal of the Evangelical Mind*, 142.

68. Ibid. Thinking that his judgments are actually accurate, Noll concludes that "the separatism and pious anti-intellectualism fostered by both Pentecostal and Holiness movements is also a thing of the past for most evangelical political theorists" (ibid., 227).

69. Jackson, *Works of John Wesley*, 8:299.

70. Ibid. For Wesley's development of the theme of "real" as opposed to "nominal" Christianity, as integral to his purpose, see Kenneth J. Collins, "Real Christianity as Integrating Theme in Wesley's Soteriology: The Critique of a Modern Myth," *Asbury Theological Journal* 51, no. 2 (Fall 1996): 15–45.

71. Francis A. Schaeffer, *The Great Evangelical Disaster* (Westchester, Ill.: Crossway, 1984), 59.

72. Colleen Carroll indicates that "studies of fundamentalist and evangelical churches have found that their members divorce at the same or higher rates than the general population." Even more troubling, "in many parts of the Protestant Bible Belt, the divorce rate is roughly 50 percent higher than the national average" (Colleen Carroll, *The New Faithful: Why Young Adults Are Embracing Christian Orthodoxy* [Chicago: Loyola Press, 2002], 270).

73. Harold Lindsell, *The New Paganism: Understanding American Culture and the Role of the Church* (San Francisco: Harper & Row, 1987), 145.

74. James W. Sire, *Habits of the Mind: Intellectual Life as a Christian Calling* (Downers Grove, Ill.: InterVarsity, 2000), 100. Cornelius Plantinga contends that there are a whole host of involuntary sins (which he defines in terms of the seven deadly sins) over which a person "may have little or, at best, only variable control" (Cornelius Plantinga Jr., *Not the Way It's Supposed to Be: A Breviary of Sin* [Grand Rapids: Eerdmans, 1995], 22).

75. Outler, *Works of John Wesley*, 1:336–37, emphasis added. Wesley makes a distinction among freedom from the *guilt* of sin (justification), the *power* of sin (regeneration), and the *being* of sin (entire sanctification) as found in his key sermons, "On Sin in Believers" and "The Repentance of Believers." See Outler, *Works of John Wesley*, 1:314–53.

76. Jackson, *Works of John Wesley*, 12:448. Wesley's definition of sin is not as simple as it might appear at first glance, for there is also sin "improperly speaking," which is any violation of a known law of God, willful or not. This sin also needs the atoning blood of Christ, though it does not issue in present guilt. Beyond this, Wesley considered sin not simply as an act but

also as a state of being, especially in terms of his doctrine of original sin. See Outler, *Works of John Wesley,* 1:314–53.

77. Telford, *Letters of John Wesley,* 3:169. For helpful treatments of Wesley's doctrine of sin, see Barry Edward Bryant, "John Wesley's Doctrine of Sin" (Ph.D. diss., King's College, University of London, 1992); and Gordon Stanley Dicker, "The Concept '*Simul Justus Et Peccator*' in Relation to the Thought of Luther, Wesley, and Bonhoeffer, and Its Significance for a Doctrine of the Christian Life" (Ph.D. diss., Union Seminary, 1971).

78. See Gregory S. Clapper, "Orthokardia: The Practical Theology of John Wesley's Heart Religion," *Quarterly Review* 10 (Spring 1990): 49–66.

79. Anthony Hoekema, "The Reformed Perspective," in *Five Views on Sanctification,* ed. Melvin E. Dieter, Anthony A. Hoekema, Stanley M. Horton, J. Robertson McQuilkin, and John F. Walvoord (Grand Rapids: Zondervan, 1987), 62.

80. Theodore W. Jennings Jr., *Good News to the Poor: John Wesley's Evangelical Economics* (Nashville: Abingdon, 1990), 142.

81. Ibid., 187.

82. Jackson, *Works of John Wesley,* 13:36.

83. Outler, *Works of John Wesley,* 1:428–29. And to the mistaken claim that there is no new birth beyond baptism, a claim inimical in so many ways, Wesley energetically responds in his *Further Appeal,* "I tell a sinner, 'You must be born again.' 'No,' say you, 'He was born again in baptism. Therefore he cannot be born again now.' Alas! What a trifling is this? What if he was *then* a child of God? He is *now* manifestly a 'child of the devil.'" See Gerald R. Cragg, ed., *The Works of John Wesley,* vol. 11, *The Appeals to Men of Reason and Religion* (New York: Oxford University Press, 1975), 107.

84. I am by no means suggesting that Christians never sin, nor does Wesley teach such a thing. The Christian life should principally be marked by holiness and sanctifying grace, but if anyone does sin, as Scripture states, "We have an advocate with the Father, Jesus Christ the righteous" (1 John 2:1). In other words, living and thriving in God's sanctifying grace should be the rule and sin the exception. Some corners of American evangelicalism, however, have turned this gospel truth on its head.

85. Jackson, *Works of John Wesley,* 10:364.

## Chapter 4

1. The first line of the major theological work of Karl Barth illustrates this point clearly: "Dogmatics is a theological discipline, but theology is a function of the church." See Karl Barth, *Church Dogmatics: The Doctrine of the Word of God,* part 1, ed. G. W. Bromiley and T. F. Torrance (Edinburgh: T & T Clark, 1936), 3.

2. Stanley J. Grenz, *Renewing the Center: Evangelical Theology in a Post-theological Era* (Grand Rapids: Baker, 2000), 220.

3. Carl F. H. Henry, *God, Revelation, and Authority,* 3 vols. (Waco: Word, 1976), 1:244–52.

4. See Gregory S. Clapper, "Orthokardia: The Practical Theology of John Wesley's Heart Religion," *Quarterly Review* 10 (Spring 1990): 49–66.

5. Roger E. Olson, *The Story of Christian Theology: Twenty Centuries of Tradition and Reform* (Downers Grove, Ill.: InterVarsity, 1999), 486, 593. Stanley Grenz uses the phrase "convertive piety" (Grenz, *Renewing the Center,* 47).

6. For an "individualistic" reading of Pietism, see Theodore Runyon, *The New Creation: John Wesley's Theology Today*, in which he writes, "One of the persistent tendencies emerging from pietism and its understanding of Christianity has been *individualism*. The essential core of Christian faith is reduced to what takes place within the individual and his or her personally experienced awareness of God." It is difficult, however, if not impossible, to make the case that Spener, Franke, and Tersteegen were individualists. In fact, these *Pietists* repeatedly emphasized the corporate, communal dimension of the church in their support of *ecclesiolae in ecclesia*. Therefore, it is simply unnecessary and indeed counterproductive to deprecate piety, the interior life of the soul, to advance external religion and social action. Indeed, the one work of grace should readily flow into the other. See Theodore H. Runyon, *The New Creation: John Wesley's Theology Today* (Nashville: Abingdon, 1998), 102; and Theodore H. Runyon, *Sanctification and Liberation: Liberation Theologies in the Light of the Wesleyan Tradition* (Nashville: Abingdon, 1981), 47. For a more balanced view of Pietism, see F. Ernest Stoeffler, "Pietism, the Wesleys, and Methodist Beginnings in America," in *Continental Pietism and Early American Christianity*, ed. F. Ernest Stoeffler (Grand Rapids: Eerdmans, 1976), 184–221.

7. Bernard Ramm, *The Evangelical Heritage: A Study in Historical Theology* (Grand Rapids: Baker, 2000), 146. Stanley Grenz observes, "A nonnegotiable principle of evangelicalism is that religion is a matter of the heart" (Stanley J. Grenz, *Revisioning Evangelical Theology: A Fresh Agenda for the Twenty-first Century* [Downers Grove, Ill.: InterVarsity, 1993], 45).

8. Stanley J. Grenz and John R. Franke, *Beyond Foundationalism: Shaping Theology in a Postmodern Context* (Louisville: Westminster John Knox, 2001), 29.

9. Nancey Murphy, *Beyond Liberalism and Fundamentalism: How Modern and Postmodern Philosophy Set the Theological Agenda* (Harrisburg, Pa.: Trinity Press International, 1996), 35.

10. Colin Gunton argues, "What, then, is wrong with foundationalism? Not, it seems to me, that it seeks a common basis for rationality, but that it seeks the wrong one and in the wrong way. It seeks the wrong basis, because it seeks one that is merely secular: something inherent within human reason and experience" (Colin Gunton, "The Trinity, Natural Theology, and a Theology of Nature," in *The Trinity in a Pluralistic Age: Theological Essays on Culture and Religion*, ed. Kevin J. Vanhoozer [Grand Rapids: Eerdmans, 1997], 91).

11. Alister McGrath, *A Passion for Truth: The Intellectual Coherence of Evangelicalism* (Downers Grove, Ill.: InterVarsity, 1996), 200.

12. Alister E. McGrath, "Evangelical Theological Method: The State of the Art," in *Evangelical Futures: A Conversation on Theological Method*, ed. John G. Stackhouse Jr. (Grand Rapids: Baker, 2000), 34.

13. McGrath, *Passion for Truth*, 119.

14. George Lindbeck, *The Nature of Doctrine: Religion and Theology in a Postliberal Age* (Philadelphia: Westminster, 1984), 34.

15. Ibid., 37.

16. Ibid., 39. Lindbeck attributes causal, determinative power to the "cultural/linguistic system" but fails to develop in a thoroughgoing way the movement in the opposite direction, that is, how that system itself was created and determined by the very men and women it affects.

17. Ibid., 118.

18. Alister McGrath, "An Evangelical Evaluation of Postliberalism," in *The Nature of Confession: Evangelicals and Postliberals in Conversation*, ed. Timothy R. Phillips and Dennis L. Okholm (Downers Grove, Ill.: InterVarsity, 1996), 35.

19. Ibid., 40.

20. Stanley J. Grenz, *A Primer on Postmodernism* (Grand Rapids: Eerdmans, 1996), 2.

21. Jean François Lyotard, *The Postmodern Condition: A Report on Knowledge,* trans. Geoff Bennington and Brian Massumi (Minneapolis: University of Minnesota Press, 1984), xxiv.

22. Dave Tomlinson, *The Post Evangelical* (London: Triangle [S.P.C.K.], 1995), 89.

23. Gene Edward Veith Jr., *Postmodern Times: A Christian Guide to Contemporary Thought and Culture* (Wheaton: Crossway, 1994), 135.

24. Grenz, *Primer on Postmodernism,* 38.

25. Peter L. Berger and Thomas Luckmann, *The Social Construction of Reality* (Garden City, N.Y.: Anchor, 1966).

26. Douglas Groothuis argues that "the postmodernist claim about truth is merely a social construction—and nothing more." But if it is only a social construction, then the statement itself cannot accurately depict the reality it purportedly describes. See Douglas Groothuis, *Truth Decay: Defending Christianity against the Challenges of Postmodernism* (Downers Grove, Ill.: InterVarsity, 2000), 106.

27. J. Richard Middleton and Brian J. Walsh, *Truth Is Stranger Than It Used to Be: Biblical Faith in a Postmodern Age* (Downers Grove, Ill.: InterVarsity, 1995), 30.

28. See John D. Caputo, ed., *Deconstruction in a Nutshell: A Conversation with Jacques Derrida* (New York: Fordham University Press, 1997).

29. See Thomas C. Oden, *Agenda for Theology: After Modernity . . . What?* (Grand Rapids: Zondervan, 1990), 43–57.

30. Jerry H. Gill, *Mediated Transcendence: A Postmodern Reflection* (Macon, Ga.: Mercer University Press, 1989), 3.

31. Ibid., 20. Gill has charted this new course by reflecting on the works of Michael Polanyi, Maurice Merleau-Ponty, and the mature Wittgenstein.

32. Ibid., 44. One can, of course, make a distinction between "beauty" and "aesthetic experience." The former term indicates that something "other" is known in and through experience that is not fully explained by or reducible to human consciousness; the latter term, on the other hand, suggests that human consciousness is all there is and that the self is locked up in its own experiences, its own world.

33. Ibid., 38.

34. Ibid., 23. Reformed theologians, historically, have taken great pains, in their articulation of the doctrine of the divine sovereignty, to maintain that the Creator is not dependent on the creation and must not, therefore, be confused with idols. See John T. McNeill, ed., *Calvin: Institutes of the Christian Religion,* 2 vols., Library of Christian Classics (Philadelphia: Westminster, 1960), 1:116–20 (I.12.1–3).

35. Donald G. Bloesch, *Essentials of Evangelical Theology,* vol. 1 (San Francisco: HarperSanFrancisco, 1982), 24–31; and Thomas C. Oden, *The Living God: Systematic Theology,* vol. 1 (San Francisco: HarperSanFrancisco, 1987), 81–82.

36. George M. Marsden, *The Outrageous Idea of Christian Scholarship* (New York: Oxford University Press, 1997), 26.

37. Ibid., 30.

38. Middleton and Walsh, *Truth Is Stranger Than It Used to Be,* 77.

39. Reinhold Niebuhr, *Moral Man and Immoral Society* (New York: Charles Scribner's Sons, 1932), 257–77.

40. James Atkinson, ed., *Luther's Works: The Christian in Society I,* vol. 44 (Philadelphia: Fortress, 1966), xi.

41. Karl Barth, "The Strange New World within the Bible," in *The Word of God and the Word of Man* (Gloucester, Mass.: Peter Smith, 1928), 28–50.

## Chapter 5

1. Ronald J. Sider, *Just Generosity: A New Vision for Overcoming Poverty in America* (Grand Rapids: Baker, 1999), 122.

2. Roger Kimball, *The Long March: How the Cultural Revolution of the 1960s Changed America* (San Francisco: Encounter Books, 2000), 41.

3. Gertrude Himmelfarb, *One Nation, Two Cultures* (New York: Knopf, 1999), 118.

4. James Davison Hunter, *Culture Wars: The Struggle to Define America* (New York: Basic Books, 1991), 118.

5. Irving Kristol, *Neo-Conservatism: The Autobiography of an Idea* (Chicago: Elephant Paperbacks, 1995), 94.

6. Robert H. Bork, *Slouching Towards Gomorrah: Modern Liberalism and American Decline* (New York: Regan Books, 1996), 61.

7. Ibid. Though I am genuinely appreciative of much of the social analysis of Robert Bork, I take exception with his description of American liberalism in terms of "radical individualism." American liberals are far less "individualistic" in my judgment than the judge contends.

8. Gertrude Himmelfarb, *On Looking into the Abyss: Untimely Thoughts on Culture and Society* (New York: Knopf, 1994), 95.

9. Ibid., 65. For two helpful accounts of the ongoing value of natural law as a moral standard, see Robert P. George, *In Defense of Natural Law* (Oxford: Oxford University Press, 1999); and John Finnis, *Natural Law and Natural Rights* (Oxford: Clarendon, 1980).

10. Kristol, *Neo-Conservatism,* x. Kristol also indicates that "neo-conservatism" is "more a descriptive term than a prescriptive one. It describes the erosion of liberal faith among a relatively small but talented and articulate group of scholars and intellectuals" (x).

11. George Gallup Jr. and D. Michael Lindsay, *Surveying the Religious Landscape: Trends in U.S. Beliefs* (Harrisburg, Pa.: Morehouse, 1999), 14.

12. E. J. Dionne and John J. Diiulio, eds., *What's God Got to Do with the American Experiment?* (Washington, D.C.: Brookings Institution Press, 2000), 63.

13. Kristol, *Neo-Conservatism,* 207.

14. Gallup and Lindsay, *Surveying the Religious Landscape,* 16.

15. Bork, *Slouching Towards Gomorrah,* 282.

16. Stephen L. Carter, *The Culture of Disbelief* (New York: Basic Books, 1993), 69.

17. Ibid. See also James Davison Hunter, *American Evangelicalism* (New Brunswick: Rutgers University Press, 1983), 112, where he maintains that "mainstream Protestantism, especially its spokespeople, is very clearly aligned with the political values and ideology of the larger, secular New Class."

18. John Schmalzbauer, "Evangelicals in the New Class: Class versus Subcultural Predictors of Ideology," *Journal for the Scientific Study of Religion* 32, no. 4 (1993): 340.

19. Ibid. Interestingly enough, Robert Wuthnow maintains that "Methodists, Lutherans, Presbyterians, Baptists, Catholics, Jews—were all divided about equally between religious conservatives and religious liberals" (Robert Wuthnow, *The Struggle for America's Soul: Evangelicals, Liberals, and Secularism* [Grand Rapids: Eerdmans, 1989], 24).

20. Ibid. For an earlier study on the effects of the new class on American evangelicals, see James Davison Hunter, "The New Class and the Young Evangelicals," *Review of Religious Research* 22, no. 2 (1980): 155–69.

21. Dionne and Diiulio, *What's God Got to Do with the American Experiment?* 160.

22. Martin E. Marty, *Politics, Religion, and the Common Good* (San Francisco: Jossey-Bass, 2000), 39. Marty also observes that "Baptist clergyman and founding father Isaac Backus believed that both religion and the State would be better off if kept separate from each other" (27).

23. Carter, *Culture of Disbelief,* 105.

24. Floyd G. Cullop, ed., *The Constitution of the United States* (New York: New American Library, 1969), 113.

25. Stephen L. Carter, *God's Name in Vain: The Wrongs and Rights of Religion in Politics* (New York: Basic Books, 2000), 74.

26. Carter, *Culture of Disbelief,* 110. For more on the issue of church and state, see Joseph Tussman, *The Supreme Court on Church and State* (New York: Oxford University Press, 1962); and William Lee Miller, *The First Liberty: Religion and the American Republic* (New York: Knopf, 1985).

27. Carter, *Culture of Disbelief,* 109. See also Leonard W. Levy, *The Establishment Clause: Religion and the First Amendment* (New York: Macmillan, 1986), 75–90.

28. Bork, *Slouching Towards Gomorrah,* 109.

29. See Cal Thomas and Ed Dobson, *Blinded by Might* (Grand Rapids: Zondervan, 1999).

30. Richard John Neuhaus, *The Naked Public Square: Religion and Democracy in America,* 2nd ed. (Grand Rapids: Eerdmans, 1996).

31. Carter, *Culture of Disbelief,* 11. This Yale Law School scholar also recounts the incident in which a television commentator questioned whether it was appropriate for Hillary Rodham Clinton, then the First Lady, to be wearing a cross around her neck for all to see during her husband's inauguration (4–5).

32. Ibid., 11.

33. Ibid., 227. The irony of all this, as Carter reveals, is that "as a group, black Americans are significantly more devout than white Americans" (60).

34. One encouraging trend, noted by Jim Wallis, is that the progressive magazine *Z* in its January 1994 issue exclaimed, "It is long past time that the American Left re-evaluated its judgment that religion is unadulterated superstition" (Jim Wallis, *The Soul of Politics* [New York: Orbis, 1994], 35).

35. Brad Miner, *The Conservative Encyclopedia* (New York: Free Press, 1996), 79.

36. Hilton Kramer and Roger Kimball, *The Betrayal of Liberalism: How the Disciples of Freedom and Equality Helped Foster the Illiberal Politics of Coercion and Control* (Chicago: Ivan R. Dee, 1999), 93.

37. Ibid., 221.

38. Bork, *Slouching Towards Gomorrah,* 78.

39. Ibid., 67. For a good discussion of the effect of some of the political ideas of the new class on evangelicals, see Boyd Reese, "The New Class and the Young Evangelicals: Second Thoughts," *Review of Religious Research* 24 (1983): 261–67.

40. Charles J. Sykes, *A Nation of Victims: The Decay of the American Character* (New York: St. Martin's Press, 1992), 163.

41. Myron Magnet, *The Dream and the Nightmare: The Sixties' Legacy to the Underclass* (San Francisco: Encounter Books, 1993), 197.

42. Ralph Reed, *Active Faith: How Christians Are Changing the Soul of American Politics* (New York: Free Press, 1996), 76.

43. Kramer and Kimball, *Betrayal of Liberalism,* 18.

44. Sykes, *Nation of Victims,* 207. Moreover, this author observes that "it is no longer necessary to engage in lengthy and detailed debate over such issues as affirmative action; it is far easier and more effective to simply brand a critic as insensitive" (17).

45. Sider, *Just Generosity,* 15.

46. Jim Wallis, *The Soul of Politics* (New York: Orbis, 1994), 37.

47. Arthur M. Schlesinger Jr., *The Disuniting of America: Reflections on a Multicultural Society* (New York: Norton, 1992), 113.

48. Robert Hughes, *Culture of Complaint: The Fraying of America* (New York: Oxford University Press, 1993), 15–16.

49. Charles J. Sykes, *The Hollow Men: Politics and Corruption in Higher Education* (Washington, D.C.: Regnery Publishing, 1990), 19.

50. See Allan Bloom, *The Closing of the American Mind: How Higher Education Has Failed Democracy and Impoverished the Souls of Today's Students* (New York: Simon & Schuster, 1987).

51. Sykes, *Hollow Men,* 138.

52. Hughes, *Culture of Complaint,* 77.

53. Sykes, *Hollow Men,* 55. Sykes also reveals that the National Association of Scholars was established as a national, nonpartisan organization to "combat the politicization of scholarship and to help reverse the intellectual decay of the universities" (312).

54. Hunter, *Culture Wars,* 216.

55. Sykes, *Hollow Men,* 54.

56. Dinesh D'Souza, *Illiberal Education: The Politics of Race and Sex on Campus* (New York: Free Press, 1991), 147.

57. Ibid., 202.

58. Ibid. Carter observes, "Had the nation tried to enforce in the 1860s or the 1960s the depressing rules for public dialogue that liberals often endorse today, our history—certainly my history, as an African American—would have been radically different . . . for the worse" (Stephen L. Carter, *The Dissent of the Governed* [Cambridge: Harvard University Press, 1998], 28–29).

59. D'Souza, *Illiberal Education,* 202. Two works that carefully explore the various transitions that have occurred in American education are George M. Marsden and Bradley J. Longfield, *The Secularization of the Academy* (New York: Oxford University Press, 1992); and George M. Marsden, *The Soul of the American University* (New York: Oxford University Press, 1994).

60. D'Souza, *Illiberal Education,* 226.

61. Carter, *God's Name in Vain,* 187. Jonathan Rauch makes the claim that there is "nothing whatever wrong with offending—hurting people's feelings—in pursuit of truth" (Jonathan Rauch, *Kindly Inquisitors: The New Attacks on Free Thought* [Chicago: University of Chicago Press, 1993], 22).

62. Hunter, *Culture Wars,* 144.

63. Schlesinger, *Disuniting of America,* 114.

64. Himmelfarb, *One Nation, Two Cultures,* 101. For a helpful discussion of some of the obstacles that prevent a proper understanding of evangelicals, see R. Stephen Warner, "Theoretical Barriers to the Understanding of Evangelical Christianity," *Sociological Analysis* 40, no. 1 (1979): 1–9.

65. Himmelfarb, *One Nation, Two Cultures,* 92.

66. Jean Hardisty, "The Resurgence of the Right: Why Now?" *Liberal Religious Education* 17 (Fall–Winter 1996–97): 31.

67. Himmelfarb reveals that "almost half of the evangelicals who are not of the religious right are Democrats. (In the election of 1998, it was reported that 40 percent of 'religious conservatives' voted Democratic)" (Himmelfarb, *One Nation, Two Cultures,* 71).

68. Carter, *God's Name in Vain,* 45.

69. Ibid., 45, 46. See also Hardisty, "Resurgence of the Right," 23–44.

70. Sider, *Just Generosity,* 217.

71. Dionne reveals that "white Evangelicals outside the National Council of Churches now outnumber white Protestants within the ecumenical fold" (Dionne and Diiulio, *What's God Got to Do with the American Experiment?* 19).

72. Kathleen Hayes, "Evangelicals for Social Action: Developing a Biblical Agenda for Public Life," *Other Side* 22, no. 3 (April 1986): 10.

73. Ibid.

74. Marty, *Politics, Religion, and the Common Good,* 83.

75. Sider, *Just Generosity,* 39.

76. Thomas and Dobson, *Blinded by Might,* 81.

77. Marvin Olasky, *Renewing American Compassion: How Compassion for the Needy Can Turn Ordinary Citizens into Heroes* (Washington, D.C.: Regnery Publishing, 1996), 66.

78. Kristol, *Neo-Conservatism,* 253.

79. Magnet, *Dream and the Nightmare,* 13.

80. Marvin Olasky, *The Tragedy of American Compassion* (Wheaton: Crossway, 1992), 179.

81. See Kramer and Kimball, *Betrayal of Liberalism,* 227–33. Magnet maintains that "poverty turned pathological . . . because the new culture that the Haves invented . . . permitted, even celebrated, behavior that, when poor people practice it, will imprison them inextricably in poverty" (Magnet, *Dream and the Nightmare,* 17).

82. Sider, *Just Generosity,* 36.

83. Olasky, *Tragedy of American Compassion,* 221. This social leader also reveals that "the New Testament does not propose redistribution of wealth and forced 'equality' for all. Instead, the emphasis is on independence from enslaving powers, spiritual or physical" (Marvin Olasky, Herbert Schlossberg, Pierre Berthoud, and Clark H. Pinnock, *Freedom, Justice, and Hope: Toward a Strategy for the Poor and the Oppressed* [Westchester, Ill.: Crossway, 1988], 130).

84. See William Ryan, *Blaming the Victim* (New York: Vintage Books, 1971).

85. Sykes, *Nation of Victims,* 106. See also Tammy Blackard, "Urban Poor: They Need More Than Good Public Policy," *Christianity Today* 34, no. 17 (November 19, 1990): 50.

86. Sykes, *Nation of Victims,* 106. See also Magnet, *Dream and the Nightmare,* 58.

87. Magnet, *Dream and the Nightmare,* 122. "Ever since Marx described capitalism as systematic exploitation," Magnet observes, "the idea of the victimized poor has cast its dispiriting shadow over the intellectual landscape of modern times" (122).

88. Marvin Olasky, *Compassionate Conservatism: What It Is, What It Does, and How It Can Transform America* (New York: Free Press, 2000), 3.

89. Wallis, *Soul of Politics,* xvi. Wallis also contends, in a very balanced way, that to "speak only of moral behavior, apart from oppressive social realities, just blames the victim" (20–21).

90. Olasky, *Renewing American Compassion,* 119–20. Moreover, Magnet observes that "the new culture of the Haves, in its quest for personal liberation, withdrew respect from the behavior and attitudes that have traditionally boosted people up the economic ladder—deferral of gratification, sobriety, thrift, dogged industry, and so on through the whole catalogue of antique-sounding bourgeois virtues" (Magnet, *Dream and the Nightmare,* 17).

91. Magnet, *Dream and the Nightmare,* 38–39. Sider points out that "neither bureaucratic government nor for-profit business is very good at teaching such things. But good families and communities are" (Sider, *Just Generosity,* 83).

92. Magnet, *Dream and the Nightmare,* 39.

93. Ibid. Beyond the virtuous practice of not having children out of wedlock, one of the most important things that the poor can do to alleviate their condition is to access American education—much of which is free. This is also an area in which the church should be involved in offering various support services (such as day care) so that the poor can acquire what education they need for a better way of life.

94. Sider, *Just Generosity,* 121.

95. John Naisbitt and Patricia Aburdene, *Megatrends 2000: Ten New Directions for the 1990s* (New York: William Morrow, 1990), 170.

96. Himmelfarb, *One Nation, Two Cultures,* 63.

97. Olasky, *Renewing American Compassion,* 137.

98. See Kathy Gilbert, "Fathers Make Important Difference in Children's Lives," *United Methodist News Service,* June 4, 2003.

99. Kristol, *Neo-Conservatism,* 67.

100. See Himmelfarb, *One Nation, Two Cultures,* 28. This scholar contends that the family needs to recover "the legal and social authority it has forfeited to the state and the morality it has ceded to the counterculture" (57).

101. Sider, *Just Generosity,* 123–24.

102. Ibid., 124.

103. Ibid., 137. Sider maintains, "Any policy or political philosophy that immediately seeks governmental solutions for problems that could be solved just as well or better at the level of family violates the biblical framework that stresses the central societal role of the family" (71).

104. Michael S. Hamilton, "We're in the Money! How Did Evangelicals Get So Wealthy, and What Has It Done to Us?" *Christianity Today* 44, no. 7 (June 12, 2000): 36.

105. Ibid.

## Chapter 6

1. Lori G. Beaman, *Shared Beliefs/Different Lives: Women's Identities in Evangelical Context* (St. Louis: Chalice Press, 1999), 90.

2. Mark Chaves, *Ordaining Women: Culture and Conflict in Religious Organizations* (Cambridge: Harvard University Press, 1997), 163.

3. Beaman, *Shared Beliefs/Different Lives,* 135.

4. Ibid., 89. Beaman is quick to note, however, that many feminisms exist, among which are "liberal feminism (Friedan, 1963), maternal feminism (Ruddick, 1984), relational feminism (Gilligan, 1982), psychoanalytic feminism (Chodorow, 1992), socialist feminism (Jaggar, 1983, 1990; Smith, 1987), radical feminism (MacKinnon, 1989; Daly 1968, 1973), postmodern feminism (Nicholson, 1990), and so on" (ibid., 93).

5. Diana Hochstedt Butler, "Between Two Worlds (Role of Evangelical Women and Scholars)," *Christian Century* 110 (March 3, 1993): 231.

6. Robert H. Bork, *Slouching Towards Gomorrah: Modern Liberalism and American Decline* (New York: Regan Books, 1996), 202.

7. James Davison Hunter, *Culture Wars: The Struggle to Define America* (New York: Basic Books, 1991), 160.

8. Bork, *Slouching Towards Gomorrah*, 197. This former judge writes, "Radical feminism is the most destructive and fanatical movement to come down to us from the Sixties. This is a revolutionary, not a reformist, movement, and it is meeting with considerable success. Totalitarian in spirit, it is deeply antagonistic to traditional Western culture and proposes the complete restructuring of society, morality, and human nature" (193).

9. Ibid., 215.

10. Beaman, *Shared Beliefs/Different Lives*, 33.

11. Daymon A. Johnson, "Reformed Neo-Traditionalists: Patriarchal Models of Womanhood and the Christian Right," *Fides et Historia* 25 (Fall 1993): 77–101.

12. Ibid., 85. Beaman views the *complementarian* argument in a slightly different way and reasons as follows: "However, there is an underlying belief that women think and reason differently. Such a conceptualization of 'equal but different' would use difference as justification for the inclusion of women in church leadership, an interesting variation on the traditional view" (Beaman, *Shared Beliefs/Different Lives*, 99).

13. Johnson, "Reformed Neo-Traditionalists," 100. For a critique of the neo-traditionalist view, see Rebecca Merrill Groothuis, "Who's Afraid of the Slippery Slope? Evangelicals and the Gender War," *Regeneration Quarterly* 1 (Fall 1995): 12–14.

14. Nevertheless, some feminist evangelicals, though they affirm basic equality of roles for men and women, draw the line with respect to women in combat.

15. Rebecca Merrill Groothuis, *Good News for Women: A Biblical Picture of Gender Equality* (Grand Rapids: Baker, 1997), 48.

16. Beaman, *Shared Beliefs/Different Lives*, 96.

17. Groothuis, *Good News for Women*, 15. In this same context, this leading evangelical scholar points out that she does not "use the term 'complementarian' . . . because I believe it to be ambiguous" (15).

18. Deane William Ferm, *Contemporary American Theologies* (San Francisco: Harper & Row, 1990), 82.

19. Ibid.

20. For an evangelical book that has as one of its headings "Feminist Spirituality: Liberation from the Text" and in its assessment section states, "In the final analysis, truth is whatever agrees with feminism," see Jim Leffel and Dennis McCallum, "The Postmodern Religious Shift: Five Case Studies," in *The Death of Truth: What's Wrong with Multiculturalism, the Rejection of Reason, and the New Postmodern Diversity,* ed. Dennis McCallum (Minneapolis: Bethany, 1996), 221–25.

21. Beaman, *Shared Beliefs/Different Lives*, 137.

22. Katherine Kersten, "How the Feminist Establishment Hurts Women: A Christian Critique of a Movement Gone Wrong," *Christianity Today* 38, no. 7 (June 20, 1994): 22. Kersten points out that "much feminist theory is no longer centrally concerned with promoting fairness and equal rights" (23).

23. Chaves, *Ordaining Women*, 1.

24. Ibid. Chaves also points out that before 1970 "women did not pursue the professional degree for clergy in significant numbers whether or not their denomination formally granted it to them; after 1970, women did pursue the degree whether or not their denomination formally granted it" (19).

25. Ibid., 30.

26. Ibid., 188.

27. Ibid., 5.

28. Ibid., 25. For a helpful study of Lutheranism's relation to the American evangelical movement, see Mark Ellingsen, "Lutheranism," in *The Variety of American Evangelicalism,* ed. Donald W. Dayton and Robert K. Johnston (Downers Grove, Ill.: InterVarsity, 1991).

29. Chaves, *Ordaining Women,* 133. Chaves reveals that "nonsacramentalist denominations are more than four times as likely to begin to ordain women in a given year than are sacramentalist denominations" (85).

30. Richard Quebedeaux, *The Young Evangelicals* (New York: Harper & Row, 1974), 114.

31. Charles Colson and Richard John Neuhaus, eds., *Evangelicals and Catholics: Toward a Common Mission* (Dallas: Word, 1995), xii.

32. Thomas C. Fox, *Sexuality and Catholicism* (New York: Braziller, 1995), 204–5.

33. Chaves, *Ordaining Women,* 87.

34. Fox, *Sexuality and Catholicism,* 204–5. For research that considers views on homosexuality as a factor in maintaining evangelical identity, see Shelia Hassell Hughes, "Homosexuality and Group Boundaries in Contemporary Evangelical Feminism: A Historical Perspective," *Quarterly Review (Methodist)* 14 (Summer 1994): 135–59.

35. As cited in Groothuis, *Good News for Women,* 109.

36. Sandra M. Schneiders, *Beyond Patching: Faith and Feminism in the Catholic Church* (Mahwah, N.J.: Paulist Press, 1991), 110.

37. Fox, *Sexuality and Catholicism,* 219.

38. Ibid. For a detailed study of a local Roman Catholic congregation that protests against Rome's diminishment of women, see Jim Naughton, *Catholics in Crisis: The Rift between American Catholics and Their Church* (New York: Penguin, 1996).

39. Jerome, "Letter to Eustochium," in *Nicene and Post-Nicene Fathers of the Christian Church, Second Series,* vol. 6, ed. Philip Schaff and Wace Henry (Grand Rapids: Eerdmans, 1892), 28.

40. Jerome, "Letter to Lucinius," in *Nicene and Post-Nicene Fathers of the Christian Church,* 153.

41. Chaves, *Ordaining Women,* 88.

42. Fox, *Sexuality and Catholicism,* 210. See also Garry Wills's assessment of the exclusion of women in key leadership roles held in place by the power of the papacy in Garry Wills, *Papal Sin: Structures of Deceit* (New York: Doubleday, 2000), 104–21.

43. Chaves, *Ordaining Women,* 119.

44. J. I. Packer, "Let's Stop Making Women Presbyters," *Christianity Today* 35, no. 2 (February 11, 1991): 13–21. Packer writes, "Since the Son of God was incarnate as a male, it will always be easier, other things being equal, to realize and remember that Christ is ministering in person if his human agent and representative is also male" (20). However, it is also likely that Christ wore a beard, so should all presbyters, then, grow beards so that we can "remember that Christ is ministering"? The reasoning here is very specious.

45. Ibid., 20.

46. As cited in Groothuis, *Good News for Women,* 105.

47. Ibid.

48. J. Lee Grady, *Ten Lies the Church Tells Women: How the Bible Has Been Misused to Keep Women in Spiritual Bondage* (Lake Mary, Fla.: Charisma House, 2000), 32.

49. Chaves, *Ordaining Women,* 89–90.

50. As indicated in Beaman, *Shared Beliefs/Different Lives,* 52. See also Nancy Nason-Clark, "Conservative Protestants and Violence against Women: Exploring the Rhetoric and the Re-

sponse," in *Sex, Lies, and Sanctity: Religion and Deviance in Modern America,* ed. Mary Jo Neitz and Marion Goldman (Greenwich, Conn.: JAI Press, 1995), 109–30.

51. Chaves, *Ordaining Women,* 101. This leading scholar adds, "But as the issue took on the symbolic weight of liberalism and modernity, and as strict inerrancy became firmly institutionalized as a symbol of resistance to the modern world, it became more and more difficult to be both an inerrantist and a supporter of women's ordination. The difficulty is mainly cultural" (116).

52. Michael S. Hamilton, "Women, Public Ministry, and American Fundamentalism, 1920–1950," *Religion and American Culture* 3 (Summer 1993): 179.

53. Ibid., 188.

54. Ibid., 179.

55. Ibid. For an excellent historical analysis of the transition from fundamentalism to evangelicalism, see George M. Marsden, "From Fundamentalism to Evangelicalism: A Historical Analysis," in *The Evangelicals,* ed. David F. Wells and John D. Woodbridge (Grand Rapids: Baker, 1977), 142–62.

56. Hamilton, "Women, Public Ministry, and American Fundamentalism," 179.

57. When I write of the Holiness movement, I am referring to the people, theological emphases, and institutions that were focused on both the doctrine of entire sanctification as the leitmotif of thought and practice and the social consequences of such a focus. This movement, gifted and valuable in so many respects, virtually broke up by the end of the twentieth century (with but a few exceptions) such that much of what remains are Holiness institutions and denominations whose earlier focus has been largely deflected by many other interests. See Kenneth J. Collins, "Why the Holiness Movement Is Dead," *Asbury Theological Journal* 54, no. 2 (Fall 1999): 27–36. See also Keith Drury, "The Holiness Movement Is Dead," *Holiness Digest* 8, no. 1 (Winter 1994), 13–15; and Richard S. Taylor, "Why the Holiness Movement Died," *God's Revivalist and Bible Advocate* 111, no. 2 (March 1999): 6–27.

58. Donald W. Dayton, *Discovering an Evangelical Heritage* (New York: Harper & Row, 1976), 86.

59. Donald W. Dayton and Lucille Sider Dayton, "Women as Preachers: Evangelical Precedents," *Christianity Today* 19 (May 23, 1975): 4.

60. Dayton, *Discovering an Evangelical Heritage,* 90.

61. Lucille Sider Dayton and Donald W. Dayton, "'Your Daughters Shall Prophesy': Feminism in the Holiness Movement," *Methodist History* 14 (January 1976): 91.

62. Dayton and Dayton, "Women as Preachers," 5.

63. Dayton, *Discovering an Evangelical Heritage,* 91.

64. Ibid., 88.

65. Ibid., 92–93.

66. Chaves, *Ordaining Women,* 115. See also Dayton and Dayton, "Your Daughters Shall Prophesy," 89.

67. Dayton and Dayton, "Your Daughters Shall Prophesy," 91.

68. Dayton and Dayton, "Women as Preachers," 6.

69. Susie C. Stanley, *Holy Boldness: Women Preachers' Autobiographies and the Sanctified Self* (Knoxville: University of Tennessee Press, 2002), xi.

70. Ibid., 28.

71. Ibid., 106. This egalitarian primitivism is linked by Stanley to nothing less than the authority of the Bible. She writes, "Wesleyan/Holiness adherents are egalitarian primitivists who

affirmed women preachers because they saw that the Bible documented women's leadership and public ministry in the early church" (7).

72. Ibid., 91. Stanley continues this line of thought and writes, "The sanctified self successfully rejected a construction of self that sought to deny women the right to speak in public. Women refused to be silenced by arguments stemming from a gendered construction of self. Women responded with evidence based on experience and Scripture, which were the primary sources of their theology" (139).

73. Ibid., 62.

74. John P. Bartkowski, "Debating Patriarchy: Discursive Disputes over Spousal Authority among Evangelical Family Commentators," *Journal for the Scientific Study of Religion* 36 (Spring 1997): 393.

75. Christian Smith, *Christian America? What Evangelicals Really Want* (Berkeley: University of California Press, 2000), 160.

76. Margaret Bendroth, "Last Gasp Patriarchy: Women and Men in Conservative American Protestantism," *Muslim World* 91, nos. 1–2 (Spring 2001): 46.

77. James Davison Hunter, *Evangelicalism: The Coming Generation* (Chicago: University of Chicago Press, 1987), 95.

78. Ibid.

79. Smith, *Christian America?* 183.

80. Hunter, *Evangelicalism,* 141. Moreover, Hunter notes that "when contemporary Evangelicals (preachers, spokesmen, family experts, lobbyists, and politicians) speak of the Christian family, the traditional family, or traditional family values, they are really referring to the prototypical nineteenth-century bourgeois family" (92).

81. Smith, *Christian America?* 175.

82. Ibid., 191. Smith fills out his thought on this score and states that "evangelicals' common constructions of male headship primarily in terms of responsibility, accountability, and self-sacrifice at times shaped their discussions of headship in an interestingly *conditional* way. Very rare were explanations of headship that unconditionally established the rights and authority of husbands" (180).

83. Ibid., 189.

84. Ibid., 190. Bartkowski sees greater diversity than has hitherto been recognized. He writes, "In this study, I have analyzed a large sample of conservative Protestant gender and family manuals to reveal a discursive multiplicity in evangelical constructions of spousal authority" (Bartkowski, "Debating Patriarchy," 406).

85. Beaman, *Shared Beliefs/Different Lives,* 64.

86. Ibid. In terms of another population, Beaman also discovered that "evangelical feminists are far less likely to accept submission as a part of their marital relationships, no matter how it is interpreted" (61).

87. Rebecca Merrill Groothuis, "Searching for Woman's Place in Evangelicalism, Review Essay," *Christian Scholar's Review* 28, no. 2 (1998): 336.

88. Ibid. R. Marie Griffith maintains that "many conservative Christians now take feminist tenets about equality for granted and take care to justify their lives to the rest of the world on those grounds" (R. Marie Griffith, "Revising Our Assessment of Evangelical Women's Groups," *Tikkun* 13, no. 1 [March–April 1998]: 19).

89. Groothuis, "Who's Afraid of the Slippery Slope?" 14.

90. Superintendent of Documents, ed., *Inaugural Addresses of the Presidents of the United States* (Washington, D.C.: United States Government Printing Office, 1969), 129–30.

91. Ronald W. Pierce, "Evangelicals and Gender Roles in the 1990s: 1 Timothy 2:8–15: A Test Case," *Journal of the Evangelical Theological Society* 36 (September 1993): 343–55.

92. Stanley, *Holy Boldness,* 7. See also the very fine study that explores the role of women preachers in historic Methodism: Paul W. Chilcote, *She Offered Them Christ: The Legacy of Women Preachers in Early Methodism* (Eugene, Ore.: Wipf & Stock, 2001).

93. Stanley, *Holy Boldness,* 132. See also Estrelda Alexander's research in terms of sanctification and African American Wesleyan women: Estrelda Alexander, "Conversion and Sanctification in Nineteenth-Century African American Wesleyan Women," in *Conversion in the Wesleyan Tradition,* ed. Kenneth J. Collins and John H. Tyson (Nashville: Abingdon, 2001), 83–102.

94. Groothuis, *Good News for Women,* 23.

95. Ibid., 14. She adds, "Religious patriarchy had been vanquished by the redemptive work of Jesus Christ. Societal patriarchy, however, remained intact" (23).

96. Leffel and McCallum, "Postmodern Religious Shift," 223.

97. Ibid., 225.

98. Groothuis writes, "The truth of equality of all persons under God is grounded in creation. Genesis 1:26–27 and 5:1–2 state that both male and female humans bear God's image equally and without distinction" (Groothuis, *Good News for Women,* 20).

99. Hunter points out that "*properly interpreted,* the text of Scripture is not inimical to women. . . . It is up to Christian feminists to call a halt to [the] inequitable handling of the Holy Word. Proper interpretation, in this case, functions to delegitimate traditional formulations" (Hunter, *Evangelicalism,* 105).

100. See Grady, *Ten Lies the Church Tells Women,* 14.

101. See Ben Witherington III, *New Testament History: A Narrative Account* (Grand Rapids: Baker, 2001); Luke Timothy Johnson, *The First and Second Letters to Timothy: A New Translation with Introduction and Commentary* (New York: Doubleday, 2001); and Donald Guthrie, *New Testament Introduction* (Downers Grove, Ill.: InterVarsity, 1975), 596–610. The fourth edition of this work was produced in July 1990. See also J. Glenn Gould, "The Pastoral Epistles: The First and Second Epistles to Timothy, the Epistle to Titus," in *Beacon Bible Commentary,* ed. A. F. Harper, Ralph Earle, W. M. Greathouse, and W. T. Purkiser (Kansas City: Beacon Hill, 1965), 541–48.

102. Gregory A. Boyd and Paul R. Eddy, *Across the Spectrum: Understanding Issues in Evangelical Theology* (Grand Rapids: Baker, 2002), 231–33.

103. Grady, *Ten Lies the Church Tells Women,* 55.

104. Richard Clark Kroeger and Catherine Clark Kroeger, *I Suffer Not a Woman: Rethinking 1 Timothy 2:11–15 in Light of Ancient Evidence* (Grand Rapids: Baker, 1992), 82.

105. Ibid.

106. As Groothuis asks, "But is the prohibition grounded in the creation account, or is it simply explained or illustrated by the creation account?" (Groothuis, *Good News for Women,* 210).

107. William Barclay, *The Letters to Timothy, Titus, and Philemon,* Daily Study Bible Series (Philadelphia: Westminster, 1975), 67.

108. Ibid.

109. Boyd and Eddy, *Across the Spectrum,* 233. These authors are laying out various views in a point/counterpoint fashion.

110. See Augustine, *On Christian Doctrine,* trans. D. W. Robertson (Indianapolis: Bobbs-Merrill Educational Publishing, 1958), section XXXVI, 30.

## Chapter 7

1. David B. Barrett, "Denominationalism," in *The Dictionary of Christianity in America,* ed. Mark A. Noll (Downers Grove, Ill.: InterVarsity, 1990), 351. Barrett lists the number in 1980 as 20,800.

2. Thomas C. Oden, *Life in the Spirit: Systematic Theology,* vol. 3 (San Francisco: Harper-SanFrancisco, 1994), 309.

3. Ibid., 309–10.

4. Ibid. See also Martien E. Brinkman, "The Common Challenge to Ecumenicals and Evangelicals: An Ecumenical Appraisal," *Exchange* 23, no. 3 (December 1994): 191–206.

5. Jon R. Stone, *On the Boundaries of American Evangelicalism: The Postwar Evangelical Coalition* (New York: St. Martin's Press, 1997), 132.

6. Ibid., 123. Robert Wuthnow asks an important question that raises the issue of disunity and cultural accommodation: "With all religious communities in flux, can religion provide a significant source of identity? Is it possible that people will simply derive their identity from the mass media and from the marketplace?" (Robert Wuthnow, *Christianity in the Twenty-first Century: Reflections on the Challenges Ahead* [Oxford: Oxford University Press, 1993], 12).

7. Stone, *On the Boundaries of American Evangelicalism,* 134. In terms of the call for unity within the evangelical household itself, see Donald G. Bloesch, *The Future of Evangelical Christianity: A Call for Unity amidst Diversity* (Colorado Springs: Helmers & Howard, 1988).

8. Brinkman, "Common Challenge to Ecumenicals and Evangelicals," 204.

9. Stanley J. Grenz, *Renewing the Center: Evangelical Theology in a Post-theological Era* (Grand Rapids: Baker, 2000), 308.

10. Though some evangelicals believe that dialogue with Eastern Orthodoxy should take precedence, I disagree. American evangelicalism, in many respects, is a "Western" phenomenon with deep roots in the Reformation and in the controversies at the turn of the twentieth century. Moreover, though theological liberalism has been supplanted in many respects by postliberal and postmodern approaches, it nevertheless continues to wield institutional power. This is likely to continue well into the twenty-first century.

11. But critical evangelical students, in other settings, were also busy critiquing some of their "fundamentalist" evangelical professors as well.

12. Alister McGrath, *A Passion for Truth: The Intellectual Coherence of Evangelicalism* (Downers Grove, Ill.: InterVarsity, 1996), 124.

13. See Theodore Jennings's description of Methodist evangelicals who consider Aldersgate to be John Wesley's conversion experience in Theodore Jennings, "John Wesley against Aldersgate," *Quarterly Review* 8, no. 3 (Fall 1988): 20, 22.

14. Alvin Plantinga provides a wonderful and informative account of how theological liberals often misuse the word *fundamentalist:* "The full meaning of the term, therefore (in this use), can be given by something like 'stupid sumbitch whose theological opinions are considerably to the right of mine'" (Alvin Plantinga, *Warranted Christian Belief* [New York: Oxford University Press, 2000], 244–45).

15. Roger E. Olson, "Whales and Elephants: Both God's Creatures but Can They Meet? Evangelicals and Liberals in Dialogue," *Pro Ecclesia* 4, no. 2 (Spring 1995): 169.

16. It is interesting to note that the "critical evangelicals" often have strong philosophical backgrounds that no doubt have prepared them for their ongoing contributions to the intellectual life of evangelicalism. Stanley Grenz, William Abraham, and Thomas Oden, among others, would qualify for this designation.

17. Alister McGrath, "Why Evangelicalism Is the Future of Protestantism," *Christianity Today* 39, no. 7 (June 19, 1995): 21.

18. See George M. Marsden, *Understanding Fundamentalism and Evangelicalism* (Grand Rapids: Eerdmans, 1991), 34–35.

19. Robert E. Webber, *The Younger Evangelicals: Facing the Challenges of the New World* (Grand Rapids: Baker, 2002), 29.

20. Michael Scott Horton, *Made in America: The Shaping of Modern American Evangelicalism* (Grand Rapids: Baker, 1991), 10.

21. See William J. Abraham, *Waking from Doctrinal Amnesia: The Healing of Doctrine in the United Methodist Church* (Nashville: Abingdon, 1995).

22. Richard G. Hutcheson, *Mainline Churches and the Evangelicals* (Atlanta: John Knox, 1981), 179.

23. Richard J. Mouw, *The Smell of Sawdust: What Evangelicals Can Learn from Their Fundamentalist Heritage* (Grand Rapids: Zondervan, 2000), 40.

24. Christian Smith, for example, working with some hard sociological data, writes, "The difference between evangelicals and liberals here is especially striking, given liberal Protestantism's long tradition of and reputation for social activism, and evangelicalism's standard critique of liberalism as being too committed to a social Gospel. Evangelicals, it appears, may ironically be the most committed carriers of a new social Gospel" (Christian Smith, *American Evangelicalism: Embattled and Thriving* [Chicago: University of Chicago Press, 1998], 37).

25. Henry H. Knight and Don E. Saliers, *The Conversation Matters: Why United Methodists Should Talk with One Another* (Nashville: Abingdon, 1999), 13.

26. Ibid. It is hoped that the distinction between "evangelical Methodist" and "ecumenically committed sacramental Methodist" is not employed by either Knight or Saliers in a way that is supposed to inform the distinction between conservative and liberal. That is, the way that the "conversation" is structured in this book at the outset may itself be problematic and therefore should rightly be questioned by progressive evangelicals. Beyond this, it would have also been interesting if Saliers had explained in a simple and cogent way what he meant by referring to himself as a "sacramental Methodist" since the sacraments are very much a part of United Methodist life and witness. Did he mean to claim, as does Rome, that a priestly class offers the sacraments in a sacerdotal way as the very instruments of salvation? Indeed, one wonders just what Saliers is affirming by such a statement that other United Methodists supposedly are not.

27. Ibid., 57.

28. Ibid., 51. For a different approach to the mainline dilemma, see Thomas C. Oden, "Mainstreaming the Mainline," *Christianity Today* 44, no. 9 (August 7, 2000): 59–61.

29. Knight and Saliers, *Conversation Matters,* 57. See also Robert Wuthnow, "Evangelicals, Liberals, and the Perils of Individualism," *Perspectives* 6 (May 1991): 10–13.

30. Knight and Saliers, *Conversation Matters,* 57. Friedrich Schleiermacher writes, "Religion is to seek this [the immediate consciousness of the universal existence of all finite things] and find it in all that lives and moves, in all growth and change, in all doing and suffering. It is to have life and to know life in immediate feeling, only as such an existence in the Infinite and Eternal" (Friedrich Schleiermacher, *On Religion: Speeches to Its Cultured Despisers* [New York: Harper Torchbooks, 1958], 36).

31. Knight and Saliers, *Conversation Matters,* 47.

32. Ibid. For a different approach in terms of dialogue between evangelicals and "ecumenicals," see Richard J. Coleman, *Issues of Theological Conflict: Evangelicals and Liberals* (Grand Rapids: Eerdmans, 1972). Moreover, as James Heidinger points out, the requirement for laity

to subscribe to the Articles of Religion was dropped in 1916. But the standard remained for clergy. See James V. Heidinger III, "Doctrine and the People Called Methodists," *Good News* 37, no. 2 (September–October 2003): 10.

33. United Methodist Church, *The United Methodist Hymnal* (Nashville: United Methodist Publishing House, 1997), 33–53. The fourth form is actually a congregational reaffirmation of the baptismal covenant.

34. United Methodist Church, *The Book of Discipline of the United Methodist Church, 2000* (Nashville: United Methodist Publishing House, 2000), 60, par. 103, sec. 3.

35. David L. Edwards and John Stott, *Evangelical Essentials* (Downers Grove, Ill.: Inter-Varsity, 1988), 93.

36. Ibid., 106.

37. Thomas P. Rausch, *Catholics and Evangelicals: Do They Share a Common Future?* (Downers Grove, Ill.: InterVarsity, 2000), 6.

38. Mark A. Noll, *American Evangelical Christianity* (Malden, Mass.: Blackwell, 2001), 113.

39. Colleen Carroll, *The New Faithful: Why Young Adults Are Embracing Christian Orthodoxy* (Chicago: Loyola, 2002), 166.

40. Richard John Neuhaus, "The Catholic Difference," in *Evangelicals and Catholics: Toward a Common Mission,* ed. Charles Colson and Richard John Neuhaus (Dallas: Word, 1995), 186.

41. Colson and Neuhaus, *Evangelicals and Catholics,* , xvi.

42. Ibid., xvi–xvii. It may be that the commonality between evangelicals and Roman Catholics, beyond serving the same Lord, consists chiefly in a shared morality, vis-à-vis the secular American state, rather than in ecclesiology, the conception of ministry, or even in terms of spirituality. In my reading, the more attention that is given to these other topics, the more will differences emerge.

43. J. I. Packer, "Crosscurrents among Evangelicals," in *Evangelicals and Catholics,* 149.

44. Colson and Neuhaus, *Evangelical and Catholics,* xvii.

45. Packer, "Crosscurrents among Evangelicals," 157.

46. Ibid., 159–60.

47. Packer, "Crosscurrents among Evangelicals," 153, 161, 167.

48. Ibid., 161. For more on the doctrine of the church as understood by evangelicals, see John H. Armstrong, *The Compromised Church: The Present Evangelical Crisis* (Wheaton: Crossway, 1998); and Robert E. Webber, *Common Roots: A Call to Evangelical Maturity* (Grand Rapids: Zondervan, 1978).

49. Neuhaus, "Catholic Difference," 197. In my judgment, it is far too much to concede to Rome that it is the "Catholic" church. Accordingly, I have employed such designations for the truly universal church, which embraces in charity and in truth Eastern Orthodoxy, the Protestant reform, and other communions of faith united in Jesus Christ. I, therefore, more accurately refer to Rome as the *Roman* Catholic Church, that is, as a particular expression of that universality.

50. Roman Catholic Church, *Catechism of the Catholic Church* (Mahwah, N.J.: Paulist Press, 1994), 224, par. 846.

51. Timothy George, "'The Gift of Salvation': A Remarkable Statement on What We Mean by the Gospel," *Christianity Today* 41, no. 14 (December 8, 1997): 34.

52. Ibid. See also Timothy George, Thomas C. Oden, and J. I. Packer, "An Open Letter about 'The Gift of Salvation,'" *Christianity Today* 42 (April 27, 1998): 9.

53. George, "Gift of Salvation," 34.

54. Arthur D. Moore, "Does 'the Gift of Salvation' Sell Out the Reformation?" *Christianity Today* 42 (April 27, 1998): 21.

55. Ibid., 17. For a reasoned analysis that compares "the gift of salvation" with the official teaching of the Roman Catholic Church, see J. Daryl Charles, "Assessing Recent Pronouncements on Justification: Evidence from 'the Gift of Salvation' and the Catholic *Catechism*," *Pro Ecclesia* 8, no. 4 (Fall 1999): 459–74.

56. Moore, "Does 'the Gift of Salvation' Sell Out the Reformation?" 21.

57. Martin Luther, *Luther's Works,* vol. 26, *Lectures on Galatians, 1535, Chapters 1–4,* ed. Jaroslav Jan Pelikan, Hilton C. Oswald, and Helmut T. Lehmann (St. Louis: Concordia, 1999), 137.

58. Mark Seifrid, "'The Gift of Salvation': Its Failure to Address the Crux of Justification," *Journal of the Evangelical Theological Society* 42, no. 4 (1999): 683.

59. John Armstrong, "Evangelicals and Catholics Together: A New Initiative or Further Confusion," *Viewpoint* 2, no. 1 (January–February 1998): 6.

60. Ibid. A similar approach is developed in John Armstrong, ed., *Roman Catholicism: Evangelical Protestants Analyze What Divides and Unites Us* (Chicago: Moody, 1994).

61. Lutheran World Federation and Roman Catholic Church, *The Joint Declaration on the Doctrine of Justification* (Grand Rapids: Eerdmans, 1999), 10–11, par. 5.

62. Richard Nyberg, "Protestant Theologians Object to Lutheran-Catholic Accord," *Christianity Today* 42, no. 7 (June 15, 1998): 12.

63. Robert Preus, *Justification and Rome* (St. Louis: Concordia, 1997), 114–15.

64. Ibid., 104.

65. Ibid., 77. See also Robert Preus, "Perennial Problems in the Doctrine of Justification," *Concordia Theological Quarterly* 45 (July 1981): 163–84.

66. Alister E. McGrath, *Iustitia Dei: A History of the Christian Doctrine of Justification from 1500 to the Present Day* (Cambridge: Cambridge University Press, 1986), 284.

67. For Luther's use of the phrase "alien righteousness" in his treatise "Two Kinds of Righteousness," see Harold J. Grimm, ed., *Luther's Works: Career of the Reformer: I,* vol. 31 (Philadelphia: Fortress, 1957), 297, 299.

68. Preus points out, "Rome objected strenuously to the Lutheran doctrine that justification was the forgiveness of sins and the imputation of Christ's righteousness to the believer since this doctrine made justification unreal, no more than a putative judgment, and therefore a fiction" (Preus, *Justification and Rome,* 70).

69. R. C. Sproul, *Faith Alone: The Evangelical Doctrine of Justification* (Grand Rapids: Baker, 1995), 97–98.

70. Lutheran World Federation and Roman Catholic Church, *Joint Declaration,* 20, par. 27, emphasis added. Preus contends that in the Catholic view justification actually becomes the process of sanctification and the Lutheran understanding of justification as a forensic doctrine is considered "peripheral" (Preus, *Justification and Rome,* 26).

71. Ibid., 13, par. 11. Clifford indicates that the Roman Catholic misunderstanding of justification as "infused grace" harkens back to difficulties with the Latin translation of a Greek term. Indeed, the Latin translation implies "making righteous," when the actual sense of the term, as generally agreed to by scholars today, implies "declaring righteous." See Alan C. Clifford, "The Gospel and Justification," *Evangelical Quarterly* 57 (1985): 254.

72. Lutheran World Federation and Roman Catholic Church, *Joint Declaration,* 45, sec. C.

73. Ibid., 19–20, pars. 26, 27. Evangelical Christians will no doubt be disappointed to learn that the *Catechism of the Catholic Church* has no separate section for the doctrine of regeneration

or the new birth. What discussion there is in the *Catechism* falls under the topic of baptism. See *Catechism of the Catholic Church,* 359, par. 1427.

74. Moreover, McGrath observes that "the very term 'justification' itself appears to have been gradually eliminated from the homiletical and catechetical literature of Catholicism." He adds, "The general reintroduction of the term into the vocabulary of Catholicism appears to date from the Second Vatican Council" (McGrath, *Iustitia Dei,* 284).

75. Lutheran World Federation and Roman Catholic Church, *Joint Declaration,* 9, preamble, par. 1: "Ruler and judge over all other Christian doctrines."

## Chapter 8

1. Alister McGrath, *Evangelicalism and the Future of Christianity* (Downers Grove, Ill.: InterVarsity, 1995), 184.

2. Ibid., 10.

3. Mark A. Shibley, *Resurgent Evangelicalism in the United States: Mapping Cultural Change since 1970* (Columbia: University of South Carolina Press, 1996), 116.

4. Mark A. Noll and Lyman Kellstedt, "The Changing Face of Evangelicalism," *Pro Ecclesia* 4, no. 2 (Spring 1995): 148.

5. Christian Smith, *American Evangelicalism: Embattled and Thriving* (Chicago: University of Chicago Press, 1998), 33.

6. McGrath, *Evangelicalism and the Future of Christianity,* 10.

7. Despite Pope Leo's claim in the nineteenth century that Anglican orders are invalid and the apostolic succession broken, I affirm the catholicity of the Anglican communion and the See of Canterbury. Rome applied a later historical construct (what it in time came to understand by the notion of a "priest") to the Anglican faith and found it wanting. The Anglican Church, on the other hand, has faithfully maintained the apostolic testimony throughout the ages through a number of means.

8. Stanley J. Grenz, *Revisioning Evangelical Theology: A Fresh Agenda for the Twenty-first Century* (Downers Grove, Ill.: InterVarsity, 1993), 44.

9. Thomas Howard, *Evangelical Is Not Enough* (San Francisco: Ignatius Press, 1984), 100.

10. This observation does not undermine the necessity of Christian apologetics in the least. It is a matter of employing various language resources in their proper venues.

11. See McGrath, *Evangelicalism and the Future of Christianity,* 83.

12. Anglicanism has been "destabilized" in the eyes of many evangelicals due to its failure to preserve the good order and teaching of the church with the consecration of Gene Robinson, an "avowed practicing homosexual," as bishop.

13. The Roman Catholic Church, *Catechism of the Catholic Church* (Mahwah, N.J.: Paulist Press, 1994), 220, par. 830.

14. Hans Küng, *The Catholic Church: A Short History* (New York: Modern Library, 2001), 40, emphasis added.

15. Ibid., 21. Moreover, Küng writes, "However, the earliest list of bishops, in Irenaeus of Lyons, according to which Peter and Paul transferred the ministry of *episkopos* to a certain Linus, is a second-century forgery. A monarchial episcopate can be demonstrated for Rome only from around the middle of the second century (Bishop Anicetus)" (22).

16. Roman Catholic Church, *Catechism of the Catholic Church,* 222, par. 837.

17. John Armstrong, ed., *Roman Catholicism: Evangelical Protestants Analyze What Divides and Unites Us* (Chicago: Moody, 1994), 163.

18. Roman Catholic Church, *Catechism of the Catholic Church*, 221, par. 834. Furthermore, the *Catechism* argues for the preeminence of Rome in the following: "Indeed, 'from the incarnate Word's descent to us, all Christian churches everywhere have held and hold the great Church that is here [at Rome] to be their only basis and foundation since, according to the Savior's promise, the gates of hell have never prevailed against her'" (221, par. 834).

19. Gerald Bray, *Evangelicalism and the Orthodox Church* (Cambridge: Acute, 2001), 86.

20. Daniel B. Clendenin, "Why I'm Not Orthodox: An Evangelical Explores the Ancient and Alien World of the Eastern Church," *Christianity Today* 41, no. 1 (January 6, 1997): 36.

21. Bray, *Evangelicalism and the Orthodox Church*, 90.

22. Ibid. Daniel Clendenin points out how the Eastern Orthodox resisted the triumphalism of Rome: "Indeed, in a letter of 865, Pope Nicholas made it clear that he intended to extend the power of the papacy 'over all the earth, that is, over every church.' Eastern Christians would hear nothing of it" (Clendenin, "Why I'm Not Orthodox," 35).

23. Clendenin, "Why I'm Not Orthodox," 36.

24. Stanley J. Grenz, *Renewing the Center: Evangelical Theology in a Post-theological Era* (Grand Rapids: Baker, 2000), 291.

25. Grenz, *Revisioning Evangelical Theology*, 49.

26. Miroslav Volf, *After Our Likeness: The Church as the Image of the Trinity* (Grand Rapids: Eerdmans, 1998), 158.

27. Ibid., 166.

28. Ibid., 164. For a much different understanding of the church, see Avery Dulles, "Church, Ministry, and Sacraments in Catholic-Evangelical Dialogue," in *Catholics and Evangelicals: Do They Share a Common Future?* ed. Thomas P. Rausch, 101–21 (Downers Grove, Ill.: InterVarsity, 2000).

29. Volf, *After Our Likeness*, 166.

30. Ibid., 275. It is this "openness" to other churches, pointed out by Volf, that is at the heart of genuine ecumenicity. For a helpful study on evangelicals and the "ecumenicals," see Martien E. Brinkman, "The Common Challenge to Ecumenicals and Evangelicals: An Ecumenical Appraisal," *Exchange* 23, no. 3 (December 1994): 191–206.

31. Volf, *After Our Likeness*, 275.

32. Ibid., 104.

33. See Gerhard Kittel, Gerhard Friedrich, and Geoffrey William Bromiley, "Kerygma," in *Theological Dictionary of the New Testament*, ed. Gerhard Kittel and Gerhard Bromiley (Grand Rapids: Eerdmans, 1995), 435.

34. Ibid.

35. "The Epistle of Ignatius to the Smyrnaeans," in *The Ante-Nicene Fathers*, vol. 1, *Translations of the Writings of the Fathers down to A.D. 325*, ed. Alexander Roberts, James Donaldson, and A. Cleveland Coxe (Grand Rapids: Eerdmans, n.d.), 1.1.4.6.0.8.

36. Bray, *Evangelicalism and the Orthodox Church*, 53.

37. The Western church was also governed in a conciliar way for a brief period when the Council of Constance, in sorting out the great Western schism in the early fifteenth century, issued the decrees *Haec sancta* and *Frequens*.

38. John Calvin, *Institutes of the Christian Religion*, trans. Henry Beveridge (Edinburgh: Calvin Translation Society, 1845–46), IV.ix.8.

39. Martin Luther, *Luther's Works,* vol. 41, *Church and Ministry III,* ed. Jaroslav Pelikan, Hilton C. Oswald, and Helmut T. Lehmann (Philadelphia: Fortress, 1966), 122.

40. Ibid., 25.

41. Martin Luther, *Luther's Works,* vol. 54, *Table Talk,* ed. Jaroslav Pelikan, Hilton C. Oswald, and Helmut T. Lehmann (Philadelphia: Fortress, 1967), 311.

42. Roman Catholic Church, *Catechism of the Catholic Church,* 26, par. 82.

43. Ibid., 27, par. 85.

44. Dulles, "Church, Ministry, and Sacraments in Catholic-Evangelical Dialogue," 115.

45. Many scholars point to the third century as the time when the use of icons began to take root in the church. See Paul Enns, "Icons," in *The Moody Handbook of Theology,* ed. Paul Enns (Chicago: Moody, 1989), 433.

46. Philip Schaff, *The Nicene and Post-Nicene Fathers Second Series,* vol. 8, *Basil: Letters and Select Works* (Peabody, Mass.: Hendrickson, 1994), ECF 3.8.1.1.0.18.

47. Clendenin, "Why I'm Not Orthodox," 37.

48. Noll and Kellstedt, "Changing Face of Evangelicalism," 159.

49. Though I share the concerns of many evangelicals with respect to icons, I nevertheless am not making the case for iconoclasm—but neither do I affirm fully the views of the iconodules. Icons, properly understood, may line the walls of churches (the side walls seem most appropriate, where icons will not likely become *the* focus of attention) and may be used with benefit in the lives of the faithful to lead them to the contemplation of the Word of God, Jesus Christ. Indeed, there is not and cannot be any knowledge of God apart from the Word. Christ is always found clothed in his promises. The same claim, however, cannot be made with any theological propriety with respect to icons. The difference is important.

50. Grenz, *Revisioning Evangelical Theology,* 108.

51. Robert E. Webber, *The Younger Evangelicals: Facing the Challenges of the New World* (Grand Rapids: Baker, 2002), 239.

52. John C. Olin, ed., *A Reformation Debate* (New York: Harper Torchbooks, 1966), 92.

53. Kim Riddlebarger, "Why Are Evangelicals Joining the Catholic Church?" in *Roman Catholicism: Evangelical Protestants Analyze What Divides and Unites Us,* ed. John Armstrong (Chicago: Moody, 1994), 238.

54. Ibid.

55. Donald G. Bloesch, *The Future of Evangelical Christianity: A Call for Unity amidst Diversity* (Colorado Springs: Helmers & Howard, 1988), 117.

56. Ibid. Bray points out that many evangelicals read the Bible from the safety net of their confessional community even "if they would not formally grant that community an authority superior to that of Scripture when rightly understood" (Bray, *Evangelicalism and the Orthodox Church,* 103).

57. Heiko A. Oberman, "Quo Vadis, Petre? Tradition from Irenaeus to Humani Generis," in *The Dawn of the Reformation: Essays in Late Medieval and Early Reformation Thought,* ed. Heiko A. Oberman (Edinburgh: T & T Clark, 1986), 269–96.

58. Each of the two "catholic" communions understands tradition in a slightly different way: Rome has a generous role for the magisterium; Eastern Orthodoxy affirms a single holy tradition that embraces both Scripture and a host of other elements.

59. I look forward to the publication of *Canonical Theism,* a work that William Abraham has edited along with Jason Vickers and Natalie Van Kirk.

60. Thomas C. Oden, *Agenda for Theology: After Modernity . . . What?* (Grand Rapids: Zondervan, 1990), 28.

61. Ibid., 25. Moreover, Oden writes, "So there is a sense in which the developing Protestant agenda for theology today must be a very Catholic agenda, but no longer in the Vatican II sense—rather in the spirit of the Counter-Reformation and Vatican I!" However, it is hard to comprehend just how the "spirit" of the Counter-Reformation, in all its anathemas, could be valuable to ecumenical evangelicals who are oriented to the truth of Scripture in a broad and generous ecumenical love that so richly bespeaks of the lordship of Christ (84).

62. Ibid., 37. See also 50–51 for a helpful definition of modernity.

63. Ibid., 160–61. Evangelical Protestants cannot affirm all that took place in the church from the year 500 to the end of the first millennium. Not only is the tradition becoming plural during this period, but many common, consensual, traditional elements, especially in terms of doctrines pertaining to Mary and the Lord's Supper, will have to be critiqued in light of the truth of Scripture.

64. Ibid., 145. So appreciative is Oden of tradition and institutional maintenance that he exclaims, "We are for the first time beginning to appreciate what was happening in the period from the Council of Trent and Ignatius Loyola and Melchior Cano through Carlos Borromeo and Roberto Bellarmine" (84). However, it must be noted that Ignatius of Loyola in his *Spiritual Exercises* counsels aspirants to put aside any thinking that differs from the tradition as articulated by the magisterium, and therefore, the faithful must obey promptly "the true spouse of Christ our Lord, our Holy Mother, the hierarchical Church." Even more emphatically, Ignatius undermines the normative value of Scripture and obscures the light of truth when he adds the following admonition: "If we wish to be sure that we are right in all things, we should always be ready to accept this principle: I will believe that the white that I see is black, if the hierarchical Church so defines it." Though Ignatius has made many lasting contributions to the church, there is little to "appreciate" in the preceding judgments. See Ignatius of Loyola, *The Spiritual Exercises of St. Ignatius,* trans. Anthony Mottola (New York: Doubleday, 1964), 139, 140–41.

65. Roman Catholic Church, *Catechism of the Catholic Church,* 222, par. 838. In a real sense, Oden's proposal for catholicity is "Roman Catholic"; Abraham's, "Eastern Orthodox"; and mine, "Protestant."

66. Susan Lynn Peterson, *Timeline Charts of the Western Church* (Grand Rapids: Zondervan, 1999), 54.

67. Cyril of Jerusalem writes, "Through Eve yet virgin came death; through a virgin, or rather from a virgin, must the Life appear: that as the serpent beguiled the one, so to the other Gabriel might bring good tidings" (Philip Schaff, *The Nicene and Post-Nicene Fathers Second Series,* vol. 7, *Cyril of Jerusalem, Gregory Nazianzen* (Peabody, Mass.: Hendrickson, 1994), 75, ECF 3.7.1.1.13.0.

68. Peterson, *Timeline Charts of the Western Church,* 64.

69. My proposal embraces the truth that Christ had two wills and thereby rejects monotheism, not on the basis of the fifth ecumenical council, though it is amply displayed there as well, but on the basis of Scripture, the teaching of the fathers, and the early history of the church. Moreover, this proposal embraces those common elements shared by the orthodox traditions during the period from 500 to the first millennium, once later Protestantism, along with its judgments and affirmations, is considered a part of the mix. In other words, the ongoing tradition, especially by the sixth century, cannot simply be accepted without the good and sufficient judgment of the Protestant community.

70. See Thomas C. Oden, *The Justification Reader* (Grand Rapids: Eerdmans, 2002).

71. Admittedly, Protestants do quite well in such a proposal since their major doctrinal emphasis of justification by grace through faith alone does not constitute a later doctrinal in-

novation, as do some of the teachings of Rome and Eastern Orthodoxy, but is very much a part of the witness of Scripture itself as well as the teaching of the early church fathers, Augustine in particular.

72. See Robert E. Webber, *Ancient-Future Faith: Rethinking Evangelicalism for a Postmodern World* (Grand Rapids: Baker, 1999).

## Conclusion

1. My thanks go out to Richard John Neuhaus, who wrote a timely work that suggested the title for my own—much different—contribution. See Richard John Neuhaus, *The Catholic Moment: The Paradox of the Church in the Postmodern World* (New York: Harper & Row, 1987).

# Bibliography

Abraham, William J. *Canon and Criterion in Christian Theology.* Oxford: Oxford University Press, 1998.

————. *The Coming Great Revival.* San Francisco: Harper & Row, 1984.

————. *The Divine Inspiration of Holy Scripture.* New York: Oxford University Press, 1981.

————. *Waking from Doctrinal Amnesia: The Healing of Doctrine in the United Methodist Church.* Nashville: Abingdon, 1995.

Abrams, Elliott. *Faith or Fear: How Jews Can Survive in a Christian America.* New York: Free Press, 1997.

Ahlstrom, Sydney E. "From Puritanism to Evangelicalism: A Critical Perspective." In *The Evangelicals,* edited by David F. Wells and John D. Woodbridge, 289–309. Grand Rapids: Baker, 1977.

Alexander, Estrelda. "Conversion and Sanctification in Nineteenth-Century African American Wesleyan Women." In *Conversion in the Wesleyan Tradition,* edited by Kenneth J. Collins and John H. Tyson, 83–102. Nashville: Abingdon, 2001.

Alexander, John F. *The Secular Squeeze: Reclaiming Christian Depth in a Shallow World.* Downers Grove, Ill.: InterVarsity, 1993.

Allen, Diogenes. *Christian Belief in a Postmodern World: The Full Wealth of Conviction.* Louisville: Westminster John Knox, 1989.

Anderson, Walter Truett. *Reality Isn't What It Used to Be.* San Francisco: Harper SanFrancisco, 1990.

Anonymous. "An Alliance of Values: Evangelical-Catholic Coalition Goes Beyond Activism." *Areopagus* 7, no. 3 (1994): 42–43.

―――――. "An Evangelical Declaration on Care of Creation." *Perspectives on Science and Christian Faith* 47 (1995): 110–11.

Armstrong, John H. *The Compromised Church: The Present Evangelical Crisis.* Wheaton: Crossway, 1998.

―――――. "Evangelicals and Catholics Together: A New Initiative or Further Confusion." *Viewpoint* 2, no. 1 (1998): 1–14.

―――――. "Guarding the Holy Fire: The Evangelicalism of John R. W. Stott, J. I. Packer, and Alister McGrath." *Reformation and Revival* 8, no. 4 (1999): 191–99.

―――――, ed. *The Coming Evangelical Crisis: Current Challenges to the Authority of Scripture and the Gospel.* Chicago: Moody, 1996.

―――――, ed. *Roman Catholicism: Evangelical Protestants Analyze What Divides and Unites Us.* Chicago: Moody, 1994.

Atkinson, James, ed. *Luther's Works.* Vol. 44, *The Christian in Society I.* Philadelphia: Fortress, 1966.

Augustine, St. *On Christian Doctrine.* Translated by D. W. Robertson. Indianapolis: Bobbs-Merrill Educational Publishing, 1958.

Aulen, Gustaf. *Christus Victor: An Historical Study of the Three Main Types of the Idea of the Atonement.* Translated by A. G. Herbert. New York: Macmillan, 1969.

Balmer, Randall. *Mine Eyes Have Seen the Glory: A Journey into the Evangelical Subculture in America.* New York: Oxford University Press, 1989.

―――――. "'A Pentecost of Politics': Evangelicals, Public Discourse, and American Culture." *Union Seminary Quarterly Review* 47, no. 1–2 (1993): 15–28.

―――――. "Trading Places: Evangelical and Mainline Protestantism at the Turn of the Twenty-First Century." *Word & World* 19, no. 1 (1999): 5–13.

Banner, Ray. "Evangelicalism in the United States." *Evangelical Quarterly* 39 (1967): 155–64.

Barclay, William. *The Letters to Timothy, Titus, and Philemon.* Daily Study Bible Series. Philadelphia: Westminster, 1975.

Barr, James. *Beyond Fundamentalism.* Philadelphia: Westminster, 1984.

Barrett, David B. "Denominationalism." In *The Dictionary of Christianity in America,* edited by Mark Noll, 351. Downers Grove, Ill.: InterVarsity, 1990.

Barron, Bruce. "Putting Women in Their Place: 1 Timothy 2 and Evangelical Views of Women in Church Leadership." *Journal of the Evangelical Theological Society* 33 (1990): 451–59.

Barth, Karl. *Church Dogmatics: The Doctrine of the Word of God.* Part 1. Edited by G. W. Bromiley and T. F. Torrance. Edinburgh: T & T Clark, 1936.

———. "The Strange New World within the Bible." In *The Word of God and the Word of Man,* 28–50. Gloucester, Mass.: Peter Smith, 1928.

Bartkowski, John P. "Debating Patriarchy: Discursive Disputes over Spousal Authority among Evangelical Family Commentators." *Journal for the Scientific Study of Religion* 36 (1997): 393–410.

Bassett, Paul. "The Fundamentalist Leavening of the Holiness Movement: 1914–1940." *Wesleyan Theological Journal* 13 (1978): 65–91.

Baum, Gregory. "The Evangelicals." *Ecumenism* 85 (1987): 2–34.

Bauman, Michael. "Why the Noninerrantists Are Not Listening: Six Tactical Errors Evangelicals Commit." *Journal of the Evangelical Theological Society* 29, no. 3 (1986): 317–24.

Beaman, Lori G. *Shared Beliefs/Different Lives: Women's Identities in Evangelical Context.* St. Louis: Chalice Press, 1999.

Bebbington, David W. "Evangelicalism in Its Settings: The British and American Movements since 1940." In *Evangelicalism,* edited by Mark Noll, David W. Bebbington, and George A. Rawlyk, 365–88. New York: Oxford University Press, 1994.

Bellah, Robert N., Richard Madsen, William M. Sullivan, Ann Swindler, and Steven M. Tipton. *Habits of the Heart.* Berkeley: University of California Press, 1985.

Bendroth, Margaret Lamberts. "Last Gasp Patriarchy: Women and Men in Conservative American Protestantism." *Muslim World* 91, nos. 1–2 (2001): 45–54.

———. "The Search for Women's Role in American Evangelicalism, 1930–1980." In *Evangelicalism and Modern America,* edited by George Marsden, 122–34. Grand Rapids: Eerdmans, 1984.

———. "Women in Twentieth-Century Evangelicalism." *Evangelical Studies Bulletin* 13 (1996): 4–6.

Bentley, William H. "Bible Believers in the Black Community." In *The Evangelicals: What They Believe, Who They Are, Where They Are Changing,* edited by David F. Wells and John D. Woodbridge, 108–21. Nashville: Abingdon, 1975.

Bercot, David W. *Will the Real Heretics Please Stand Up*. Tyler, Tex.: Scroll Publishing, 1989.

Berger, Peter L. "Religion in Post-Protestant America." *Commentary* 81, no. 5 (1986): 41–46.

———, and Thomas Luckmann. *The Social Construction of Reality*. Garden City, N.Y.: Anchor Books, 1966.

Blackard, Tammy. "Urban Poor: They Need More Than Good Public Policy." *Christianity Today* 34, no. 17 (1990): 50.

Bloesch, Donald G. *Essentials of Evangelical Theology*. Vol. 1. San Francisco: HarperSanFrancisco, 1982.

———. *Essentials of Evangelical Theology*. Vol. 2. San Francisco: HarperSan-Francisco, 1982.

———. *The Evangelical Renaissance*. Grand Rapids: Eerdmans, 1973.

———. *The Future of Evangelical Christianity: A Call for Unity amidst Diversity*. Colorado Springs: Helmers & Howard, 1988.

———. "The New Evangelicalism." *Religion in Life* 41 (1972): 327–39.

Bloom, Allan. *The Closing of the American Mind: How Higher Education Has Failed Democracy and Impoverished the Souls of Today's Students*. New York: Simon & Schuster, 1987.

Boice, James Montgomery. *What Makes a Church Evangelical?* Wheaton: Crossway, 1999.

———, and Benjamin E. Sasse, eds. *Here We Stand: A Call from Confessing Evangelicals*. Grand Rapids: Baker, 1996.

Bonhoeffer, Dietrich. *The Cost of Discipleship*. 2nd ed. New York: Macmillan, 1960.

Bonicelli, Paul J. "Testing the Waters or Opening the Floodgates? Evangelicals, Politics, and the 'New' Mexico." *Journal of Church and State* 39 (1997): 107–30.

Bork, Robert H. *Slouching towards Gomorrah: Modern Liberalism and American Decline*. New York: Regan Books, 1996.

Boyd, Gregory A., and Paul R. Eddy. *Across the Spectrum: Understanding Issues in Evangelical Theology*. Grand Rapids: Baker, 2002.

Brand, Chad Owen. "Is Carl Henry a Modernist? Rationalism and Foundationalism in Post-War Evangelical Theology." *Trinity Journal* 20 (1999): 3–21.

Bray, Gerald. *Evangelicalism and the Orthodox Church*. Cambridge: Acute, 2001.

Briggs, John. "A Lot in Common: Orthodox and Evangelicals Compare Notes." *One World* 209 (1995): 12–14.

Brinkman, Martien E. "The Common Challenge to Ecumenicals and Evangelicals: An Ecumenical Appraisal." *Exchange* 23, no. 3 (1994): 191–206.

Brow, Robert. "Evangelical Megashift." *Christianity Today* 34, no. 3 (1990): 12–14.

Brown, Harold O. J. "What's in a Name? (Perspective)." *Fundamentalist Journal* 3, no. 11 (1984): 21–22.

Brown, Ralph. "The Evangelical Succession? Evangelical History and Denominational Identity." *Evangelical Quarterly* 68, no. 1 (1996): 3–13.

Bruce, Steve. *The Rise and Fall of the New Christian Right.* Oxford: Clarendon, 1990.

Brushaber, George K. "Religious Leaders Join Scientists in Ecological Concerns." *Christianity Today* 35, no. 9 (1991): 49.

Burnham, Frederic B. *Postmodern Theology: Christian Faith in a Pluralist World.* New York: Harper & Row, 1989.

Butler, Diana Hochstedt. "Between Two Worlds (Role of Evangelical Women and Scholars)." *Christian Century* 110 (1993): 231–32.

Cagney, Mary. "Do Christian Colleges Treat Their Women Faculty Fairly?" *Christianity Today* 41, no. 14 (1997): 72.

Calhoun-Brown, Allison. "Still Seeing in Black and White: Racial Challenges for the Christian Right." In *Sojourners in the Wilderness,* edited by Corwin E. Smidt and James M. Penning, 115–37. Lanham, Md.: Rowman & Littlefield, 1997.

Caputo, John D., ed. *Deconstruction in a Nutshell: A Conversation with Jacques Derrida.* New York: Fordham University Press, 1997.

Carpenter, Joel A. "Fundamentalist Institutions and the Rise of Evangelical Protestantism, 1929–1942." *Church History* 49 (1980): 62–75.

———. *Revive Us Again: The Reawakening of American Fundamentalism.* New York: Oxford University Press, 1997.

———. "The Scope of American Evangelicalism: Some Comments on the Dayton-Marsden Exchange." *Christian Scholar's Review* 23, no. 1 (1993): 53–61.

Carroll, Colleen. *The New Faithful: Why Young Adults Are Embracing Christian Orthodoxy.* Chicago: Loyola Press, 2002.

Carter, Stephen L. *The Culture of Disbelief.* New York: Basic Books, 1993.

————. *The Dissent of the Governed.* Cambridge: Harvard University Press, 1998.

————. *God's Name in Vain: The Wrongs and Rights of Religion in Politics.* New York: Basic Books, 2000.

————. *Integrity.* New York: Basic Books, 1996.

Cerillo, Augustus, Jr. "A Survey of Recent Evangelical Social Thought." *Christian Scholar's Review* 5, no. 3 (1976): 272–80.

————, and Murray W. Dempster. "Carl F. H. Henry's Early Apologetic for an Evangelical Social Ethic, 1942–1956." *Journal of the Evangelical Theological Society* 34, no. 3 (1991): 365–79.

Chadwick, Samuel. *The Gospel of the Cross.* Salem, Ohio: Schmul Publishing, n.d.

Charles, J. Daryl. "Assessing Recent Pronouncements on Justification: Evidence from 'the Gift of Salvation' and the Catholic *Catechism.*" *Pro Ecclesia* 8, no. 4 (1999): 459–74.

Chaves, Mark. *Ordaining Women: Culture and Conflict in Religious Organizations.* Cambridge: Harvard University Press, 1997.

Chilcote, Paul W. *She Offered Them Christ: The Legacy of Women Preachers in Early Methodism.* Eugene, Ore.: Wipf & Stock, 2001.

Clendenin, Daniel B. "Why I'm Not Orthodox: An Evangelical Explores the Ancient and Alien World of the Eastern Church." *Christianity Today* 41, no. 1 (1997): 33–38.

Cole, Graham A. "The Evangelical and Scholarship: Personal Reflections." *Themelios* 24 (1998): 3–12.

Cole, Stewart G. *The History of Fundamentalism.* Brooklyn: Braunworth & Co., 1931.

Coleman, Richard J. *Issues of Theological Conflict: Evangelicals and Liberals.* Grand Rapids: Eerdmans, 1972.

Collins, Kenneth J. "Children of Neglect: American Methodist Evangelicals." *Christian Scholar's Review* 20, no. 1 (1990): 7–16.

Colson, Charles, and Richard John Neuhaus, eds. *Evangelicals and Catholics: Toward a Common Mission.* Dallas: Word, 1995.

Conn, Joseph L., ed. "Marriage of Convenience: The Growing Catholic-Fundamentalist Alliance and What It Means for Church-State Separation." *Journal of Church and State* 47 (1994): 103–7.

Cook, Guillermo. "The Evangelical Groundswell in Latin America." *Christian Century* 107 (1990): 1172–79.

Cook, Sharon Anne. "'A Gallant Little Band': Bertha Wright and the Late Nineteenth-Century Evangelical Woman." *Journal of the Canadian Church Historical Society* 37 (1995): 3–21.

Cox, Harvey. *Religion in the Secular City.* New York: Simon & Schuster, 1984.

Cullop, Floyd G., ed. *The Constitution of the United States.* New York: New American Library, 1969.

Davis, John Jefferson. "Future Directions for American Evangelicals." *Journal of the Evangelical Theological Society* 29, no. 4 (1986): 461–67.

Dayton, Donald W. *Discovering an Evangelical Heritage.* New York: Harper & Row, 1976.

———. "The Embourgeoisement of a Vision: Lament of a Radical Evangelical." *Other Side* 23, no. 8 (1987): 19.

———. "Evangelical Roots of Feminism." *Covenant Quarterly* 34 (1976): 41–56.

———. "Piety and Radicalism: Ante-Bellum Social Evangelicalism in the U.S." *Radical Religion* 3, no. 1 (1976): 36–40.

———. "Rejoinder to Historiography Discussion." *Christian Scholar's Review* 23, no. 1 (1993): 62–71.

———. "The Search for the Historical Evangelicalism: George Marsden's History of Fuller Seminary as a Case Study." *Christian Scholar's Review* 23, no. 1 (1993): 12–33.

———. "Some Doubts about the Usefulness of the Category 'Evangelical.'" In *The Variety of American Evangelicalism,* edited by Donald Dayton and Robert K. Johnston, 245–51. Downers Grove, Ill.: InterVarsity, 1991.

———. *The Theological Roots of Pentecostalism.* Grand Rapids: Francis Asbury Press, 1987.

———. "Yet Another Layer of the Onion: Or Opening the Ecumenical Door to Let the Riffraff In." *Ecumenical Review* 40 (1988): 87–110.

———, and Lucille Sider Dayton. "Women as Preachers: Evangelical Precedents." *Christianity Today* 19 (1975): 4–7.

———, and Robert K. Johnston, eds. *The Variety of American Evangelicalism.* Downers Grove, Ill.: InterVarsity, 1991.

Dayton, Lucille Sider, and Donald W. Dayton. "'Your Daughters Shall Prophesy': Feminism in the Holiness Movement." *Methodist History* 14 (1976): 66–91.

DeYoung, Curtiss Paul. "Tensions in North American Protestantism: An Evangelical Perspective." *Journal of Ecumenical Studies* 35, nos. 3, 4 (1998): 400–405.

Dieter, Melvin Easterday. *Revivalism and Holiness.* Philadelphia: Temple University, 1972.

———. "Telling the Arminian Story: Some Observations on Revivalistic Evangelicalism Past and Present." *Evangelical Journal* 10 (1992): 47–54.

Dionne, E. J., and John J. Diiulio, eds. *What's God Got to Do with the American Experiment?* Washington, D.C.: Brookings Institution Press, 2000.

Dobson, Edward. "Fundamentalism and Evangelicalism: A Comparison and Contrast." *Fundamentalist Today* 5, no. 3 (1986): 12.

Dockery, David S. *The Challenge of Postmodernism: An Evangelical Engagement.* Wheaton: Bridgepoint, 1995.

Dollar, George W. *The History of Fundamentalism in America.* Greenville, S.C.: Bob Jones University Press, 1973.

Dorrien, Gary. *The Remaking of Evangelical Theology.* Louisville: Westminster John Knox, 1998.

Dray, Stephen. "A Sickness unto Death?" *Evangel* 15, no. 3 (1997): 65–66.

D'Souza, Dinesh. *Illiberal Education: The Politics of Race and Sex on Campus.* New York: Free Press, 1991.

Dulles, Avery. "Church, Ministry, and Sacraments in Catholic-Evangelical Dialogue." In *Catholics and Evangelicals: Do They Share a Common Future?* edited by Thomas P. Rausch, 101–21. Downers Grove, Ill.: InterVarsity, 2000.

Dunnavant, Anthony L., ed. *Poverty and Ecclesiology.* Collegeville, Minn.: Liturgical Press, 1992.

Edge, Findley B. "The Evangelical Concern for Social Justice." *Religious Education* 74, no. 2 (1979): 487–89.

Editor. "Evangelicals Attack Environmentalists." *Christianity Today* 117, no. 14 (2000): 497–98.

———. "God vs. God: Two Competing Theologies Vie for the Future of Evangelicalism." *Christianity Today* 44, no. 2 (2000): 34–35.

Edwards, David L., and John Stott. *Evangelical Essentials.* Downers Grove, Ill.: InterVarsity, 1988.

Ellingsen, Mark. *The Evangelical Movement: Growth, Impact, Controversy, Dialog.* Minneapolis: Augsburg, 1988.

————. "Lutheranism." In *The Variety of American Evangelicalism,* edited by Donald Dayton and Robert K. Johnston, 222–44. Downers Grove, Ill.: InterVarsity, 1991.

Enns-Rempel, Kevin. "Interpretation of Evangelicalism: An Annotated Bibliography." *Direction* 20, no. 1 (1991): 67–71.

Erickson, Millard J. *Postmodernizing the Faith: Evangelical Responses to the Challenge of Postmodernism.* Grand Rapids: Baker, 1998.

————. *Where Is Theology Going? Issues and Perspectives on the Future of Theology.* Grand Rapids: Baker, 1994.

Fackre, Gabriel. "Whither Evangelicalism?" *Pro Ecclesia* 6, no. 1 (1997): 12–15.

Fairbanks, E. LeBron, Roger Hahn, Frank M. Moore, Jack Stone, and J. K. Warrick, eds. *Manual: Church of the Nazarene.* Kansas City: Nazarene Publishing House, 2001.

Fea, John. "American Fundamentalism and Neo-Evangelicalism: A Bibliographic Survey." *Evangelical Journal* 11 (1993): 21–30.

Ferm, Deane William. *Contemporary American Theologies.* San Francisco: Harper & Row, 1990.

Finney, Charles G. *Lectures on Systematic Theology.* New York: D. H. Doran, 1878.

Finnis, John. *Natural Law and Natural Rights.* Oxford: Clarendon, 1980.

Fox, Thomas C. *Sexuality and Catholicism.* New York: George Braziller, 1995.

Frame, Randy. "Evangelicals, Catholics Issue Salvation Accord." *Christianity Today* 42, no. 1 (1998): 61–63.

Frank, Douglas W. *Less Than Conquerors: How Evangelicalism Entered the Twentieth Century.* Grand Rapids: Eerdmans, 1986.

————. "The Triumph of Illusion: Evangelicalism's Tenacious Tendency to Fervent Self-Deceit." *Other Side* 23, no. 8 (1987): 12–25.

Fuller, Daniel P. "Response to Donald W. Dayton." *Christian Scholar's Review* 23, no. 1 (1993): 41–43.

Furniss, Norman F. *The Fundamentalist Controversy, 1918–1931.* New Haven: Yale University Press, 1954.

Gallup, George, Jr., and Jim Castelli. *The People's Religion: American Faith in the 90s.* New York: Macmillan, 1989.

————, and Timothy Jones. *The Next American Spirituality.* Colorado Springs: Cook Communications Ministries, 2000.

————, and D. Michael Lindsay. *Surveying the Religious Landscape: Trends in U.S. Beliefs.* Harrisburg, Pa.: Morehouse, 1999.

————, and David Poling. *The Search for America's Faith.* Nashville: Abingdon, 1980.

Garrett, James Leo, Jr., E. Glenn Hinson, and James E. Tull. *Are Southern Baptists Evangelicals?* Macon: Mercer University Press, 1983.

Gasper, Louis. *The Fundametalist Movement 1930–1956.* Grand Rapids: Baker, 1981.

Gaustad, Edwin Scott. *The Great Awakening in New England.* New York: Harper, 1957.

Gay, Craig M. "The Uneasy Intellect of Modern Evangelicalism." *Crux* 26, no. 3 (1990): 8–11.

George, Robert P. *In Defense of Natural Law.* Oxford: Oxford University Press, 1999.

George, Timothy. "Evangelicals and Catholics Together: A New Initiative." *Christianity Today* 41, no. 14 (1997): 34–35.

————. "'The Gift of Salvation': A Remarkable Statement on What We Mean by the Gospel." *Christianity Today* 41, no. 14 (1997): 34.

————. "The Gospel Statement Revisited." *Christianity Today* 44, no. 2 (2000): 50–51.

————. "If I'm an Evangelical, What Am I?" *Christianity Today* 43, no. 9 (1999): 62.

————, Thomas C. Oden, and J. I. Packer. "An Open Letter about 'the Gift of Salvation.'" *Christianity Today* 42 (1998): 9.

Gibson, Dennis L. "The Obsessive Personality and the Evangelical." *Journal of Psychology and Christianity* 2, no. 3 (1983): 30–35.

Gilbreath, Edward. "Catching up with a Dream: Evangelicals and Race Thirty Years after the Death of Martin Luther King Jr." *Christianity Today* 42, no. 3 (1998): 21–29.

Gill, Jerry H. *Mediated Transcendence: A Postmodern Reflection.* Macon, Ga.: Mercer University Press, 1989.

Goldberg, Bernard. *Bias: A CBS Insider Exposes How the Media Distort the News.* Washington, D.C.: Regnery Publishing, 2002.

Gordon-McCutchan, R. C. "The Irony of Evangelical History." *Journal for the Scientific Study of Religion* 1, no. 20 (1981): 309–26.

Gould, J. Glenn. "The Pastoral Epistles: The First and Second Epistles to Timothy, the Epistle to Titus." In *Beacon Bible Commentary,* edited by

A. F. Harper, Ralph Earle, W. M. Greathouse, and W. T. Purkiser, 541–48. Kansas City: Beacon Hill, 1965.

Grady, J. Lee. *Ten Lies the Church Tells Women: How the Bible Has Been Misused to Keep Women in Spiritual Bondage.* Lake Mary, Fla.: Charisma House, 2000.

Grass, Tim, ed. *Evangelicalism and the Orthodox Church.* London: Paternoster, 2001.

Green, Joel B. "Reconstructing the Authority of Scripture for Christian Formation and Mission." In *The Wesleyan Tradition: A Paradigm for Renewal,* edited by Paul W. Chilcote, 38–51. Nashville: Abingdon, 2002.

Grenz, Stanley J. *A Primer on Postmodernism.* Grand Rapids: Eerdmans, 1996.

———. *Renewing the Center: Evangelical Theology in a Post-theological Era.* Grand Rapids: Baker, 2000.

———. *Revisioning Evangelical Theology: A Fresh Agenda for the Twenty-first Century.* Downers Grove, Ill.: InterVarsity, 1993.

———, and John R. Franke. *Beyond Foundationalism: Shaping Theology in a Postmodern Context.* Louisville: Westminster John Knox, 2001.

———, and Roger E. Olson. *Twentieth-Century Theology: God and the World in a Transitional Age.* Downers Grove, Ill.: InterVarsity, 1992.

———, and Roger E. Olson. *Who Needs Theology? An Invitation to the Study of God.* Downers Grove, Ill.: InterVarsity, 1996.

Griffith, R. Marie. "Revising Our Assessment of Evangelical Women's Groups." *Tikkun* 13, no. 1 (1998): 18–19, 90.

Groothuis, Douglas. *Truth Decay: Defending Christianity against the Challenges of Postmodernism.* Downers Grove, Ill.: InterVarsity, 2000.

Groothuis, Rebecca Merrill. *Good News for Women: A Biblical Picture of Gender Equality.* Grand Rapids: Baker, 1997.

———. "Searching for Woman's Place in Evangelicalism, Review Essay." *Christian Scholar's Review* 28, no. 2 (1998): 333–39.

———. "Who's Afraid of the Slippery Slope? Evangelicals and the Gender War." *Regeneration Quarterly* 1 (1995): 12–14.

Gros, Jeffrey. "Recent Evangelical Engagement in the Ecumenical Movement." *Ecumenical Trends* 19 (1990): 101–3.

Grudem, Wayne A., and Grant R. Osborne. "Do Inclusive-Language Bibles Distort Scripture?" *Christianity Today* 41 (1997): 26–34, 36–39.

Gundry, Robert. "On Oden's 'Answer.'" *Christianity Today* 7, no. 2 (2001): 14.

———. "Why I Didn't Endorse 'the Gospel of Jesus Christ: An Evangelical Celebration' . . . Even Though I Wasn't Asked To." *Christianity Today* 7, no. 1 (2001): 6.

Gundry, Stanley N., and Alan F. Johnson. *Tensions in Contemporary Theology.* 2nd ed. Grand Rapids: Baker, 1976.

Gunton, Colin. "The Trinity, Natural Theology, and a Theology of Nature." In *The Trinity in a Pluralistic Age: Theological Essays on Culture and Religion,* edited by Kevin J. Vanhoozer, 88–103. Grand Rapids: Eerdmans, 1997.

Gushee, David P., ed. *Toward a Just and Caring Society: Christian Responses to Poverty in America.* Grand Rapids: Baker, 1999.

Guthrie, Donald. *New Testament Introduction.* Downers Grove, Ill.: InterVarsity, 1975.

Hahn, Scott and Kimberly. *Rome Sweet Home.* San Francisco: Ignatius, 1993.

Hamilton, Michael S. "The Dissatisfaction of Francis Schaeffer: Thirteen Years after His Death, Schaeffer's Vision and Frustrations Continue to Haunt Evangelicalism." *Christianity Today* 41, no. 3 (1997): 22–30.

———. "We're in the Money! How Did Evangelicals Get So Wealthy, and What Has It Done to Us?" *Christianity Today* 44, no. 7 (2000): 36–43.

———. "Women, Public Ministry, and American Fundamentalism, 1920–1950." *Religion and American Culture* 3 (1993): 171–96.

Hammond, Phillip E. "An Approach to the Political Meaning of Evangelicalism in Present-Day America." *Annual Review of Social Sciences of Religion* 5 (1981): 186–202.

———. "Evangelical Politics: Generalizations and Implications." *Review of Religious Research* 27, no. 2 (1985): 189–92.

———. "In Search of a Protestant Twentieth Century: American Religion and Power since 1900." *Review of Religious Research* 24, no. 4 (1983): 281–94.

———. "Is America Experiencing Another Religious Revival: What Would Tocqueville Say?" *Social Compass* 38, no. 3 (1991): 239–56.

Handy, Robert T. *A Christian America: Protestant Hopes and Historical Realities.* New York: Oxford University Press, 1971.

———. "Fundamentalism and Modernism in Perspective." *Religion in Life* 24 (1955): 381–94.

Hardisty, Jean. "The Resurgence of the Right: Why Now?" *Liberal Religious Education* 17 (1996–97): 23–44.

Harrell, David E., Jr. *Varieties of Southern Evangelicalism*. Macon, Ga.: Mercer University Press, 1981.

Hasker, William, ed. "What Is Evangelicalism?" *Christian Scholar's Review* 23, no. 1 (1993): 10–89.

Hatch, Nathan O. *The Democratization of American Christianity*. New Haven: Yale University Press, 1989.

———. "Our Shackled Scholars: Evangelical Institutions Are Circling the Wagons and Withdrawing from Wider Discourse." *Christianity Today* 37, no. 14 (1993): 12–13.

———, and Michael S. Hamilton. "Can Evangelicalism Survive Its Success?" *Christianity Today* 36, no. 11 (1992): 20–31.

Hayes, Kathleen. "Evangelicals for Social Action: Developing a Biblical Agenda for Public Life." *Other Side* 22, no. 3 (1986): 10–11.

———. "Opening up the Club: Are Evangelicals Finally Ready to Bring Women in from the Fringes?" *Other Side* 30 (1994): 44–47.

Heidinger, James V., III. "Doctrine and the People Called Methodists." *Good News* 37, no. 2 (2003): 10–11.

Henry, Carl F. H. "American Evangelicals in a Turning Time." *Christian Century* 97 (1980): 1058–62.

———. *God, Revelation, and Authority*. Waco: Word, 1976.

———. *The Uneasy Conscience of Fundamentalism*. Grand Rapids: Eerdmans, 1947.

———. "The Vagrancy of the American Spirit." *Faculty Dialogue,* no. 22 (1994): 5–18.

Hickman, James T. "The Polarity in American Evangelicalism." *Religion in Life* 44 (1975): 47–58.

Himmelfarb, Gertrude. *One Nation, Two Cultures*. New York: Knopf, 1999.

———. *On Looking into the Abyss: Untimely Thoughts on Culture and Society*. New York: Knopf, 1994.

Hodge, Charles. "Systematic Theology." In *Theology in America: The Major Protestant Voices from Puritanism to Neo-Orthodoxy,* edited by Sydney E. Ahlstrom, 253–92. Indianapolis: Bobbs-Merrill Educational Publishing, 1967.

Hoekema, Anthony. "The Reformed Perspective." In *Five Views on Sanctification,* edited by Melvin E. Dieter, 59–90. Grand Rapids: Zondervan, 1987.

Hoke, Donald E., ed. *Evangelicals Face the Future.* Pasadena: William Carey Library, 1978.

Horton, Michael Scott. *Made in America: The Shaping of Modern American Evangelicalism.* Grand Rapids: Baker, 1991.

———. "Recovering the Plumb Line." In *The Coming Evangelical Crisis: Current Challenges to the Authority of Scripture and the Gospel,* edited by John Armstrong, 245–65. Chicago: Moody, 1996.

Howard, Thomas. *Evangelical Is Not Enough.* San Francisco: Ignatius, 1984.

Hubbard, David Allan. *What We Evangelicals Believe.* Pasadena: Fuller Theological Seminary, 1979.

Hudson, Don. "The Dance of Truth: Postmodernism and the Evangelical." *Mars Hill Review* 12 (1998): 13–22.

Hudson, Winthrop S. *Religion in America: An Historical Account of the Development of American Religious Life.* New York: Charles Scribner's Sons, 1973.

Hughes, Robert. *Culture of Complaint: The Fraying of America.* New York: Oxford University Press, 1993.

Hughes, Shelia Hassell. "Homosexuality and Group Boundaries in Contemporary Evangelical Feminism: A Historical Perspective." *Quarterly Review (Methodist)* 14 (1994): 135–59.

Hunter, James Davison. *American Evangelicalism.* New Brunswick: Rutgers University Press, 1983.

———. *Culture Wars: The Struggle to Define America.* New York: Basic Books, 1991.

———. *Evangelicalism: The Coming Generation.* Chicago: University of Chicago Press, 1987.

———. "The New Class and the Young Evangelicals." *Review of Religious Research* 22, no. 2 (1980): 155–69.

Hutchens, S. M. "My Brother, Be He Ne'er So Vile? The Difficulty and Promise of Catholic-Evangelical Rapprochement: An Address to an Evangelical Congregation." *Touchstone (US)* 8 (1995): 13–16.

Hutcheson, Richard G. *Mainline Churches and the Evangelicals.* Atlanta: John Knox, 1981.

Hylson-Smith, Kenneth. *Christianity in England from Roman Times to the Reformation.* Vol. 3, *From 1384–1558.* London: SCM, 2001.

Hynson, Leon. "The Inerrancy Question: A Misplaced Debate." *Evangelical Journal* 5 (1987): 30–34.

Jacobs, Anton K. "Ideology, Self-Esteem, and Religious Doctrine: Toward a Socio-Psychological Understanding of the Popularity of Evangelicalism in Modern, Capitalist America." *Ultimate Reality and Meaning* 13 (1990): 122–33.

Jacobsen, Douglas. "The Center and Boundaries of Evangelical/Fundamentalist Faith: A Review Essay." *Christian Scholar's Review* 28, no. 2 (1998): 340–44.

————. "Purity or Tolerance: The Social Dimension of Hermeneutics in the Calvinist, Arminian, and American Evangelical Traditions." *Evangelical Journal* 11 (1993): 3–20.

————. "The Rise of Evangelical Hermeneutical Pluralism." *Christian Scholar's Review* 16, no. 4 (1987): 325–35.

James, William. *The Varieties of Religious Experience*. Harmondsworth: Penguin, 1982.

Jennings, Theodore W., Jr. *Good News to the Poor: John Wesley's Evangelical Economics*. Nashville: Abingdon, 1990.

Jerome. "Letter to Eustochium." In *Nicene and Post-Nicene Fathers of the Christian Church,* second series, edited by Philip Schaff and Wace Henry VI, 22–40. Grand Rapids: Eerdmans, 1892.

————. "Letter to Lucinius." In *Nicene and Post-Nicene Fathers of the Christian Church,* second series, edited by Philip Schaff and Wace Henry VI, 151–54. Grand Rapids: Eerdmans, 1892.

John Paul II, Pope. *Crossing the Threshold of Hope*. New York: Knopf, 1994.

Johns, Cheryl Bridges. "Partners in Scandal: Wesleyan and Pentecostal Scholarship." *Pneuma* 21, no. 2 (1999): 183–97.

Johnson, Alan F., and Robert E. Webber. *What Christians Believe: A Biblical and Historical Summary*. Grand Rapids: Zondervan, 1989.

Johnson, Daymon A. "Reformed Neo-Traditionalists: Patriarchal Models of Womanhood and the Christian Right." *Fides et Historia* 25 (1993): 77–101.

Johnson, Gary L. W. "A Prophet for Our Times: The Jeremiads of David F. Wells." *Reformation and Revival* 7, no. 3 (1998): 207–13.

Johnson, Luke Timothy. *The First and Second Letters to Timothy: A New Translation with Introduction and Commentary*. New York: Doubleday, 2001.

Johnston, Robert K. "American Evangelicalism: An Extended Family." In *The Variety of American Evangelicalism,* edited by Donald Dayton and Robert K. Johnston, 252–72. Downers Grove, Ill.: InterVarsity, 1991.

———. *Evangelicals at an Impasse: Biblical Authority in Practice.* Atlanta: John Knox, 1979.

Jones, Charles Edwin. *Perfectionist Persuasion: The Holiness Movement and American Methodism, 1867–1936.* Metuchen, N.J.: Scarecrow Press, 1974.

Jones, Preston. "More Scandals of the Evangelical Mind." *First Things* 84 (1998): 16–18.

Jordan, Philip D. "Immigrants, Methodists, and a 'Conservative' Social Gospel, 1865–1908." *Methodist History* 17 (1978): 16–43.

Kantzer, Kenneth S., and Carl F. H. Henry. *Evangelical Affirmations.* Grand Rapids: Zondervan, 1990.

Kellstedt, Lyman. "Simple Questions, Complex Answers: What Do We Mean by 'Evangelicalism'? What Difference Does It Make?" *Evangelical Studies Bulletin* 12, no. 2 (1995): 1–4.

Kelly, J. N. D. *Early Christian Doctrines.* San Francisco: Harper & Row, 1960.

Kennedy, John W. "Hunting for Heresy: Prominent Evangelical Christians—Campolo, Mains—Come under Withering Attack for Controversial Writings." *Christianity Today* 38, no. 6 (1994): 38–40.

Kersten, Katherine. "How the Feminist Establishment Hurts Women: A Christian Critique of a Movement Gone Wrong." *Christianity Today* 38, no. 7 (1994): 20, 22–25.

Keysor, Charles. "American Methodism at 200: The Case for Despair." *Christianity Today* 28, no. 16 (1984): 24–26.

Kierkegaard, Søren. *Stages on Life's Way.* Translated by Howard V. Hong and Edna H. Hong. Princeton: Princeton University Press, 1988.

Kimball, Roger. *The Long March: How the Cultural Revolution of the 1960s Changed America.* San Francisco: Encounter Books, 2000.

Kincheloe, Joe L., Jr. "European Roots of Evangelical Revivalism: Methodist Transmission of the Pietistic Socio-Religious Tradition." *Methodist History* 18 (1980): 262–71.

Kittelson, James. "Enough Is Enough! The Confusion over the Augsburg Confession and Its Satis Est." *Lutheran Quarterly* 12 (1998): 249–70.

Knapp, Steve. "Radical Evangelicals: Who Are They? and Where in the World Are They Headed?" *Other Side* 88 (1979): 34–39.

Knight, Henry H. *A Future for Truth: Evangelical Theology in a Postmodern World.* Nashville: Abingdon, 1997.

———, and Don E. Saliers. *The Conversation Matters: Why United Methodists Should Talk with One Another.* Nashville: Abingdon, 1999.

Kostlevy, William. *Holiness Manuscripts: A Guide to Sources Documenting the Wesleyan Holiness Movement in the United States and Canada.* Metuchen, N.J.: Scarecrow Press, 1994.

Koyzis, Anthony A. "Evangelical Christian Education in America: The Ideas, the Innovations, and the Enterprise." *Christian Educational Journal* 13–15, no. 2 (1995): 70–87.

Kramer, Hilton, and Roger Kimball. *The Betrayal of Liberalism: How the Disciples of Freedom and Equality Helped Foster the Illiberal Politics of Coercion and Control.* Chicago: Ivan R. Dee, 1999.

Kraus, C. Norman. "Evangelicalism: A Mennonite Critique." In *The Variety of American Evangelicalism,* ed. Donald W. Dayton and Robert K. Johnston, 184–203. Downers Grove, Ill.: InterVarsity, 1991.

Kristol, Irving. *Neo-Conservatism: The Autobiography of an Idea.* Chicago: Elephant Paperbacks, 1995.

Kroeger, Catherine Clark. "The Apostle Paul and the Greco-Roman Cults of Women." *Journal of the Evangelical Theological Society* 30, no. 1 (1987): 25–38.

———. "1 Timothy 2:12: A Classicist's View." In *Women, Authority, and the Bible,* edited by Alvera Mickelsen, 225–44. Downers Grove, Ill.: InterVarsity, 1986.

Kroeger, Richard Clark, and Catherine Clark Kroeger. *I Suffer Not a Woman: Rethinking 1 Timothy 2:11–15 in Light of Ancient Evidence.* Grand Rapids: Baker, 1992.

Küng, Hans. *The Catholic Church: A Short History.* New York: Modern Library, 2001.

Kushiner, James Mark. "No Cure in Sight? An Encounter with an Evangelical-Roman Catholic Impasse." *Touchstone* 8 (1995): 44–46.

———, ed. "Mid-Life Crisis or Golden Years?" *Touchstone* 5 (1992): 29–33.

LaCugna, Catherine Mowry. *God for Us: The Trinity and Christian Life.* San Francisco: HarperSanFrancisco, 1991.

Larson, Edward J. *Summer for the Gods: The Scopes Trial and America's Continuing Debate over Science and Religion.* New York: Basic Books, 1997.

Leffel, Jim, and Dennis McCallum. "The Postmodern Religious Shift: Five Case Studies." In *The Death of Truth: What's Wrong with Multiculturalism, the Rejection of Reason, and the New Postmodern Diversity,* edited by Dennis McCallum, 215–34. Minneapolis: Bethany, 1996.

Levy, Leonard W. *The Establishment Clause: Religion and the First Amendment.* New York: Macmillan, 1986.

Limbaugh, David. *Persecution: How Liberals Are Waging War against Christianity.* Washington, D.C.: Regnery Publishing, 2003.

Lindbeck, George. *The Nature of Doctrine: Religion and Theology in a Postliberal Age.* Philadelphia: Westminster, 1984.

———, George Hunsinger, Alister McGrath, and Gabriel Fackre. "Evangelicals and Postliberals Together." *Books & Culture* 2 (1996): 26–28.

Lindsell, Harold. *The Battle for the Bible.* Grand Rapids: Zondervan, 1976.

———. *The New Paganism: Understanding American Culture and the Role of the Church.* San Francisco: Harper & Row, 1987.

Longfield, Bradley. "The American Evangelical Tradition." *Journal of Ecclesiastical History* 48 (1997): 498–506.

Lucas, Sean Michael. "Fundamentalisms Revived and Still Standing: A Review Essay." *Westminster Theological Journal* 60 (1998): 327–37.

Lundin, Roger. "Deconstructive Therapy." *Reformed Journal* 36, no. 1 (1986): 15–20.

Lyotard, Jean François. *The Postmodern Condition: A Report on Knowledge.* Translated by Geoff Bennington and Brian Massumi. Minneapolis: University of Minnesota Press, 1984.

Macculloch, Diarmaid. *The Boy King: Edward VI and the Protestant Reformation.* New York: Palgrave, 1999.

Machen, J. Gresham. *The Christian Faith in the Modern World.* New York: Macmillan, 1936.

———. *Christianity and Liberalism.* Grand Rapids: Eerdmans, 1990.

MacIver, Martha Abele. "Mirror Images? Conceptions of God and Political Duty on the Left and Right of the Evangelical Spectrum." *Sociological Analysis* 51, no. 3 (1990): 287–95.

Magnet, Myron. *The Dream and the Nightmare: The Sixties' Legacy to the Underclass.* San Francisco: Encounter Books, 1993.

Mahan, Asa. *The Baptism of the Holy Ghost.* Noblesville, Ind.: Newby Book Room, 1972.

Maldonado, Jorge E. "Evangelicalism and the Family in Latin America." *International Review of Mission* 82 (1993): 189–202.

Marsden, George M. *Evangelicalism and Modern America.* Grand Rapids: Eerdmans, 1984.

———. "From Fundamentalism to Evangelicalism: A Historical Analysis." In *The Evangelicals,* edited by David F. Wells and John D. Woodbridge, 142–62. Grand Rapids: Baker, 1977.

———. *Fundamentalism and American Culture.* New York: Oxford University Press, 1980.

———. *The Outrageous Idea of Christian Scholarship.* New York: Oxford University Press, 1997.

———. *Reforming Fundamentalism: Fuller Seminary and the New Evangelicalism.* Grand Rapids: Eerdmans, 1987.

———. "Response to Don Dayton." *Christian Scholar's Review* 23, no. 1 (1993): 34–40.

———. *The Soul of the American University.* New York: Oxford University Press, 1994.

———. *Understanding Fundamentalism and Evangelicalism.* Grand Rapids: Eerdmans, 1991.

———, and Bradley J. Longfield. *The Secularization of the Academy.* New York: Oxford University Press, 1992.

Marty, Martin E. *Modern American Religion.* Vol. 1, *The Irony of It All, 1893–1919.* Chicago: University of Chicago Press, 1986.

———. *Modern American Religion.* Vol. 2, *The Noise of Conflict, 1919–1941.* Chicago: University of Chicago Press, 1991.

———. *Modern American Religion.* Vol. 3, *Under God Indivisible, 1941–1960.* Vol. 3. Chicago: University of Chicago Press, 1996.

———. *Politics, Religion, and the Common Good.* San Francisco: Jossey-Bass, 2000.

———. "Religion in America since Mid-Century." *Daedalus* 3 (1982): 149–63.

———. "Tensions within Contemporary Evangelicalism: A Critical Appraisal." In *The Evangelicals: What They Believe, Who They Are, Where They Are Changing,* edited by David F. Wells and John D. Woodbridge, 170–88. Nashville: Abingdon, 1975.

Massey, James Earl. "Race Relations and the American Holiness Movement." *Wesleyan Theological Journal* 31 (1996): 40–50.

Mathisen, Robert R. "Evangelicals and the Age of Reform, 1870–1930: An Assessment." *Fides et Historia* 16, no. 2 (1984): 74–85.

McCallum, Dennis. *The Death of Truth: What's Wrong with Multiculturalism, the Rejection of Reason, and the New Postmodern Diversity.* Minneapolis: Bethany, 1996.

McCune, Rolland D. "The Formation of the New Evangelicalism (Part 1): Historical and Theological Antecedents." *Detroit Baptist Seminary Journal* 3 (1998): 3–34.

McGrath, Alister E. *Christian Theology: An Introduction.* Cambridge: Blackwell, 1994.

———. "An Evangelical Evaluation of Postliberalism." In *The Nature of Confession: Evangelicals and Postliberals in Conversation,* edited by Timothy R. Phillips and Dennis L. Okholm, 23–44. Downers Grove, Ill.: InterVarsity, 1996.

———. *Evangelicalism and the Future of Christianity.* Downers Grove, Ill.: InterVarsity, 1995.

———. "Evangelicalism in the Twenty-first Century: Issues and Challenges." *Jian Dao* 12 (1999): 143–53.

———. *A Passion for Truth: The Intellectual Coherence of Evangelicalism.* Downers Grove, Ill.: InterVarsity, 1996.

———. "Why Evangelicalism Is the Future of Protestantism." *Christianity Today* 39, no. 7 (1995): 18–23.

McKim, Donald K. *Theological Turning Points: Major Issues in Christian Thought.* Atlanta: John Knox, 1988.

McLoughlin, William G. *The American Evangelicals, 1800–1900: An Anthology.* Gloucester, Mass.: Harper & Row, 1968.

———. "Is There a Third Force in Christendom?" *Daedalus* 96, no. 1 (1967): 43–68.

———. *Revivals, Awakenings, and Reform.* Chicago: University of Chicago Press, 1978.

McNeill, John T., ed. *Calvin: Institutes of the Christian Religion.* Vol. 1. Library of Christian Classics. Philadelphia: Westminster, 1960.

Middleton, J. Richard, and Brian J. Walsh. *Truth Is Stranger Than It Used to Be: Biblical Faith in a Postmodern Age.* Downers Grove, Ill.: InterVarsity, 1995.

Miller, Albert G. "The Rise of African-American Evangelicalism in American Culture." In *Perspectives on American Religion and Culture,* edited by Peter W. Williams, 259–69. Oxford: Blackwell, 1999.

Miller, Glenn T. "Trying the Spirits: The Heresy Trials of the Nineteenth Century as Cultural Events." *Perspectives in Religious Studies* 9 (1982): 49–63.

Miller, Perry. *The Life of the Mind in America.* New York: Harcourt, Brace & World, 1965.

Miller, William Lee. *The First Liberty: Religion and the American Republic.* New York: Knopf, 1985.

Miner, Brad. *The Conservative Encyclopedia.* New York: Free Press, 1996.

Moberg, David. *The Great Reversal: Evangelism versus Social Concern.* Philadelphia: Holman, 1972.

Mohler, R. Albert, Jr. "Contending for Truth in an Age of Anti-Truth." In *Here We Stand: A Call from Confessing Evangelicals,* edited by James Montgomery Boice and Benjamin E. Sasse, 59–76. Grand Rapids: Baker, 1996.

Moore, Arthur D. "Does 'the Gift of Salvation' Sell out the Reformation?" *Christianity Today* 42, no. 5 (1998): 17, 21.

Morgan, Timothy C. "First Stride in a Long Walk: Evangelicals Labor to Heal Old Hurts." *Christianity Today* 39, no. 2 (1995): 48.

Morris, Leon. *The Apostolic Preaching of the Cross.* Grand Rapids: Eerdmans, 1976.

———. *The Cross in the New Testament.* Grand Rapids: Eerdmans, 1965.

Mouw, Richard J. "Evangelicals in Search for Maturity." *Theology Today* 35 (1978): 42–51.

———. *The Smell of Sawdust: What Evangelicals Can Learn from Their Fundamentalist Heritage.* Grand Rapids: Zondervan, 2000.

Murch, James DeForest. *Cooperation without Compromise: A History of the National Association of Evangelicals.* Grand Rapids: Eerdmans, 1956.

Murphy, Cullen. "Protestantism and the Evangelicals." *Wilson Quarterly* 5 (1981): 105–16.

Murphy, Nancey. *Beyond Liberalism and Fundamentalism: How Modern and Postmodern Philosophy Set the Theological Agenda.* Harrisburg, Pa.: Trinity Press International, 1996.

Naisbitt, John, and Patricia Aburdene. *Megatrends 2000: Ten New Directions for the 1990s.* New York: William Morrow, 1990.

Nash, Ronald. *Evangelical Renewal.* Westchester, Ill.: Crossway, 1987.

————. *Evangelicals in America: Who They Are, What They Believe.* Nashville: Abingdon, 1987.

————. *The New Evangelicalism.* Grand Rapids: Zondervan, 1963.

Nason-Clark, Nancy. "Conservative Protestants and Violence against Women: Exploring the Rhetoric and the Response." In *Sex, Lies, and Sanctity: Religion and Deviance in Modern America,* edited by Mary Jo Neitz and Marion Goldman, 109–30. Greenwich, Conn.: JAI Press, 1995.

Nathan, Rich, and Ken Wilson. *Empowered Evangelicals: Bringing Together the Best of the Evangelical and Charismatic Worlds.* Ann Arbor, Mich.: Vine Books, 1995.

Naughton, Jim. *Catholics in Crisis: The Rift between American Catholics and Their Church.* New York: Penguin, 1996.

Neff, David. "Divided by Faith?" *Christianity Today* 44, no. 11 (2000): 34–55.

————. "Fighting the Good Fight: A Plea for Healthy Disagreements." *Christianity Today* 41 (1997): 35–37.

————. "The Gospel of Jesus Christ: An Evangelical Celebration." *Christianity Today* 43, no. 7 (1999): 49.

————. "When Christians Fight Christians." *Christianity Today* 41, no. 11 (1997): 28–34.

Neuhaus, Richard John. "The Catholic Difference." In *Evangelicals and Catholics Together: Toward a Common Mission,* edited by Charles Colson and Richard John Neuhaus, 175–227. Dallas: Word, 1995.

————. *The Catholic Moment: The Paradox of the Church in the Postmodern World.* New York: Harper & Row, 1987.

————. *The Naked Public Square: Religion and Democracy in America.* 2nd ed. Grand Rapids: Eerdmans, 1996.

————. "A Typology of Evangelicalism." *First Things* 37 (1993): 48.

Nevins, Albert J. *Answering a Fundamentalist.* Huntington, Ind.: Our Sunday Visitor Publishing Division, 1990.

Nicholls, Bruce J. "Our Evangelical Conscience." *Evangelical Review of Theology* 18, no. 3 (1994): 196–284.

Niebuhr, Reinhold. *Moral Man and Immoral Society.* New York: Charles Scribner's Sons, 1932.

Noll, Mark A. *American Evangelical Christianity.* Malden, Mass.: Blackwell, 2001.

————. *Between Faith and Criticism.* Grand Rapids: Baker, 1991.

————. "Evangelicalism at Its Best." *Harvard Divinity Bulletin* 27, nos. 2–3 (1998): 8–12.

————. "The Evangelical Mind." In *The Evangelical Landscape,* edited by Garth M. Rosell, 13–40. Grand Rapids: Baker, 1996.

————. "Evangelicals and the Study of the Bible." *Reformed Journal* 34, no. 4 (1984): 11–19.

————. *The Scandal of the Evangelical Mind.* Grand Rapids: Eerdmans, 1994.

————. "The Swelling Tide of Revivalism." In *Eerdmans Handbook to Christianity in America,* edited by Mark A. Noll, Nathan O. Hatch, George M. Marsden, David F. Wells, and John D. Woodbridge, 172–87. Grand Rapids: Eerdmans, 1983.

————. *Turning Points: Decisive Moments in the History of Christianity.* Grand Rapids: Baker, 1997.

————, David W. Bebbington, and George A. Rawlyk. *Evangelicalism.* New York: Oxford University Press, 1994.

————, Nathan O. Hatch, and George M. Marsden. *The Search for Christian America.* Westchester, Ill.: Crossway, 1983.

————, and Lyman Kellstedt. "The Changing Face of Evangelicalism." *Pro Ecclesia* 4, no. 2 (1995): 146–64.

————, Cornelius Plantinga, and David Wells. "Evangelical Theology Today." *Theology Today* 51 (1995): 495–507.

Nord, Warren A. *Religion and American Education.* Chapel Hill: University of North Carolina Press, 1995.

Oberman, Heiko A. "Quo Vadis, Petre? Tradition from Irenaeus to Humani Generis." In *The Dawn of the Reformation: Essays in Late Medieval and Early Reformation Thought,* edited by Heiko A. Oberman, 269–96. Edinburgh: T & T Clark, 1986.

Oblinger, Peter. *Religious Mimesis: Social Bases for Holiness Schism in Late Nineteenth-Century Methodism.* Monograph Studies, 1. Evanston, Ill.: Institute for the Study of American Religion, 1973.

Oden, Thomas C. *Agenda for Theology: After Modernity . . . What?* Grand Rapids: Zondervan, 1990.

————. "A Calm Answer . . . to a Critique of 'the Gospel of Jesus Christ': An Evangelical Celebration." *Christianity Today* 7, no. 2 (2001): 12.

————. "Form and Freedom: Evangelicals Enter the Twenty-First Century." *Regeneration Quarterly* 4 (1998): 44–45.

———. *The Justification Reader.* Grand Rapids: Eerdmans, 2002.

———. *Life in the Spirit.* Systematic Theology. Vol. 3. San Francisco: Harper-SanFrancisco, 1994.

———. *The Living God.* Systematic Theology. Vol. 1. San Francisco: Harper-SanFrancisco, 1987.

———. "Mainstreaming the Mainline." *Christianity Today* 44, no. 9 (2000): 59–61.

———. *The Word of Life: Systematic Theology.* Vol. 2. San Francisco: Harper-SanFrancisco, 1992.

Offner, Kevin F. "American Evangelicalism: Adrift with Amnesia." *Regeneration Quarterly* 1 (1995): 6–9.

Olasky, Marvin. *Compassionate Conservatism: What It Is, What It Does, and How It Can Transform America.* New York: Free Press, 2000.

———. *Renewing American Compassion: How Compassion for the Needy Can Turn Ordinary Citizens into Heroes.* Washington, D.C.: Regnery Publishing, 1996.

———. *The Tragedy of American Compassion.* Wheaton: Crossway, 1992.

———, Herbert Schlossberg, Pierre Berthoud, and Clark H. Pinnock. *Freedom, Justice, and Hope: Toward a Strategy for the Poor and the Oppressed.* Westchester, Ill.: Crossway, 1988.

Olin, John C., ed. *A Reformation Debate.* New York: Harper Torchbooks, 1966.

Olson, Mark. "Over Great Waters: As a Religious Movement, Evangelicalism Offers Incredible Strengths—and Incredible Dangers." *Other Side* 30 (1994): 32–55.

———. "Socially Concerned Evangelicals: Where Next?" *Other Side* 30 (1994): 32–38.

Olson, Roger E. "Don't Hate Me Because I'm Arminian." *Christianity Today* 43, no. 10 (1999): 87–90, 92–94.

———. *The Story of Christian Theology: Twenty Centuries of Tradition and Reform.* Downers Grove, Ill.: InterVarsity, 1999.

———. "Whales and Elephants: Both God's Creatures but Can They Meet? Evangelicals and Liberals in Dialogue." *Pro Ecclesia* 4, no. 2 (1995): 165–89.

———, and Christopher A. Hall. *The Trinity.* Grand Rapids: Eerdmans, 2002.

Osborne, Grant R. "Christianity Challenges Postmodernism." *Evangelical Journal* 15 (1997): 1–17.

Paauw, Glen. "Virtual Christianity: Evangelicals, America, and the Big Show." *Christian Research Journal* 18 (1995): 52–53.

Packer, J. I. "Crosscurrents among Evangelicals." In *Evangelicals and Catholics: Toward a Common Mission,* edited by Charles Colson and Richard John Neuhaus, 147–74. Dallas: Word, 1995.

———. *Fundamentalism and the Word of God.* Grand Rapids: Eerdmans, 1980.

———. "Let's Stop Making Women Presbyters." *Christianity Today* 35, no. 2 (1991): 13–21.

———. "What Did the Cross Achieve? The Logic of Penal Substitution." *Tyndale Bulletin* 25 (1974): 3–45.

Parker, David. "Evangelical Spirituality Reviewed." *Evangelical Quarterly* 63, no. 2 (1991): 123–48.

Parker, T. H. L. *John Calvin: A Biography.* Philadelphia: Westminster, 1975.

Perrin, Robin D., Paul Kennedy, and Donald E. Miller. "Examining the Sources of Conservative Church Growth: Where Are the New Evangelical Movements Getting Their Numbers?" *Journal for the Scientific Study of Religion* 36, no. 1 (1997): 71–80.

Peterson, Susan Lynn. *Timeline Charts of the Western Church.* Grand Rapids: Zondervan, 1999.

Phillips, Timothy R., and Dennis L. Okholm. *Christian Apologetics in the Postmodern World.* Downers Grove, Ill.: InterVarsity, 1995.

———. *The Nature of Confession: Evangelicals and Postliberals in Conversation.* Downers Grove, Ill.: InterVarsity, 1996.

Pickering, Ernest D. *The Tragedy of Compromise: The Origin and Impact of the New Evangelicalism.* Greenville, S.C.: Bob Jones University Press, 1994.

Pierard, Richard. "The Quest for the Historical Evangelicalism: A Bibliographical Excursus." *Fides et Historia* 11 (1979): 60–72.

———. *The Unequal Yoke: Evangelical Christianity and Political Conservatism.* Philadelphia: J. B. Lippincott, 1970.

Pierce, Ronald W. "Evangelicals and Gender Roles in the 1990s: 1 Timothy 2:8–15: A Test Case." *Journal of the Evangelical Theological Society* 36 (1993): 343–55.

Piggin, Stuart. "Evangelical Christianity in Crisis: Is There a Need for a New Paradigm?" *Lucas* 23 (1997): 141–60.

————. "Evangelical Christianity in Crisis: Is There a Need for a Paradigm?" *Lucas* 23–24 (1997–98): 141–60.

Pinnock, Clark. "Evangelicals and Inerrancy: The Current Debate." *Theology Today* 35 (1978): 65–69.

————. "Fuller Theological Seminary and the Nature of Evangelicalism." *Christian Scholar's Review* 23, no. 1 (1993): 44–47.

————, Richard Rice, John Sanders, William Hasker, and David Basinger. *The Openness of God: A Biblical Challenge to the Traditional Understanding of God.* Downers Grove, Ill.: InterVarsity, 1994.

Plantinga, Alvin. *Warranted Christian Belief.* New York: Oxford University Press, 2000.

Plantinga, Cornelius, Jr. *Not the Way It's Supposed to Be: A Breviary of Sin.* Grand Rapids: Eerdmans, 1995.

Quebedeaux, Richard. *The Worldly Evangelicals.* San Francisco: Harper & Row, 1978.

————. *The Young Evangelicals.* New York: Harper & Row, 1974.

Rabey, Steve. "Conversation or Competition? Pentecostals, Roman Catholics in Long-Standing Talks to Resolve Conflicts, Discover Some Commonalities." *Christianity Today* 42, no. 10 (1998): 22–23.

Ramm, Bernard. "Are We Obscurantists?" *Christianity Today* 1 (1957): 14–15.

————. *The Evangelical Heritage: A Study in Historical Theology.* Grand Rapids: Baker, 2000.

Rauch, Jonathan. *Kindly Inquisitors: The New Attacks on Free Thought.* Chicago: University of Chicago Press, 1993.

Rausch, Thomas P. *Catholics and Evangelicals: Do They Share a Common Future?* Downers Grove, Ill.: InterVarsity, 2000.

Rauschenbusch, Walter. *A Theology for the Social Gospel.* Nashville: Abingdon, 1981.

Reed, Ralph. *Active Faith: How Christians Are Changing the Soul of American Politics.* New York: Free Press, 1996.

Reese, Boyd. "The New Class and the Young Evangelicals: Second Thoughts." *Review of Religious Research* 24 (1983): 261–67.

Richey, Russell E., and Donald G. Jones. *American Civil Religion.* New York: Harper & Row, 1974.

Riddlebarger, Kim. "Why Are Evangelicals Joining the Catholic Church?" In *Roman Catholicism: Evangelical Protestants Analyze What Divides and Unites Us,* edited by Alister McGrath, 221–44. Chicago: Moody, 1994.

Robb, Edward W., Jr. "American Methodism at 200: The Case for Hope." *Christianity Today* 28, no. 16 (1984): 20–23.

Roels, Shirley J. "The Business Ethics of Evangelicals." *Business Ethics Quarterly* 7, no. 2 (1997): 109–22.

Rogers, Jack B., and Donald K. McKim. *The Authority and Interpretation of the Bible.* San Francisco: Harper & Row, 1979.

Roman, Bill D. S. "Worlds Apart: Why Black Christians Don't Feel at Ease with Evangelicals." *Other Side* 30 (1994): 40, 42–43, 54–55.

Roman Catholic Church. *Catechism of the Catholic Church.* Mahwah, N.J.: Paulist Press, 1994.

Rosell, Garth M., ed. *The Evangelical Landscape: Essays on the American Evangelical Tradition.* Grand Rapids: Baker, 1996.

Ryan, William. *Blaming the Victim.* New York: Vintage Books, 1971.

Samples, Kenneth R. "What Think Ye of Rome? An Evangelical Appraisal of Contemporary Catholicism (Part 2)." *Christian Research Journal* 15 (1993): 32–42.

Sandeen, Ernest R. *The Roots of Fundamentalism: British and American Millenarianism, 1800–1930.* Grand Rapids: Baker, 1978.

Scanzoni, Letha, and Nancy Hardesty. *All We're Meant to Be.* Waco: Word, 1975.

Schaeffer, Francis A. *A Christian Manifesto.* Westchester, Ill.: Crossway, 1981.

———. *The Great Evangelical Disaster.* Westchester, Ill.: Crossway, 1984.

Schleiermacher, Friedrich. *On Religion: Speeches to Its Cultured Despisers.* New York: Harper Torchbooks, 1958.

Schlesinger, Arthur M., Jr. *The Disuniting of America: Reflections on a Multicultural Society.* New York: W. W. Norton, 1992.

Schmalzbauer, John. "Evangelicals in the New Class: Class versus Subcultural Predictors of Ideology." *Journal for the Scientific Study of Religion* 32, no. 4 (1993): 330–42.

Schneiders, Sandra M. *Beyond Patching: Faith and Feminism in the Catholic Church.* Mahwah, N.J.: Paulist Press, 1991.

Scott, J. Julius, Jr. "Some Problems in Hermeneutics for Contemporary Evangelicals." *Journal of the Evangelical Theological Society* 22 (1979): 67–77.

Seifrid, Mark. "'The Gift of Salvation': Its Failure to Address the Crux of Justification." *Journal of the Evangelical Theological Society* 42, no. 4 (1999): 679–88.

Sernett, Milton G. "Black Religion and the Question of Evangelical Identity." In *The Variety of American Evangelicalism,* edited by Donald W. Dayton and Robert K. Johnston, 135–47. Downers Grove, Ill.: InterVarsity, 1991.

Shelley, Bruce L. *Evangelicalism in America.* Grand Rapids: Eerdmans, 1967.

———. "Sources of Pietistic Fundamentalism." *Fides et Historia* 5 (1972): 68–78.

Sherman, Amy L. *Restorers of Hope: Reaching the Poor in Your Community with Church-Based Ministries That Work.* Wheaton: Crossway, 1997.

Shibley, Mark A. *Resurgent Evangelicalism in the United States: Mapping Cultural Change since 1970.* Columbia: University of South Carolina Press, 1996.

Sider, Ronald J. "An Evangelical Theology of Liberation." *Christian Century* 97 (1980): 314–18.

———. *Just Generosity: A New Vision for Overcoming Poverty in America.* Grand Rapids: Baker, 1999.

Sire, James W. *Discipleship of the Mind: Learning to Love God in the Ways We Think.* Downers Grove, Ill.: InterVarsity, 1990.

———. *Habits of the Mind: Intellectual Life as a Christian Calling.* Downers Grove, Ill.: InterVarsity, 2000.

———. *The Universe Next Door: A Basic World View Catalog.* Downers Grove, Ill.: InterVarsity, 1976.

Smidt, Corwin E. *Contemporary Evangelical Political Involvement.* Lanham, Md.: University Press of America, 1989.

Smith, Christian. *American Evangelicalism: Embattled and Thriving.* Chicago: University of Chicago Press, 1998.

———. *Christian America? What Evangelicals Really Want.* Berkeley: University of California Press, 2000.

Smith, David L. *A Handbook of Contemporary Theology: Tracing Trends and Discerning Directions in Today's Theological Landscape.* Wheaton: Bridgepoint, 1992.

Smith, Timothy L. "The Evangelical Kaleidoscope and the Call to Unity." *Christian Scholar's Review* 15, no. 2 (1986): 125–40.

———. *Revivalism and Social Reform.* Baltimore: Johns Hopkins University Press, 1980.

Spencer, Aída Besançon, and William David Spencer, eds. *The Global God: Multicultural Evangelical Views of God*. Grand Rapids: Bridgepoint, 1998.

Spener, Philip Jacob. *Pia Desideria*. Edited by Theodore G. Tappert. Philadelphia: Fortress, 1964.

Stackhouse, John G., Jr. "By Their Books Ye Shall Know Them: Books That Have Shaped American Evangelicals in the Last Forty Years." *Christianity Today* 40, no. 10 (1996): 58–59.

———. "History Clearly Teaches—What? The Uses of History in Evangelical Gender Debates." *Crux* 36, no. 1 (2000): 11–15.

———. "The Perils of Left and Right: Evangelical Theology Is Much Bigger and Richer Than Our Two-Party Labels." *Christianity Today* 42, no. 9 (1998): 58–59.

———. "Perpetual Adolescence: The Emerging Culture of North American Evangelicalism." *Crux* 29, no. 3 (1993): 32–37.

———. "Why Johnny Can't Produce Christian Scholarship." *Crux* 32, no. 1 (1996): 13–23.

———, ed. *Evangelical Futures: A Conversation on Theological Method*. Grand Rapids: Baker, 2000.

Stanley, Susie C. *Holy Boldness: Women Preachers' Autobiographies and the Sanctified Self*. Knoxville: University of Tennessee Press, 2002.

Steuernagel, Valdir R. "Social Concern and Evangelization: The Journey of the Lausanne Movement." *International Bulletin of Missionary Research* 15 (1991): 53–56.

Stoll, David. "A Protestant Reformation in Latin America?" *Christian Century* 107 (1990): 44–48.

Stone, Jon R. *On the Boundaries of American Evangelicalism: The Postwar Evangelical Coalition*. New York: St. Martin's Press, 1997.

Stookey, Stephen M. "In God We Trust? Evangelical Historiography and the Quest for a Christian America." *Southwestern Journal of Theology* 41 (1999): 41–69.

Stott, John R. W. "Are Evangelicals Fundamentalists?" *Christianity Today* 22 (1978): 44–46.

———. *The Cross of Christ*. Downers Grove, Ill.: InterVarsity, 1986.

Sundberg, Walter. "Religious Trends in Twentieth-Century America." *Word & World* 20, no. 1 (2000): 22–31.

Sweeney, Douglas A. "The Essential Evangelicalism Dialectic: The Historiography of the Early Neo-Evangelical Movement and the Observer-Participant Dilemma." *Church History* 60 (1991): 70–84.

———. "Historiographical Dialectics: On Marsden, Dayton, and the Inner Logic of Evangelical History." *Christian Scholar's Review* 23, no. 1 (1993): 48–52.

Sweet, Leonard I. *The Evangelical Tradition in America.* Macon, Ga.: Mercer University Press, 1984.

———. "Wise as Serpents, Innocent as Doves: The New Evangelical Historiography." *Journal of the American Academy of Religion* 56, no. 3 (1988): 397–416.

Sykes, Charles J. *The Hollow Men: Politics and Corruption in Higher Education.* Washington, D.C.: Regnery Publishing, 1990.

———. *A Nation of Victims: The Decay of the American Character.* New York: St. Martin's Press, 1992.

Synan, Vinson. *The Holiness-Pentecostal Movement in the United States.* Grand Rapids: Eerdmans, 1987.

Tapia, Andres. "L.A. after the Ashes: Churches Struggle to Overcome Racial Tensions, Poverty, and Inner-City Violence." *Christianity Today* 37, no. 11 (1993): 42–46.

———. "The Myth of Racial Progress." *Christianity Today* 37, no. 11 (1993): 16–27.

———. "Why Is Latin America Turning Protestant?" *Christianity Today* 36, no. 4 (1992): 28–39.

Taylor, Richard S. *God's Integrity and the Cross.* Nappanee, Ind.: Francis Asbury Press, 1999.

Thomas, Cal, and Edward G. Dobson. *Blinded by Might.* Grand Rapids: Zondervan, 1999.

———. "Hostage to an Illusion: The Religious Right Lost Its Moorings and Sold Its Soul When It Chose to Play by the Politicians' Rules." *Sojourners* 28 (1999): 18–21.

Tolson, Jay. "The New Oldtime Religion." *U.S. News & World Report* 135, no. 20 (2003): 38–44.

Tomlinson, Dave. *The Post Evangelical.* London: Triangle (S.P.C.K.), 1995.

Torrance, James B. *Worship, Community, and the Triune God of Grace.* Downers Grove, Ill.: InterVarsity, 1996.

Torrey, R. A., and A. C. Dixon, eds. *The Fundamentals: A Testimony to the Truth*. Grand Rapids: Baker, 1980.

Toulouse, Mark G., and James O. Duke. *Makers of Christian Theology in America*. Nashville: Abingdon, 1997.

Treloar, Geoffrey, Barry N. Hankins, and Al Beck. "Evangelical Historical Scholarship 1994." *Lucas* 19–20 (1995–96): 217–41.

Trever, John C. "A Closer Look at the Meaning of 'Evangelical Christianity.'" *Brethren Life and Thought* 32 (1987): 148–53.

Tussman, Joseph. *The Supreme Court on Church and State*. New York: Oxford University Press, 1962.

Van Die, Marguerite. "In Search of Piety." *Touchstone* 11 (1993): 4–15.

Vanhoozer, Kevin J., ed. *The Trinity in a Pluralistic Age: Theological Essays on Culture and Religion*. Grand Rapids: Eerdmans, 1997.

Veith, Gene Edward, Jr. *Postmodern Times: A Christian Guide to Contemporary Thought and Culture*. Wheaton: Crossway, 1994.

———. *The Spirituality of the Cross: The Way of the First Evangelicals*. St. Louis: Concordia, 1999.

Volf, Miroslav. *After Our Likeness: The Church as the Image of the Trinity*. Grand Rapids: Eerdmans, 1998.

Wacker, Grant. "How Evangelicals Won the South: And What They Lost in the Process." *Christianity Today* 42, no. 5 (1998): 80–82.

Wagner, Donald. "Evangelicals and Israel: Theological Roots of a Political Alliance." *Christian Century* 115 (1998): 1020–26.

Wallace, Daniel B. "Granville Sharp: A Model of Evangelical Scholarship and Social Activism." *Journal of the Evangelical Theological Society* 41, no. 4 (1998): 591–613.

Wallis, Jim. "Our Common Struggle." *Post American* 3 (August–September 1974): 3–29.

———. *The Soul of Politics*. New York: Orbis, 1994.

Walsh, Brian J., and Richard J. Middleton. *The Transforming Vision: Shaping a Christian World View*. Downers Grove, Ill.: InterVarsity, 1984.

Ware, Bruce A. *God's Lesser Glory: The Diminished God of Open Theism*. Wheaton: Good News Books, 2000.

Warner, R. Stephen. "Theoretical Barriers to the Understanding of Evangelical Christianity." *Sociological Analysis* 40, no. 1 (1979): 1–9.

Webber, Robert E. *Ancient-Future Faith: Rethinking Evangelicalism for a Postmodern World*. Grand Rapids: Baker, 1999.

———. *Common Roots: A Call to Evangelical Maturity.* Grand Rapids: Zondervan, 1978.

———. *Evangelicals on the Canterbury Trail: Why Evangelicals Are Attracted to the Liturgical Church.* Harrisburg, Pa.: Morehouse, 1985.

———. *The Younger Evangelicals: Facing the Challenges of the New World.* Grand Rapids: Baker, 2002.

———, and Donald Bloesch. *The Orthodox Evangelicals: Who They Are and What They Are Saying.* Nashville: Thomas Nelson, 1978.

Weber, Timothy P. "How Evangelicals Became Israel's Best Friend." *Christianity Today* 42, no. 11 (1998): 38–49.

———. "Premillennialism and the Branches of Evangelicalism." In *The Variety of American Evangelicalism,* edited by Donald W. Dayton and Robert K. Johnston, 5–21. Downers Grove, Ill.: InterVarsity, 1991.

Wellings, Martin. "What Is an Evangelical?" *Epworth Review* 21, no. 3 (1994): 45–53.

Wells, David F. *No Place for Truth, or Whatever Happened to Evangelical Theology?* Grand Rapids: Eerdmans, 1993.

———, and John D. Woodbridge. *The Evangelicals.* Grand Rapids: Baker, 1977.

———, and John D. Woodbridge, eds. *The Evangelicals: What They Believe, Who They Are, Where They Are Changing.* Nashville: Abingdon, 1975.

White, Ronald C., Jr., C. Howard Hopkins, and John C. Bennet. *The Social Gospel.* Philadelphia: Temple University Press, 1976.

Wilcox, Bradford W., and John P. Bartkowski. "The Conservative Protestant Family: Traditional Rhetoric, Progressive Practice." In *What's God Got to Do with the American Experiment?* edited by E. J. Dionne and John J. Diiulio, 32–40. Washington, D.C.: Brookings Institution Press, 2000.

Wilkinson, Loren. "How Christian Is the Green Agenda?" *Christianity Today* 37, no. 1 (1993): 16–20.

Williams, Philip J., and Anna L. Peterson. "Evangelicals and Catholics in El Salvador: Evolving Religious Responses to Social Change." *Journal of Church and State* 38 (1996): 873–97.

Wills, Garry. *Papal Sin: Structures of Deceit.* New York: Doubleday, 2000.

Wilson, John F. *Public Religion in American Culture.* Philadelphia: Temple University Press, 1979.

Wilson, John, ed. "The Year's Best Books: Annual Books Issue." *Christianity Today* 42 (1998): 26–35, 70–87.

Winner, Lauren F. "Finding Power in Submission: Two Feminist Scholars Write about Women You'll Recognize." *Christianity Today* 42, no. 5 (1998): 70–72.

Witherington, Ben, III. *New Testament History: A Narrative Account.* Grand Rapids: Baker, 2001.

Woodham, G. H. "What Is an Evangelical?" *Congregational Quarterly* 28 (1950): 165–72.

Wright, R. K. McGregor. *No Place for Sovereignty.* Downers Grove, Ill.: Inter-Varsity, 1996.

Wuthnow, Robert. *Christianity in the Twenty-first Century: Reflections on the Challenges Ahead.* Oxford: Oxford University Press, 1993.

———. "Evangelicals, Liberals, and the Perils of Individualism." *Perspectives* 6 (1991): 10–13.

———. "Living the Question: Evangelical Christianity and Critical Thought." *Cross Currents* 40 (1990): 160–75.

———. *The Struggle for America's Soul: Evangelicals, Liberals, and Secularism.* Grand Rapids: Eerdmans, 1989.

Yancey, Philip. "Christian McCarthyism." *Christianity Today* 38, no. 8 (1994): 72.

Zizioulas, John D. *Being as Communion.* Crestwood, N.Y.: St. Vladimir's Seminary Press, 1985.

Zoba, Wendy Murray, and Helen Lee. "Ministering Women: Enough Already on Men's and Women's Expectations. What Does God Want from Eve's Daughters?" *Christianity Today* 40 (1996): 14–21.

# Index